WAINWRIGHT
ON THE
LAKELAND MOUNTAIN PASSES

Also by A. Wainwright and Derry Brabbs

FELLWALKING WITH WAINWRIGHT
WAINWRIGHT ON THE PENNINE WAY
WAINWRIGHT'S COAST TO COAST WALK
WAINWRIGHT IN SCOTLAND
WAINWRIGHT'S FAVOURITE LAKELAND MOUNTAINS

By A. Wainwright and Ed Geldard

WAINWRIGHT IN THE LIMESTONE DALES

WAINWRIGHT
ON THE
LAKELAND MOUNTAIN PASSES

with photographs by
DERRY BRABBS

Michael Joseph – London

MICHAEL JOSEPH LTD

Published by the Penguin Group
27 Wrights Lane, London W8 5TZ, England
Viking Penguin Inc., 375 Hudson Street, New York,
New York 10014, USA
Penguin Books Australia Ltd, Ringwood, Victoria, Australia
Penguin Books Canada Ltd, 10 Alcorn Avenue, Toronto, Ontario,
Canada, M4V 3B2
Penguin Books (NZ) Ltd, 182–190 Wairau Road, Auckland 10,
New Zealand

Penguin Books Ltd, Registered Offices, Harmondsworth,
Middlesex, England

First published April 1989
Second impression March 1992

First published in Mermaid Books April 1992

A CIP catalogue record for this book is available from the British
Library

ISBN 0 7181 2815 X hbk
ISBN 0 7181 3267 X pbk

Typeset in 10½ on 13pt Linotron Ehrhardt
by Cambrian Typesetters, Frimley, Surrey
Colour reproduction by Anglia Graphics, Bedford
Printed and bound in The Netherlands by
Royal Smeets Offset b.v., Weert

CONTENTS

MAPS BY BORIS WELTMAN
Illustration on half-title page: *High Sweden Bridge*
title page: *Honister Pass*
page 4: *Hallin Fell from the pier at Howtown*

INTRODUCTION

THE LAKE DISTRICT is a compact mass of high and rugged ground soaring abruptly from surrounding valleys and the coastal plain of Cumbria, almost as distinctive and well defined as a volcanic island rising from the sea. Within its natural boundaries, mountains and fells crowd together, there being over 200 separate and named summits. As in all mountainous terrain, the peaks are linked by ridges intersected by skyline gaps or depressions that permit ease of crossing from one valley to another; a few carry roads but most are accessible only on foot. These relatively simple ways of crossing high ranges are known as passes. Long before men explored the lofty summits for pleasure, the passes were used by nomadic tribes and later by the early settlers and, where negotiable by packhorses, by enterprising traders as commercial routes.

Left *Helvellyn from High Tove*   Above *The road over Honister Pass*

Lakeland is not fashioned for motorists: cars can penetrate the interior only in a few places. It is largely a preserve of walkers. The most exhilarating and rewarding form of pedestrian travel is fellwalking, a pastime that has grown greatly in popularity in recent decades, but it is available only to the physically fit. Most visitors to the district, however, are content to stroll along the lovely valleys and beside the lakes, preferring not to risk the hazards of the higher ground above; some even have a primeval fear of mountains as places of danger. But there is an intermediate class of walkers who admire mountain scenery and favour the loneliness of the wild recesses, yet because of disability or lack of energy in their later years cannot aspire to the ultimate summits and dare not venture too far upwards. Such are catered for by the passes, away from the sight and sound of traffic, where the peaks can be viewed in intimate detail and in the silence of solitude.

Deepdale

For those who can walk in moderation and choose to do so sedately and without fear of going astray, the passes offer ideal expeditions. People get lost on the mountains but very rarely on the passes. Here distinct paths have formed through centuries of use although they are often still narrow and rough; cairns provide comfort in places of doubt; the natural configuration of the ground, rising on both sides, confines walkers to the trodden ways, and the streams descending from the passes are infallible guides to direction. All these reassuring factors make the passes practicable in any weather conditions except deep snow, and on days when heavy cloud rules the tops out of bounds the passes can be walked in safety.

The passes may of course be walked in either direction. In this book, I have described them in the direction most usually followed or which provides the greater interest or excellence in forward views. In a few cases where passes have no official name, I have given them appropriate ones.

Every skyline gap or depression on a mountain ridge, sometimes referred to as cols, may be regarded as a pass of sorts if approachable on both sides, and there are hundreds of such places in Lakeland. Most of those remote from tourist paths will have been crossed by shepherds or foxhunters or Ordnance surveyors at one time or another, but many are virgin and have never been trodden by man. These latter are outside the scope of this book which is concerned only with those that carry distinct paths and are in common use.

Some of the passes are short and can be reversed to the starting point in the course of a day's walk. But most are of several miles and a single crossing is enough for one day. Walkers who are travelling from one bed-and-breakfast to another in a different valley have no problems, but those encumbered by cars must plan to return to them. The best arrangement in such cases is to team up with friends who also have their own transport, the two parties leaving their cars at either extremity of the pass at agreed parking places and doing the walk in opposite directions, swapping car keys as they meet midway, thus ensuring a comfortable return to base.

No day in the Lake District needs be wasted because of inclement weather. The mountains are inhospitable in bad conditions and better avoided, and touring the gift shops in the valleys and sheltering in doorways and cafés quickly palls. The friendly passes offer the perfect answer. You'll still get wet, of course, and despair at the shroud of mist that masks the beauty all around, but the exercise will do you good and after a rousing supper in dry clothes you will vote the day a very satisfactory one after all. Walking the passes is the next best thing to walking on the mountains and often no less rewarding.

Each pass is the subject of a separate chapter, the description of the route being accompanied by a simple location map with a mile-scale, north being at the top. Heights are given in English feet and distances in English miles despite the current regrettable practice of quoting them in foreign metres and kilometres to which the author, a jingoistic Englishman, refuses to comply. This book is about the English Lake District. Let's go on thinking of it as English!

1 BLACK SAIL PASS, 1800′
Wasdale Head – Ennerdale

WASDALE HEAD, the most impressive inhabited place in Lakeland, is so deeply inurned amongst high mountains that there appears to be no easy escape from it other than by reversing the usual line of approach on the road alongside Wastwater. Only the glen of Lingmell Beck coming down on the right below the shapely pyramid of Great Gable seems to offer a possible way out of the valley: this is the walkers' way to Sty Head. Less obvious is a route entering the side valley of Mosedale on the left: this climbs to a skyline depression or saddle between Kirk Fell and Pillar and descends from there into Ennerdale.

This is the Black Sail Pass.

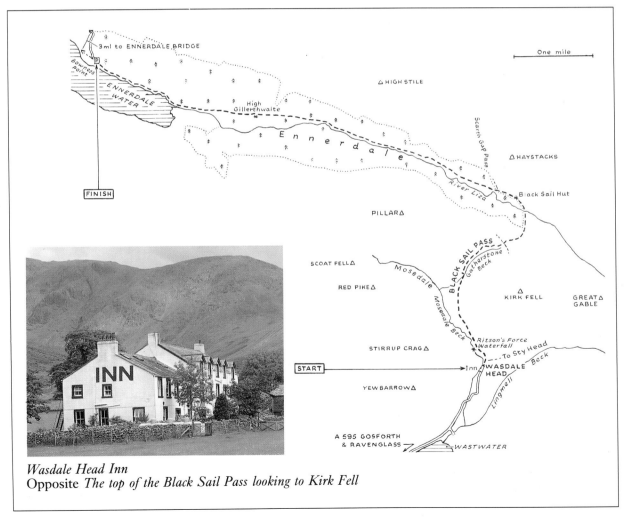

Wasdale Head Inn
Opposite *The top of the Black Sail Pass looking to Kirk Fell*

Wasdale Head

THE ROUTE STARTS from Wasdale Head Inn which has reverted to its former name after being known as Wastwater Hotel for many years, inappropriately because the lake is a mile distant. Modernisation has destroyed the old atmosphere of this venerable inn, a Mecca for the pioneers of rockclimbing of a hundred years ago.

When I first went there, the passages were littered with climbing ropes, hobnailed boots and drying clothes. Meals were served at a long table, with no choice of food, in a room hung with enlarged photographs by Ashley Abraham, whose camera work incidentally has never been bettered, of the classic rock climbs around Wasdale and the brave men who made the first ascents. The talk then was exclusively of adventures on the crags. Mine host in those early years of the sport was Will Ritson, a great character and practical joker: it was said of Wasdale Head in those days that it had the highest mountain, the deepest lake and the biggest liar in the country, the latter distinction being earned by Ritson himself.

Those times are over. Today all is changed. The inn has been tidied, the horses and traps have been replaced by cars, and sandals are as likely to be seen as heavy boots. I liked it better as it was.

A short lane leaves the inn heading towards Kirk Fell which most closely overlooks the dale, and a good path turns left above the intake walls and enters Mosedale. Just below, lined by trees, is Mosedale Beck, momentarily excited by a waterfall known as Ritson's Force; across the stream rise the towering slopes of Yewbarrow, surmounted by the cliffs of Stirrup Crag. Ahead, the desolate hollow of Mosedale comes into view, dominated by the ramparts of Red Pike and terminated by Scoat Fell.

The path trends to the right as the slopes of Kirk Fell decline. It climbs steadily to come alongside the tumbling waters of Gatherstone Beck, its name apparently derived from the boulders that litter its bed. This is forded, the path rising on the far bank in zigzags before straightening into a steady climb towards the depression ahead. A newer track branching to the left is used by walkers ascending Pillar. Views here on Gatherstone Head are restricted to Yewbarrow behind and Kirk Fell across the beck, but gradually the gradient eases and a ruined wire fence marking the top of Black Sail Pass is reached.

Mosedale   Above *Ritson's Force*

At the top of the pass a splendid view unfolds ahead. Ennerdale is below in a dark shroud of conifer plantations contrasting sharply with the bare slopes of the upper reaches of the valley. Haystacks is directly in front and the lofty High Stile ridge rises in fine array to the left. At this point, however, the most arresting sight is Kirk Fell nearby, its shattered and craggy slopes soaring into the sky with dramatic effect: it looks rough, and it is.

The fence crosses the top of the pass, keeping to the watershed; westwards it serves as a perfect guide to Pillar, eastwards it climbs sharply into the fastnesses of Kirk Fell, bravely accompanied by a thin track.

The path goes forward and descends into Ennerdale, coming alongside the edge of the plantations and crossing the River Liza by a footbridge. Now in sight are the two giants of Ennerdale, Great Gable and Pillar: the former descends in smooth slopes from the rim of crags fringing its perfect dome while Pillar is very rough from top to toe and has an unbecoming skirt of spruce fir.

Black Sail Hut is a few minutes further on.

Opposite *Black Sail Hut*   Above left *View in Ennerdale and* (right) *the River Liza*

The Black Sail Hut, once a shepherd's bothy but now converted and extended into a Youth Hostel, is a lonely outpost indeed, far from other habitations, but a first-class centre for fellwalking expeditions. A cart track, now used as a forest road, leads down the valley through the plantations, some relief from a monotonous trudge being afforded by the lively Liza alongside. Another Youth Hostel at High Gillerthwaite is passed after an hour's walk in the close company of trees, the forest road continuing to run alongside the north shore of Ennerdale Water, where there is a fine retrospective view of Pillar, to a public car park at Bowness Point. If no car is waiting, the walk can be continued by a lakeside path to the little community of Ennerdale Bridge to sample the fleshpots on offer there, these consisting of an inn, a shop and an infrequent bus to Whitehaven.

2 BOARDALE HAUSE, 1200'
Patterdale – Boardale or Martindale

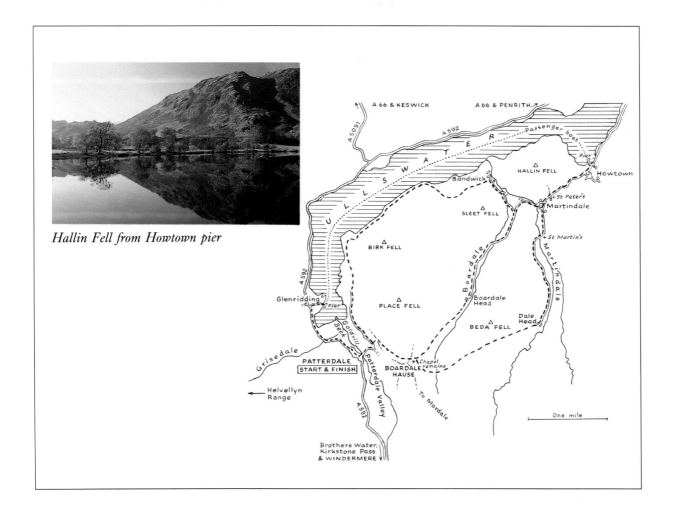

Hallin Fell from Howtown pier

THE EASTERN SIDE of the upper reaches of Ullswater rises abruptly in the steep and rough slopes of Place Fell, effectively barring a direct approach to the valleys that lie in the folds of the hills beyond. These valleys are hidden from the sight of the crowds of tourists who visit the lake, are unsuspected and remain unspoilt. By road, they can be reached by a long and circuitous journey around the north end of the lake and, having no through routes, are of little appeal to motorists, but walkers are blessed with a choice of two lovely paths. One runs along the lakeside, rounding the north end of Place Fell, and is in my opinion the most beautiful walk in Lakeland; the other climbs to and crosses a low ridge at the south end.

This latter pass is Boardale Hause.

Opposite *Patterdale from Boardale Hause*

Deepdale from Boardale Hause

FROM PATTERDALE VILLAGE, a side road crosses Goldrill Beck and gives access to the open fellside. The well-trodden path to the right is followed, taking the higher branch when it forks and climbing steadily to the easier ground of Boardale Hause.

The views on this ascent are of superlative beauty. Ahead is Brothers Water and Kirkstone Pass, deep-set amongst encroaching heights; behind is a glorious prospect of the Patterdale valley with the massive bulk of the Helvellyn range towering beyond the deep trench of Grisedale. Ullswater completes a delightful picture.

Boardale Hause is a walkers' crossroads, five paths leaving here for different destinations and needing care in selection. On the hause is a ruined enclosure resembling a derelict sheepfold, but in fact it is the site of a medieval chapel, as a few carved stones lying around testify. On large-scale maps, this is named Chapel in the Hause. Its isolated situation on the ridge, midway between Patterdale and Boardale, was presumably intended to give equal facility of access to the good folk of both valleys. Some years ago, the confusion of paths was further compounded by the construction of an aqueduct across the hause when the pipe-laying operations and tractors carved new routes over the top, but nature is doing its best to remove the scars.

Boardale Hause is the popular springboard for the ascent of Place Fell and a track climbs to the left with the summit as objective; another goes right for the long upland crossing to Mardale, but the main path, for Boardale and Martindale, leads forward over the crest, forking at once for Boardale, to the left, and Martindale, to the right.

The path into Boardale (spelt Boredale by early writers and map-makers) descends to the head of this valley which takes the form of a narrow defile between the slopes of Place Fell and Beda Fell. A good track goes down to the first habitation, Boardale Head, where it matures into a narrow road which, after a further mile or so, branches left to Sandwick; here the lakeside path may be taken to return to Patterdale, thus completing the circuit of Place Fell. The right fork links with Martindale and goes on to Howtown.

The path to Martindale is in no hurry to descend and circles around the head of Boardale to the south ridge of Beda Fell, beyond which it declines steadily into the much larger valley of Martindale, where there is a long-established deer sanctuary. It reaches the first habitation at Dale Head, a farmhouse notable for its massively buttressed walls. Here starts a pleasant road that proceeds along this quiet and lovely valley in the shadow of Beda Fell and joins the road from Boardale. Before the junction, a detour to the old church of St Martin is recommended: this was built in 1653 on the site of an ancient chapel, but was closed in 1881 because of decay. A new church, St Peter's, was built in 1882, but a few summer services are still held in the old church which has been restored.

Boardale   *Dale Head*

Below *The old church of St Martin*

From the road opposite St Peter's church a wide grass path – a joy to tread even in bare feet – leads to the top of Hallin Fell, and if time permits a half-hour's diversion, this simple stroll should not be missed. This is the easiest of all fellwalks and the visual rewards more than recompense the slight effort needed. Martindale is seen full length and in all its glory, and a bird's-eye view of Ullswater presents itself when the highest point is reached at 1271'. The summit is crowned by a fine obelisk of cut stone twelve feet tall. The man who built it not only indicated the top of the fell but erected for himself a permanent memorial.

There is a rise in the road beyond St Peter's church and at the top Ullswater is revealed ahead. The lakeside hamlet of Howtown is also in view amongst trees at the foot of a long descent made easier for cars by a series of wide loops.

Martindale from Hallin Fell

Howtown has a pier and is a calling place for the passenger boats that ply on Ullswater in summer. With pre-knowledge of the timetable, arrival can be timed to meet the boat for Glenridding, a mile from Patterdale, which gives a very pleasant return to the starting point of the walk. There is no more beautiful scene in the district than the head of Ullswater and no better way to enjoy its delights than to approach leisurely over the water.

Opposite *The road curling down to Ullswater*   Below *The pier at Howtown*

3 THE BURNMOOR CORPSE ROAD, 900′
Wasdale Head – Eskdale

BEFORE THE EARLY settlers at Wasdale Head were granted the present small patch of consecrated ground their fatal casualties had to be conveyed for burial elsewhere, at first to the mother church at St Bees and later to the churchyard just outside the village of Boot in Eskdale. The route adopted for these sad journeys to Boot lay over the low moor around Burnmoor Tarn, this being preferred to the longer and circuitous way on the primitive roads of that time. The coffins were strapped to the backs of horses, wheels being unable to negotiate the rough ground. The route was known as the Corpse Road and, now classed as a bridleway, is in popular use by today's walkers.

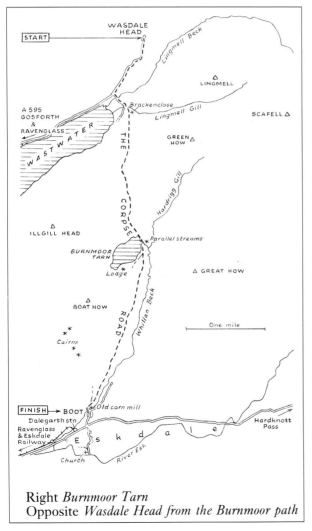

Right *Burnmoor Tarn*
Opposite *Wasdale Head from the Burnmoor path*

TURN OFF the road from Wasdale Head near the head of Wastwater where a lane to the left crosses an area that still bears traces of a devastating cloudburst in Lingmell Gill many years ago when an avalanche of boulders and rubble thundered down on the fields below, the debris being later partially cleared by prisoners of war. Beyond is the handsome building of Brackenclose, headquarters of the Fell and Rock Climbing Club since 1937. From here the route heads south on a gradual incline between the rising slopes of Green How and Illgill Head, to reach the bare summit of the pass, where Burnmoor Tarn and the fells around Eskdale come into view. The path goes on to the tarn.

Burnmoor Tarn is a large and unattractive sheet of water in a desolate landscape; a former gamekeeper's lodge is the only habitation in sight. The path skirts the eastern shore and here an odd natural curiosity will be seen: the main feeder of the tarn, Hardrigg Gill coming off Scafell, and the issuing stream, Whillan Beck, occur side by side and only a few paces apart without any apparent watershed between them.

After a marshy tract the path commences a long straight descent to Boot in the close company of Whillan Beck with the scene ahead becoming more pleasant with every step.

Walkers with archaeological interests and time to spare should deviate by climbing the low moor on the right to its summit, Boat How, thence descending south through an area of Bronze Age occupation with at least five stone circles and many ancient cairns as evidence. At the foot of the slope a bridleway will be reached, this going down to join the main path as it enters Boot.

Illgill Head

Ruins near Boat How

On the outskirts of Boot, before going down to the main street, the fellside immediately south is of nostalgic interest, being scarred with the remains of disused iron mines that were served by a narrow-gauge industrial railway along the base of the fell. The track is plain to see, although robbed of its lines, as is the site of the former Boot Station, passengers also being carried on the railway. This section was closed when the mines were abandoned, but half a mile down the valley the railway is open for passenger traffic; miniature trains offer a sylvan ride from Ravenglass to a new terminus at Dalegarth, where there is a shop and café. This popular railway is the Ravenglass and Eskdale Railway, affectionately known as Ratty, and links with the main railway at Ravenglass.

The old railway track at Boot

The village of Boot is entered by crossing a bridge over Whillan Beck and here is a building of character: the old corn mill, long disused but restored to working order by Cumbria County Council in 1975.

The scenery upstream is charming and a short walk on a woodland path from the bridge brings into view a delightful section of the beck, its waters tumbling in cataracts amongst rocks.

Boot is the 'capital' of mid-Eskdale although having only a few cottages and a tiny population. It is a friendly place and apart from its visual delights, has an hotel, shops and cafés that cater mainly for the summer invasions of visitors brought by the miniature railway to the terminus nearby. And there is a church and graveyard worth visiting, and of course the lovely River Esk. Boot is favoured.

The corn mill at Boot

Whillan Beck

4 CARLSIDE COL, 2250'
Millbeck – Barkbeth

ANYONE TRAVELLING between the Vale of Keswick and the countryside west of Skiddaw will almost certainly make the journey by road and only the odd eccentric with time to kill will consider the alternative walking route described in this chapter, this involving a steep and stony scramble in terrain unfamiliar to tourists. The route provides an introduction to the twin valleys of Southerndale and Barkbethdale coming down from Skiddaw, rarely visited and known intimately only by the local farmers. Other walkers are not likely to be met. Solitude reigns.

THE WALK STARTS at the pleasant hamlet of Millbeck nestling amongst trees at the base of Skiddaw where a path leads north and soon comes alongside the stream issuing from the obvious defile ahead. Directly in front is the dark pyramid of Carsleddam, a heathery offshoot of the greater fell of Carl Side beyond. The stream, Slades Beck, comes round the obstacle on the east side, down a stony ravine with Skiddaw Little Man towering high above and the parent fell ahead. The walk by the stream is so totally enclosed that it becomes claustrophobic: there is little of beauty in this arid scene. When confronted by the great mass of Skiddaw the route trends left and climbs steeply and stonily to an obvious col on the skyline where a deserved halt may be taken and the way onward prospected. Carl Side rises on the left, terminating a ridge formed by Long Side and Ullock Pike. A track bound for Skiddaw crosses the col and ascends a stony slope littered with slate fragments, some loose, some in embedded upright flakes. Nearby is the insignificant Carlside Tarn.

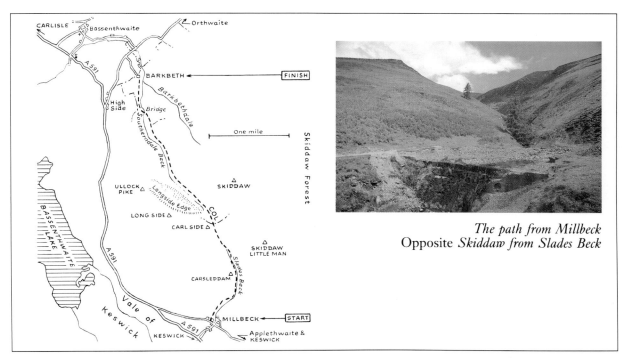

The path from Millbeck
Opposite *Skiddaw from Slades Beck*

Above *Long Side and Ullock Pike from Carlside Col*
Left *Southerndale*

Over the crest of the col the way is downhill on steep pathless slopes into the head of Southerndale, a shy valley completely dominated by the ramparts of Longside Edge high above, from which fans of scree scar the fellsides. When Southerndale Beck takes shape, a thin track above its eastern bank will, if it can be found, ease the walk down the valley to a bridge, and here there is an impressive retrospect of the valley with Skiddaw now in view.

From the bridge, a rough lane, with thorn bushes and trees which soften the landscape, leads to the farmstead of Barkbeth at the foot of a parallel valley, Barkbethdale, along which is an imposing view of Skiddaw.

A farm access lane goes down to a tarmac road leading left to High Side, which has a bus stop on the Keswick–Carlisle service. Or alternatively, a side road goes to the nearby village of Bassenthwaite (locally called Bass) which is likely to have refreshments on offer.

Above *The path to Barkbeth*   Below *Barkbeth Farm*

5 COLEDALE HAUSE, 2000'
Braithwaite – Lanthwaite

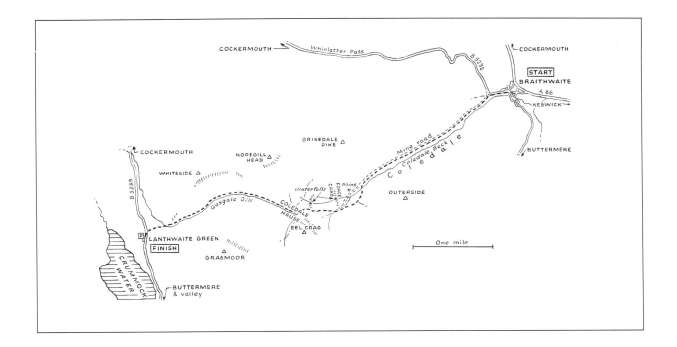

T HE NORTH-WESTERN fells form a compact mass, the individual summits being closely linked, and although the boundaries of the group are clearly defined by surrounding valleys, there are no easy ways through the high ground.

The only recognised pass in common use is Coledale Hause, the usual route to it being along the straight channel of Coledale, leading into the heart of wild uplands, an approach also popular as a fast way to the summits of the enclosing heights, especially when starting from the village of Braithwaite. The through route is interesting rather than impressive, views being restricted, but the journey is a splendid half-day's expedition.

Opposite *Coledale*
Right *Braithwaite*

STARTING FROM Braithwaite, advantage can be taken of a long and easy mine road leading straight as an arrow in the direction of the hause. The village is left by the Whinlatter Pass road and around the first corner the mine road leaves on the left. There is a short cut to it blazed by the boots of the thousands of walkers bound for Grisedale Pike which dominates the scene, but the original start is much easier. The mine road enters the long valley of Coledale and heads purposefully for a barytes mine at its terminus: this section is tedious but gives a fast approach on a good surface along the base of Grisedale Pike; opposite is the shapely peak of Outside rising sharply from Coledale Beck alongside the road. When the mine is within easy reach, the beck is crossed and a rising path ascends grassy slopes to outflank the imposing barrier of Force Crag directly behind the mine and forming a precipitous background. The dark cliffs are relieved by the silver thread of Low Force cascading over the rim.

As height is gained along the path, another wall of crags comes into view above the other, these upper cliffs also having a slender waterfall, High Force.

Force Crag

Coledale and Force Crag mine from High Force

Now having the impending mass of Eel Crag on the left, the path continues to climb easily to the flat expanse of Coledale Hause, passing many industrial relics on the adjacent ground. On the hause itself is a disused water cut that formerly diverted the stream of Gasgale Gill, coming down on the left, from its natural course over the watershed to provide supplies for the mines.

Most walkers arriving at the hause leave the path here to ascend Eel Crag or Grasmoor on the left, or Hopegill Head or Grisedale Pike on the right; all these fine summits are often visited in a circular expedition from Braithwaite using the hause only as a crossing place.

The through route to Lanthwaite and Crummock Water goes forward over the watershed and descends steeply into the ravine of Gasgale Gill on a path now much rougher underfoot but compensated by the lovely vistas appearing through the portals of the gill as the walk proceeds.

All around is wild desolation, ahead is enchantment.

As height is lost, the confining fells rise starkly into the sky. On the left is Grasmoor, the highest of the group, its steep slopes not inviting ascent; and on the right, even more repelling, are the crags and scree runs of Whiteside in an awesome downfall.

Between the two heights, the stream and the path run close together and emerge in a rocky passage at the exit to the gill; immediately a beautiful prospect is revealed as an easy slope goes down to the road at Lanthwaite Green. The formidable slopes of Grasmoor fall away abruptly to permit a view of the Buttermere valley with the High Stile ridge supreme. Over the pastures of Lanthwaite, rise the twin summits of Mellbreak, a stretch of Crummock Water also being seen.

The whole scene is exquisite and becomes more so on close acquaintance; only the procession of cars along the road disturb the tranquillity of this loveliest part of Lakeland. The road remains narrow despite the influx of summer motorists who must continue to suffer inconvenience: it would be sacrilege to widen and improve this road to modern standards, so destroying the charm of a delightful journey in scenery of superlative beauty.

Mellbreak and Lanthwaite   Above *Gasgale Gill*

Above *High Stile and Crummock Water*

Below *Crummock Water and Loweswater*

6 DALEHEAD TARN, 1900'
Newlands – Honister Pass

THE HEAD OF Newlands is so tightly encircled by mountains that there seems at first sight to be no way of crossing this barrier except by serious climbing. And these mountains are formidable. Blocking the direct route south is Dale Head, defended by cliffs always in shadow and effectively terminating the valley. Nor are its near neighbours of kinder appearance: high on the left is the mile-long escarpment of Eel Crags, a place for rockclimbers only, and to the right rise interminable slopes, capped by cliffs and scree, to the top of Hindscarth, neither having anything to offer the average walker.

Newlands Beck points the way of escape. It is seen coming down easier ground to the left of Dale Head and a path follows its course upwards without difficulty and leads on to an easy descent to the road at the top of Honister Pass.

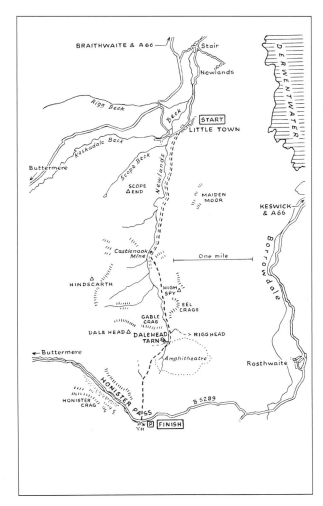

A CART-TRACK leaves the road at Little Town in Newlands and heads south following Newlands Beck upstream for two miles along the floor of the valley with little gain in height. The track is distinct, having been used for centuries by traffic from the many mines hereabouts, all now disused, and in modern times by the boots of walkers. On the left is Maiden Moor, with relics of lead mines and quarries, and on the right Scope End rises abruptly in a dark covering of heather that conceals the spoil of the once-famous Goldscope Mine; although the levels driven into the fellside can still be found, they should not be entered.

Opposite *The upper Newlands valley*
Below *Dale Head*

Hindscarth and Scope End from Little Town

This mine was abandoned over a hundred years ago after intermittent operation for six centuries: one of the oldest mines in the district, it was also the most important in output, having rich veins of lead and copper, and silver and gold have also been extracted. Its early development on a large scale was undertaken by German miners, and its long history has been marked by many incidents and much litigation.

Higher in the valley the old mine of Castlenook occupies a prominent headland alongside the track and beyond is revealed the final reaches in the form of a grassy ampitheatre deep-set amongst rising fellsides. Directly in front, leaving nobody in doubt that Newlands has come to an end, towers the immense facade of Dale Head with Gable Crag conspicuous. On the left skyline is the intimidating array of Eel Crags, and Hindscarth on the right is capped by a barrier of broken cliffs and has no welcome to offer. The ampitheatre, however, is a rewarding place for those with an interest in things past: there are mine shafts and ruined huts, and it is still possible to trace a well-graded path going up to the old copper mine on Dale Head, now in sad decay but worthy of inspection.

Newlands Beck is seen coming down from a depression to the left of Dale Head and a path follows it up to a plateau of easy but undulating and confusing ground. A track branches left to Rigg Head and descends to Rosthwaite past the extensive disused quarries.

For Honister, the path goes forward, still alongside the stream, passing Dalehead Tarn which cannot be seen but is indicated by a tributary issuing from it. A thin track leaves the side of the tarn bound for the summit of Dale Head which towers behind.

It will now be appreciated by walkers that the name of Dalehead Tarn heading this chapter is not really appropriate. The true pass or watershed is seen half a mile further on above a slight slope, the stream still descending from it. The path continues easily, crossing an old wire fence to join the main path from Honister Pass to the top of Dale Head. At the watershed, a glorious panorama of well-loved mountains is suddenly displayed ahead with stunning effect across the trench of Honister, and makes a magnificent background as the path descends gradually to the road at the top of Honister Pass.

Right *Dalehead Tarn*
Below *The view south from the watershed*

7 DEEPDALE HAUSE, 2150'
Dunmail Raise – Deepdale

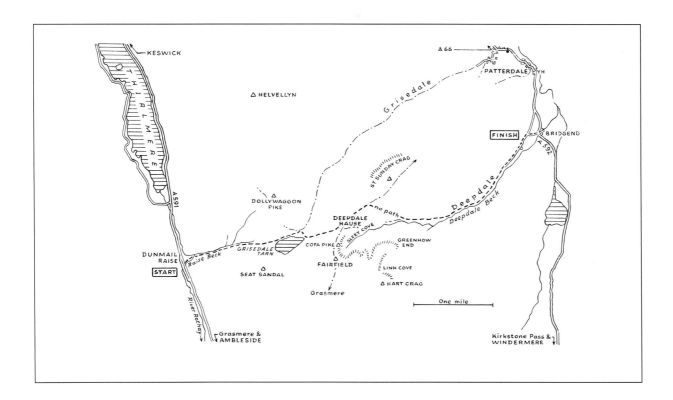

WHEN I FIRST explored the eastern fells, there was no semblance of a path from Grisedale Tarn to the obvious depression of Deepdale Hause on the high skyline between St Sunday Crag and Fairfield. Since those early days, a thin track has formed, not, however, intended to assist the crossing of the hause into the valley of Deepdale beyond but to reach the excellent path going up from the hause to St Sunday Crag after following the ridge down from Fairfield. Rarely indeed is the hause used as a pass into Deepdale since most walkers arriving at the tarn from Grasmere prefer the easier route provided by continuing along the bridleway down Grisedale and so to the Patterdale valley, of which Deepdale is a part. But if Grisedale is busy with pedestrian traffic, as it often is, Deepdale Hause is the key to a lonely alternative with mountain scenery of a high order, and for the person who likes undisturbed solitude it has special appeal for there is very little possibility of meeting other walkers. Here a buzzard may circle overhead and sheep will be grazing but no other sign of life need be expected. On its wild upper reaches, Deepdale becomes your very own.

Opposite *Deepdale Hause from Grisedale Tarn*

GRISEDALE TARN is invariably reached by way of the popular Grasmere–Patterdale path but there is a shorter and quieter route to the tarn from the west. This starts from the A591 on the top of Dunmail Raise.

Clear of the tarmac and the things that speed along it, the moor is crossed to come alongside Raise Beck issuing from a rough watercourse forming the north boundary of Seat Sandal. The beck, a happy tumble of cataracts, is no longer destined exclusively for the Rothay, as nature intended, but has been diverted to feed Thirlmere. A stony track climbs along the bank emerging, as Seat Sandal declines, into open grassland with Grisedale Tarn in full view ahead, backed by the St Sunday Crag and Fairfield range with Deepdale Hause clearly identifiable. Nearby is the massive bulk of Dollywaggon Pike carrying a dusty path to Helvellyn.

From the outlet of the tarn, a beeline can be made for the hause, keeping a lookout for the new track to ease the ascent of the rough fellside. When attained, there is a comprehensive view of the Helvellyn range seen over the great gulf of Grisedale, but the most imposing feature within close proximity is the sharp pinnacle of Cofa Pike, concealing its parent fell, Fairfield.

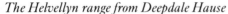

The Helvellyn range from Deepdale Hause   Above *Raise Beck*

Used as a pass, a descent must now be made into the head of Deepdale without the help of a path, and the scenery is immediately awesome: the crags of Cofa Pike plunge precipitously into Sleet Cove and beyond is seen the massive wall of Fairfield in a succession of cliffs and scree gullies which terminate in the towering buttress of Greenhow End. There is no difficulty in finding a way down the valley: after initial steepness, the descent is on easy grass and Deepdale Beck soon forms to give infallible guidance – indeed, one has a feeling of watching a tremendous convulsion of nature from a comfortable seat in the front row of the stalls.

When the wild upper recesses are left behind, a path materialises and leads around the base of St Sunday Crag in surroundings of lessening drama to the cultivated fields, trees and scattered homesteads as the A592 road and creature comforts are reached in Patterdale.

Above *Cofa Pike*

Below *The northern precipices of Fairfield*

8 DUNMAIL RAISE, 782'
Grasmere – Thirlmere

THE MAIN ARTERY of communication in the Lake District is the A591 road which takes advantage of the only easy breach in the high fells. Recent road improvements have made this a fast highway for cars but, because of the weight of traffic, heavy lorries are precluded from using it.

The name of the pass derives from Dunmail, the last King of Cumberland, who was defeated in battle in 945 by King Edmund of England, and whose remains, according to legend, are buried beneath the huge pile of stones on the summit of the pass. This cairn or mound was preserved during a realignment of the road some years ago and now occupies an island formed by a dual carriageway.

Freed from the delays caused by heavy vehicles, cars use the road as a racetrack. Pedestrians are advised to keep off the tarmac as much as they can and may do so as described below.

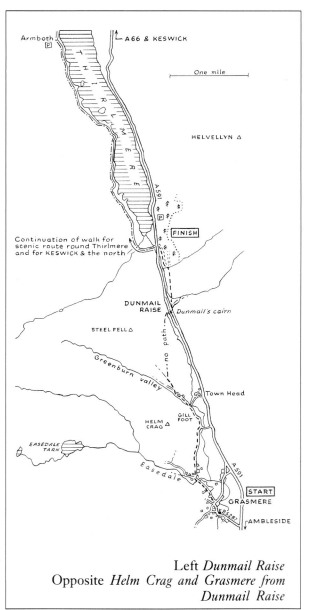

Left *Dunmail Raise*
Opposite *Helm Crag and Grasmere from Dunmail Raise*

INSTEAD OF following the A591 north from Grasmere, travellers on foot would do far better by taking the side road to Easedale, leaving it at the first junction on the right where a quiet and pleasant byway runs below Helm Crag to the secluded dell of Gill Foot and continues along a track that leads into the side valley of Greenburn. This is left near the last two cottages in favour of a path climbing the south ridge of Steel Fell. When clear of the intakes, which still feature a pillbox where the folk of Grasmere intended to repel German invaders who never came, a beeline can be made to Dunmail Raise, now clearly in sight, by contouring the pathless fellside and crossing an area of drumlins left by a glacier. Walkers arrive exactly at the top of the pass, indicated by Dunmail's cairn.

The alternative to continuing on the road is provided by a stile in the wall on the east side, which admits to a field where the old road can be joined to cross an ancient bridge at the foot of a series of waterfalls before entering a conifer plantation and debouching on the main road opposite the junction of the scenic route around Thirlmere. If instead the A591 is followed down to Thirlmere, a tear-jerking plaque set in the wall on the right, and not noticed by speeding motorists, deserves a brief halt: this pays a glowing tribute to a horse that gave his master a lifetime of faithful service and 'whose only fault was dying'.

Walkers bound for places north of Thirlmere, or Keswick, should escape from the A591 and take to the scenic route, a much quieter and more attractive alternative starting at the junction where a signpost still points to Armboth although nothing is left of Armboth now but its name which is used for the car park and the fell (*see* page 100).

9 ESK HAUSE, 2490'
Eskdale – Borrowdale

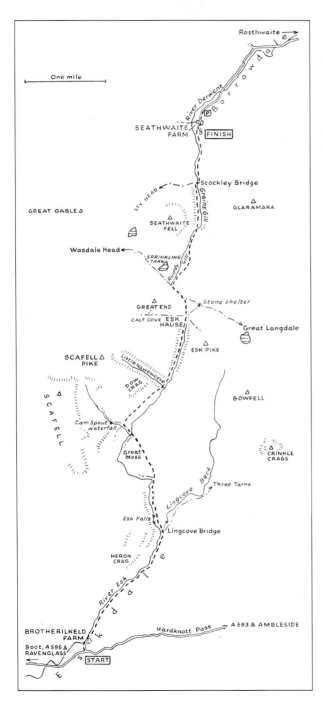

ESK HAUSE – the true Esk Hause, not the misnamed one – forms a watershed between the two lovely valleys of Eskdale and Borrowdale, and is the highest pass in Lakeland. This distinction is not recognised by popularity, for although it crosses magnificent terrain it is rarely used as a pass. In fact, I have never seen anybody engaged on the through route and, truth to tell, I have never done it myself. One reason for its neglect may be that the course of the route runs alongside the Scafell range and most red-blooded walkers, in fine weather, cannot resist the greater appeal of the high-level traverse of the ridge.

The head of Eskdale is confusing topographically, a tangle of rough ground in a bowl formed by the Scafells, Esk Pike, Bowfell and Crinkle Crags, and one of the wildest areas in the district. But the route to Esk Hause is clearly defined by the River Esk, this being followed closely to its source just below the hause and pointing the way exactly. Over the hause, territory much frequented by walkers is reached and the loneliness of the approach is dispelled.

But make no mistake. An afternoon start is too late. Esk Hause deserves a full day.

ESKDALE'S ROAD is left at the foot of Hardknott Pass near Brotherilkeld Farm, the only habitation seen on the journey until Seathwaite Farm is reached at the end of the day. A distinct path goes up the valley in typical Lakeland scenery and comes alongside the delightful River Esk, a watercourse of pools and splashes and happy gurgles, but today its charms must be resisted: it must not detain. The long precipice of Heron Crag, high on the left, is passed and a confluence of waters is reached, the picturesque stone arch of Lingcove Bridge being just beyond and spanning Lingcove Beck coming down from Bowfell.

Opposite Esk Hause

Above *Brotherilkeld looking towards Bowfell*

Below *Lingcove Bridge*

Hereabouts, the Esk changes direction, the river issuing from a spectacular gorge through which plunge the Esk Falls. The gorge is manifestly inaccessible and is avoided by crossing Lingcove Bridge to a path rising along the fellside high above. Almost at once the great wall of the Scafells comes into view ahead, a thrilling moment calculated to stop in his tracks anyone carrying a camera. The path goes forward towards the imposing scene and reaches a vast marshland, the Great Moss, once a deer preserve owned by Furness Abbey. Now the Scafells are seen in full stature and majesty, rising sharply from the flat strath of the Moss. A popular route of ascent is indicated by the waterfall of Cam Spout directly ahead, but the route to Esk Hause follows the river up the valley opening on the right and after gingerly picking a way through the marshy ground, join a firm path.

Above *Esk Falls*

The Scafells from Great Moss

The path continues upriver, the valley narrowing as the fells crowd in on both sides. The formidable cliff of Dow Crag, sometimes referred to as Esk Buttress, is prominent on the left and succeeded by the great chasm of Little Narrowcove, a rough and menacing ravine beset by crags and bringing a tributary down to join the Esk, which is now in its infancy. As it traverses stony ground the path becomes intermittent as it still keeps close to the stream. The eastern flanks of the valley throughout this section of the walk from Great Moss belong to Esk Pike.

The hause is now seen ahead above a rough steep slope; the stream and the path give up the ghost, having fulfilled their roles as guides, and a final stiff pull lands the walker on Esk Hause, with a new landscape in front of him.

Above *Esk Pike*

Below *Looking north from Esk Hause*

Grains Gill

On the grassy expanse of Esk Hause life becomes exciting again. The ground in front falls away gradually towards Borrowdale between the massive dome of Great End, half left, and Esk Pike high to the right. Well-worn paths are met here. A track blazed by thousands of boots each year winds up into Calf Cove on a popular route to Scafell Pike; another goes off to climb Esk Pike. Another, also part of the Scafell Pike route, comes up over easy grass from a wind shelter of stones on the path crossing below between Great Langdale and Wasdale Head; this shelter is commonly regarded as Esk Hause, quite wrongly.

To proceed, it was formerly necessary to go down to the shelter and turn along the Wasdale path, but a fairly new track has been trodden from the hause and descends directly to the Wasdale path at the top of Grains Gill after passing alongside Great End and revealing a view of Great Gable. Grains Gill is the key to the last few miles of the walk. At its head, alongside the Wasdale path, it has the name of Ruddy Gill, the red subsoil having an iron content. Five minutes further towards Wasdale, the path comes alongside the shores of a delightful sheet of water, Sprinkling Tarn, a great time-waster and not on today's crowded itinerary: it should be saved for a leisurely visit and a long halt. Having resisted this detour, the stream issuing from Ruddy Gill is crossed and a steep descent follows, skirting a deep ravine from which the stream emerges as Grains Gill. This too is forded to a path that goes down with the stream to Stockley Bridge; the stream becomes the River Derwent below the bridge. The crowds met here should not be assumed to be a welcoming party; nothing is further from their minds. Some are picnickers; some casual strollers. We are back in tourist country. A wide, dusty and often busy path leaves the bridge for the short journey to Seathwaite Farm, always a welcome sight. There is a car park here which is the terminus of the Borrowdale valley road.

Above *The top of Floutern Pass looking to Buttermere*

Below *Ennerdale from Floutern Pass*

10 FLOUTERN PASS, 1300'
Ennerdale – Buttermere

IF WALKERS WERE called upon to vote for the Lakeland pass they considered least attractive, there is little doubt that Floutern Pass would top the poll with a thumping majority. This pass is the easiest and shortest way of crossing the fells between the Buttermere valley and Ennerdale Water. It starts well and finishes well but the intermediate stages are without charm or beauty and contain an extensive quagmire from which few walkers escape dryshod. Nor have the surrounding fells any visual appeal: they are barren, lack character, are without features of interest, undistinguished in outline and share in the general hopelessness of the landscape. It is the sort of place that once visited will ever afterwards be approached with trepidation. Some reward for misery will be gained by walking the pass in the direction here indicated, suffering being forgotten in the sylvan beauty of Buttermere with Scale Force as a special bonus to revive drooping spirits. Floutern, frankly, is a mess.

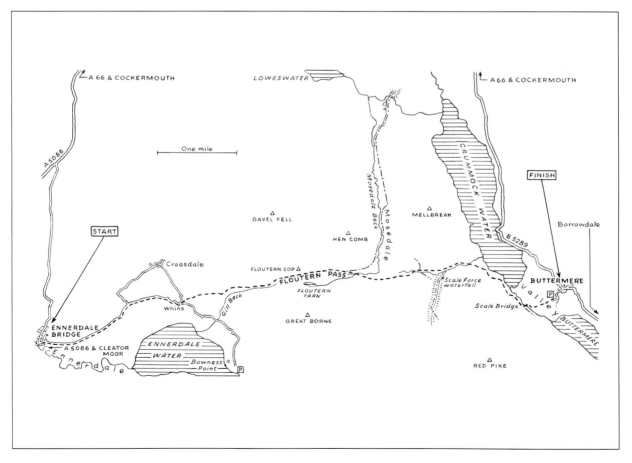

THE VILLAGE of Ennerdale Bridge is left by the Croasdale road, from which a lane cuts a corner to reach a no-through road, much used in summer, going down to a large car park at Bowness Point on the side of Ennerdale Water. The path to Floutern Pass leaves this road at Whins and climbs steadily alongside Gill Beck to a wire fence crossing the watershed and marking the highest point of the walk. The views fore and aft are in total contrast. Behind are the green pastures and thriving husbandry of Ennerdale with a glimpse of its lovely lake, a pleasing scene, but ahead is seen a dreary wasteland without invitation or welcome – Bunyan's Slough of Despond in person, but with a hint of better things in the far distance. Only the diminutive peak of Floutern Cop nearby tries to give distinction to the scene. On the right, the ground rises to Great Borne, also known as Herdhouse or Herdus, and Floutern Tarn comes into sight as the walk proceeds, being revealed as an elongated sheet of water with attractions only for anglers and not worth a visit.

The path descends into a vast hollow, dark with peaty marshland and threaded by the stream issuing from the tarn. The stream has the good sense to escape into a side valley, one of Lakeland's five Mosedales, and a path goes with it along the base of Mellbreak to the sweet countryside of Loweswater. But walkers bound for Buttermere must contemplate the morass ahead and find a way across it, gingerly treading the wet ground and making abortive searches for firm footing in a series of trials and errors before soaked feet make a nonsense of patient investigation and a beeline is ploughed to the greenery ahead. Finally clear of the glutinous mud, a slight slope is climbed and at the top a view is revealed that makes it all seem worthwhile.

The marshes of Floutern Pass

Crummock Water and the Buttermere Fells
Right *Scale Force*

After the damp rigours of the Floutern crossing, the prospect from the top of the rise beyond is a soothing balm. Crummock Water appears in a frame of colourful fells to make a lovely picture. On the descent, a popular path turns off to the rocky chasm of Scale Force, its 125-ft plunge making it the highest of Lakeland's waterfalls and the highlight of the Buttermere area. Victorian ladies and gentlemen visiting the force were brought by boat to a landing on the shore of Crummock Water, but today's Elizabethans must use a wet path through the lakeside trees. This is the path that ends the walk from Ennerdale, crossing Scale Bridge to enter Buttermere village in surroundings of such exquisite beauty that Floutern seems like a bad dream. But if the path is crowded and noisy, as is all too often the case, even lonely Floutern will be seen to have some merit after all.

11 GARBURN PASS, 1450'
Troutbeck – Kentmere

THERE IS little doubt that in late medieval times before the present lines of communication were established, a primitive road cut across the fells in the south-east corner of the Lake District between Windermere and Shap. The initial section of this ancient highway took advantage of a dip in the high skyline of the Ill Bell range to cross from Troutbeck to Kentmere, the depression being known as Garburn Pass, originally spelt Garbourn. Ordnance Survey maps still name the long lane leading to it as Garburn Road. Today, reduced in status to a bridleway, it is a route only for walkers, pony trekkers and motorbike scramblers.

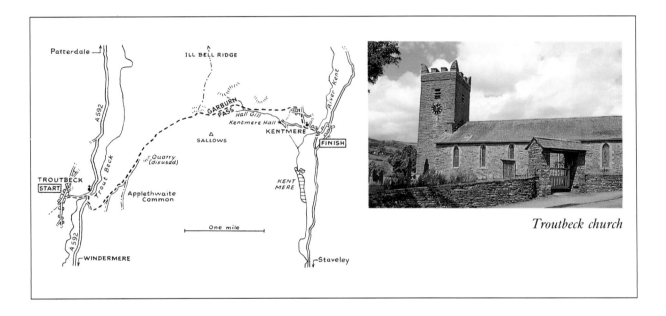

Troutbeck church

A SHADY LANE leaves the A592 near Troutbeck church and climbs steadily among trees to reach open country where it is joined by a rough road coming from the south. The fellside here is Applethwaite Common, the venue of annual sheepdog trials.

The lane continues to ascend between stone walls and soon reaches the disused Applethwaite Quarry. Most old quarries are gloomy and repelling, with an air of desolation, but this one, masked by trees, is worthy of inspection since it still retains its weighbridge and other relics of abandoned industry. This apart, there is little to relieve the tedium of the steady climb except for an excellent aerial view of the Troutbeck valley, improving with every step.

When the summit is gained, there is a comprehensive panorama to the west, the high fells of Lakeland forming the distant horizon. A rough track turns off here over marshy ground to the Ill Bell ridge, but the cart-track goes forward through a gate between sturdy stone walls.

Opposite *Looking to The Tongue and Threshthwaite Mouth*

Above *Applethwaite Quarry*

Below *Garburn Pass looking down to Windermere*

With the Kentmere valley now in sight, the descent there commences on a deteriorating but distinct path following Hall Gill down below an escarpment of crags high on the left. In pleasant surroundings, the pele tower of Kentmere Hall comes into sight below and the new Kent Mere beyond. As the first buildings appear ahead, a huge isolated rock may be noticed in a field over the wall on the right: this is Badger Rock, also known as Brock Stone. It resembles a small cliff, large enough to provide rock climbs, but is in fact a boulder fallen from the heights above.

Pass through a picturesque complex of cottages and farm buildings to a tarmac road which leads to Kentmere church and the village beyond.

Pele tower at Kentmere Hall   Above *Badger Rock*

12 GATESCARTH PASS, 1950'
Longsleddale – Mardale

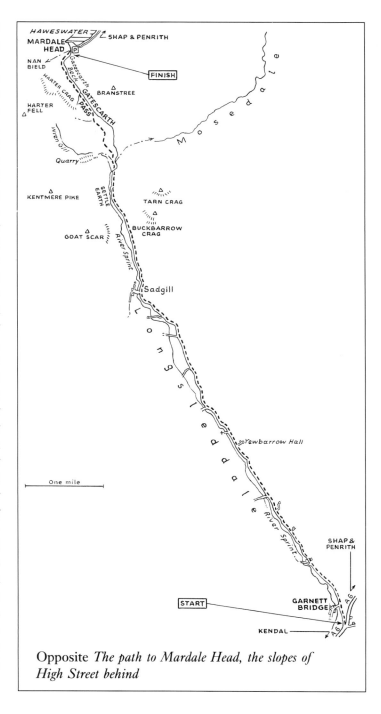

MOTORISTS TRAVELLING north from Kendal along the A6 are rewarded for preferring this old turnpike to the modern M6 by a brief glimpse of a lovely valley opening between bare fells on the left after five miles of the journey. This valley is seen emerging, straight as a furrow, from a distant mountain surround, and patterned by pasture and woodland and an occasional white farmhouse. With the River Sprint running alongside, it is a delightful place.

This is Longsleddale, the most easterly of the major valleys of Lakeland and lacking nothing of the beauty of the others; indeed, preserving the romantic charm that some have lost. Because of its seclusion and the absence of a through passage for vehicles, and having neither an inn nor a shop in its eight-mile length, it has happily suffered little from the intrusion of tourists: its one road remains narrow between fragrant hedges and stone walls. It is an oasis of pastoral tranquillity amidst inhospitable fells, looking very much as it did three centuries ago. Man has nurtured it, not spoilt it. The only disturbance to its rural security occurred some fifty years ago when Manchester Corporation cut a five-mile trench along the eastern slopes to contain their aqueduct from Haweswater, but they restored the ground commendably and nature has since clothed the scars. More recently a second aqueduct was planned but the project was abandoned after angry protests from the inhabitants. The people of Longsleddale may be few in number but they love their valley and are right to be proud of it. Longsleddale is delightful.

Opposite *The path to Mardale Head, the slopes of High Street behind*

Longsleddale
Right *Garnett Bridge*

THE VALLEY ROAD branches from the A6 and descends sharply to the only hamlet, Garnett Bridge, where a cluster of cottages around a former bobbin mill makes a picturesque study for the camera. Then the road goes on, mile after mile, passing the oldest building in the dale, the medieval pele tower of Yewbarrow Hall, and the little church before finally reaching the farmsteads of Sadgill. Here the road ends. Cars can go no further and are often parked on the verges by the bridge, sometimes awkwardly to the annoyance of the few residents of this lonely outpost. Car parks never improve the scenery and usually detract from it, but at Sadgill Bridge a small one is now needed.

At Sadgill, the view ahead is of wild grandeur. The mountains crowd in, revealing the desolate upper reaches of the valley through the rugged portals of Goat Scar and Buckbarrow. The crossing of Gatescarth Pass starts here, for travellers on foot only. The tarmac road gives place to a rough cart-track between stone walls. The green pastures continue for a further half-mile. In 1845, a reservoir was planned here with the authority of an Act of Parliament to regulate the flow of the river to the water-powered mills lower down the valley, but it was never proceeded with because of the huge cost. Cultivation ends abruptly where a gravel dam, built to retain the stones brought down by the river, crosses the valley floor.

Now the track starts to climb into a scene of grim desolation. On the left rises the precipitous face of Goat Scar, this being succeeded by the gloomy mountain hollow of Settle Earth, a haven for foxes; the summit above is Kentmere Pike. On the right towers Buckbarrow Crag, its discharge of stones littering the ground; amongst them but not discernible from the track is a massive boulder rivalling in size the famous Bowder Stone in Borrowdale. The height above is Tarn Crag which has on its summit the crumbling remains of a stone survey post, one of three erected above the line of the aqueduct from Haweswater, here in a tunnel over a thousand feet below the surface.

The steeper sections of the track are roughly paved with stones set in horizontal courses to serve as brakes for the horses bringing down heavy loads of slate from Wrengill Quarry, long disused. Alongside tumbles the infant Sprint in a series of cataracts and waterfalls.

The head of Longsleddale

The cart-track escapes from its confining walls when the gradient eases and a gate is reached, the wall on the right turning up the fellside and that on the left continuing on the line of march. The landscape here is dreary, the walk proceeding with open grassland on the right, rising gradually to a depression on the skyline. A path branches in this direction over rough and marshy ground: this is the way to Mosedale.

A stile in the accompanying wall admits to the vast disused Wrengill Quarry, and for walkers with an interest in industrial archaeology a detour over the wall will be most rewarding.

Wrengill Quarry has vertical man-made cliffs, tunnels, a derelict tramway, water channels, a terrace of cottages and ancillary buildings, all in sad decay.

On my first visit, the cottages were substantially intact. I once spent a night here amongst the skeletal ghosts of an abandoned industry, an eerie experience in the graveyard of dead workings. The only pleasure I can remember on this occasion was provided by the extensive carpet of wild thyme on the cliff tops: I uprooted a few plants for my garden at home but they obviously preferred the loneliness of Wrengill Quarry and soon withered in an alien habitat in suburbia.

At the far extremity of the quarry, Wren Gill enters in a fine waterfall, disappearing into two potholes and continuing underground before emerging as the River Sprint.

The quarry was last worked by prisoners during the First World War. It is a sad place today.

Waterfall in River Sprint

Summit of Gatesgarth Pass
Right *Harter Crag*

Resuming the walk to Mardale, the track rises steadily over grass slopes, now unenclosed, and ascends in a series of zigzags, engineered centuries ago to ease the passage of laden packhorses. Higher, the gradient lessens and the summit of Gatescarth Pass is reached at a gate in a wire fence crossing the watershed. A new landscape opens up ahead framed by the crags of Harter Fell and the steep declivities of Branstree. The prospect is pleasing as the track descends into Mardale, at first gently and, when the ground steepens, in a succession of sharp zigzags so delightful to follow that there is no inducement to short cuts; consequently there is little erosion and the path remains in pristine condition. Gatescarth Beck is a lively companion alongside.

To the left, split by a great gully, tower the cliffs of Harter Crag. It was here that a pair of golden eagles, the first seen in Lakeland for 150 years, built an abortive eyrie two decades ago. Later they adopted a nesting site on another crag a mile away where, under the watchful eyes of wardens of the Royal Society for the Protection of Birds, they settled successfully and reared families.

High Street and Haweswater come into view during the descent and the path from Nan Bield joins in for the final hundred yards to the public car park at Mardale Head situated at the terminus of the road alongside Haweswater.

13 GOATS HAUSE, 2100'
Coniston – Duddon Valley

GOATS HAUSE, as the name implies, is undoubtedly a pass, and it is true that by crossing it a walker may travel between Coniston and the Duddon Valley, but few ever will because the Walna Scar 'road' is so obviously the most direct way from one to the other. Only for anyone wishing to extend the walk and having a couple of hours to spare can Goats Hause be recommended. The route, however, has one great merit: it passes through one of the grandest scenes in the district where the awesome precipices of Dow Crag soar high above Goats Water. Also introduced is Seathwaite Tarn, a large sheet of water shyly hidden in a fold of the hills and not often seen by Lakeland's visitors.

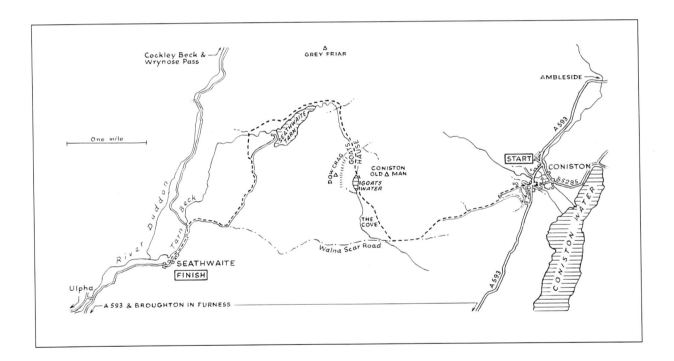

APPROACHING FROM Coniston, leave the Walna Scar cart-track just beyond the rock gateway where a track branches to the right and rises into a hollow, The Cove, with Dow Crag coming into sight ahead. When Goats Water is suddenly reached after a rise in the path, a dramatic picture unfolds with stunning effect. Dow Crag is now revealed in full stature as an array of massive buttresses split by deep gullies and overtopping steep slopes of scree and boulders falling to the water's edge. Goat's Water is uninviting, its outlet choked by boulders and its shores fringed with debris from above.

Opposite *Dow Crag*

When I first visited this impressive scene, there was an upright memorial stone, roughly inscribed CHARMER 1911, on a grassy bank amongst the boulders at the outlet of Goat's Water. Charmer was a foxhound killed in a fall on Dow Crag, and it is nice to reflect that a faithful dog was revered in this way. Then came the vandals. On a later visit, I found the memorial uprooted and cast among the stones in the bed of the issuing stream. Later still I could find no trace of it and hope it has been carried down by floodwaters to a safer haven. Charmer deserved better than this.

The rockclimbers' way to Dow Crag fords the outlet and slants upwards across the scree to a cave formed by a huge boulder at the foot of the cliff, this being the usual base of operations. Lesser mortals take a rough track along the eastern shore of the tarn, reaching easy slopes that rise to the dip in the skyline ahead. This is Goats Hause, traversed by a path linking Dow Crag and Coniston Old Man, the latter having been on the right throughout the walk thus far. There is a fresh landscape in front but it is the sight of Dow Crag that still rivets the attention.

Goats Water and Dow Crag from Goats Hause

Seathwaite Tarn
Right *Gully on Dow Crag*

Continuing, a long simple slope descends into the valley in front where Seathwaite Tarn, almost a mile in length, occupies the centre of the stage, the backcloth being formed by the bulky fell of Grey Friar, an outlier of the Coniston range. Around the head of the tarn, which has been adapted as a reservoir, are relics of the Seathwaite Copper Mines, a dead industry; there are open mine levels here that are dangerous to enter. This area is featured in Richard Adams' *The Plague Dogs*.

A path on the northern shore of the tarn leads to the reservoir access road and this is followed down, in scenes of increasing loveliness and thriving husbandry, to join the Walna Scar road before it meets the main valley road a pleasant half-mile north of Seathwaite. Dancing alongside in the final stages of the walk is Tarn Beck on its way to meet the River Duddon.

14 GRASSGUARDS, 1180′
Duddon Valley – Eskdale

FOR A WALK of sustained delight, the crossing of the broad ridge dividing the Duddon Valley and Eskdale must rank high in the itinerary of visitors enjoying a stay in the southern part of Lakeland. The start and finish are amid scenery of idyllic loveliness, sadly marred by recent extensive conifer plantations on the Duddon flank of Harter Fell but the forest so created is skirted rather than entered and does not detract from the pleasures of a summer walk.

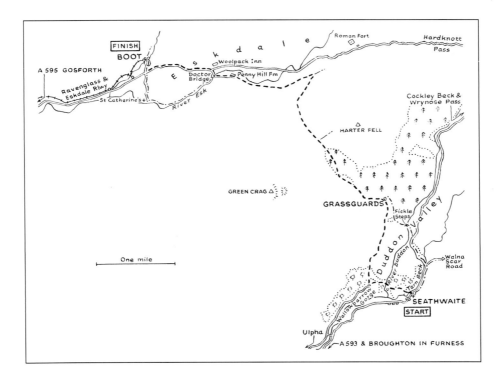

THE ISOLATED BUILDINGS of Grassguards may be reached by either of two routes from the Duddon Valley. From Seathwaite church a path leads through woodlands, crossing Tarn Beck, to a bridge that has replaced stepping stones on the River Duddon in a setting joyful to behold: here the river is seen issuing from the steep confining slopes of Wallowbarrow Gorge, a ravine bedecked with heather and trees, and always a place of bewitching beauty. Over the bridge, the path turns west to join a cart-track used by the scattered farms hereabouts and this climbs steadily to open countryside and Grassguards.

The alternative route leaves the road a mile north of Seathwaite and crosses a pasture to reach the river, where the huge stepping stones of Fickle Steps admit to the wooded slope on the far bank. This too is a charming spot although the crossing may cause some apprehension. Safely accomplished, a path rises through native trees to emerge at Grassguards.

Opposite *From the bridge in Wallowbarrow Gorge*

Upper Eskdale from Harter Fell; Hardknott Fort is visible in the centre

From Grassguards, the path heads north-west, with open undulating country on the left and, when the trees are left behind, the beckoning pyramid of Harter Fell rising in colourful slopes. An insignificant watershed is crossed, marked by a broken wall, and Eskdale starts to take shape ahead. When a track branches off, obviously bound for the summit of Harter Fell, the ascent of this fine mountain should be considered: the climb, amongst heather, is rewarded with fine views of Eskdale, the summit is exciting, the highest inches reached only by simple scrambling up naked rock. The northern panorama of the head of Eskdale, backed by the Scafells and Bowfell, with a nearer aerial view of Hardknott Roman Fort, is truly magnificent. If two parties have arranged to do the walk from opposite directions, it needs to be discussed beforehand whether Harter Fell is to be included; if so, the summit makes a grand meeting place.

Resuming the main path and with Eskdale gloriously displaying its lovely plumage in front, descend into the valley. It is well to keep strictly to the path and not attempt short cuts on the lower slopes, since the bracken of Eskdale is the highest in the district and impenetrably dense. At the foot of the descent, a lane is joined and followed down-river, to pass Penny Hill Farm – a place of happy memories where I was first introduced to the life of a Lakeland farmer – and arriving at Doctor Bridge over the River Esk. The lane joins the valley road near the Woolpack Inn, and the village of Boot is a short mile to the left.

But to enjoy some delectable river scenery, an enchanting path leaves Doctor Bridge and follows the Esk down-river as it rounds a wooded hill and leads to St Catherine's church, the parish church of Eskdale, a plain structure built in the seventeenth century and more remarkable for the contents of the graveyard than for those of the interior. Here is Tommy Dobson's grave, marked by a headstone inscribed with his own likeness, a fox, a hound and horn: a masterpiece in granite. Tommy's name has not lived on as has John Peel's, yet his local reputation as a Master of Foxhounds was even greater. Foxhunting was his whole life and his memorial reflects this passion.

A lane from the church leads to journey's end in the friendly village of Boot.

Tommy Dobson's grave
Below left and right *Penny Hill Farm*

Above *Far Easedale*

Below *Greenup Gill*

15 GREENUP EDGE, 1995'
Grasmere – Borrowdale

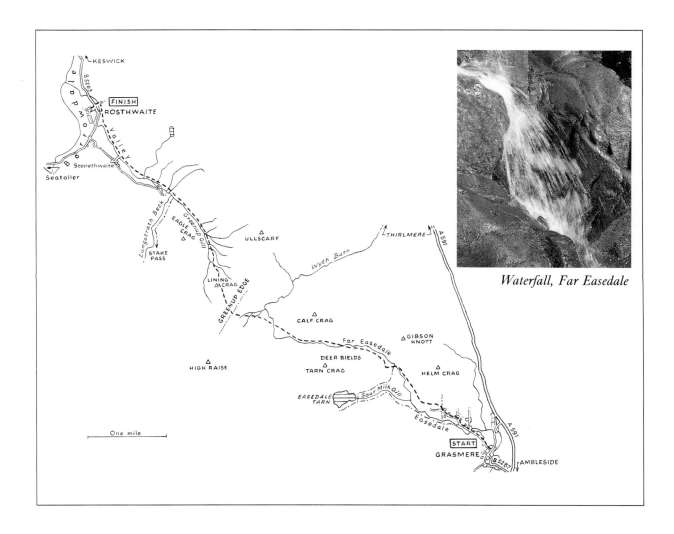

Waterfall, Far Easedale

TRAVELLERS ON FOOT between Grasmere and Borrowdale have little choice of route if they seek the shortest and most direct way. The central mass of fells must be crossed at a high level and the key to the easiest passage is Greenup Edge, a gap on the ridge joining High Raise and Ullscarf but, unfortunately for many walkers who have gone astray, not an obvious one when approached from Grasmere. The Edge is wild and lonely and provides a sharp contrast with the initial and final stages of the walk which are verdant and beautiful. Greenup Edge links two of the most popular parts of Lakeland and is in daily use.

LEAVE GRASMERE by the road to Easedale, from which a very popular path turns off to cross Easedale Beck and climb by the side of Sour Milk Gill, a delightful cataract, to Easedale Tarn. This is a prime objective of most sojourners at Grasmere – even in Victorian times when refreshments could be obtained at a stone hut near the outflow, but this has gone and today's visitors must take their own picnic lunches.

The route to Borrowdale, however, still with a tarmac surface, follows the main valley into Far Easedale, passing some desirable residences, and from it another well-trodden path leads upwards to another much visited objective, Helm Crag. This is better known as the Lion and the Lamb, to which the summit rocks bear a fancied resemblance.

These off-route attractions have no place in the itinerary of walkers bound for Borrowdale. The road is continued to its extremity where it becomes a rough lane alongside Far Easedale Beck which, when the last walls are passed, is crossed at Stythwaite Steps to a path heading upstream in open country. The path is unmistakable and cannot be lost even in mist, the sound of rushing water giving direction. Up on the left is the formidable Deer Bields Buttress, jutting from the lofty ridge that divides the two Easedales; on the right are the colourful slopes of Gibson Knott, continuing the skyline from Helm Crag. In places, the path crosses marshy ground where bog asphodel is rampant and then, after a rocky scramble, reaches the watershed marking the head of the valley of Far Easedale.

Looking towards Grasmere from the Easedale Tarn path

Easedale Tarn

Below Summit of Greenup Edge

The head of Far Easedale was formerly crossed by a wire fence of which a forlorn iron stepstile is the sole remaining relic. Beyond, the ground declines to a valley draining to the right, and walkers under the mistaken belief that the watershed is Greenup Edge may descend in that direction thinking it will lead down to Borrowdale. It won't: this is the valley of Wythburn going down to the head of Thirlmere, nowhere near Borrowdale, and containing extensive tracts of marshy ground indicated on Ordnance maps as The Bog. Greenup Edge is still half a mile distant and at a higher level; it can be discerned in front, slightly to the left of the ridge declining from the facing fell of Ullscarf. The path to it declines gently at first and then rises steadily, crossing several streams draining into Wythburn.

The path over Greenup Edge is a simple promenade on easy ground between the rough declivities of High Raise on the left and the smoother slopes of Ullscarf on the right, and either of these summits may be climbed from this point by walkers with energy to spare. But most will go forward for the distant glimpse of the Borrowdale heights and a bird's-eye view of the valley of Greenup Gill curving steeply down on the next stage of the journey.

With the flat top of the Edge left behind, the path starts the long descent, soon bypassing the rocky upthrust of Lining Crag and coming alongside Greenup Gill and fording the many tributaries joining in from Ullscarf. The descent continues below the cliffs of Eagle Crag (the best known of a dozen Eagle Crags in Lakeland, all named when golden eagles were resident in the district in past centuries) and out of its shadow reaches valley level at a lovely watersmeet where Langstrath Beck joins Greenup Gill from a wide opening on the left. Great slabs of rock are a feature of the confluence and they are a much favoured halting place. A drowning tragedy here is commemorated by a memorial bridge.

Right *Lining Crag*
Greenup Gill meets Langstrath Beck

Eagle Crag from Stonethwaite Beck

The finish of the walk is along the Stonethwaite Valley directly ahead, a mile of exquisite beauty where the distinctive charm of Victorian Lakeland is still preserved. Out of sight and sound of the Borrowdale traffic, the Stonethwaite Valley is an Arcadia of delight, its huddle of cottages and farm buildings an architectural gem, and living a life unchanged for centuries. The environs of wooded fellsides, sparkling streams and emerald pastures make Stonethwaite, in my opinion, the most charming of Lakeland's side valleys. Nothing is orderly as modern planners would have it; a carefree untidiness pervades the scene and hits exactly the right key in bewitching enchantment. The whole is an epitome of rural peace and serenity in a landscape of romance. Here is a surviving example of Lakeland's unique charm that has to such a large extent been destroyed by the very same people who come in search of it.

The path ends in the busy main street of Rosthwaite, a metropolis after Stonethwaite. Here, back in civilisation, advantage can be taken of the Borrowdale bus to go to Keswick for a connection to Grasmere if it is desired to return to the starting point of the walk. It must be grudgingly conceded that despite the damage done to the twentieth-century Lakeland scene by the internal combustion engine, buses can sometimes be a blessing.

16 GRISEDALE HAUSE, 1929'
Grasmere – Patterdale

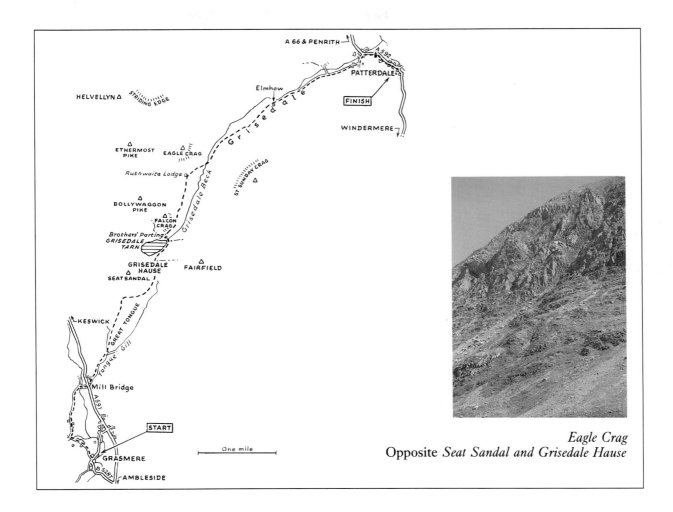

Eagle Crag
Opposite *Seat Sandal and Grisedale Hause*

THE ROYAL ROAD for walkers journeying between Grasmere and Patterdale lies over Grisedale Hause, and indeed there is no other direct way that does not call for serious climbing. It is a route used for centuries by the dalesmen and later adopted in part for the ascent of Helvellyn when the fashionable method of reaching the summit was on the backs of ponies.

It is a splendid walk through the mountains in contrasting scenery, beautiful at the extremities and grimly austere in its higher sections, and is much used as a springboard for the ascent of the many popular heights that flank the route.

With the possible exceptions of the Sty Head and Rossett passes, Grisedale Hause may well be the most trodden of the high crossings amongst the fells that are and will always remain the exclusive preserve of travellers on foot.

Above *Grisedale Tarn*

Below *The Vale of Grasmere from Grisedale Hause*

A SIGNPOST on the A591 at Mill Bridge, just above the Travellers' Rest, points the way along a pleasant lane with Tongue Gill in close company. This ends when confronted by a steep conical slope that seems to bar further progress. This is Great Tongue, Tongue being a name common in Lakeland where a sharp upthrust of land divides a valley into two parallel descending sections. But here, as in most such cases, paths go round the obstacle on both sides. The left fork is usually taken, this being the way the ponies went, and the breast of Seat Sandal is ascended on a grass path before contouring to the stony rise below the hause. The right fork is easier initially but terminates in a steep rough scramble alongside waterfalls to join the other. The final rise to the hause is short but arduous on loose stones. At the crest, crossed by a sturdy wall, fine views fore and aft reward earlier effort.

The outlet of Grisedale Tarn

Ahead, Grisedale Tarn comes suddenly into view, backed by the featureless slopes of Dollywaggon Pike, up which winds a well-worn and dusty track; this was the former pony route to Helvellyn but nowadays is usually littered by countless humans, some struggling upwards, many fallen by the wayside. On the right beyond the tarn rise the even steeper slopes of St Sunday Crag, and between the two heights is the V-shaped gap that contains the valley of Grisedale. It is a barren landscape that greets the walker at Grisedale Hause, but look back to see, in total contrast, the verdant Vale of Keswick, Coniston Water and the undulating lesser fells of southern Lakeland.

From the hause, tracks go off to Seat Sandal, left, and Fairfield, right, but the main route goes forward, descending slightly to the outlet of the tarn, this being easily forded; here the path to Helvellyn turns left and the pass route to Patterdale follows the direction of the issuing stream, Grisedale Beck.

A short distance below the outlet, on a slope littered by fallen boulders is one of special significance; this is an inscribed boulder known as the Brothers' Parting, marking the spot where William Wordsworth said a last farewell to his brother John in 1805. They never met again, John being drowned in the ship he commanded shortly afterwards.

The path goes forward into Grisedale, descending slightly at first and revealing the shadowed cliffs of Falcon Crag high on the left before reaching a solitary stone hut, Ruthwaite Lodge, built originally as a shooting lodge but taken over by a mountaineering club. The stream cascading down the fellside nearby deserves a second glance: note the old mine level at the side.

From Ruthwaite Lodge the path descends more steeply to the floor of the valley, again crossing Grisedale Beck. Up on the left is the near-vertical precipice of Eagle Crag, a haunt not of eagles but of rockclimbers. Towering on the right are the unremitting slopes of St Sunday Crag, nearly 2000 feet above and topped by a fringe of cliffs down which a woman fell to her death recently after going astray on the summit of the mountain.

From here on the walking is easy, the path becoming a cart-track and affording impressive retrospects of Dollywaggon Pike which now assumes the form of a slender pyramid, and neighbouring Nethermost Pike, starkly etched against the sky above a line of crags.

Above *Ruthwaite Lodge*

Below left *Eagle Crag*   and right *Nethermostcove Beck*

Grisedale

Below *Patterdale church*

In scenery of increasing loveliness, the first buildings are reached at the farm of Elmhow. I once spent a night in a barn here without permission. The occasion was Coronation Day 1953, a public holiday, and I arrived at dusk after walking over the tops from Ambleside. I found a comfortable bed of straw but, being apprehensive of discovery, was unable to sleep and chain-smoked through the hours of darkness (I was on cigarettes in those days) without setting the barn on fire. I was off at dawn before the farmer started his morning rounds. I had to be in Kendal at nine o'clock to open the office, and walked over to Grasmere to catch the first morning bus. The day was memorable because it brought the news that Hillary and Tensing had reached the summit of Everest, an event that interested me more than the Coronation, for I had long cherished an impossible ambition to be the first man to reach the top of the highest mountain in the world. The news effectively burst a silly bubble.

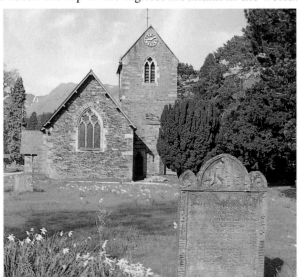

Further down the valley, the cart-track becomes a tarmac road used as an unofficial parking place for the cars of motorists who take to their legs for the ascent of Helvellyn by way of Striding Edge. The road leads down through an avenue of trees to join the A592 near Patterdale church, the village and refreshments for which the body has been clamouring being around the corner to the right.

The A592 has infrequent bus services and wise people wishing to avail themselves of these facilities will have studied the timetables in advance and kept an eye on their watches.

17 HARDKNOTT PASS, 1290'
Duddon Valley – Eskdale

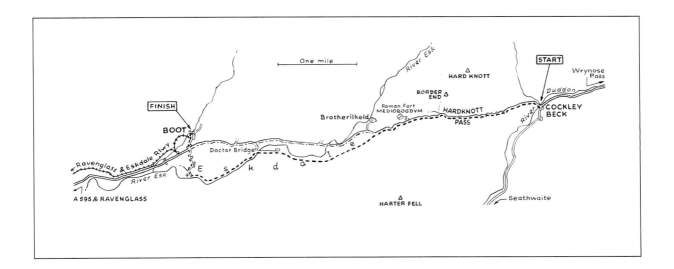

SEVEN OF THE mountain passes in Lakeland are crossed by motor roads, all of them having steep gradients on both sides, but quite the most notorious, challenging the skill and nerve of car drivers, is Hardknott Pass between the Duddon Valley and Eskdale.

Hardknott is almost a twin to Wrynose and usually both passes are crossed on the same journey, but motorists who have come over Wrynose from the east must expect a much stiffer climb over Hardknott and should approach it with the utmost concentration. It is no place for learner drivers. Height is not the problem, the altitude at the top being modest and lower than most of the others: it is the steepness of certain sections. Even the Romans baulked at the steepest part and sacrificed pride and principles by adopting a detour to circumvent the difficulties.

Opposite *The top of Hardknott Pass*
Right *The Scafell range from Border End*

THE ROAD STARTS to climb innocuously from the River Duddon at Cockley Beck Bridge but soon springs to life in a heart-stopping series of sharp and narrow hairpin bends with a gradient of 1 in 3, without respite until an easier incline to the top of the pass is reached. It is not unusual to find cars and their owners stranded on the unenclosed verges, or halted for breath on the more accommodating summit. Over the pass, with a glorious view of Eskdale ahead, there is a steep and awkward corner to negotiate before the road settles down in a long decline to the valley.

Towards the end of this descent, on an elevation to the right of the road, is the best preserved of the Roman forts in Lakeland: this is Mediobognvm, commonly referred to as Hardknott Castle, and should certainly be visited. Dating from the second century and identified beyond doubt by inscribed stones and

discoveries on the site, the fort is a pattern of drystone walls, some partly restored, with four gateways, the complex comprising the commandant's house, the barracks of the garrison, a granary and bath houses, while on the fellside above was a parade ground. Imagination is needed to comprehend the scale of the encampment and to appreciate the lonely life of the soldiers exiled here, far from home. Mediobognvm was of strategic importance to the Romans, defending the approach from the coast at a point of great vantage. It is in the care of English Heritage.

Above *Cockley Beck Bridge*

Hardknott Fort

Returning to the road, the descent continues to the floor of the valley, occupied by the River Esk and generously endowed with lush fields and lovely trees, and goes on to the village of Boot amidst scenery of unspoilt charm. At Boot, a miniature railway makes a delightful seven-mile journey to connect with the main line at Ravenglass.

Walkers over Hardknott Pass have little chance of escaping from the traffic on the Duddon side, the verges being too rough and boggy for easy progress, but upon reaching the top they should leave the road and scramble higher to the crest of Border End for a magnificent prospect of the Scafells and Bowfell and the other wild mountains circling upper Eskdale. After visiting the Roman fort, they should proceed down the valley by footpath from the bottom of the hill, enjoying the idyllic surroundings of the River Esk flowing nearby. At Doctor Bridge, the road may be joined for the last mile to Boot or, pleasanter, the river may be followed around a wooded hill on an enchanting path to the humble parish church of Eskdale, where the remarkable memorial to Tommy Dobson in the graveyard should be inspected (*see* page 73). A short lane then leads to the village.

Above *Remains of Hardknott Fort*

Eskdale

18 HART CRAG COL, 2520′
Rydal – Deepdale

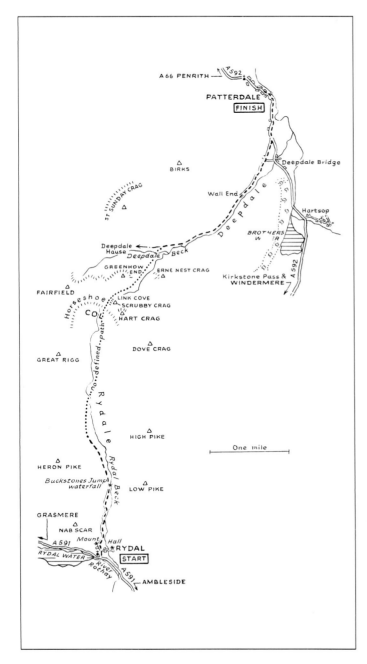

A66 PENRITH →
A592
PATTERDALE
FINISH

Deepdale Bridge

BIRKS

ST SUNDAY CRAG

Wall End

Hartsop

Deepdale

BROTHERS WR

Deepdale Hause

Deepdale Beck

GREENHOW END
ERNE NEST CRAG

Kirkstone Pass & WINDERMERE
A592

FAIRFIELD

Horseshoe COL
LINK COVE
SCRUBBY CRAG
HART CRAG

GREAT RIGG

DOVE CRAG

Rydale Beck

no-defined path

One mile

HIGH PIKE

HERON PIKE

Buckstones Jump waterfall

LOW PIKE

GRASMERE
NAB SCAR
A591
Mount Hall
RYDAL
START
RYDAL WATER
River Rothay
A591 → AMBLESIDE

AN EXCEPTION to the general rule that the passes offer simple walking is provided by the abrupt gap, formerly known as The Step, on the ridge linking Hart Crag and Fairfield. It is not the actual crossing of the gap that is arduous, but the approaches to it, especially on the Rydale side, and walkers who like to preserve a dignified bearing will not enjoy the steep and stony scramble to reach the crest. It is, however, the most direct way across the high range dividing the Rothay valley at Rydal from Deepdale and Patterdale; it is the shortest in distance but not in time. The route has other merits, too, being unfrequented, remote from traffic, and pleasantly approached from either side on easy paths, only the middle mile calling for strenuous effort.

Opposite *Fairfield*
Below *Head of Rydale*

RYDAL IS LEFT by a side road from the A591, passing between the church and Rydal Mount on the left and Rydal Hall on the right, initially negotiable by cars. This soon degenerates into a rough lane and then a path; when clear of trees, there is a comprehensive view of the Fairfield Horseshoe ahead. The long valley opening in front is conveniently but unofficially known as Rydale. The surroundings are impressive and become more so as the walk proceeds up the valley alongside a wall, with Rydal Beck flowing nearby; there is a minor interruption at the small waterfall of Buckstones Jump. The dominant height in a lofty skyline is Great Rigg, falling in a rough declivity, and beyond this the valley is terminated by the high barrier of Fairfield and Hart Crag, the gap between them being the next objective. The hard work starts when the wall turns away and the path fades to nothing. The ground rises ahead and soon becomes unremittingly steep, upward progress not being helped by the absence of a path. The only guidance is given by the infant Rydal Beck which should be crossed and kept on the left during the final ascent. After a long and arduous struggle against gravity, the col is gained suddenly and with profound relief.

Rydale

Deepdale from the col

Although both sides of Hart Crag Col are virgin, untrodden and silent, the narrow crest has been blazed white by thousands of boots each year engaged on the very popular Fairfield Horseshoe walk, this spot being the only place where deviations are ruled out by the ruggedness of the terrain. It is also the most spectacular. The Rydal side has no terrors other than steepness and indeed has a tranquil view, but the Deepdale side has a fearsome aspect of wild country flanked by crags.

This is a true col, a narrow causeway poised above steep and inhospitable acclivities. The walk continues down a bouldery slope without the help of a foot-track, but the gradient eases as a way is made below the impending cliffs of Scrubby Crag. A stream joins the route of descent as it issues from the hanging valley of Link Cove, and takes over as guide on the next part of the walk.

Again the ground steepens as the stream plunges in cascades to the floor of the valley, passing below the tremendous buttress of Greenhow End in the shadow of Erne Nest Crag to join Deepdale Beck as it emerges from the wild recesses of Fairfield. This is a lonely place indeed: a silent sanctuary almost encircled by steep fellsides and dark crags with only the stream to point a way of escape. The vast sprawling slopes of St Sunday Crag fill the background as the waters of the beck are forded to gain the comfort of a path running above the far bank. Looking back from this point, the great tower of Greenhow End is seen as the impressive termination of the northern precipices of Fairfield.

Greenhow End

The rest is easy. The path curves around the base of St Sunday Crag and gradually the scene becomes less confined as trees, walls and cultivated fields mark the final stages of Deepdale. Across the beck flowing alongside rises the high but declining ridge of Hartsop above How, ending in woodlands above Brothers Water; on the left the steep and craggy slopes of St Sunday Crag and Birks rise to heaven. At the first farm of Wall End, the path merges into a lane with a few scattered houses, reaching the A592 near Deepdale Bridge. Patterdale village is a mile along the road to the left; a beautiful finish.

Above *View down Deepdale to Bridge End*

Deepdale Bridge

19 HAUSE GATE, 1150′
Newlands – Manesty

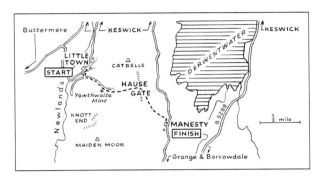

HAUSE GATE is a favourite objective although not well known by name. It is easily reached on a summer evening's stroll, rewarding the small effort with views of surpassing beauty. Everybody knows Catbells. The Hause (there is no gate, the word here meaning an open passage) is the grassy saddle on the ridge south of this popular summit, and is a place to halt awhile and try to memorise a scene to relive during moments of urban depression.

NEWLANDS IS LEFT at the hamlet of Little Town where an old mine road branches left and rises below the cliffs of Knott End to an area despoiled by the disused Yewthwaite Mine where there are still dangerous shafts and levels that call for caution if being explored, having already accounted for a fatal casualty. Beyond, the path rises in bracken to the top of the ridge at Hawes Gate, revealing a ravishing view of Derwentwater and its environs: a picture to bring tears of joy. A delectable grass path descends the fellside, every step a pleasure to tread, but there is such an eye-catching view ahead that it is advisable to halt on the uneven path when surveying the glorious scene.

At Manesty, the west Derwentwater road is joined and can be followed on to Grange in Borrowdale and its bus service.

Opposite *Derwentwater from Hause Gate*   Below *Borrowdale from Hause Gate*

20 HIGH TOVE, 1665'
Thirlmere – Borrowdale

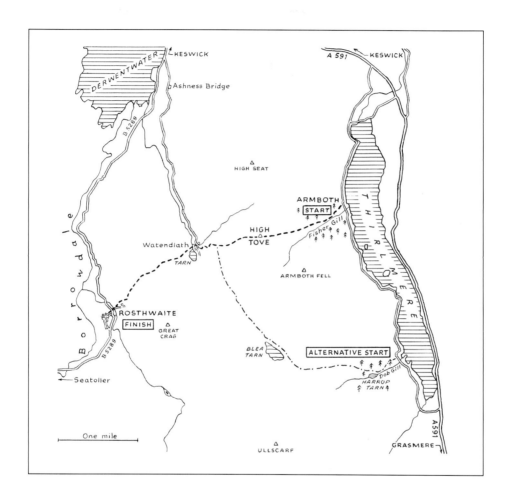

THERE ARE TWO paths along which walkers may cross the long central ridge that divides the Thirlmere valley and Borrowdale. One, giving a fine walk, leaves the west side of Thirlmere at Dob Gill near the south end of the reservoir, passes through the plantations around Harrop Tarn and crosses the indefinite ridge to descend to Watendlath by way of Blea Tarn. But this route is more in the nature of a cross-country walk than a pass.

The other path leaves the west side of Thirlmere near the north end of the reservoir and makes a beeline across the moorland of High Tove, actually visiting the summit, before descending to Watendlath. This route also hardly qualifies as a pass, traversing a low summit and not a depression, but passes over a watershed, being the most direct way, and has long been in use.

Opposite *Watendlath*

BEFORE MANCHESTER CORPORATION acquired rights to convert the natural lake of Thirlmere into a reservoir, Armboth House was the principal residence on the west shore, the centre of a small community connected to the east side by a picturesque wooden footbridge across the narrowest part of the lake. The house, other buildings and footbridge were all casualties of the reservoir and nothing was left of Armboth except its name, which curiously has survived on signposts. The slopes falling from the ridge have since been tightly afforested but directly above the site at Armboth a wide breach in the trees has been left unplanted to accommodate the old path over to Borrowdale. This climbs a bouldery slope alongside the plantation with outcropping rocks nearby and Fisher Gill in close attendance, and reaches a wall marking the upper limit of the plantations. The path passes through a gate and emerges on a wide moorland of heather and marsh, where it ascends more gradually to the cairned summit of High Tove, a place with no pretensions to interest or beauty, its one redeeming feature being as a viewpoint.

High Tove is a minor undulation on the long ridge forming the spine of central Lakeland. To the north, after a slight descent, the ground rises to High Seat; southwards, the nearest neighbour of note is Ullscarf, seen in the distance over the soggy morass of Armboth Fell. Over the watershed, the path descends gradually at first, and then, when Watendlath comes into sight ahead, much more steeply between two ravines, the gradient being eased by zigzags.

Watendlath is delightful and its qualities unique. There is no other place like it. A tiny cluster of white cottages and stone barns set at odd angles without pattern, a tarn, a stream and a bridge, all deeply inurned amongst surrounding fells and hidden from outside gaze: here are all the attributes of a perfect picture, a scene to enrapture artists and photographers. Apart from the intrinsic joys of this little hamlet in a fold of the hills, there are literary associations to attract visitors since this was the home of Judith Paris in the Herries novels by Hugh Walpole. Watendlath's link with the world outside is a narrow ribbon of tarmac branching from the Borrowdale road above Ashness Bridge, a three-mile journey of enchantment which, unfortunately, has been discovered by the touring motorist who often causes severe congestion. Watendlath should always be approached on foot; noise is sacrilege here. This is hallowed ground.

Watendlath Bridge

Watendlath is always left with regret and many a lingering look back. Sparing a crumb for the ducks, the walk is continued on a path that gets no rest from boots, and steadily climbs to the ridge that still hides Borrowdale; there are superb retrospective views of the hamlet and tarn on the way. This, if a census were taken, would be proved to be one of the most populated footpaths in Lakeland and, after topping the low ridge and starting the descent into Borrowdale, the reason for its popularity is clear. The upper reaches of this most beautiful of valleys unfold in a lovely pageant of colour and charm, the green strath and shaggy fells making a perfect canvas. With dragging steps, Rosthwaite is entered and the magic dispelled by tourist traffic.

Borrowdale

Below View towards Grisedale Pike from High Tove

21 HONISTER PASS, 1190'
Borrowdale – Buttermere

UNTIL THE MID-NINETEENTH century, when the turnpikes were improved for stagecoach traffic, and the railways came to Windermere and Keswick, the Lake District was a world apart, rarely visited by people from outside the area but, as early adventurers and the Lake Poets extolled its unique beauties, more were attracted to see for themselves. These were mainly professional gentlemen and their ladies.

In Victorian times, these visitors were conveyed in horse-drawn wagonettes on sightseeing tours along the few dusty and roughly metalled roads negotiable by wheeled vehicles, a romantic form of travel that vanished with the coming of tarmacadam and motor cars and omnibuses. Of these early tours, the great adventure, enjoyed on payment of a toll, was provided by the crossing of Honister Pass, a fearsome and exciting journey. Today the romance has been savaged out of existence by the procession of cars using this popular route linking Borrowdale and Buttermere, but the scenic grandeur of the past remains.

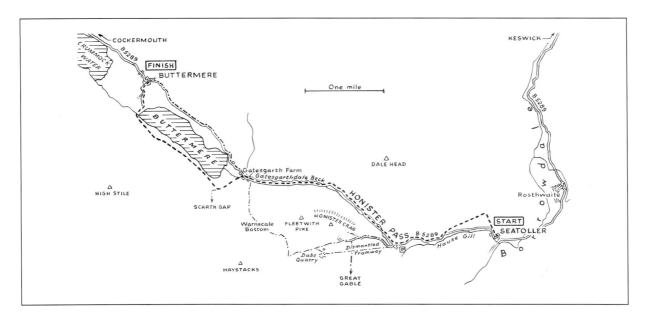

SEATOLLER IS THE bus terminus at the head of Borrowdale and from this attractive group of buildings the ascent to the pass starts at once and in earnest, the initial steepness being relieved by the sparkling cascades of Hause Gill alongside in a bower of trees, after which a bare landscape is entered as the unenclosed road rises more gently to the summit. Walkers can avoid most of the hard road to the top and the hazard of speeding cars by preferring the old toll road which is grassy, abandoned and much kinder to the feet: this branches off the road on the right after leaving Seatoller, and after a sharp turn heads directly for the pass at a higher level, joining the motor road below the top.

Opposite *Honister Pass*

103

Below *The cutting sheds, Honister Quarry*

Seatoller

Honister Pass is extremely impressive. The great feature is Honister Crag, a towering cliff honeycombed with quarries and a network of steep tracks used for bringing down the handsome slate that for colour, texture and durability has earned international renown. In the formative years of the industry, horse-drawn sleds were used to convey the blocks of slate to the cutting sheds; later a tramway served this purpose; this in turn was superseded by lorries making the perilous descent. Now all is silent: the centuries-old workings were closed recently and activity has come to an end. Honister Crag has had the heart torn out of it but has not been tamed.

There is a Youth Hostel on the top of the pass in addition to the quarry buildings, and limited space for the parking of cars; there is always activity here. It is a starting point for the ascent of Great Gable, using the old tramway, and on the north side an easy ridge can be climbed to the summit of Dale Head, where there is a classic view of Newlands and the Vale of Keswick backed by Skiddaw.

The High Stile range from Gatesgarth

Over the pass, the road descends steeply under a bridge built to carry a private cart-track from quarries on the side of Dale Head, and then winds down into a boulder-strewn defile. The gradient eases as Gatesgarthdale Beck comes alongside and a splendid view of the High Stile range unfolds ahead. The soaring slopes on the left gradually decline to valley level; a white cross on the lower rocks is a memorial to a girl accidentally killed here in 1887. The rugged crest of Haystacks appears in a wider landscape, and trees, welcome after the sterile crossing, enhance the majestic scene as the first habitation of Gatesgarth Farm is reached.

From Gatesgarth, the road continues for two lovely miles to Buttermere village with glimpses of the lake seen below. Walkers have a charming alternative on this final stage by following a lakeside path on the north-east side.

Fellwalkers who have a rooted objection to travelling along hard roads may follow a parallel course from the top of the pass by climbing up the old tramway on the left side and continuing on a good path skirting Dubs Quarry and descending to Gatesgarth along an old quarry road through Warnscale Bottom. This route is more arduous but in the matter of views better by far.

Kirkstone Pass looking north and (below) *south*

22 KIRKSTONE PASS, 1489'
Ambleside – Patterdale

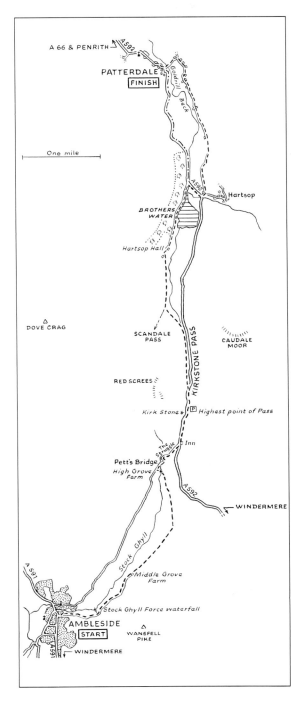

KIRKSTONE PASS is the high crossing that most excites the tourists who inspect the Lake District from the comfort of a car or coach. The environs of the pass are spectacular, a narrow road winding through a gap between the rugged downfall of Red Screes and the scree slopes of Caudale Moor. It is a wild defile of tumbled rocks and mountain debris, but the loneliness that characterised it a century ago, when horse-drawn carriages braved the rigours of the journey carrying parties of awestruck Victorians, has been dispelled by the procession of motorists who today throng the limited confines of the road. The atmosphere of frightening solitude has been lost and is fleetingly regained only when winter snowfalls block the pass.

A road climbs steeply to the summit from Ambleside, there joining the busy A592 from Windermere for the long descent to the Patterdale Valley. The weight of traffic on most days of the year makes this a route to be avoided by travellers on foot who would do well to favour instead the quiet and unfrequented track over Scandale Pass although this alternative bypasses Kirkstone's exciting scenery. However, the route described in this chapter enables walkers to make acquaintance with the pass on footpaths that avoid the motor road except for a long mile across the highest part. Even so, Kirkstone Pass is best appreciated when the summer visitors have departed.

LEAVE AMBLESIDE along the signposted road to Stock Ghyll Force, this delightful waterfall being seen by a walk through the woods alongside Stock Ghyll. In former days, an admission charge was made for the privilege of entry, but today access is free and a well-worn path leads up to the impressive plunge of the stream in a bower of foliage. It is a charming scene for Stock Ghyll Force is the most beautiful waterfall in the Lake District.

Near Middle Grove

The ruins near High Grove
Right *Red Screes*

A path above the fall leads back to the road which continues upstream to Middle Grove Farm along the lower flanks of Wansfell with Kirkstone Pass in sight ahead. Beyond the farm, a cart-track goes on to the ruins of High Grove Farm, from which a path crosses to join the motor road from Ambleside at Pett's Bridge. Originally the track went directly forward, climbing to join the A592. It is likely that this route by the Grove farms was the usual way to Kirkstone Pass before the road from Ambleside was constructed.

From Pett's Bridge, the motor road rises very steeply to the summit of the pass, this section being known as The Struggle for reasons that must have been very obvious when wheeled traffic was horse-drawn. At the top of this incline, the road meets the A592 at the Kirkstone Pass Inn, once known as the Travellers' Rest where there is an ample and well-patronised car park. This is a popular halt for refreshment or for gazing up at the formidable ramparts of Red Screes, up which there is a steep and arduous track from this point. The gentle slopes behind the inn provide simple ski runs when snow has been cleared from the road and cars can reach the inn. On a high shoulder of Caudale Moor overlooking the pass is a memorial cairn to Mark Atkinson, mine host at the inn for many years until his death in 1930.

The highest point of the pass is a short distance beyond the inn, and here a dramatic view forward is revealed, the long descent into Patterdale commences, the road being tightly enclosed between stone walls. A car park has been provided to discourage motorists from stopping on the edge of the road to admire the scene. Nearby is a massive fallen boulder, the Kirk Stone, from which the pass was named; its appearance on the skyline when approaching from the north resembles the steeple of a church tower. All around is chaotic convulsion of nature, a primeval desolation.

Opposite *The north side of Kirkstone Pass*   Above *Patterdale*

A signpost on the roadside lower down indicates a footpath along which pedestrians can escape from the hazards of speeding cars, this leading pleasantly down to valley level; there the path from Scandale Pass joins in. The walk proceeds, with views of Dove Crag, to Hartsop Hall, a farmhouse unusually distinguished by having a public right of way through the building as a result of the erection of an extension over a bridleway that formerly passed alongside.

A wooded lane continues the walk along the shore of Brothers Water, which was named Broad Water until two brothers lost their lives here by drowning on separate occasions early in the nineteenth century. The A592 is rejoined at the end of the lane and may be followed for two lovely miles to Patterdale village, but if traffic is heavy it is advisable to go back about 200 yards to the Hartsop junction, there taking a parallel and pleasant by-road where there is less danger of being annihilated by a car.

Thus ends an enjoyable ten-mile walk in contrasting surroundings, nature being displayed both in the raw and at its supreme best. For walkers already familiar with Kirkstone Pass, however, it is preferable to make the journey by way of Scandale Pass, which is innocent of wheels, rather shorter in distance, requires little more effort and is blessed with a profound solitude: *see* page 161.

23 THE LOFT BECK CROSSING, 1900′
Ennerdale – Borrowdale

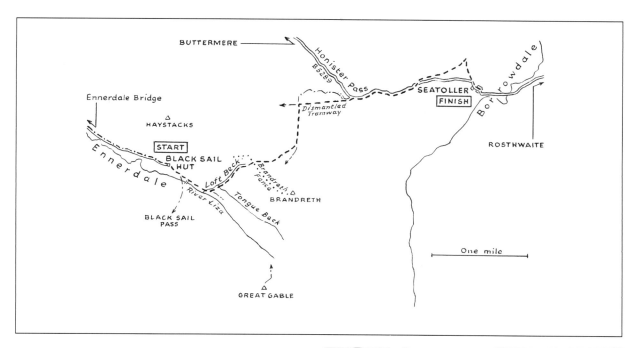

A USEFUL TIME-SAVING route between the Black Sail Hut in Ennerdale and Honister Pass is available by climbing up to the grassy plateau crossed by the Brandreth fence: this is a route not generally recognised as a pass but has the attributes if not the appearance of one. There is now a distinct track and this should be kept strictly underfoot in misty conditions, the highest part of the crossing being without landmarks. The track joins the broad path coming down from Great Gable for the descent to Honister Pass, from which the well-known delights of Borrowdale can be reached by an easy hour's march.

Left *Loft Beck*
Opposite *Great Gable from the River Liza*

A PATH FROM the Black Sail Hut goes up the valley of the River Liza towards Great Gable, ignoring the footbridge, to the point where the tributary of Loft Beck comes down steeply on the left. Loft Beck is the key to the route: it is followed up closely on a steep and rough track, passing a confluence of waters where Tongue Beck joins in, until the climbing ends on an extensive upland prairie. With Ennerdale now lost to sight behind, the path trends to the right across a grassy expanse with no distinctive features other than the old Brandreth fence, which is crossed to join the Great Gable path at a large cairn. Although the immediate environs are dreary and without interest, the views of the Buttermere fells and valley are of classical beauty.

Left *The Brandreth fence*
Below *The Buttermere fells*

Honister Pass

There are no problems of route finding when the Great Gable path is reached, this having been worn to the dimensions of a road, albeit a rough one, as the result of daily flagellation by countless boots. It goes easily down to the top of the old quarry tramway above Honister Pass and this is descended to the motor road on the summit of the pass.

Here, if continuing to Borrowdale, the road to the right leads down to Seatoller, and the bus terminus, but travellers on foot should, for the comfort of their feet, branch left along the old toll road, now no more than a grass cart-track, which reaches Seatoller much more pleasantly.

24 THE MARDALE CORPSE ROAD, 1670′
Mardale Head – Swindale

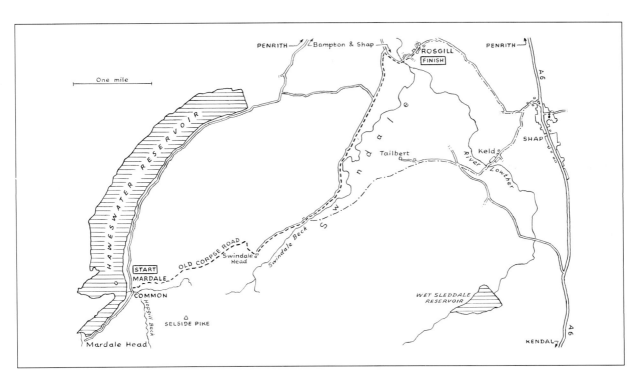

THE EARLY SETTLERS in the Lake District, living in isolated communities amongst the fells, faced many problems, one of them being the disposal of their dead. Some had a church with burial rights nearby, but others had to devise routes across high country to the nearest consecrated ground. Such a community lived at Mardale Green, a lonely hamlet later to be drowned beneath Haweswater Reservoir in 1937. Before a church was built here in the seventeenth century, bodies were conveyed to Shap, eight miles distant, the coffins strapped to the backs of horses. The shortest way was due east, over Mardale Common, and is still known today as the Old Corpse Road.

Opposite *Mardale Head from the Old Corpse Road*
Right *The road around Haweswater Reservoir*

A STEEP PATH, rising in zigzags to ease the gradient, climbed directly from the little group of buildings at Mardale Green. It is probable that this path was engineered primarily as a sledgate for bringing peat down from Mardale Common, peat then being the main source of fuel, but it served the funeral corteges also and is best remembered for this purpose. The lower section of this path was engulfed and submerged by the reservoir, and a little higher is interrupted by the new road to Mardale Head which cuts across it, a signpost indicating the path's continuation up the fellside; this is the point at which modern walkers start the crossing to Swindale.

For several hundred feet the ascent is unremittingly steep, a series of delightful turns and twists, on a distinct path. Hopgill Beck nearby displays a long white ribbon of cascading waters: a pretty sight. Two roofless stone huts, built for the drying and storing of peat, are reached and then another.

The retrospective view of Mardale Head is superb, the encircling mountains appearing in fine array around the deep valley and presenting a scene that, in my opinion, is unrivalled in Lakeland. Above the huts, the steepness abates and the path continues as a narrow track across a wide grassy upland, reaching its highest point amidst undulating moors overtopped by Selside Pike. Then the path trends easily downhill into Swindale, reaching a road terminus at the farm buildings of Swindale Head.

Opposite *Swindale*
Below *Hopgill Beck*

This road goes down the valley, breasts a small hill where it is crossed by the Haweswater access road and descends to Rosgill, between Bampton and Shap. This is the end of the Mardale Head-Swindale pass but for the early mourners was only the first stage of their sad journey, Shap being still six miles distant, their route crossing Swindale and contouring around the facing fells to the last resting place at Shap.

It is interesting to note that when the church at Mardale Green was dismantled and demolished in 1936 as a casualty of the reservoir, the graves in the churchyard were exhumed and the coffins taken by an easier mode of transport to Shap for re-interment, thus reuniting the remains of the more recent dead with those of their ancestors who came the hard way along the Old Corpse Road.

This walk serves also as an introduction to Swindale, a quiet and lovely valley rarely visited by tourists and quite unspoilt. Swindale Beck did not escape the eyes of Manchester Corporation and its waters have been plundered, but thankfully unobtrusively and with little disturbance to the environment, being taken through a tunnel to augment Haweswater Reservoir.

25 MICKLEDORE, 2650'
Eskdale – Wasdale

MICKLEDORE IS the well-defined gap between Scafell and Scafell Pike crossed by a narrow ridge linking the two in a situation of awesome grandeur and amidst highly exciting rock scenery. I consider Mickledore to be the most impressive place in Lakeland: it compels attention to the exclusion of all else. Here is nature in the raw – savage, primeval, immense. In such surroundings man is a speck, insignificant and unimportant.

The ridge across the gap is short, the crest is narrow and the sides steep, and no deviations are possible from the blazed path along it. With towering crags at both ends, the gap is a natural pass yet the ridge is rarely used as such. The crossing from Eskdale to Wasdale Head is arduous. Why suffer all this effort when a simple walk by Burnmoor Tarn connects the two valleys? Almost invariably the Mickledore ridge is traversed by walkers passing between Scafell and Scafell Pike, this being the only feasible way from one to the other, and not as a pass between valleys, although in appearance it is the grandest pass of all.

Mickledore is high drama.

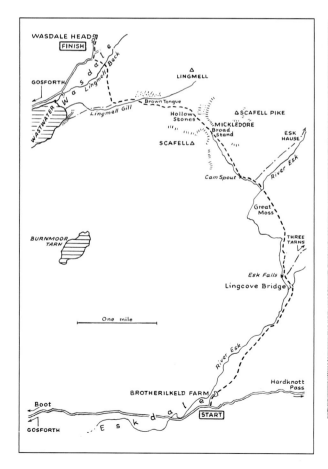

Cam Spout
Opposite *Mickledore*

WITH A FULL DAY ahead and emergency rations in the rucksack, the road along Eskdale is left near the foot of Hardknott Pass and the Esk followed upriver from Brotherilkeld Farm for two miles to Lingcove Bridge, spanning a tributary just above the confluence of waters. The main river here comes round a bend on the left, emerging from a deep gorge in which are the Esk Falls, a series of spectacular waterfalls and cataracts defying close access. The bridge is crossed to a path rising at a higher level in the same direction. The Scafells soon appear ahead, with Mickledore seen as a high gap on the skyline between the two giants in the range. The path continues easily to the foot of the tremendous mountain wall, crossing the flat and marshy expanse of Great Moss. The next objective is the slender waterfall of Cam Spout, this being reached after fording the Esk which is seen winding down from its headwaters below Esk Hause but is left behind at this point.

The ascent now starts in earnest up a steep path alongside Cam Spout. The stream pouring over the lip of the waterfall comes down from Mickledore and, ignoring tributaries joining from the left, gives direction to the remainder of the climb. Easier ground is reached above the waterfall, but the uphill trudge is relentless, flanked by the lower crags of Scafell and the stony slopes of Scafell Pike and in surroundings of extreme wildness and desolation. Timid pedestrians may well suffer apprehension as the track mounts higher towards even grimmer fastnesses ahead. An obvious gully opening on the left offers a scrambling route to the summit of Scafell by way of Foxes Tarn, but for Mickledore the route is directly ahead. It passes into the shadow of the vertical cliffs of Scafell's East Buttress and, beyond, the gaping mouth of Mickledore Chimney which, mercifully, does not have to be entered. Now on a treadmill of scree, with the gap of Mickledore close ahead, the final scramble is alongside a wall of crags split by two vertical cracks; the second, Fat Man's Agony, gives access to the notorious Broad Stand, a rockclimbers' short cut to Scafell but definitely not for lesser fry. After a few more slithering steps, the ridge is reached for a deserved halt.

I always find it difficult to tear myself away from Mickledore, always feel it a great privilege to be allowed admittance to such a wonderful place. Not because there is beauty here. The scene is brutal, uncompromising, yet fascinating and a little frightening. Massive towers of naked rock soar majestically into the sky on all sides. Here is nature's architecture, and it is overwhelming, reducing man to insignificance and a reverent humility. These vertical precipices are repelling: surely they could never be scaled? 'Nobbut a fleeing thing could get up theer,' said old Will Ritson a hundred years ago, yet since that time a network of climbing routes has been forged by expert pioneers on Scafell Crag and the neighbouring cliffs. Legs turn to jelly at the merest thought. Brave men, these, and I am not amongst them.

The Mickledore ridge is not razor-sharp nor a tightrope but is extremely narrow. Within two paces of reaching the crest, steps are immediately downhill on a funnel of scree, descending into a wild hollow below Scafell Crag, the most magnificent of Lakeland's cliffs, rising vertically on the left and far above. On the right, Pulpit Rock and Pikes Crag, outliers of Scafell Pike, enclose the amphitheatre effectively. There is grass here and many huge boulders, some of which offer crude shelter. This sanctuary is known as Hollow Stones.

Opposite *Scafell East Buttress from Mickledore*

Above *Hollow Stones*

Lingmell Beck and Wastwater

Wastwater

A night's bivouac in Hollow Stones is an experience long remembered. The hours of darkness are distinctly eerie, the impending crags around appearing as black silhouettes and the silence being that of the grave. Dawn brings a rich reward, the gloom gradually being dispelld as the first rays of the sun touch the uppermost tips of Scafell Crag and then very slowly diffuse the whole rock face in a rosy pink glow.

But those who prefer a comfortable bed will continue easily down towards Wasdale, now in sight, passing the long fans of scree brought down from Scafell Pinnacle during a tremendous electric storm in 1958, overlaying earlier stonefalls. A path forms at the top of a long descending spur, Brown Tongue, this emerging from the claustrophobia of the crags and enjoying the wider landscape ahead.

At the foot of Brown Tongue, Lingmell Gill is forded, this also carrying the debris of a violent cloudburst, and the path rounds a corner to reveal splendid views of Wastwater and the patchwork fields of Wasdale Head backed by the Pillar range. With the latter prospect in view, the path descends to the valley, slanting down the breast of Lingmell End, a delightful finish to the day. Those who use Mickledore as a pass will never regret their choice over the soft option of Burnmoor. This has been a walk to remember and its memories will be evergreen.

26 MOOR DIVOCK, 1000'
Pooley Bridge – Helton

THE EASY CROSSING of Moor Divock would appeal not only to sedate walkers but also to those with archaeological and geological interests. The Moor is a wide grassy upland forming a broad saddle between Heughscar Hill where limestone is much in evidence, and the greater bulk of Loadpot Hill at the north end of the High Street range. At first sight, the moor seems to be a featureless expanse without landmarks, but appearances deceive. The bland surface of the ground abounds in surprises, but they are not obvious and need searching out. Moor Divock is in fact a rich field of exploration and discovery, a graveyard of relics of prehistoric occupation: stone circles, ancient cairns, burial mounds, settlements, standing stones and avenues. Here too is the famous Roman road, High Street, and even earlier than this is the wide path across the moor that probably originated in neolithic times. For the geologist, there are shakeholes and sinkholes galore, indicating a limestone bedrock, and for the simple walker a pleasant stroll amongst ghosts of the past. Moor Divock is history.

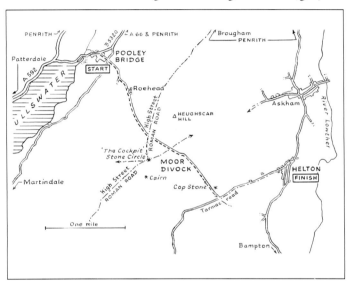

Opposite *Moor Divock*

The Roman Road

The stone circle

A LANE RISES south-east from Pooley Bridge, passing Roehead and reaching open country beyond, its continuation being a wide track, with branches to the left used by pony trekkers. The track ascends gently to a large cairn where it is crossed by the Roman road coming down from High Street on its way to Brougham. At this point, a recommended diversion follows the Roman road to the right, reaching a large stone circle alongside; about thirty yards in diameter and named on Ordnance maps as The Cockpit, it is worthy of leisurely inspection.

Returning to the main path, preferably by retracing steps to avoid the bogs met on short cuts, the walk is resumed, still ascending slightly and passing a line of shakeholes on the right. Near an old boundary stone, a path branches left for Askham. Ignoring this, the path goes on, in places as wide as a motor road. Across the moor on the right are the Pulpit Holes, a group of shakeholes which, on my first and only visit, were depositories for the carcasses and skeletons of sheep: this is not a diversion to be recommended! On the left side of the path reached by short detours is a series of small circles, cairns and burial mounds some of which have obviously been excavated or disturbed. These remains are not as complete as reported by nineteenth-century investigators, and it seems likely that some of the stones have been removed for use in the construction of shooting butts nearby: a double sacrilege.

Ahead on the skyline is a prominent upright boulder, the Cap Stone, thought to be a survivor of a former avenue of stones akin to the one at Shap and possibly a continuation of it. Just beyond, the path debouches on an unenclosed tarmac road, with wide verges often occupied by parked cars and this, followed to the left, leads down to the village of Helton, in the valley of the River Lowther.

This walk across Moor Divock, however, is so effortless and the path so pleasant that, on arrival at the tarmac, most walkers will simply turn round and return to Pooley Bridge the same way with the extra bonus of lovely views of Ullswater on the descent.

Above *A burial mound*

Above right *The Cap Stone* and below *Ullswater*

27 THE MOSEDALE WATERSHED, 1600'
Longsleddale – Swindale or Wet Sleddale

THERE ARE FIVE Mosedales in the Lake District, all of them justifying the interpretation of the name as 'Dreary Valley', and this one, the highest of them, is not merely dreary, but wild and lonely. It provides a crossing out of Longsleddale to Swindale or Wet Sleddale, passing between the high fells of Tarn Crag and Branstree, and was once in regular use but today is unfrequented and the path in parts has gone to seed.

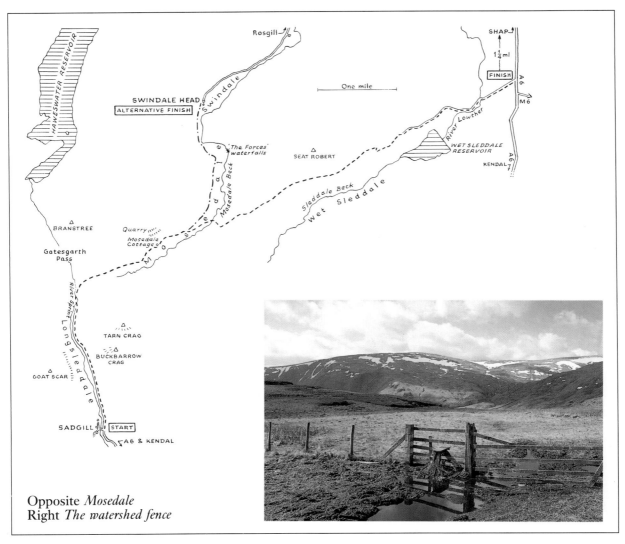

Opposite *Mosedale*
Right *The watershed fence*

FROM SADGILL BRIDGE in Longsleddale, where the motor road ends, a continuing cart-track goes forward into the head of the valley through a rocky portal formed by the cliffs of Goat Scar and Buckbarrow Crag. This section has many features of interest (described in the chapter on Gatescarth Pass, page 61). When the track escapes from its confining walls at a gate at the top of a steep rise, a path soon branches to the right from the Gatescarth route and aims for a wide depression in the skyline between the declining slopes of Tarn Crag and Branstree. The ascent to it is gentle; however, the original path, once of commercial use but now abandoned and taken over by nature, is obscure and interrupted by marshes as it rises to a gate in a wire fence crossing the depression. This is now seen to be a watershed as the ground beyond slowly declines and a new landscape appears ahead. The path goes on, indistinctly, across a vast grassy prairie for a further mile, maintaining a level contour. Mosedale Beck forms nearby, sluggishly confirming, against the visual evidence, that the watershed has indeed been crossed and the ground trending down. The path becomes clearer when a solitary building comes in sight: this is Mosedale Cottage, an overnight refuge for shepherds. On the fellside behind is the large disused Mosedale Quarry. These names confirm that we are now in Mosedale, although the bare and featureless terrain at such a high altitude bears little resemblance to a dale.

Mosedale Cottage and Quarry   *The Forces*

Wet Sleddale

Beyond the cottage, which is surely the loneliest in Lakeland, the path divides, the left branch contouring the slope and turning north with Mosedale Beck into Swindale. In the later stages of the descent, the beck provides a display of waterfalls known as The Forces before the road terminus is reached at the farm buildings of Swindale Head.

The main branch goes ahead to cross Mosedale Beck at a primitive bridge as its waters drain north into Swindale. The facing slope is rounded and then follows a long and gradual descent into Wet Sleddale on a distinct track, once a cart road but later reduced to the status of a bridleway. Wet Sleddale is a long deep valley flanked by lesser fells and its details are well seen from the track which maintains a high level above it. Down in the bottom of the valley may be discerned the stone walls, 12 feet high, of a medieval deer trap, unique in the district. Further on is the new Wet Sleddale Reservoir, Manchester's latest and hopefully last, with its attendant casualties of ruined buildings and broken walls.

The track slants down to valley level, becoming tarred to serve the remaining active farms; it passes a Victorian postbox set in a wall before crossing the River Lowther to join the A6 a mile south of Shap.

Nobody will rank the crossing of this Mosedale amongst the best of Lakeland passes, much of it being dull and unexciting, and Wet Sleddale has an atmosphere of forlorn sadness, but on a day of fine weather it provides a satisfactory nine-mile walk.

28 MOUSTHWAITE COMB, 1350'
Scales – Mungrisdale

A SHORT AND simple pass walk is available on the eastern fringe of the Northern Fells, crossing a low col to enter the little-known valley of the River Glenderamackin and passing below the long escarpment of Bannerdale Crags before reaching the village of Mungrisdale. It is a pleasant expedition in unfrequented terrain, requiring little effort and suitable for a short half-day after a morning's rain.

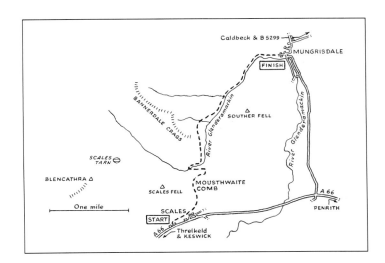

FROM THE HAMLET of Scales on the A66 east of Threlkeld starts a popular path over Scales Fell to Blencathra, skirting a hollow in the fells known as Mousthwaite Comb.

Crossing this hollow and ignoring the well-trodden path up Scales Fell and another branching left to Scales Tarn, the head of the hollow is reached at a col on the east side, whence a descending path slants down to a bridge over the River Glenderamackin and joins another path on the far bank.

The course of the Glenderamackin is interesting, suggesting an early problem in deciding the direction of flow. From its source, it heads south-east, turns east on finding its way barred by Mousthwaite Comb, is then turned north by Souther Fell and when the latter declines to valley level flows east through Mungrisdale and then due south and finally west to join the River Greta, almost completing a circuit of Souther Fell.

Across the river rises the long southern slope of Bannerdale Crags, and the path on the far bank contours round its base, following the river as it turns north and soon bringing into view the mile-long escarpment of Bannerdale Crags. These are palpably inaccessible except at one point where a steep ridge comes down to the valley, yet has ruins of old mines high amongst the cliffs. When the river turns east, a tributary beck is forded and an improving path, becoming a lane, leads into the attractive small village of Mungrisdale, two miles by road from the A66 and its bus service.

Opposite *Blencathra from Mousthwaite Comb*

29 NAN BIELD, 2100′
Kentmere – Mardale

OF ALL THE Lakeland passes, I rank Nan Bield amongst the finest. It conforms most to my concept of a true mountain pass or col, being delicately sculptured, narrow at its crest and steeply descending on both sides. It is poised high, a lonely gap between lofty fells, and retains features from long ago when it served as a trade route for packhorses. Unmarred by wheeled traffic, this is a way only for travellers on foot and wearing stout boots.

Nan Bield provides a direct link between the Kentmere valley and Mardale, and six miles of rough and in places steep ground separate their road termini. The road to Kentmere leaves the A591 at Staveley, midway between Kendal and Windermere: the A591 is the usual approach to the Lake District from the south and the turn to Kentmere is often overlooked or, being a dead end, ignored by motorists hurrying to reach Windermere which, for many of them, marks the start of Lakeland. The four miles to the little community of Kentmere are consequently relatively quiet and mainly used by local traffic and the discerning few who disagree that Lakeland starts at Windermere. These four miles along a winding valley are lovely, the River Kent pursuing a rapid course through pleasant pastures and woodlands where daffodils and bluebells are a springtime delight. Of course Lakeland doesn't start at Windermere; here in the Kentmere valley, natural charm typical of the district is all around and no less enchanting. Here romance is allied to beauty.

Opposite *Nan Bield*

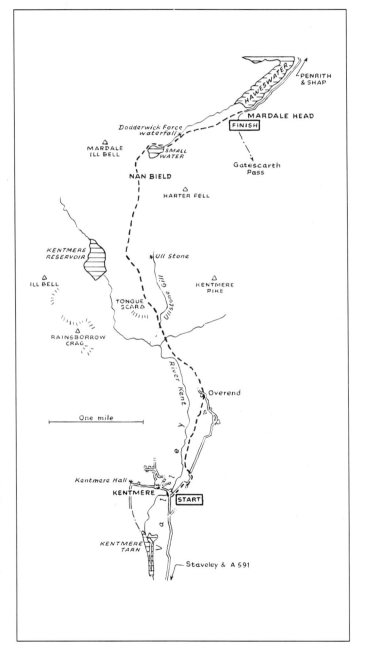

Unlike the neighbouring Longsleddale, the Kentmere valley curves, revealing a succession of fresh scenes and occasional sightings of the mountains ahead. After passing a former asbestos works, open ground is reached and there is a distant view of the church on a hill. Across fields is the new Kent Mere. On the flat strath south of the church was formerly a shallow lake, the Kent Mere that gave its name to the valley and village. This was drained in 1840 to provide more land for cultivation – a purpose not entirely achieved, much of the reclaimed ground remaining too marshy for the plough and for grazing. Analysis of the former bed of the lake in the present century disclosed the presence of rich deposits of diatomaceous earth which, when extracted and processed, proved a valuable insulation material and led to the establishment of a works on the site. During these operations, the remains of two primitive boats in the form of dugout canoes, believed to be of the Viking period, were discovered; the better of the two specimens is now at the National Maritime Museum. The draining of the lake in 1840 was probably a factor in the erratic flow of the river that led to the promotion of an Act of Parliament to create a reservoir in the upper reaches of the valley. Today, with supplies of diatomaceous earth exhausted and the industry closed, a new Kent Mere has come into being on the same site: a narrow sheet of water half a mile in length.

Nearby is the site of an ancient British village settlement and the valley has other evidences of prehistoric occupation. Not far from the church is Kentmere Hall, with a ruined fourteenth-century pele tower: this was the birthplace in 1517 of Bernard Gilpin, who had a distinguished career in the Church and became known as 'The Apostle of the North'.

Rainsborrow Crag

Ill Bell and Kentmere Reservoir

Southern approach to Nan Bield

THE ROADS in the village are narrow and unsuitable for the parking of cars: it is usual to take advantage of an open space alongside the church. The way to Nan Bield, now on foot, starts from the bridge where the Low Bridge Inn was formerly. Here turn up a side road heading north until a signpost (to Mardale) indicates a path with the River Kent nearby rushing through a tree-lined gorge in a series of cataracts and waterfalls. The footpath leads to the farm buildings of Overend, the last outpost of civilisation, and continues beyond, passing a quaint bridge used for access to fields across the river. The scenery now is very impressive, the dominant feature being Rainsborrow Crag on the other side of the valley, backed by Ill Bell and its satellites. On the right, colourful slopes rise to Kentmere Pike, 1600 feet above. Ahead, blocking the valley, is Tongue Scar, a craggy upthrust at the foot of which are long-established badger setts. The river curves to the left amongst many disused quarries to the outflow from Kentmere Reservoir, but the path to Nan Bield goes ahead.

A tributary beck is crossed in a pretty dell, and the path then climbs the east slope of the Tongue, the route being indicated by a line of cairns erected by Kendal schoolboys. At one point, where a quarry road branches to the right, is an upright stone slab bearing the inscription 'To Mardale': a relic of packhorse days. On the fellside to the right, across Ullstone Gill, is a disused quarry and below it a huge boulder, the Ull Stone, provides shelter for sheep.

When abreast of the top of the Tongue, the gradient eases and a splendid view unfolds of the mountains around the head of the valley, and Kentmere Reservoir comes into sight down below on the left. Nan Bield is seen a mile ahead as a lofty gap between Mardale Ill Bell, left, and Harter Fell, right; the path aims directly towards it and becomes a narrow track over open grassland. The ground steepens on the final rise to the pass, upward progress being helped by a series of zigzags, skilfully engineered not for the benefit of pedestrians but for the comfort of laden packhorses. At the top of the slope, the crest of Nan Bield is reached, adorned with a large wind shelter of stones, its back to the prevailing wind. A crude shelter that many a stormbound traveller has been glad to enter.

On a day of clear visibility the view northwards from Nan Bield is excellent. Mardale is seen ahead and below, and the long line of the Pennines closes the distant horizon. Retrospectively, the Kentmere valley is well displayed, the Tongue dwarfed to insignificance by the enclosing mountains.

The descent into Mardale commences at once, and after only a few paces Small Water and Haweswater come into sight far below: an arresting picture for the camera.

The path on the Mardale side of the pass, originally in the form of well-graded bends and twists to ease the descent, has unfortunately been cut to ribbons by the tread of impatient boots, the way down being a river of sliding stones where there is a need to walk circumspectly with regard to the placing of every step as the eye searches for firm footing; this is a bad case of erosion by careless walkers. The fine view ahead demands attention but should be observed only by halting; here the scenery should not be viewed while in motion or mishaps will occur.

At the foot of this unpleasant descent, the shores of Small Water are reached. This is one of the finest mountain tarns, deep-set in a wild surround of craggy heights, a gem of its kind, best appreciated when you are not in the company of others.

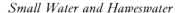

Small Water and Haweswater

Small Water   Below *Shelters by Small Water*

The path skirts the edge of the tarn, passing three stone shelters, these presumably being constructed long ago for the benefit of travellers overtaken by storm or darkness; they are still serviceable and can be entered by crawling, to the consternation of the resident spiders.

The path fords the outlet of the tarn and descends along a pony route by which early visitors were taken to Small Water. The issuing stream leaps alongside and, lower down in a hidden gorge, makes a final plunge at Dodderwick Force before proceeding quietly to enter Haweswater. The path crosses a declining moorland below the crags of Harter Fell and joins a track coming down from Gatescarth Pass for the last 100 yards to the road terminus and car park at Mardale Head.

A strong walker may return to Kentmere by way of Gatescarth Pass and Sadgill in Longsleddale. But not many will. For the weary, the temptation of a soft seat in a car and an effortless drive alongside Haweswater will be too great to resist. Nan Bield is enough for one day.

30 NEWLANDS HAUSE, 1096'
Newlands – Buttermere

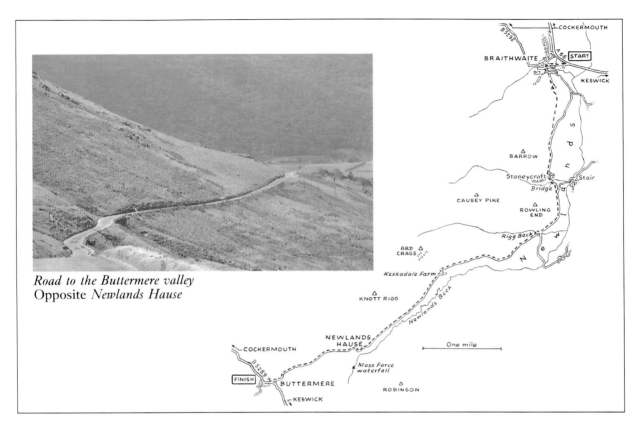

Road to the Buttermere valley
Opposite *Newlands Hause*

NEWLANDS HAUSE, often wrongly referred to as Buttermere Hause, carries a narrow motor road, non-commercial and normally quiet but much used by summer and weekend visitors to the district. The lovely valley of Newlands is patterned with country roads, any of which may be taken at the start of the journey. The most direct leaves the village of Braithwaite, then rounds the abrupt hill of Barrow which still bears the scars of disused lead mines, crosses Stonycroft Bridge over a stream where relics of mining activity can be seen in the form of a watercut, now dry, and passes along the base of Rowling End, elevated above the valley pastures. At Keskadale the road, fairly straight thus far, escapes from an impasse by steep curves to resume a direct ascending course to the hause rising along the flanks of Knott Rigg. Across the narrowing valley is the massive bulk of Robinson Fell. On the hause is ample space for parking cars from where Knott Rigg may be climbed or a waterfall, seen on the left, visited. Around the corner, the Buttermere valley comes into view with its attendant heights, a prospect full of promise; then the road starts a long decline to the village, allowing a more intimate appraisal of the delightful environs.

The road is not exclusively the preserve of motorists, and walkers can and often do use it but there is little opportunity to escape from the hard surface and at busy times it is best left to those who travel on wheels. Fortunately there is a direct alternative for walkers avoiding the hause, which is free from noise other than the tinkling of streams. This is the route alongside Rigg Beck (*see* page 151).

31 ORE GAP, 2575'
Eskdale – Borrowdale

THERE IS A splendid alternative route between Eskdale and Borrowdale, less spectacular than that over Esk Hause and having a considerable amount of rough and pathless walking, but because the way is guided by streams, there is little danger of going astray. This is a walk rarely undertaken, the adjoining mountains having the greater appeal, but in misty conditions when the tops are obscured it has merit as a foolproof route. However, it should not be underestimated; for most walkers it will prove a full day's expedition. Novice fellwalkers should not attempt the journey. In bad weather, it is safer to go from Boot to Wasdale Head by way of Burnmoor Tarn and thence over Sty Head to Borrowdale.

The route aims for the narrow col between Esk Pike and Bowfell, named Ore Gap and identifiable when reached by the red subsoil of a vein of hematite that gives the place its name which, occasionally and obviously wrongly, is spelt Ewer Gap.

View up Esk Valley to Bowfell
Opposite *View to Eskdale from Ore Gap*

THE ESKDALE ROAD is left at the foot of Hardknott Pass, passing the farm of Brotherilkeld and continuing up the valley of the River Esk on a distinct path with an exciting mountain prospect ahead. The walking here is pleasant and the Esk a delightful companion, but after passing below the formidable cliff of Heron Crag, high on the left, the terrain becomes rougher as a confluence of waters is reached at the picturesque arch of Lingcove Bridge. Here the Esk changes direction, coming down a deep gorge on the left, the bridge spanning a tributary, Lingcove Beck. The way to Ore Gap does not cross the bridge, but proceeds on a path climbing alongside the beck, which here displays a series of waterfalls. Bowfell and Crinkle Crags rear up massively in front, and after passing the opening of another Mosedale on the right, in surroundings of wild and chaotic desolation, the path goes forward to a grassy basin on the left. This is Green Hole and here the hard work starts.

The valley of the River Esk

Yeastyrigg Gill

Ore Gap looking up to Esk Pike

Abreast of Green Hole, the path thus far followed from Lingcove Bridge heads purposefully north-east, bound for the depression of Three Tarns between Bowfell and Crinkle Crags, but here is left in favour of a pathless crossing of Green Hole alongside the principal watercourse, Lingcove Beck. This stream emerges from a long and stony ravine, Yeastyrigg Gill, an uninviting chasm with the sole merit of pointing the way exactly to Ore Gap, not yet in view. The scramble up the bed of the stream is arduous, and better progress will be made on the adjoining slopes of Bowfell, which now appears as a massive pyramid of stones. At length, after an exhausting ascent, the ravine ends on an open fellside, the stream becomes a trickle, and Ore Gap is now clearly in sight ahead and reached with mute cheers. This is the end of uphill walking for the day.

Langstrath

A much-trodden path crosses Ore Gap, linking Bowfell and Esk Pike, and a distant view to the north opens up, revealing a kinder landscape with the promise of easier travel. Over the crest of the col, the way down starts immediately on a thin track aiming for Angle Tarn, seen as a dark circular pool in a green hollow below, and comes alongside it after a rough descent.

At the outlet of the tarn, the popular pedestrian highway coming over Rossett Pass and bound for Wasdale Head is met. The comfort of a well-trodden path is short-lived, the stream issuing from the tarn being followed down into the great hollow of Langstrath immediately in front and appearing verdant and restful after the arid wastes so far traversed. Ahead is a green and refreshing landscape, a valley set deep amongst enclosing fells: Allen Crags and Glaramara on the left and Rossett Pike on the right. The way down, on grass, does not have the advantage of a good path, but it is a pleasure to accompany the lively stream, here named Angletarn Gill and in maturity Langstrath Beck. Lower down a thin track forms and after two miles of walking from the tarn a distinct path is joined, this coming over Stake Pass from Great Langdale. Langstrath is now seen stretching far ahead, and tired feet will testify to the interpretation of its name as 'Long Valley'. But even tired feet will find the remainder of the walk a joy to tread.

Special delights of Langstrath are related to its charming beck, which flows along an alluring channel in a succession of bathing pools and cataracts and waterfalls. The enclosing heights, too, become more impressive, Sergeant's Crag and Eagle Crag rising very steeply to a rim of cliffs. Adding to the beauty of the lower reaches of the valley, trees appear in profusion and extend up fellsides which are coloured by heather and bracken.

Langstrath terminates at a delightful meeting of waters where a stream joins from Greenup Edge, the combined waters turning left into the Stonethwaite valley.

A bridge across the beck before the watersmeet and a path therefrom enters a rural lane that leads very pleasantly into the unspoilt hamlet of Stonethwaite, the cottages here being the first habitations seen since leaving Brotherilkeld.

This is a lovely corner of the district, typical of the romantic natural beauty of Lakeland and here still defended against modern intrusions.

A motor road connects with the nearby valley of Borrowdale at Rosthwaite. A pleasanter option, however, is to take the path alongside the beck for the final stage of the walk.

Above *Langstrath Beck*

The Stonethwaite valley

32 RIGG BECK, 1200'
Newlands – Buttermere

THE RIGG BECK route provides a direct way between Newlands and Buttermere exclusively for travellers on foot: it is not so much a pass as a deep cutting through mountainous terrain, rising gently to a low watershed from which streams descend on both sides. So confined and clearly defined is this crossing that only a genius could possibly go astray.

Opposite The valley of Rigg Beck looking towards Newlands Valley
Right Ard Crags

A GOOD PATH leaves the Newlands Hause road at the point where Rigg Beck comes down a pleasant valley from the west; there is limited parking for cars on the verges near the bridge. The path rounds a curve to enter a long straight furrow through the steepening fellsides of Ard Crags and Causey Pike. With Rigg Beck gurgling alongside, the path proceeds to its head waters; Ard Crags give place to Knott Rigg and Causey Pike is succeeded by Scar Crags, Sail and Eel Crags without any noticeable variation in the high skyline. These lofty enclosing walls effectively shut out distant views, but when the slight watershed is reached, the Buttermere Fells are seen in their full glory ahead. Past the divide, the role of guide is taken over by Sail Beck, the path following faithfully all the way down to the village of Buttermere in an environment of increasing beauty, being joined in its final stages by the path coming down from Whiteless Pike. Thus ends a walk greatly to be preferred to the hard road over Newlands Hause (*see* page 143).

33 ROSSETT PASS, 2000'
Great Langdale – Wasdale Head

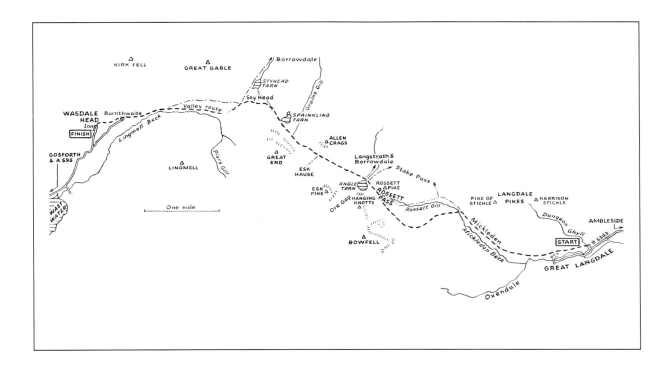

PASS WALKING has not the exhilaration and excitement of fellwalking, nor are the views as extensive as those seen from the ridges and summits. Lacking too is the interest of route planning and route findings: most passes have no easy variations from the well-trodden paths and there is no fear of going astray. For newcomers to the fells, walking the passes is a good apprenticeship for walking on the tops.

But there is one popular pass in Lakeland that comes near to the excellence of a high-level fell walk, one that affords intimate acquaintanceship with grand mountains, winds through contrasting and impressive landscapes, climbs to a considerable altitude and is exposed to the elements: in short, it deserves to rank as a first-class mountain expedition. This is the crossing between Great Langdale and Wasdale Head, generally and indeed almost always referred to as the Esk Hause route although this is a misnomer because the path does not reach or cross the true Esk Hause. It may perhaps be more accurate to refer to the route as Rossett Pass which is certainly crossed on the walk from Great Langdale although succeeded by higher ground before the descent to Wasdale Head commences. Two sections of the walk are uncomfortably rough and stony but can be avoided by grass alternatives mentioned in the chapter.

For full appreciation a whole day should be allowed for the journey.

Opposite *Rossett Pass*

BEYOND DUNGEON GHYLL, Great Langdale divides into two valleys, Oxendale and Mickleden. The path travels the two easy miles of Mickleden below the towering skyline of the Langdale Pikes, with the Band of Bowfell rising on the left. The valley terminates abruptly at the base of Rossett Pike, where a path branches right to climb to Stake Pass, the main path trending left and arriving at the foot of Rossett Gill. Nobody ever said a kind word about Rossett Gill. The direct climb is abominably rough, up a river of sliding stones through a height of a thousand feet; a torment of the flesh that only hardened masochists will enjoy. I had toiled up this ladder of loose stones dozens of times before discovering on an old map that there was formerly a pony track that made the ascent by a circuitous route across the lower slopes of Bowfell. I traced this old way on the ground without difficulty, finding it quiet, well graded and pleasant, and never again did I suffer the discomforts of the direct route. This alternative I recommend.

Langdale Pikes and Mickleden from Rossett Gill

It leaves the floor of Mickleden short of the head of the valley, fording the beck at a point I've never been able to identify exactly but no matter; the stream may be crossed at any convenient place and the pathless fellside beyond climbed half-right and across a landslide to a line of ancient cairns. The route thus far has been indistinct underfoot although, like many old tracks, plainly seen from a distance. Once found, with the help of the cairns, the path is a joy to follow, quite easy and within sight of the crowds struggling up Rossett Gill. It rises more steeply to a hollow threaded by many waterslides coming off Bowfell and crosses a causeway at a pool. Nearby is an old sheepfold, screened from sight of the valley below where, I was told by a Langdale historian, the dalesmen hid their sheep during the border raids. Within easy reach on a grassy mound, is a cross of stones laid on the ground, marking the grave of a packwoman who used to call at the Langdale farms carrying articles for sale and whose remains were found at this spot 200 years ago.

Angle Tarn

The pony route then heads directly to the top of Rossett Pass, appearing as a straight groove in its later sections, and here joining the direct climb up the gill. Some pony routes were devised for the pleasure of visitors and others, like this, were trade routes in the days of packhorses.

Rossett Pass, with grass succeeding stones, is a welcome relief to the feet, but a wild and inhospitable landscape meets the eyes. High on the left, the Hanging Knotts of Bowfell plunge into the waters of Angle Tarn; the tarn has been variously described as dark and sinister or as calm and lovely in its solitude. There is a short descent to the outlet of the tarn, and here you can see that the issuing stream crosses the path and descends into the valley of Langstrath, a vast hollow on the right leading down into Borrowdale. Indeed, beyond Rossett Pass, all the ground in sight is within the Borrowdale watershed, and the path over the so-called Esk Hause, straight ahead and much higher, is for some miles, until the descent of Wasdale Head from Sty Head, the catchment area of Borrowdale's rivers.

Esk Pike

From Angle Tarn the path goes ahead, climbing gradually to a wall shelter of stones, the highest point of the journey and commonly known as Esk Hause, although the true Esk Hause – i.e. the pass from Eskdale – is the higher ridge seen on the left between Esk Pike and Great End. The site of the shelter, at 2386ft, qualifies as a pass but only a minor one. The main watershed, at 2490ft, divides the gathering grounds of Eskdale and Borrowdale at Esk Hause proper and is not visited on this walk.

The journey becomes more exciting as the path leaves the shelter and descends gently, coming alongside Ruddy Gill where the vein of hematite seen at Ore Gap is again in evidence; this colourful ravine curves to the right, heading for Borrowdale via Grains Gill and a path accompanies it. The main path continues forward below the massive cliff of Great End, riven by gullies and dominating all else. Soon the shore of Sprinkling Tarn is reached: a lovely sheet of water that cries out for a halt; invariably rucksacks are cast off here for a rest while those walkers with cameras inevitably take the classic picture of Great End seen soaring above the indented shore.

Resuming the walk, the feature that compels attention is the immense pyramid of Great Gable directly ahead and increasing in stature as the path descends gradually towards it to arrive at Sty Head, a walkers' crossroads known to all who frequent the fells and from which tracks radiate in all directions. Away to the right is the inky pool of Styhead Tarn.

Great End from Sprinkling Tarn

Below *Great Gable*

From Sty Head, the path for Wasdale Head turns a corner on the left, a fine viewpoint and, with the promised land of Wasdale coming into sight as an inviting green oasis, makes a beeline for it. But over-use has turned the surface of the path into an uncomfortable channel of loose stones. Much better is the original path, now rarely used, known as the Valley Route, reached by descending at once from Sty Head into the grassy depths on the left to join the stream there: this, augmented by the flow from Piers Gill, becomes Lingmell Beck. The path follows it closely, arriving at the cultivated fields of Burnthwaite, from which a short lane leads to the inn at Wasdale Head and journey's end.

There are few, if any, grander cross-country walks than this. It will remain an evergreen memory.

Looking towards Newlands

Below *The summit of Sail Pass*

34 SAIL PASS, 2050'
Newlands – Buttermere

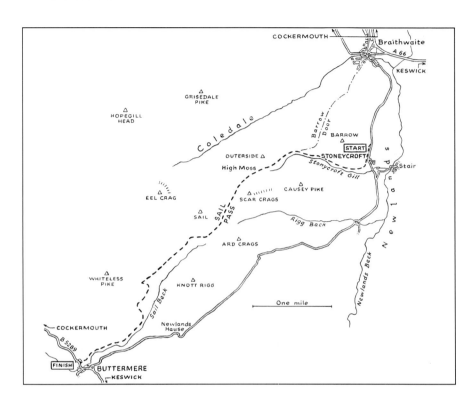

IN ADDITION TO the two crossings between Newlands and Buttermere by way of Newlands Hause (No.30) and Rigg Beck (No.32), there is another, rather more arduous, that takes advantage of an old mine road and gives much grander mountain views. This leads to a former cobalt mine of which a few traces remain, crosses a ridge beyond and descends to join the Rigg Beck route to reach Buttermere.

THE MAIN ROAD leaves Newlands at Stoneycroft, branching off at the valley road from Braithwaite, and soon starts to climb steadily up the side valley of the Stonycroft Gill overlooked by the imposing peak of Causey Pike and the heathery slopes of Barrow. It is joined after a mile by an alternative route from Braithwaite through Barrow Door, itself a pass, and becomes less distinct as it crosses the marshy plateau of High Moss before finally rising to the site of the old mine. There's a striking view hereabouts of the head of Coledale down below on the right and closely confined by the impending heights of Eel Crag, Hopegill Head and Grisedale Pike. Beyond the mine, the route, now reduced to a thin track, reaches a depression in the ridge above. This is Sail Pass, carrying a ridge path in popular use. Over the pass is the deep valley of Rigg Beck and a slender track, probably used by miners but little used today, slants down across the breast of Sail to the watershed of Rigg Beck and Sail Beck, the latter then being followed down on a good path to enter the village of Buttermere, arriving there in sylvan surroundings on a parallel course with the motor road over Newlands Hause.

159

35 SCANDALE PASS, 1680'
Ambleside – Patterdale

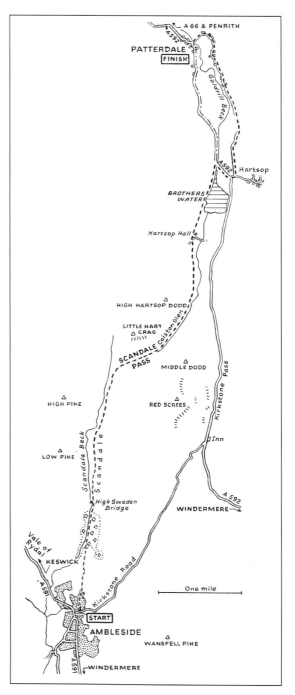

A CENSUS OF the travellers making the journey between Ambleside and Patterdale via (a) Kirkstone Pass and (b) Scandale Pass, would show the former route to be used almost exclusively and the latter, having no motor road, hardly at all. Even those who travel on foot seem to prefer the animation of Kirkstone to the loneliness of Scandale. Scenically, Kirkstone is the grander of the two by far, its untamed wildness being very impressive despite the tourist traffic it attracts. Scandale cannot compete in the matter of scenery, being tedious and dull by comparison, and its more limited appeal is due to its quietness and solitude.

AMBLESIDE IS LEFT by way of Sweden Bridge Lane, branching from the Kirkstone road near the old church. The lane climbs into an enviable suburbia, but when the residences and tarmac are left behind at a gate it becomes a rough cart-track. The next mile is perfect bliss, the rising lane affording exquisite views of the Vale of Rydal and the surrounding fells, while nearby Wansfell Pike assumes a stature that belies its rather modest altitude.

Opposite *The head of Scandale in summer Red Screes' summit rocks*

High Sweden Bridge in Scandale

The lane enters a woodland glade and here is an avenue of loveliness, especially when dappled by sunlight; a musical accompaniment to the scene is provided by the rushing waters of Scandale Beck, hidden in a gorge down on the left. The lane is another of Ambleside's many treasures and is well patronised by visitors, their objective coming into sight at the end of the trees. Here is the picturesque High Sweden Bridge, a gem of its kind, its one simple arch spanning the stream. Everybody with a camera takes photographs at this romantic spot.

The bridge is the great attraction for the many people who walk the two miles from Ambleside, the prize they seek, and few aspire further along the valley to its head at Scandale Pass. This is not surprising; it must be conceded that the scenery beyond the bridge compares unfavourably with the beauty of the approach to it.

The higher reaches of Scandale are therefore likely to be of interest only to walkers bound for Patterdale. The cart-track continues upstream, not crossing the bridge, and rises gently, enclosed by walls, to reveal a different landscape, a barren wilderness where the many stone walls are the only signs of human intervention in the dreary scene. The track descends to a marshy amphitheatre hemmed in by the high ridge of Low Pike and High Pike on the left and flanked by the featureless slopes of Red Screes which reserves its interest for the savage Kirkstone face. Ahead is the pass, overtopped by the twin peaks of Little Hart Crag. The hollow is crossed and the ground rises steeply, trending to the right to gain the top of Scandale Pass, crossed by a sturdy stone wall.

The ascent of Red Screes may be made from the top of the pass, the wall serving as guide, but this side of the mountain exhibits nothing of the ruggedness displayed to the crowds at the Kirkstone Pass Inn.

The descent from the pass starts at once along the steeply declining valley of Caiston Glen, equally dreary and even more shut in by fells but having a vista of verdant greenery in front framed by the slopes of High Hartsop Dodd and Middle Dodd, the former terminating in a downfall of crags and scree where, in 1948, the efforts of the local dalesmen to rescue two trapped terriers won headlines in national newspapers for several days until the dogs were finally released.

With the high ground falling away sharply alongside, the surroundings become more open, trees making a welcome appearance, and then the path from Kirkstone Pass joins for the pleasant walk down the Patterdale Valley to the farm of Hartsop Hall, whence a lane continues the route along the shores of Brothers Water and to the A592. The village of Patterdale is two miles further or, if the road is busy, a parallel by-road from the Hartsop junction is to be preferred.

There is rural loveliness and quiet serenity at both ends of the Scandale Pass, but only drab desolation in its middle section. For walkers who choose not to be in close proximity to cars and enjoy solitude, this route is greatly to be preferred to the popular Kirkstone Pass with its endless traffic and noise. You will never see a buzzard or an eagle in the sky above Kirkstone; over Scandale you might.

The head of Scandale in winter

36 SCARTH GAP, 1400′
Buttermere – Ennerdale

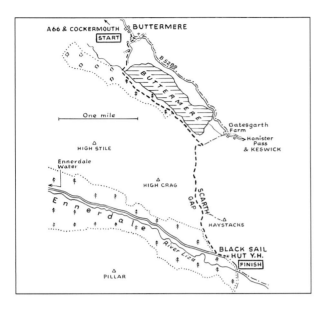

THERE IS NO WAY across the mountain barrier separating Buttermere and Ennerdale that does not call for serious fellwalking at a high level, and those who wish to travel from one valley to the other with minimum output of energy must have recourse to the Scarth Gap path which skirts the range to the east. This is a splendid walk, not long in distance but endowed with magnificent views; the camera is as essential as boots. Scarth Gap, often referred to as Scarf Gap in earlier days, is the depression between High Crag, one of the trinity of peaks forming the High Stile range, and Haystacks which is a lesser summit. The path is distinct, without deviations, and poses no problems of route finding.

Opposite *The summit of Scarth Gap*
Buttermere

FROM BUTTERMERE VILLAGE, either side of its lake may be followed, the more direct way being along the south-west shore, reached by a bridge over the outflow. Then amongst trees, some natural and some planted, the charming lakeside path leads for a mile below the majestic presence of High Stile, almost to the head of the lake where a cairned path branches off and climbs the open fellside.

This point may be reached more quickly by crossing the pastures from Gatesgarth Farm, this alternative saving a mile of walking but missing the delights of the lakeside.

The path rises steadily over grass slopes in the direction of Haystacks. Halts are justified by the excellence of the retrospective view over the Buttermere valley to Grasmoor. Scarth Gap is obvious in front, and the path leads unerringly to a large cairn marking the summit of the path.

There are signs at Scarth Gap that men have been at work recently trying to combat erosion caused by boots; in particular, steps have been made in the scree slope leading up to Haystacks. Early guidebooks dismissed Haystacks as of little consequence and barely worth a mention, but in recent years it has deservedly become a popular objective of fellwalkers. I cannot agree, however, that steps should be provided to ease the ascent. Erosion of paths by over-use is a growing problem, but steps are not the answer. Steps up a mountain are incongruous, out of place. Steps are for going upstairs to bed, not for climbing mountains. Unfortunately, there are now many examples: there are flights of steps on Loughrigg and Nab Scar, and worst of all a stairway to the top of Mam Tor in Derbyshire – with hand rail provided. Heaven forbid, at least in Lakeland. No, the cure for erosion is for walkers to tread carefully and firmly on paths, not to kick them to bits.

A scene of grandeur greets the eyes on the descent into Ennerdale. Great Gable and Pillar rear up proudly across the gulf, Great Gable naked and unashamed, Pillar wearing an unbecoming skirt of foreign conifer plantations which have draped across the lower slopes for the last few decades. They reach all the way down Ennerdale and have no natural beauty. I saw Pillar before the trees came, in full stature, and it was a glorious sight. Now, its tears of lost pride and dignity swell the River Liza at its base. I weep with it. This should not have happened.

Gatesgarth Farm

Great Gable from Scarth Gap

The path from Scarth Gap goes stonily down to come alongside the dark cloak of a plantation, and reaches the cart-track now used as a forest road that follows the River Liza down-river for several miles to the scattered habitations near Ennerdale Water; there is a Youth Hostel midway. But at the point of arrival from Scarth Gap the only sign of civilisation is the solitary Black Sail Hut, most remote and isolated of Lakeland's Youth Hostels. Failing accommodation here, there is no alternative to the long trek down the valley with no respite from regimented avenues of battery-reared skeletons of trees. Where now is the beauty that was Ennerdale?

Pillar from Scarth Gap

The path to Skiddaw House

Below *Skiddaw Forest*

37 SKIDDAW FOREST, 1500'
Keswick – Orthwaite or Mosedale

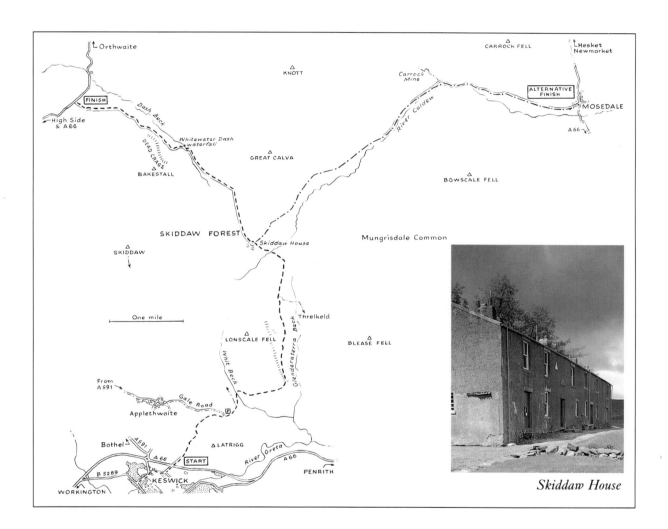

Skiddaw House

THE NORTHERN fells of Lakeland rise in complete isolation from the Vale of Keswick and extend to the coastal plain of Cumbria as a huge natural barrier topping 3000 ft in altitude. This high mass, roughly circular in plan, is dissected by watercourses to form a score of separate summits. They are individually named and closely linked and nowhere permit easy passage between them except by two low crossings which divide the area into three segments, each having its own group of fells. These crossings are remarkably easy considering the high ground they penetrate, and are even negotiable by cars in parts. They start as one from the Vale of Keswick, branching in the heart of Skiddaw Forest; the main route goes on to the farming communities north-west of Skiddaw, the other follows the River Caldew east to Mosedale.

Dead Crags

STARTING FROM KESWICK, the small hill of Latrigg, 'Skiddaw's cub', must be rounded after crossing the new A66, either by way of Spooney Green Lane on foot, or by motor road via Applethwaite to the terminus of Gale Road; here the two routes converge and there is parking for cars. Here commences the time-honoured path to Skiddaw, heading north for the mountain. Around the first bend, the path to Skiddaw Forest branches to the right, makes a wide sweep to cross Whit Beck and contours along the lower slopes of Lonscale Fell, a terrace walk with lovely views of the Greta valley. The path turns north abruptly, in places cut out of the living rock, above the deep watercourse of Glenderaterra Beck, and now having the immense slopes of Blease Fell opposite. With Lonscale Fell displaying its rugged eastern face, culminating in a fine tower of rock, the path aims directly forward, passing an area of abandoned lead mines of which a few relics remain, and being joined by a path from Threlkeld. Walls come alongside, a gate is reached on a minor watershed, and the path trends left to the lonely buildings of Skiddaw House, built as a gamekeeper's lodge and later occupied by shepherds. A small plantation behind serves as a windbreak.

Here we are in Skiddaw Forest, a vast tract of open moorland extending into the far distance, a forest without trees, once a hunting ground and now a spacious pasture for sheep. Note that the sheepfolds hereabouts are circular, conforming to the Scottish pattern, and not rectangular as elsewhere in Lakeland. The forest is a wilderness, dreary under cloud, yet having a haunting beauty when sunlight dapples the landscape. The solitude is profound.

Skiddaw House is served by a rough access road, and if the objective is the pastoral countryside north-west of Skiddaw, this is followed below the shattered cliffs of Dead Crags into the valley of Dash Beck which has a spectacular but little-known waterfall called Whitewater Dash. Soon the fells are left behind and, amongst cultivated fields, a quiet motor road is reached between Orthwaite and High Side, the latter having a bus service.

The alternative route, for Mosedale: from Skiddaw House, the way slowly declines north-eastwards into the valley of the River Caldew; a thin track goes towards this pleasant watercourse and then comes alongside it. The track follows the river downstream on its north bank for three lonely but enjoyable miles as it develops bathing pools along its slaty bed. The track joins a tarred road below Carrock Mine, this leading into the hamlet of Mosedale along the base of the rugged declivities of Carrock Fell. From Mosedale a country road goes south for three miles to reach the A66 and its bus service.

Valley of the River Caldew

Above *Whitewater Dash*

38 STAKE PASS, 1576'
Great Langdale – Borrowdale

THE LAKE DISTRICT was not designed for motorists who, to pass from one valley to the next, must in many cases travel up to ten times further than the crow can fly because of intervening high ground. Walkers are better favoured although, even with greater mobility, they can rarely make crowlines or beelines and must seek the easiest contours. Nature obviously never intended Lakeland to be overrun by men on wheels, nor by timid pedestrians; it was fashioned as a rugged wilderness to be enjoyed only by lovers of solitude and primitive landscapes. One should be thankful for this.

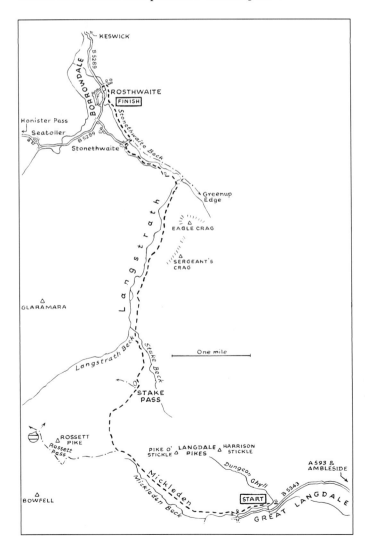

Thus the two valleys most populated by modern tourists, Great Langdale and Borrowdale, have no linking road and cars must make a wide detour around Keswick to pass from one to the other. But walkers have one possible route that avoids rough climbing and reveals glories that motorists never see.

This is the Stake Pass.

Opposite *Mickleden
Stake Pass*

Langstrath

BEYOND DUNGEON GHYLL at the head of Great Langdale a much-used level path proceeds along the branching valley of Mickleden, set deep between the ramparts of the Langdale Pikes on one side and the rising shoulder of Bowfell on the other. After two miles of easy walking, Rossett Pike presents an insuperable impasse directly ahead and the path bifurcates, the main branch trending left to Rossett Pass and the other ascending grassy slopes on the right to the skyline depression formed by Stake Pass. The climb is unremitting and the original well-engineered zigzags have unfortunately been abused by impatient walkers who have yet to learn that a staggered path following the easiest slopes gives by far the most enjoyable mode of progression: these untidy short cuts are invariably made, not in ascent but by clumsy walkers descending at speed, and are inexcusable. All mountain paths should be savoured slowly and treated with respect even in bad weather or when there's a bus to catch. They are the walker's greatest help in his wanderings amongst the fells and should be preserved with care, not kicked into unsightly ribbons of loose stones which can also cause accidents. I love zigzag paths and it pains me to see them wrecked unmercifully by walkers who do not appreciate their worth and do not deserve the privilege of freedom on the fells.

The ascent is dull, relieved only by the growing stature of Bowfell behind, but when the top of the pass is reached and crossed, a glorious prospect unfolds ahead as the environs of Borrowdale come into sight. On the right, the Langdale Pikes assume an unfamiliar outline, appearing insignificant over a wide moorland.

Gradually the path leads down into the long valley of Langstrath, promising a few miles of pleasant travel as a prelude to Borrowdale. And so it proves. Langstrath is lovely.

Down in the valley acquaintance is made with Langstrath Beck, an exuberant rushing of waters attractively endowed in its lower reaches with waterfalls and rocky pools. The path accompanies it along the valley, passing Gash Rock, a huge fallen boulder providing a few rock climbs. Across the beck rises the massive whaleback of Glaramara, and soaring above the pass are the unassailable heights of Sergeant's Crag and, further, Eagle Crag, both falling in scree slopes from dark towers of rock.

Langstrath has many temptations to linger over, but in due course a bridge spans the beck and admits to a lane in surroundings more akin to heaven than earth; rich carpeted fellside and woodland glades and the sparkling beck make the turn into the Stonethwaite valley a sylvan delight.

The unspoilt hamlet of Stonethwaite is reached with envy of those who live in this secluded community where little has changed since men first settled here and which still has an aura of seventeenth-century Lakeland. A tarred road shatters the illusion, reminding us that the days of horses and carts are over; this leads into the main valley road of Borrowdale, half a mile distant.

If Rosthwaite is the objective, a bridge over the beck can be crossed and a pleasant path followed to this hospitable village amongst trees and pastures; a most fitting finish to the walk that emphasises again that travelling on foot is so greatly preferable to motoring.

One is poetry, the other prose.

Gash Rock   *Langstrath Beck*

39

STICKS PASS, 2420'
Stanah (Thirlmere) – Glenridding

ONLY ONCE HAVE I walked from one end of Sticks Pass to the other (once being enough), although perforce having to use sections of it on many occasions subsequently. It is almost sacrilege to describe any of Lakeland's paths as unattractive, but this high crossing of the Helvellyn range has little to commend it except as an exercise for the legs; it is tedious and drab and in places badly scarred by abandoned lead-mining activities. Sticks Pass is the only crossing between Thirlmere and Ullswater served by a continuous path, its one distinction being that it is the highest pass in the district in regular use. Formerly the highest part of the path was marked by a line of wooden posts, hence the name, but these have vanished.

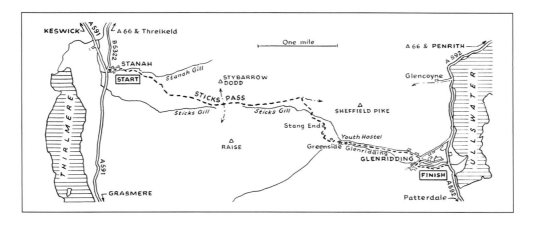

Opposite *The summit of Sticks Pass*

Looking west from Sticks Pass

STANAH IS A little group of buildings reached by a short lane from the A591 at the point where a road branches to St John's in the Vale. A path leaves here, crosses a small bridge, and climbs very steeply above the deep ravine of Stanah Gill, a gloomy chasm with many waterfalls.

The gradient eases when a sheepfold is reached, the cairned path then slanting across an open moor, the sprawling west slope of Stybarrow Dodd, to overlook the valley of Sticks Gill which is followed up to the source of the stream. Across it are the bare slopes of Raise which are normally unfrequented except when presenting animated scenes in snowy winters, being much favoured by skiers.

The final rise to the summit of the pass is steep. At the top the ascents of Stybarrow Dodd, left, and Raise, right, may be made.

The prospect ahead is not one to inspire enthusiasm. It is a scene without beauty, an arid and sterile landscape.

Stanah Gill
Stybarrow Dodd

The path starts a long descent and is soon joined by another Sticks Gill. This is the only instance of streams descending from a watershed in opposite directions having the same name. At length a small reservoir constructed to serve the Glenridding lead mine is reached: this, having outlived its usefulness, has been abandoned and now appears as an unlovely muddy waste, and has been removed from the latest Ordnance maps. Beyond the bed of the old reservoir, a path goes forward and descends to Glencoyne but the main route, now faced by the slopes of Sheffield Pike, turns to the right and enters an area of industrial devastation at Stang End where there are many traces of departed enterprise, notably a long flue that discharged at a chimney, now derelict, on the lower slopes of Raise.

With the Glenridding valley and Ullswater coming into sight, the path drops sharply in zigzags to the site of the Greenside lead mine, its scars grassed over and some of the buildings converted to other uses including a Youth Hostel. From here a road goes down to the lakeside village of Glenridding, its economy no longer based on mining but on catering for the many visitors to Ullswater. Here are hotels, guest houses, shops, a bus service and facilities for sailing on the lake.

Mining relics
The valley of Glenridding from Stang End

40 STILE END, 1100'
Kentmere – Longsleddale

IF, AS IS SUPPOSED, Garburn Pass was the first section of an old road across the south-eastern corner of Lakeland, its logical continuation from Kentmere must have been the cart-track into Longsleddale, referred to here in the absence of a name as the Stile End crossing. The way is distinct underfoot but happily sufficiently rough to break the springs of a car and is now classed as a bridleway.

Incredibly, an insensitive county council some years ago planned to transform this pleasant path into a modern road for the benefit of tourists but the scheme was quite rightly howled down by public outrage.

Kentmere village is left by the rising no-through road to Hallow Bank, this being departed from short of the hamlet where a signposted lane turns off to the right and climbs gently to Stile End; here two stone barns make a good foreground to the classic view of the head of Kentmere beyond. Through a gate, the track continues easily across open grassland to its highest point and then descends to Longsleddale ahead. In one steep section, the track has been badly eroded, an effective barrier to wheels, but is followed by a better surface as the track turns north below Sadgill Wood with a splendid view of the head of Longsleddale in front. It ends at Sadgill Bridge at the terminus of a motor road to the A6 and Kendal.

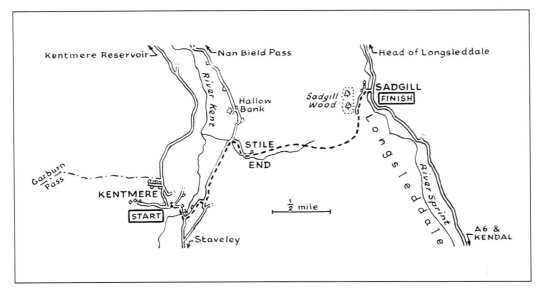

HAVING COME THUS far, which route would the old road take beyond Sadgill? Here it would be faced by an insuperable obstacle, high fells barring a straight continuation. The only feasible way for horse-drawn traffic was to ascend to the head of Longsleddale by cart-track (later used as the Wrengill Quarry road) thence heading across Mosedale and down Wet Sleddale to join the Great North Road (now the A6) at Shap.

This is amateur conjecture only.

Opposite *The head of Kentmere from Stile End*

41 THE STRAITS OF RIGGINDALE

WHEN IS A PASS not a pass? The essential requirement of a mountain pass is that it must permit access from either side, allowing a crossing from one valley to the next.

Seen from a distance, or on a map, the Straits of Riggindale would seem to qualify, appearing as a pronounced dip in a high skyline where the declining ridge of High Street falls briefly before rising sharply to Rampsgill Head; the name too (Straits = a narrow passage) promises a through route – but this is not so.

A footpath from Patterdale by way of Boardale Hause and Angle Tarn crosses an extensive area of foothills before rounding The Knott and slanting upwards to the Straits where it meets the Roman road traversing the ridge. Here one arrives at the brink of the yawning gulf of Riggindale, the way forward being abruptly stopped by a very steep downfall of rocks and scree with no possibility of continuing the line of approach by direct descent into Riggindale although this valley is soon to lead straight to Mardale. True, an adventurous walker may pick his way carefully down the crags and stone gullies but I write for ordinary mortals.

Riggindale is inexpressibly wild and has become a sanctuary for deer and fell ponies, foxes and golden eagles since the only habitation was demolished during the construction of the Haweswater Reservoir and the hamlet at its foot, Mardale Green, has vanished beneath the engulfing waters.

Prudent walkers arriving at the Straits of Riggindale and bound for Mardale complete the journey by going over Kidsty Pike and descending the easy slopes beyond. The Straits form only half a pass, and therefore are no pass at all.

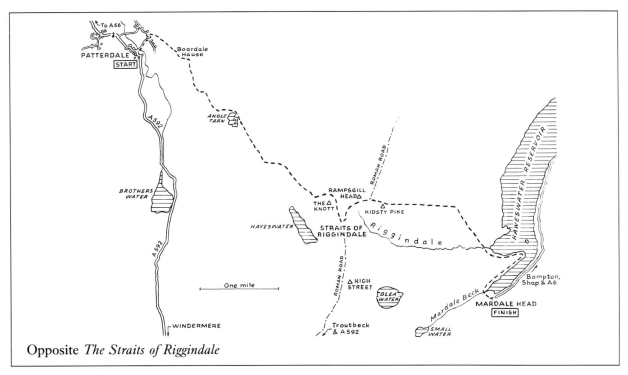

Opposite *The Straits of Riggindale*

42 STY HEAD, 1600'
Borrowdale – Wasdale Head

The top of Sty Head

SOONER OR LATER a very active walker in the Lake District arrives at Sty Head, usually on the crossing between Borrowdale and Wasdale, and most call here frequently during the course of their wanderings. It is a popular halt and there are few days in the year when walkers are absent from its well-trodden paths. The distance from one valley to the other is short, but the mountain barrier intervening is so impregnable that motorists wishing to make the journey must take a circuitous route of forty-five miles. This inconvenience led to an ill-fated proposal many years ago that a motor road be constructed over the pass; thankfully the proposal never got off the drawing board because of the weight of public opposition. Sty Head is a sanctuary of silence and peace amongst the grandest mountains in the country and should remain so. It is a place of outstanding scenic quality, staging a permanent exhibition of awesome impressiveness. This is a part of Lakeland that has never changed. Today's visitors see it as it has always been; to an old man it appears just as it was in the days of his youth, only the paths can show evidence of greater use and the cairns have grown in size.

Dalesmen have been familiar with the route for centuries, and there are signs that the steeper sections were originally skilfully graded and roughly metalled to ease the passage of laden horses.

'Sty Head' means 'The top of the ladder'. To many of us it also means Lakeland at its best.

Opposite *Sty Head and Great Gable*

Seathwaite   Below *Stockley Bridge*

THE WALK STARTS at the farmstead of Seathwaite at the terminus of the Borrowdale road where it is usual to find dozens of cars parked on the verges of the tarmac. Seathwaite is the wettest inhabited place in England, suffering an average annual rainfall of around 140 inches, and has been the scene of devastating floods; yet it offers a friendly welcome to the many visitors who pass through the farmyard all day long.

There is a choice of two routes. The original and usual path continues up the valley to Stockley Bridge, a picturesque stone arch above the rocky channel of Grains Gill. The path has been trodden to dust by endless processions of pedestrians most of whom, ill-shod and ill-equipped for rough walking, settle on the rocks by the bridge and go no further. Hardier souls bound for Sty Head cross the bridge and choose from a variety of tracks up the facing slope, which has been cut to shreds by the clumsy boots of those who see no virtue in following the well-engineered gradients of the original path and prefer short cuts. This section is a disgrace: verges have been trampled and vegetation stripped. Nature never gets a chance to heal the scars. On easier ground above, the path reverts to its old course by Styhead Gill, crossing it at a footbridge.

The alternative route from Seathwaite is quieter and more exciting. It was formerly little known and was late in appearing on Ordnance maps. This starts along a short lane from the farm buildings to a bridge across the Derwent, then following the river up the valley on the west bank through moist and rough pastures. The Derwent is formed by the meeting of Grains Gill and Styhead Gill, but before the confluence the path turns steeply up the fellside to enter the rocky confines of Taylorgill Force, a splendid waterfall. The path here is awkward in places as it hugs a wall of cliffs on the right before emerging into open country above the waterfall and continuing alongside Styhead Gill to join the usual and more frequented path at a footbridge.

A short distance further the shore of Styhead Tarn is reached.

Above *Taylorgill Force*

Styhead Tarn

Ahead is the massive dome of Great End and the giants of the Scafell range behind. On the left is Seathwaite Fell which, like the tarn, keeps its own rainfall records, and high on the right rise the vast slopes of Green Gable and Great Gable, split by the immense fissure of Aaron Slack. The wildness of the scene is accentuated rather than softened by the dark waters of Styhead Tarn.

The path proceeds to the highest point of the pass, a most important crossroads for walkers, furnished with a stretcher box for casualties.

From the large cairn, paths radiate in all directions. Here starts the popular Breast Route to the top of Great Gable, and a secondary and less obvious path contours to Kern Knotts and the Girdle Traverse of Gable. To the left goes the path to Esk Hause and Great Langdale, with the Corridor Route to the Scafells branching from it. The main path to Wasdale Head goes forward, turning a corner to face Lingmell's dark cliffs and the huge gash of Piers Gill.

Lingmell

Wasdale Head from Sty Head

The main path aims directly for Wasdale Head, slanting down across the flanks of Great Gable; through over-use it has become an uncomfortable channel of loose stones, appearing from afar as a great wound slashed by a giant knife across the mountainside. During the long descent, Wasdale Head comes into sight as a patchwork of small fields bordered by stone walls: a welcome green oasis enclosed by bare mountains.

An alternative way down from Sty Head is provided by the original path, known as the Valley Route, once long abandoned but recently restored to favour. This descends at once in the direction of Lingmell, easy grass slopes leading down to the stream flowing from Great End. A path accompanies this to the confluence with the waters of Piers Gill. High above is the long escarpment of Lingmell, and on the right Great Gable towers into the sky, seen foreshortened but imposing a majestic presence upon the landscape. The combined waters take the name of Lingmell Beck (on early Ordnance maps named as Cawfell Beck – a rare aberration) and a path continues alongside very pleasantly until it ends at a junction with the usual direct path. All that now remains is a stroll through cultivated fields to Burnthwaite Farm and a short lane to the little cluster of buildings at Wasdale Head.

There have been changes here since my early days. The primitive inn that was the Mecca of the pioneer rockclimbers has become a sophisticated hotel and cars have brought a new and growing clientele. Once all visitors wore heavy boots; today sightseers have introduced sandals. I liked it better as it was . . . But of course the mountain scene is unaffected by happenings in the valley and remains superb. Wasdale Head is wonderfully situated in a green hollow below an array of challenging peaks, Great Gable in particular rising starkly as a shapely pyramid. In this magnificent setting, minor irritations simply don't matter.

43 THREE TARNS, 2250'
Great Langdale – Eskdale

MOTORISTS WISHING TO travel between Great Langdale and Eskdale must make a roundabout and up and down journey over Wrynose and Hardknott Passes, but others unencumbered by wheels have available a splendid direct cross-country route with a single ascent and descent which, moreover, leads through impressive mountain scenery.

This is the Three Tarns route, taking advantage of a pronounced depression in the Crinkle Crags–Bowfell skyline, occupied by small tarns, usually considered to be three in number although there is a lesser fourth.

Coming up from Great Langdale, there is invariably the company of others engaged on the ascent of Bowfell, but beyond the tarns the way is unfrequented and rough underfoot as it threads a passage through a barren waste of rocks and stones undisturbed down the ages. The scene is primeval, but softens as Eskdale opens in front, waterfalls giving a foretaste of the manifold delights to come.

Opposite *The Links of Bowfell and Three Tarns*   *Bowfell*

FROM DUNGEON GHYLL at the head of Great Langdale, a level strath is crossed on a farm road to Stool End, and the steep buttress immediately beyond is climbed on a distinct path suffering from popularity. This is a shoulder of Bowfell known as The Band and the path rises steadily between the valleys of Mickleden and Oxendale. The ascent is tedious but relieved by fine views on either side – the Langdale Pikes arrayed above Mickleden and Pike o' Blisco overlooking Oxendale. The serrated top of Crinkle Crags, ahead to the left, demands increasing attention as height is gained.

Crinkle Crags from the Band
Below *The Band and Stool End*

Great Langdale

Below *One of the Three Tarns*

The path up The Band was formed for the ascent of Bowfell, and is the usual route to the summit of that noble mountain. When the ground steepens into the final rugged pyramid, it trends to the left to find an easy way to the top, arriving there ascending a stony and badly eroded breach in the rough ground above the depression occupied by the Three Tarns. The path is left when the tarns come into sight and an easy walk leads to them. From higher ground nearby, there is a retrospective view of Great Langdale.

The dominating feature of the Three Tarns depression is the extraordinary line of cliffs high on the side of Bowfell, deeply furrowed by a dozen steep and stony parallel gullies known as the Links and looking as though they were scratched out of the rocks by a giant comb; a formation unique in the district. I once descended one of these boulder-filled cracks and it was not a happy experience.

The tarns are unattractive, giving no cause to linger, and the route continues on a thin track south-west in the direction of Eskdale.

The track goes down along the base of the steeply rising buttresses of Crinkle Crags, its course amply cairned through a desert of loose stones and fallen boulders. When I first came along here, a very long time ago, there was little semblance of a path, the way being indicated by a series of very small cairns, simply one stone placed on another, and it was fun looking for the next. One stone balanced on another is all that is necessary in clear weather; too many Lakeland cairns have grown into immense piles, encouraging in mist or snow, but are today obsolete as paths have been trodden wider and more obvious during the growth of fellwalking since the last war. Too many cairns can be more misleading than too few especially when they have been erected off-route to mark a viewpoint or a dangerous cliff or a rockclimbers' track, all leading into difficult situations. But on the whole cairns are a great comfort when walkers are uncertain of their next move, and even the most experienced have often been glad to see one marking a path in bad weather conditions. During my early explorations in uncharted wastes, I was often mightily relieved to see a cairn that led me to a path. I love mountain cairns but not too many of them.

During the descent, a great rift appears in the side of Crinkle Crags: this is Rest Gill, offering a pathless and scrambling route direct to the top of the highest Crinkle; this is for adventurers only, while walkers bound for Eskdale continue down the stony track, reaching easier ground when Lingcove Beck comes alongside after crossing the grassy hollow of Green Hole. Looking back, Bowfell appears as a gigantic heap of stones, an untrodden wilderness. Bowfell's many attractions are all on the Langdale side.

Lingcove Beck and the path now go down into Eskdale side by side. Soon the cliffs of Crinkle Crags recede to give place to a wide grassy opening with a descending stream: this is another Mosedale, as dreary as the others of its kin but a pass in its own right, the crossing of its low watershed giving an easy route to Cockley Beck in the Duddon Valley.

Bowfell from Lingcove Beck

Mosedale

Lingcove Beck enlivens the continuing descent with waterfalls as the path comes down to the rustic arch of Lingcove Bridge and Eskdale is seen ahead.

Without crossing the bridge, the path goes down to greet the River Esk issuing from a spectacular gorge on the right, and then continues pleasantly along to the farmstead of Brotherilkeld and the Eskdale Valley road. The village of Boot, two miles further, may be reached by the road passing the Youth Hostel and the Woolpack Inn or, if these establishments are not of immediate interest, the village may be reached by a pleasant riverside path. Either way, the beauties of the valley will be seen and appreciated.

Eskdale with Lingcove Bridge

44 THRESHTHWAITE MOUTH, 1920'
Troutbeck – Patterdale

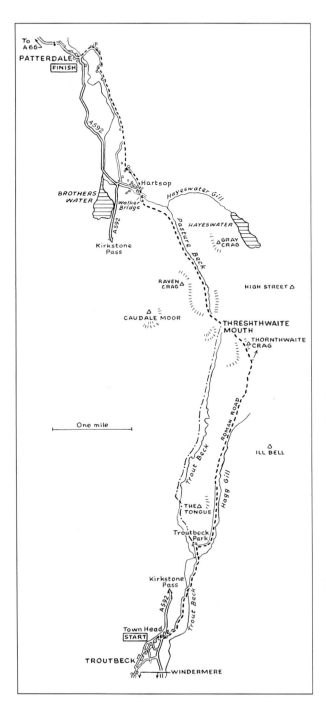

TRAVELLERS BETWEEN Troutbeck and Patterdale, whether on foot or on wheels, invariably make the journey by way of the popular A592 over the Kirkstone Pass. Walkers, however, can avoid the crowds of tourists and the hazards of the pathless tarmac by using a little-known route, roughly parallel, and proceed in blissful silence, out of sight and sound of traffic, over a pass in a wild setting between Caudale Moor and Thornthwaite Crag. This is a watershed named Threshthwaite Mouth and, although lacking the guidance of a distinct path, it is well defined by descending streams, and there need be no fear of straying.

Opposite *The view north from Threshthwaite Mouth Hagg Gill*

THE A592 IS LEFT at Troutbeck village by a side road at Town Head that heads north along the valley floor amongst pleasant pastures and copses, and crosses the tree-fringed Trout Beck to reach its terminus at the remote farmstead of Troutbeck Park in a lovely situation at the foot of a wooded hill that appears to bar further progress. This hill is The Tongue and may be bypassed on either side, preferably on the right where a good track originated by the Romans goes upstream alongside Hagg Gill.

Hagg Gill is deeply enclosed; The Tongue rises steeply on the left and a lofty mountain range of which Ill Bell, scarred by old quarries, is the dominant height forms the skyline on the right.

At the head of this defile, the path most in use starts to rise in grassy grooves up the fellside on the right to the ridge high above. This is the line of the Roman road over High Street and is here known as Scot Rake, the reputed scene of a skirmish where the native Britons routed a band of Scottish invaders.

Troutbeck Park

Ullswater from Threshthwaite Mouth

Departing from the Roman road, the way to Threshthwaite Mouth goes forward alongside a wall until it turns away left as the declining slopes of The Tongue come down to eye level. Here the valley is again wide and the way ahead clear, although nothing better than a thin track need be expected on the final rise to the gap ahead over rough ground littered by boulders. Caudale Moor is a fine object half-left, rising in craggy tiers to a shapely summit; opposite is the steep downfall of Thornthwaite Crag, fans of scree dropping from a rim of cliffs overtopped by a tall obelisk. Trout Beck is rejoined, here in infancy, and in mist is useful as a sure pointer to the watershed at the head of the valley. This is Threshthwaite Mouth, crossed by a tumbled wall, and suddenly revealing an inspiring view to the north, a tangle of fells and a glimpse of Ullswater: a thrilling revelation.

The Tongue from Threshwaite Mouth
Raven Crag

Retrospectively, too, the view is pleasing, the Troutbeck valley being seen winding down to Windermere in the far distance and The Tongue dwarfed to insignificance by the greater heights around. It is always gratifying to look back aerially over a line of approach.

Threshthwaite Mouth is a lonely place, and in many visits I have yet to see another walker there.

The route continues over descending grassland towards a deep valley ahead and then drops more steeply to the formative waters of Pasture Beck which is followed downstream, a path forming on the left bank, along a narrow glen deeply enclosed by fellsides rimmed with crags. The path passes below the black precipice of Raven Crag, a haunt for rockclimbers, and across the beck slopes rise sharply to the long ridge of Grey Crag. A more friendly and open landscape with trees is entered as the pleasant environs of Low Hartsop are reached and the confines of the fell are left behind. Grass succeeds stones.

Pasture Beck from Walker Bridge

Below *Low Hartsop*

The path leaves Pasture Beck as it joins Hayes-water Gill in an area of former mining activity and goes on to cross the combined waters at Walker Bridge, an old one-arch span in a charming setting.

Low Hartsop is an old settlement and a few buildings preserve features that belong to the distant past. It is a living museum of seventeenth-century Lakeland. Regrettably it is now defaced by an incongruous modern car park alien to its surroundings. It is surely wrong to invite motorists to disturb this tranquil backwater; horses and carts would suit the environment better.

On tarmac again, the short lane through the hamlet joins the busy A592 coming down from the Kirkstone Pass and the illusion fades: we're back in the twentieth century. At the junction, a quiet by-road leads into Patterdale village two miles further and is greatly to be preferred to walking along the busy main road.

45

WALNA SCAR, 1990'
Coniston – Duddon Valley

FOR PEDESTRIANS, cyclists and horses the only easy passage between Coniston and the Duddon Valley is an ancient way that skirts the high mass of the Coniston Fells on their south side. This has long been known as the Walna Scar Road and in days gone by was maintained sufficiently to accommodate wheeled traffic, being much used for the conveyance of slate from the quarries alongsides. Both ends of the road are still accessible by vehicles. In its vicinity are identifiable remains of an early civilisation and, spanning the ages, this is where a local youth in 1954 took the first-ever photograph of a flying saucer (?).

It is a straightforward walk on a clear track made obvious by centuries of use, not in itself exciting but affording extensive panoramas of Coniston Water and the coastline of Morecambe Bay and over the watershed a glorious view over Duddon to the distant heights of the Scafell Range. The highlight, seen only by a short detour off-route, is provided by Dow Crag and Goat's Water, together forming one of the grandest scenes in the district.

Opposite *Sunrise: view south from the Walna Scar Road*
Right *Looking back from the summit of the Walna Scar Pass*

CONISTON IS LEFT along a tarmac road rising sharply to the site of the former railway station which, in its heyday, was the terminus of a branch line from Foxfield Junction. This rural line, provided for the benefit of visitors approaching the district from the Furness area, and for commercial freight, was a casualty of the growth of motorised traffic, the passenger service being withdrawn in 1958. Above the buildings, the road climbs steeply, enclosed by walls and hedges, for a short mile further. At this point, a quarry road serving Coniston's main source of the handsome and durable slate that has won international renown, branches to the right and is commonly used for the ascent of Coniston Old Man. The Walna Scar track goes forward, having been improved in recent years since the reopening of another quarry ahead. Still rising, a small reedy pool, Boo Tarn, is passed and the reopened quarry is seen up the fell side on the right. Deprived now of its new surface but still very distinct, the track continues along the base of the Old Man with a wide moorland gradually declining on the left: this is the desolate terrain upon which important relics of the Bronze Age were discovered. After passing through a natural rock gateway, a branch path leaves on the right, this leading across a green hollow, The Cove, to a most impressive scene. The precipitous cliffs of Dow Crag are poised high above the bouldery shore of Goat's Water; if time permits, this short detour should be made.

Coniston Old Man

Dow Crag from Goat's Water

The Scafell range from Walna Scar

The main track continues, crossing the primitive Cove Bridge and then rising steadily with improving views of Coniston Water and the distant coastline. A small slate shelter with very limited accommodation is passed as the ground steepens on the final rise to the highest point of the walk, a watershed between Brown Pike on the right and the long level top of Walna Scar easily attained on the left. But, on a clear day, it is the superb view ahead that compels attention.

After the austere surroundings so far, the prospect from the top of the pass is as refreshing as springtime following a hard winter. Below is the valley of the River Duddon in a wealth of lovely woodlands and the green fields and scattered farmsteads of a contented husbandry. Standing sentinel above this realm of beauty is its guardian angel, Harter Fell, sprouting conifers instead of wings, and in the blue haze of distance, overtopping all, the Scafell range and the other heights of upper Eskdale.

The descent starts at once. The huge ramifications of the disused Walna Scar Quarry appear on the left and the track becomes a walled lane; it reaches the valley road a mile north of Seathwaite and its friendly inn. This last mile is delightful. Tarn Beck, a tributary of the River Duddon and often mistaken for it, races and dances alongside, embowered in trees. The main river in this part of the valley is hidden in a spectacular gorge.

The Duddon Valley is also known as Dunnerdale, this now appearing on Ordnance maps. It is a name I don't like and have never used. The Duddon Valley seems to me a sweeter name and more appropriate to this lovely environment.

46 WHINLATTER PASS, 1043'
Braithwaite – Lorton

WHINLATTER PASS has long been the recognised way from the Vale of Keswick to the Vale of Lorton and the Loweswater area, having had a road across it since early times. A century ago it was in commission by wagonettes on a popular sightseeing tour from Keswick, later becoming used for a bus service: today it is a fast highway for all forms of wheeled traffic. It is less accommodating to walkers who cannot conveniently escape the footpaths and must have recourse to the grass verges or forest roads wherever possible. It is an easy pass with few steep gradients and is sheltered by large plantations bordering the tarmac which unfortunately conceal nearby mountains from view. The plantations on the Braithwaite side are old, being indicated on maps 150 years ago; however they have been greatly extended and are continuous for many miles to the top of the pass and beyond.

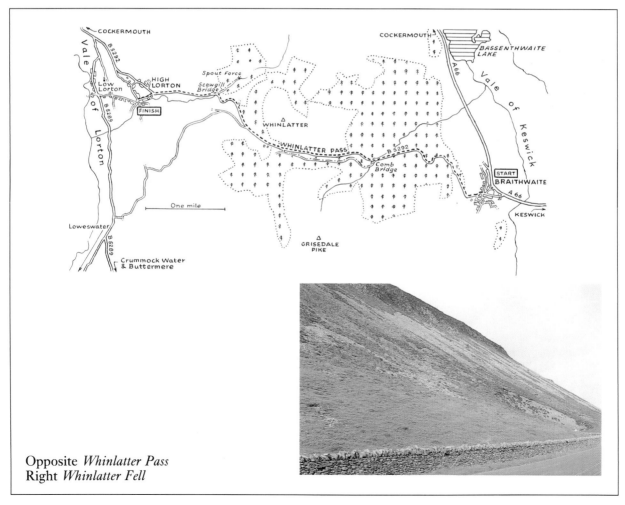

Opposite *Whinlatter Pass*
Right *Whinlatter Fell*

THE ROAD CLIMBS immediately out of Braithwaite, rising steadily with many curves, and soon becomes an avenue of trees which relent at one point to permit a lovely view of Bassenthwaite Lake and Skiddaw; this is a favourite halting place for both motorists and pedestrians.

Then follows a straight mile, passing a solitary building that was formerly an isolation hospital. Beyond, at Comb Bridge, walkers can pass into the silence of the trees on a forest road, from which branches another that runs parallel to the motor road and joins it beyond the highest part of the pass. Or the more adventurous may continue along the road from Comb Bridge and leave it to climb the heathery slopes of Whinlatter, which has escaped plantings. Walkers on this route first attain the ridge and then traverse this to the wind shelter on the summit, there enjoying a splendid view denied to those who pursue the road closely; Grisedale Pike, in particular, soars majestically from its skirt of conifers. It should be mentioned, however, that the direct descent to rejoin the road is both rough and steep.

Over the pass, there is a break in the plantations on the left and the lane branches away: this was the route adopted by the horse-drawn coaches on the Grand Tour in Victorian times. It is still, for walkers, the most direct way to the delights of Loweswater and Crummock.

The present road descends more steeply to Scawgill Bridge.

Bassenthwaite Lake

Scawgill Bridge

Spout Force

A halt should be made at Scawgill Bridge. Not long ago a peep over the parapet would have given a view of the diminutive bridge Scawgill replaced but this has now disappeared. Scawgill Bridge is the point of departure for a walk upstream to locate the handsome yet little-known waterfall of Spout Force. My first visit here entailed a desperate struggle through a new plantation, the forestry workers having completely disregarded the public footpath – a fault since remedied.

From the bridge, the road gradually descends to Lorton, a village in two parts, High and Low, which achieved a measure of fame when Wordsworth was moved to write a poem about a venerable yew he found there. Roads go south to Loweswater and Buttermere and north to Cockermouth through a lovely countryside that also deserves poems of praise.

High Lorton

47 WIND GAP, 2600'
Ennerdale — Wasdale Head

ALTHOUGH NOT CLASSED as a pass in guidebooks and not often used as such, the sharp col at the top of Windgap Cove between Pillar and Scoat Fell has all the characteristics of a true pass and indeed is one of the best defined in Lakeland. The ridge connecting the two mountains is short, a matter of yards only, and the crest is so narrow that ascent to it becomes descent from it in a few paces. The situation of the col is exceedingly grand; like an eyrie, the col overlooks a savage untamed landscape of crags and rivers of scree where solitude is absolute and silence unbroken. This is Wind Gap, attained from below only by rough and steep scrambling, and in terms of effort a poor alternative to the much easier Black Sail Pass. Wind Gap is for the adventurous and the lover of grim mountain scenery.

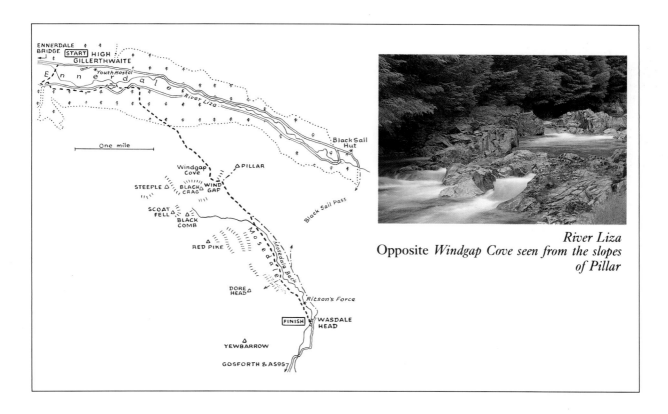

River Liza
Opposite *Windgap Cove seen from the slopes of Pillar*

APPROACHING FROM ENNERDALE, the first problem is to find a breach in the plantations to give access to the open fellside ahead, and this is provided as a footbridge over the River Liza near the Gillerthwaite Youth Hostel; this indicates a forest ride or firebreak that points the way to a stile in the upper enclosing fence. Clear of the trees, an exciting view of Windgap Cove is disclosed ahead.

Windgap Cove

Pillar rises as a ridge on the left, Steeple is the tremendous declivity on the right, and the skyline directly in front is formed by the Black Crag of Scoat Fell. Wind Gap appears as the walk proceeds into the wild hollow of Windgap Cove littered with debris fallen from the heights around. The path is sketchy but the direction obvious as altitude is gained on steepening ground and, with Steeple becoming more imposing and intimidating with every step, the col is at length attained.

The summit of Pillar can quickly be reached from this point on a rough track rising on the left and it would be a pity to miss its extensive view at the cost of so little extra effort.

The path crossing the gap continues on the other side over the top of Black Crag to Scoat Fell. Ahead is a new landscape.

The valley seen far below and continuing towards the majestic mountains encircling Wasdale Head is the best known of the many Mosedales, and the path down into it is both steep and stony; much care should be taken. A long and tedious descent ends when the valley floor is reached and Mosedale Beck is alongside, its main flow issuing from the craggy recesses of Blackem (Back Comb) Head on the right. This is a natural sanctuary where few people ever go and the starry saxifrage grows profusely among the wet rocks and in moist crevices without fear of human disturbance.

Either side of the beck may be followed down the valley, the Ordnance Survey preferring the left bank and I the right, where a narrow trod leads below the beetling crags of Red Pike and passes a large split boulder known to the climbing fraternity as the Y Boulder; this provides a short climb that experts can accomplish feet first. The path improves when joined by the scree run from Dore Head, beyond which, with the beck now tree-fringed and deserving a deviation to Ritson's Force, it descends gradually through green fields along the base of Yewbarrow to the bridge and buildings of Wasdale Head.

Mosedale

48 WINDY GAP, 2450′
Sty Head – Ennerdale

WINDY GAP IS almost a twin, even in name, to Wind Gap, having the same features: a narrow col linking two mountains reached in ascent over very rough ground, and rarely used as a pass. It is, in fact, only of use as a pass for travellers coming from the east by Sprinkling Tarn and seeking a direct course for Ennerdale or Buttermere or vice versa in which case the long descent to Wasdale Head is avoided.

Like Wind Gap, it calls for arduous efforts and rewards those who do it with scenes of mountain grandeur.

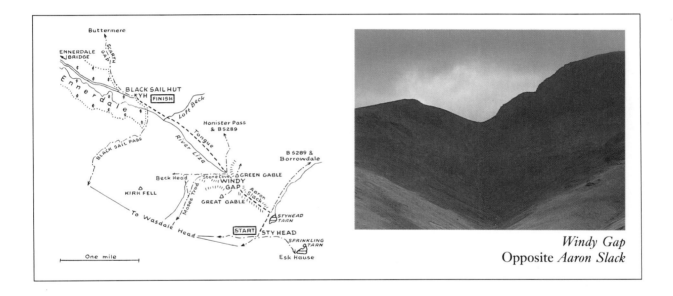

Windy Gap
Opposite *Aaron Slack*

THE FELLSIDE WEST of Styhead Tarn is cleft by a great ravine, given the name of Aaron Slack by pioneer adventurers who had a liking for biblical names. A track, often obscured by loose stones, goes up this defile, soon becoming deeply confined by the enclosing slopes that shut out all distant views. The effect is claustrophobic. Although not excessively steep, progress is slow and tedious, over tumbled stones and unremitting with no couches of greenery inviting halts. This strange cutting, between Great Gable and Green Gable, leads directly to Windy Gap.

After the arid and dusty recesses of Aaron Slack, arrival at Windy Gap is a relief; here too the awesome loneliness of the ascent is often dispelled by the sight and sound of walkers crossing the gap on a popular route to the summit of Great Gable. From this point, the top of Great Gable's summit is a tough proposition, its ascent and return to Windy Gap taking an hour, and longer if the superlative views from the top are to be studied at leisure. Apart from this tempting detour, the next stage of the journey, the descent into Ennerdale, can be prospected from the crest of Windy Gap, this valley being seen framed by Pillar and the High Stile range and identifiable by a dark covering of conifers.

Windy Gap

The descent starts unpromisingly amongst the boulders of Stone Cove without the help of a clear path, a way having to be threaded through a maze of rock debris, difficult to negotiate and needing care. Some recompense is provided as the cliffs of Green Gable come into sight, seen intimately at close range nearby. But the eyes turn quickly as the great arc of Gable Crag is fully revealed high above on the left, a formidable precipice split by intimidating gullies and cracks.

Green Gable crags   *Stone Cove*

Ennerdale from Windy Gap

The infant River Liza trickles from the desert of boulders in Stone Cove, soon becoming a defiant watercourse heading directly for Ennerdale and a perfect guide in mist. When welcome grass comes underfoot, the best stage to easy progress is provided on the right bank of the stream, where a thin track will be found on the long descending spur of Green Gable called the Tongue. This is crossed by Moses Trod on its way from Honister to Beck Head and Wasdale.

During the descent, the depression of Beck Head succeeds Gable Crag with Kirk Fell rising steeply from it. Beck Head also qualifies as a pass between Wasdale Head and Ennerdale, but few people will have used it as such since Moses made his regular journeys with his cargo of slate and whisky, the usual route from one valley to the other being the much easier and more direct crossing of Black Sail Pass.

At the foot of the Tongue, a tributary of the Liza, Loft Beck, is forded and a simple path continues forward to Black Sail Youth Hostel, passing a field of drumlins like giant molehills. At the hostel are the only beds for miles around; to find others in the valley a trip of several miles on forest roads is necessary – an anticlimax to the excitement of Windy Gap.

49 WRYNOSE PASS, 1270′
Little Langdale – Duddon Valley

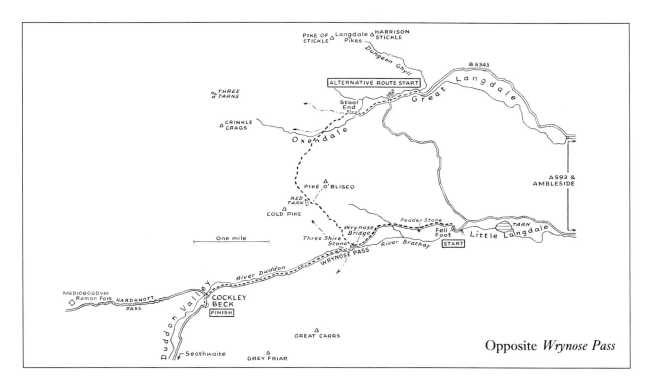

Opposite *Wrynose Pass*

WHEN THE ROMAN surveyors were planning a network of roads to link their forts in the north-west, they were faced with difficulties in finding easy passages for the movement of men and supplies in the mountainous terrain of Lakeland. Ease of passage, however, was secondary to directness of route; here, as elsewhere, a straight course from A to B was preferred. Their High Street is the best example of their fixation for directness, climbing to 2700 feet although simple but more circuitous routes were available. Another example is the road they made between their forts at Galava (Ambleside) and Glannaventa (Ravenglass). In this case, however, by placing a ruler on their maps they found that advantage could be taken of two passes through the mountain barrier. Little Langdale pointed the direction to a gap in the skyline beyond, now known as Wrynose Pass (Wrayene in twelfth-century records = path of the stallion); this was succeeded a few miles further by Hardknott Pass. From here it was an easy march to the west coast.

The Romans adopted this route and their primitive road can still be traced in parts although it is mostly overlaid by a modern surface: a narrow strip of tarmac winds unenclosed in a wild and untamed landscape and gives motorists the thrill of mountaineering without leaving their cars. During the last war, the road was requisitioned for military training and badly cut up by tanks and other heavy vehicles, but it was repaired and restored after the cessation of hostilities. It has remained narrow and unenclosed over the pass, calling for care and negotiation, in an atmosphere which, on a busy day, is charged with the expletives of frustrated motorists.

219

Fell Foot

THE CLIMB TO Wrynose Pass starts at Fell Foot, once an inn, at the head of Little Langdale; here the farm children used to man a gate giving access to the road beyond, but the gate and the children have long gone, as has so much of the Lakeland I knew fifty years ago. The road rises at once, giving a view of the Langdale Pikes and becoming unenclosed beyond the intake walls. A flat-topped boulder at the side of the long incline has the name of Pedder Stone, being a resting place for the pedlars who in olden days carried their wares in backpacks and found it a convenient height for taking the weight off their shoulders.

The road to Wrynose Pass

The stream coursing down the valley on the left is the Brathay, formerly a boundary between Westmorland and Lancashire. The incline halts briefly at Wrynose Bridge, crossing a tributary from Pike o' Blisco, and then continues at a steeper gradient with the Roman road in evidence alongside; it levels out towards the top.

On flat ground usually occupied by parked cars near the highest point of the pass stands a simple monolith, the Three Shire Stone, erected in 1816 to mark the meeting of three counties, Westmorland, Cumberland and Lancashire. All became Cumbria at midnight on 31 March 1974, and Lancashire lost its proud claim to own a part of the Lake District.

A path leaves here for Crinkle Crags and Pike o' Blisco and further, on the left, another path trends off for the ridge of Great Carrs and the Coniston fells.

Over the pass, the road descends sharply into the Duddon Valley below the steep slopes of Grey Friar, becoming level as the infant Duddon forms alongside on the two miles to Cockley Beck Bridge where Highland cattle may be seen grazing and the first habitation since Fell Foot is reached.

The road goes on down the valley but a branch crosses the bridge bound for Hardknott Pass. This is the way the Romans went.

The Duddon Valley   Above *The Three Shires Stone*

Wrynose Pass is not kind to pedestrians, who can only escape from the hard surface of the road and its traffic, in the absence of a footpath, by tramping along the rough verges. Nevertheless, it is a fine walk, best enjoyed in winter when all is quiet.

Walkers starting from Dungeon Ghyll in Great Langdale, however, can avoid much of the road and arrive at the summit of Wrynose by an alternative route along the Oxendale path from Stool End, climbing steeply out of this valley on a track that crosses a minor pass at Red Tarn and descends to the Three Shire Stone at the top of Wrynose Pass. This alternative route requires more effort than walking on the road but is infinitely to be preferred; the ascent to the tarn and its vicinity affords scenes of mountain splendour not seen from the road.

Red Tarn

INDEX

Bold type indicates the passes and their main entries; *italic* type indicate illustrations.

patient

AND

person

To Charles, and the person you are

Patient
AND
Person

Developing interpersonal skills
in nursing

Jane Stein-Parbury

SECOND EDITION

CHURCHILL
LIVINGSTONE

Sydney Edinburgh London New York Philadelphia St Louis Toronto

Churchill Livingstone
is an imprint of Elsevier Science

Elsevier Science | Harcourt Australia
30–52 Smidmore Street, Marrickville, NSW 2204

National Library of Australia Cataloguing-in-Publication Data

---

Stein-Parbury, Jane
Patient and person.

2nd ed.
Bibliography.
Includes index
ISBN 0 443 06291 9.

1. Nurse and patient. 2. Interpersonal relations.
I. Title.

610.730699

Publishing Editor: Vaughn Curtis
Publishing Services Manager: Helena Klijn
Edited and project managed by Rowena Lennox
Cover design, internal design and typeset by Toni Darben, Darben Design
Index by Russell Brooks
Printed in Australia by Southwood Press, Sydney

CONTENTS

PREFACE TO THE SECOND EDITION

A lot can happen in seven years and the period between the first edition of *Patient and Person*, published in 1993, and now is no exception. Health care has changed dramatically in relation to the time that nurses and patient have to spend with each other. For example, day surgery is quickly taking the place of longer postoperative recovery care in a hospital setting. Nevertheless meaningful interactions between those trying to help, nurses, and those in need of help, patients, remain at the heart of good patient care. Nurses still need to understand patient needs in whatever context and for however long they interact; and ascertaining and understanding those needs requires effective interpersonal skills.

One the major changes in the second edition of *Patient and Person* is the addition of relevant research findings that serve to reinforce the practice wisdom and expert opinion that filled the pages of the first edition. Discussion and analysis of relevant research material challenge readers to expand their theoretical understanding of the practical skills of relating to patients.

Selecting appropriate research findings from the variety of available published studies proved both challenging and rewarding. One challenge arose in focusing and limiting the amount of information so that the book did not become unduly long or lose its ease of reading, which characterised the first edition. Chapter 2 in this edition reflects the selection process and includes extensive literature on research into caring in nursing.

Another challenge was the type of evidence that is available on the topic of patient–nurse relationships. Much of the research evidence about patient–nurse relationships is descriptive and theoretical in nature. Those readers who are familiar with the evidence-based practice movement will appreciate that this is not the 'strongest' evidence possible in the sense that cause-effect relationships between health-care interventions and patient outcomes are not established. The type of evidence provided is appropriate because the material in this book is not concerned with clinical interventions as such. It is not a book about psychotherapy, that is, intervening in particular ways of talking to patients in order to alter their thoughts, feelings or behaviours. Rather, it a book with information about how nurses can be therapeutic in their everyday interactions with patients.

Locating and incorporating research evidence into the text also proved rewarding when the available evidence reinforced the material almost exactly as it appeared in the first edition. At other times using research evidence resulted in changes in the manner in which material is presented. Changes that are most pronounced can be found in chapter 7 (chapter 6, Intervening skills in the first edition) in which material has been revamped and re-ordered under the headings of Comforting, Supporting and Enabling. Although the material in the revised chapter is not fundamentally different from that of its predecessor, readers familiar with the first edition will notice a different sequence and emphasis in the new chapter.

Regrettably, Sue Nagy and Jackie Crisp did not make a direct contribution to this edition. The material they contributed for the first edition now forms Chapters 8 and 9 of this edition, and the content of their initial contribution remains essentially intact.

Reinforcing the content with research evidence has resulted in a book that is more academically oriented and perhaps more demanding of readers. Nevertheless, I have tried to retain the ease of reading and practical value that characterised the first edition of *Patient and Person*. I hope I have provided a text that remains useful for all levels of nurses.

JSP, Sydney, 2000

PREFACE TO THE FIRST EDITION

This book is for nurses who want to learn about establishing interpersonal contact with patients, not *as* patients but as people whose unique experiences as patients are significant. In caring for patients, nurses need to understand patients' experiences not simply on a theoretical level but on a personal level. One way they can do this is through the effective use of the interpersonal skills described in this book. Through relating to and interacting with patients *as* persons, nurses place themselves in a position to understand the experience of the person who is the patient.

Most nurses would desire to understand patients' experiences. Nevertheless, the best intentions can be meaningless unless they are accompanied by skilled know-how in making interpersonal contact with patients. The focus of this book is on the development of interpersonal skills. Readers are encouraged to appreciate the significance of these skills through presentation of the theoretical basis of the use of these skills. The theoretical aspects of the skills are presented as underpinning skill development, therefore the approach of this book is not so much the application of theory as it is the integration of theory with skills.

The starting point of this book is that nurses need to recognise that interactions with patients are central to their care. Most nurses know that. But in 'knowing that' nurses also need to 'know how' to make these interactions meaningful. 'Knowing that' interacting with patients is central must be accompanied by 'knowing how' to make these interactions meaningful.

In chapters 3 through 7, each skill is first isolated. They are then discussed in context in chapters 8 and 9. The final chapter focuses on the need for effective relationships with nursing colleagues, as the skills used in relating to patients are also important in colleague interaction.

Experiential learning activities are incorporated throughout chapters 2–9. These activities are designed to focus on the development of skills in a practical, workable manner.

A potential pitfall of a skills-based approach is that nurses may know how to use each of the skills but may lack awareness of which skills are suitable for a particular situation. The stories interspersed throughout the text are designed to illustrate particular contexts in the use of the skills. All stories are based on real-life experiences. While these stories have not been fabricated for the text, the details of each have been altered in order to retain the anonymity of the persons involved. The stories are not case studies in the traditional sense, but are told as dramatic illustrations of particular concepts.

One of the most challenging aspects of writing a book about interpersonal aspects of nursing is the tension between the need to capture the complexity of interpersonal connections and the need to present concrete guidelines and general rules for beginning nurses. Beginning nurses, like novices in any discipline, rely on guidelines and rules. In presenting rules and guidelines there is an inherent danger of a 'cookbook' approach. Such an approach assumes that there is a rational, objective, 'right' way for nurses to interact with patients. Recipes such as *Combine 3 open-ended questions with 2 empathic statements, add 1 large tablespoon of support and reassurance, then mix well for 10 minutes during an interaction with a patient*, are simple to understand but inadequate in addressing the intricacy of patient–nurse interactions.

In meeting this challenge, I have tried to avoid an oversimplified approach to the use of interpersonal skills by including discussion of the contextual variables that need to be considered. I have done so in the hope that the guidelines and rules presented in this book will not be interpreted as prescriptions or recipes.

Patient and Person is intended primarily for use as a textbook for undergraduate nursing courses. The material has been prepared in a manner that also will assist educators who are planning a program of interpersonal skill development in these courses. The material in chapters 1–7 will suit early stages of an undergraduate nursing course, while chapters 8–11 are more appropriate to later stages of a course.

Although the intended audience is undergraduate students of nursing and their educators, this book will also be useful to practising nurses who will find the information beneficial in extending and refining their interpersonal skills, regardless of the extent of their nursing experience. Although written from a nursing perspective, the material in this book is applicable to any health-care professional.

The use of the word *patient* is purposive. While I do not want to perpetuate the problems of treating patients as passive recipients of nursing care, this term is one that is most frequently recognised in nursing. The central point of the book, that patients should be treated as persons, speaks for itself about the humanistic basis of my philosophical beliefs. The term *nurse* is used in the generic sense to refer to any level of nurse, from students of nursing to experienced registered nurses.

Finally, I want to emphasise that I realise that skills are not learnt simply by reading about them in a book. While this book offers guidelines and suggestions for the development of interpersonal skills in nursing, the best way to learn them is through interacting with patients. In listening to and understanding patients' experiences of health and illness, nurses will come to appreciate that their real teachers are the persons who happen to be patients.

JSP, Sydney, 1993

ACKNOWLEDGMENTS

A special note of appreciation is extended to all of the students of nursing whom I have had the pleasure of teaching over the years. Your questions, although often challenging, expanded my thinking, sharpened my focus and enriched my insights into the struggles of learning interpersonal skills. The many experiences that you shared in class helped in the development of the stories in this book. Also, your comments on the activities used in this book assisted in their development and refinement.

Thanks also to my colleagues and the numerous people who have provided feedback on the first edition. Your comments were encouraging and helpful in the production of the second edition.

I appreciate the assistance provided by Harcourt Australia, especially Helena Klijn and Rowena Lennox.

Finally, I would like to acknowledge my family. I am grateful to my Mum and Dad, who enabled me to understand interpersonal connections by providing open, honest interactions. Thanks to Richard and Russell, who always found ways of distracting me and making me laugh when I needed to. My most enthusiastic applause goes to Charles, who understood my frustration and shared my joy during the writing of this book. Without this support I am not sure I could have sustained the effort.

JSP

HOW TO USE THIS BOOK

Patient and Person is a textbook about the practice and theory of developing interpersonal skills in nursing.

Incorporated throughout chapters 2–9 are various learning activities designed to provide a means by which skills can be developed and theoretical concepts understood. The text that precedes and follows each activity reinforces the point of that activity. For this reason it is essential that the activities be used in their context, that is, that they *not* be separated from the text.

Activities throughout the text adhere to a standard format. Importantly, this serves to develop a working pattern of reflection and enquiry. The activity structure comprises two major sections: *process* and *discussion*. The process includes detailed instructions for completing the activity, setting the parameters of the learning experience. The discussion contains exploratory statements and questions designed to encourage reflection on and dialogue about the learning experience, focusing attention on the theoretical concepts highlighted in the learning experience.

Defining learners as both *participants* and *members* in activities is an intended feature. Participants denotes an entire learning group; members specifically refers to people within a smaller group, that is, participants who are part of a subdivided total group.

Some activities are identified with the symbol ➥ (followed by a page number), which indicates that there is further material in the appendix, primarily intended for those instructors who are facilitating learning through the use of the activity. (It is useful to note at this point that the appendix itself is organised on a chapter-by-chapter basis, preceded by some very useful information to assist facilitators conducting practical sessions.) When an activity in the text is identified with the symbol ➥ it should immediately alert the facilitator to read the additional information for that activity in the appendix, on the page indicated, before proceeding. Activities are marked by symbols in the left margin.

indicates that the activity is to be completed in solitude.

indicates that the activity requires group interaction and discussion.

indicates that the activity can be completed in solitude, although learning is enhanced through group interaction.

The use of cross-referencing between chapters is of considerable value, due to the overlap between concept and skills. Readers can therefore refer back and forth between chapters, reinforcing and building their understanding of both theory and skills.

The book is not intended for use as a workbook, therefore it is recommended, finally, that readers record all written responses and notes to activity instructions on separate sheets of paper. These should be retained in a folder (or similar) for later revision and future reference, especially because some activities build on the results of previous activities.

LIST OF ACTIVITIES

Part I

INTRODUCTION

The two chapters in part I reinforce each other by pursuing the same intention, to distil the overall significance of interpersonal skills in nursing. Although similar in intent, each chapter realises its aim through different means. The stories in chapter 1 engage the reader though identification and serve as illustrations that reassert the subject of this book. Chapter 2 presents theoretical evidence that reinforces the importance of interpersonal skills in nursing practice. The evidence is a synthesis of relevant and meaningful research into the nature of therapeutic relationships between nurses and patients. The presentation of stories juxtaposed with discussion of research sets a scene that is carried throughout the remainder of the chapters.

CHAPTER I

WHY INTERPERSONAL SKILLS?

INTRODUCTION

Nurses need to know how to effectively relate to and interact with people in their care. As such nursing is a social activity. In addition to being technically proficient, nurses need to be socially competent. As professionals they need to know what to do for patients, know how to do it, and know how to be while they are doing it. That is, nursing involves knowing, doing and being. *Knowing how* and *doing that* is accompanied by *being with* patients in ways that are helpful and healthful. This book deals with the 'being with' part of nursing, the social aspects of nursing that are therapeutic to patients.

Throughout the course of their professional lives nurses are with a variety of people, in a variety of contexts and for a variety of reasons. During these social interactions they need to be able to relate to other people, especially those in their care, the people nurses call patients.

Numerous other professions also involve the ability to interact with and relate to people. In fact, good interpersonal skills are needed for successful employment across a range of disciplines. In this respect nursing is not unique. What differs in the nursing context is what qualifies as 'effective' within the context of patient interaction. 'Effective' in the nursing care context refers to interpersonal interactions between nurses and patients that are helpful to patients. In effective patient–nurse interactions there is an orientation on the part of the nurse *to be* of benefit to the patient, and, more importantly, the patient feels assisted in some way by the interaction.

The helpful nature of patient–nurse interactions is important to bear in mind because effective interaction in other contexts would have other meanings and orientations. For example, an effective interaction in the world of business sales is oriented toward company profit. While assisting the customer is important to successful ongoing interactions, the intention of the business sales interaction is the exchange of money for goods and services. Furthermore, customers in a sales transaction are not vulnerable; they are not dependent on the salesperson for their wellbeing. Persons in need of health-care often are in such a position: they are vulnerable.

Nurses interacting with people called patients need to demonstrate sensitivity to the patient's vulnerability. In reducing the patient's vulnerability

3

nurses need to operate from a position of 'being for' the patient, that is, they need to function as a useful resource. This is a necessary condition for successful fulfilment of an intention to be helpful. 'Being for' patients reflects an attitude and a value; it is a moral positioning on the part of the nurse. Such positioning has its origins in the writings of Florence Nightingale's expressed notion of placing the person in the best position for nature to cure. For example, the restful state of feeling reassured by knowing what to expect, through preparation for a procedure, is of benefit to patients. Fear, anxiety and worry are not part of an environment most conducive to healing. Decreasing a patient's fear of the unknown through explanations requires interpersonal skills to effectively communicate and relate. These are some examples of how interpersonal skills demonstrate 'being for' a patient.

The significance of interpersonal skills in nursing practice is sometimes difficult for beginning nurses to appreciate. The completion of skilled tasks often comes to the foreground and interpersonal contact is something that happens after tasks are completed. Focusing on interpersonal aspects of nursing does not mean that attention to task-related nursing functions is diminished. Interpersonal contact increases the therapeutic effectiveness of nursing activities. The physical act of caring for the patient involves an ability to make contact with the person who is the patient.

Chapter overview

This chapter contains a series of stories that illustrate the importance of interpersonal aspects of nursing care. All possible concepts of the interpersonal aspects of nursing are not covered in this chapter. Rather, a selection has been made in an attempt to highlight the significance and centrality of interpersonal contact in nursing.

Understanding Margaret

Taking the time and expending the effort to understand the world as the patient experiences it results in nursing care that integrates the patient's experiences. Consider the following story, told by a nurse:

> I was in my second undergraduate year at university when I met Margaret. We met during my clinical placement at a large public health-care facility that was established to provide rehabilitation services for people who were disabled and/or chronically ill. There were over a thousand patients in this facility and the sheer mass of this humanity hit me like a ton of bricks on the first day. We were taken on a grand tour of the entire facility on that day and told that the average age of the residents was 72. It was 'so young', we were told, because there were a few patients in their thirties and forties who were suffering from progressive conditions such as multiple sclerosis. To me the place looked like an enormous nursing home. Although I had an overview of all patients who lived in this facility, I only came to recognise the 50 who resided in the ward to which I was assigned, and one of these patients became well known to me. Margaret caught my attention on that first day I was on the ward. She was a frail looking lady who sat in a wheelchair the entire day, being transported from bed to dining table and back to bed at various times during the day.

Margaret captured my attention because she kept repeating the same phrase over and over again. 'Why am I being chastised?' she kept saying. The word 'chastise' struck me as quaint and curious, as if it was a relic from a bygone era. I had to look in a dictionary to find its meaning. Once I discovered the meaning of the word, I became intrigued by Margaret's thought that she was being punished. 'Punished for what?' I thought. What is making Margaret feel she is being punished? I thought to myself that being a permanent resident of this facility could be perceived as punishment, but there was more than this in Margaret's experience.

I set out to learn more about Margaret. It did not take long for me to get to know her. The fact that I was willing to sit with her and listen to her was sufficient to establish a rapport. During the two days a week that I spent on the ward I sat next to her and listened, mostly to her thoughts about being punished. For what, I still did not know. I accepted her feelings although in the back of my mind there were nagging thoughts about the reason for them.

Whenever we talked, I could not get past her expression of the feeling that she was being chastised, so I went to the records to learn more about Margaret. There I saw the words 'legally blind' and 'nearly deaf'. I began to wonder how much sensory input Margaret was receiving and how much this was contributing to her feelings. I located material in my textbooks that described the possible effects of reduced sensory input (in Margaret's case, near blindness and near deafness). I learnt that one of these effects is suspicious feelings.

I also discussed Margaret with the regular staff working in this ward. They told me that Margaret was a 'bit crazy' and definitely 'paranoid'. Because I thought there was more to Margaret than her suspicion, labelling her as paranoid did not satisfy me. Although the label of 'paranoid' seemed insufficient to me, I could see how easily such a label could dismiss Margaret's reality. I still wanted to learn more about Margaret and only she could help me to do so. Week after week I came to Margaret, sat next to her, expressed my interest in her and then just listened.

Eventually Margaret began to share with me more than just her feelings of being punished. We talked about her family and discussed other things. Eventually I learnt more about Margaret, beyond her paranoia. I think just being there, showing interest in her and listening to her was enough to enable her to open up and share her thoughts. As I listened to Margaret's story I began to piece together bits of what she said.

She mentioned that when she entered this facility her handbag had been taken away and put into a room somewhere. She often spoke of the handbag and the room where it was held. I began to realise that the handbag was significant to Margaret. I asked, 'What's in the handbag?' She told me it contained a card that had her nephew's address written on it. Her nephew, who lived in the next state, was her only living relative. Margaret's husband had died and so had all of her brothers and sisters. She had no children. Her nephew was her only link with her family and she didn't have his address! Margaret wanted desperately to write to this nephew but could not.

Through my perseverance and with the aid of my clinical instructor, I located the room that held Margaret's possessions. They had been taken from her when she was admitted and placed for 'safe keeping' in this room. Fortunately, I was able to retrieve the handbag and, sure enough, inside was a card from her nephew that was sent to her shortly before Margaret entered this facility. Margaret was ecstatic about the find. With it came the possibility of re-establishing contact with her family. I penned Margaret's words to her nephew and made sure the letter was posted to him. Margaret seemed to settle after this, although she continued to complain about being punished and I continued to wonder why this feeling persisted.

While the contact with her nephew had helped to calm Margaret, she remained quite anxious about being in this facility. So I kept listening. One day she mentioned that sitting near the window hurt her eyes. Her diminishing eyesight was the result of cataracts and the bright summer sun through the window created discomfort for her. Each day after lunch she was wheeled to the window to 'enjoy the sunshine'. But instead of enjoying this afternoon ritual Margaret found the experience quite uncomfortable. Could this be perceived by Margaret as punishment? I explored my hunch with Margaret, directing my questions toward the subject of her daily seating near the window. She confirmed my hunch. In Margaret's mind, the afternoon ritual of being placed in the sun was equivalent to a daily punishment. For what reason, she was not certain. But in her mind she thought it was because she had done something wrong and this was punishment for the transgression. With this revelation came my understanding of Margaret's reality. Her feelings of being punished made more sense to me.

My next plan of action was to try to get the other staff on the ward to appreciate Margaret's experience. I spoke with the nursing staff and they realised what was happening to Margaret. They agreed that placing her in direct contact with the sunshine was counterproductive to what was intended by the move. Even placing her near the sun but not in its direct flow would help her. No longer would Margaret be placed in the direct sunlight.

When it came close to the time that I would be leaving this placement I could hardly contain my feelings of sadness. Saying goodbye to Margaret was going to be difficult for me. When the time finally came to do so, Margaret reached into her 'newly found' handbag, pulled out an embroidered handkerchief and placed it in my hand. 'Here,' she said, 'this is for you.' In the back of my mind I recalled the warnings I had heard about accepting gifts from patients. I ignored the warnings, placed the handkerchief in the pocket of my uniform and thanked Margaret. We had shared a special understanding and the handkerchief became a symbol of this understanding. I cherished this gift because it served as a reminder of the importance of being interested in patients, listening to and accepting their reality and, most importantly, understanding their experiences.

This story illustrates the essence of this book: the significance and value of taking the time to understand patients as people, of taking the time to notice, of being concerned enough to explore and understand their world as they experience it. Interpersonal skills enable nurses to make contact with the private, subjective experiences of patients.

Responding to Tony's father

'How can you be a nurse and witness suffering and pain?' is a question often asked of nurses. It reflects feelings of distress at the thought of human pain and implies that such pain often is hard to bear. But the fact that nurses do encounter situations of human suffering means that they cannot avoid it. Not only must nurses face such realities but, on a personal and professional level, they need to learn how to make contact with people who are experiencing human pain and suffering.

The situations that nurses encounter often create feelings of helplessness within them when the patient's circumstances cannot be changed. Nurses may fear that because they cannot change the situation there is nothing else that can be done. When this happens, nurses may avoid interaction and interpersonal contact, or limit contact with patients to those times when physical aspects of care require attention.

Other times nurses recognise the comfort and solace that comes as a result of establishing interpersonal contact. Consider the following story, told by a nurse:

> Tony, age five, was hospitalised as a result of serious injuries he sustained in a motor vehicle accident. He was a passenger in the vehicle driven by his mother, who also sustained injuries and required hospitalisation in a different facility to Tony. Although Tony's mother was in hospital, her injuries were minor. Because Tony's injuries were to his head and spine, he was initially admitted to the intensive care unit of the hospital, but eventually was transferred to a general medical ward. This is when we first met.
>
> Tony's father remained by his son's side day and night throughout the entire hospitalisation. He did not say much and most of our interactions were either nonverbal or limited to brief and factual information about Tony's condition. I noticed that Tony's father looked increasingly tired and drained as the days went by.
>
> After five days on the ward Tony's condition deteriorated, necessitating a transfer back to the intensive care unit. This setback was overwhelming for Tony's father. I could see it in his face. Initially I concerned myself with the details of getting the transfer underway. After the transfer was complete Tony's father returned to the ward area to collect his son's belongings. He didn't look at me and seemed quite distant. I wanted to say something to him in an effort to offer some degree of comfort but knew better than to deliver a trite cliché such as 'It will be all right'. After all, how was I to know it would be? Instead I approached him in the hallway as he was about to leave the ward area and told him how sorry I was that his son had to be transferred back to intensive care. I expressed my genuine sympathy for the turn of events that led to the transfer. He didn't respond but rather looked at me with a vacant stare, as if he was looking through and past me. I wanted to say more. I could not leave it at just that. So I said: 'I can only imagine one-hundredth of what you must be feeling. It seems like Tony has taken two steps forward and three steps back.'
>
> Tears welled in his eyes and he said, 'I keep hoping…but something always happens.' He began to cry and talk about how much he loved his son and how helpless he felt in this situation. I placed my hand on his shoulder and guided him to a private area of the ward. He expressed his thoughts and feelings about what was happening to his son, describing his condition in detail and expressing feelings of despair. Although I too felt extremely sad for Tony and his father, I maintained control over my emotions at the moment because I wanted to focus on him, not me (although I did cry later). I said nothing but simply placed my hand on his hand and squeezed it. It seemed enough. After a few minutes he composed himself, told me how much he appreciated my concern, thanked me and left the ward. I recall how helpless I felt about Tony's situation. It was likely that he would not walk again.

Although I felt helpless I focused my energy on making contact with Tony's father. I *had* to make contact and was glad I found the courage to do so. In some small way I knew my concern for him and his son helped Tony's father. I could not change the situation but I was there for him. I demonstrated that I cared and that I wanted to understand how he felt, no matter how helpless this made me feel.

This story illustrates how conveying concern and understanding enables nurses to connect with patients and their families. The clinical reality of Tony's injuries was not altered, but the emotional pain that Tony's father was experiencing was shared by this nurse.

This story also demonstrates that the helpless feelings nurses sometimes experience, as a result of clinical realities that are devastating and sad, does not mean that *they* are helpless. It does not mean that nothing more can be done. Being with patients in a manner that is wholly human and caring is more than just something that can be done. It may be everything.

Responding to anger

As the previous story illustrates, patients themselves are not the only people with whom nurses need to establish interpersonal contact. Connecting with the friends and relatives of patients is often part of connecting with patients. When anger and frustration are being experienced by patients or their family and friends, the challenge of establishing contact with them is especially daunting for nurses. Consider the following story, told by a nurse:

> As I came on duty to begin my night shift in the paediatric ward, I noticed two distraught women in the nursery. They were engaged in what appeared to be a heated discussion. One of the women was Eve, the nurse who was finishing her evening shift. The other woman was Tracey, the mother of one of the babies in the nursery. Tracey's child was hospitalised for respiratory problems. I caught only the tail end of their conversation and although I could not understand the content, I sensed hostility and anger in both of them. Tracey was walking away from Eve as I entered the nursery. I sat down to receive the handover report from Eve and she began to tell me of her frustration with Tracey. 'It seems that I cannot do anything to make her happy,' Eve said. She then went on to tell of the numerous complaints made by Tracey. I listened to Eve, knowing in the back of my mind that I would have to listen to Tracey as well. I told Eve I would try to sort out the situation and would see her the next day. She seemed relieved.
>
> After the report I went to find Tracey. She was packing her baby's belongings and informed me that she was taking her baby home. I knew from the report that Tracey's baby had not taken any fluids by mouth during the previous shift and was at risk of dehydration. I was quite concerned about Tracey's plan to leave. Slowly I said, 'I know you are upset—' but was cut off mid-sentence by Tracey.
>
> 'That nurse is typical of everything here, just typical. You bet I'm upset.' She continued to pack her belongings. 'And I don't want to discuss it. I'm going home with my baby.'
>
> At this point I felt at a loss, but also knew I had to try and make contact with Tracey, even though she was shutting me out.

'Look,' I said in an almost pleading manner, 'I want to help but I don't know what is going on. I don't know what is wrong.'

Tracey picked up her belongings and her baby and said, 'Well, it's too late to start worrying now.'

I protested, 'I *am* worried, even if it is too late. I am concerned for you and your baby.'

'Don't give me that, nobody cares around here, not you or any of the other nurses,' she said.

I blurted out, 'Oh, is that what's wrong?'

She looked straight at me for the first time, 'Yes, that's exactly what's wrong.'

I knew I had to think fast. The contact that I had made with her seemed tenuous and I wanted to strengthen it. I did not want this mother to leave. 'Please, let's talk,' I said, 'I was just about to have a cup of coffee. Come with me and I'll get you one too.' To my relief she agreed. I added, 'And I'll get a bottle for your baby.'

We went together into the kitchen area where I prepared coffee for us and a bottle for Tracey's baby, who had been crying the entire time we had been talking. I didn't want to take over but thought it essential to get the baby settled. Her distressed baby could have been half of Tracey's problem. When the bottle was ready I asked Tracey if she would like to feed her baby.

She replied, 'Look, that's what I've been trying to do all evening. He just won't take anything. I can't do it, and he'll end up needing a drip.'

I sensed her anger and frustration which was now starting to escalate again. 'Okay' I said, 'I'll feed the baby and you drink your coffee.' I noticed how directive I'd become, but decided that Tracey needed some concrete assistance in settling her baby. Besides, it was becoming increasingly difficult to carry on a conversation in the presence of the crying baby.

'Nobody has been able to feed him today and they said he may need a drip. They expect me to feed him but what can I do when he keeps fussing and refusing to suck,' she explained. She felt useless and helpless, while at the same time responsible. She was trapped by the circumstances. I decided to take over a bit more. In proceeding to feed her baby, I explained how his respiratory problems were interfering with his ability to suck. Thankfully, Tracey's baby began to feed and settle. At this point I turned to Tracey and said, 'You must be so frustrated and angry. I know I would be if I were you.' I held my breath, hoping that this statement would connect with Tracey. She nodded and looked at me, some of her anger was dissipating. I continued, 'Sometimes it's hard for us to know exactly when to take over and when to let mothers care for their own babies.'

I really didn't expect her to have much sympathy for the plight of the nurses, but fortunately I had struck a chord with Tracey. She responded by saying, 'Right now, I do need for you to take over and care for my baby. I can't bear the thought that he would get a drip because I am unable to feed him.' With this statement I began to understand what this mother was going through.

Eventually Tracey's baby settled and I managed to put him to bed and get him off to sleep. Tracey also prepared to settle for the night. She was lying down in the bed next to her baby's cot as I prepared to leave the nursery. As I began to exit, she called me over and whispered, 'Thank you.' Even though I now had what seemed like a hundred other chores to complete, I knew I had spent my time wisely. I looked at my watch. Twenty minutes was all that it had taken to turn these events around. I had taken the time to become involved in what might have been a most unfortunate situation. I had taken the time to understand. I felt satisfied.

Situations like this are demanding of nurses. They must contain their natural instincts to defend themselves, their colleagues and their nursing care. Tracey was distressed because she felt unable to care for her baby. She felt responsible for her baby's deteriorating condition and blamed the nurses for not assuming what she perceived to be *their* responsibility.

When this nurse arrived on the scene, the situation was almost out of control. By involving herself in a non-defensive, concerned manner she was able to make contact with Tracey and begin to see the situation through her eyes. This took effort, energy and time, all of which she knew were well spent in the end.

Often nurses believe that no time exists to listen to and understand what patients are experiencing. While this is sometimes the case, lack of time can become an easy excuse for not becoming involved in difficult and emotionally draining interactions. What might have happened if the nurse in this situation had not taken the time to understand?

Listening to Pita

Interactions with patients occur in a particular context. Often this context is that of caring for patients in ways that are not exclusively interpersonal. That is, nurses often find that they engage in meaningful interaction with patients as they are going about what seems to be routine nursing care. Consider the following story, told by a nurse:

> When I answered her call light I did not know much about Pita Gottleib, other than the fact that she had undergone a surgical procedure, an abdominal hysterectomy, two days ago. I had not cared for her during her hospitalisation but was aware of her clinical situation and knew her postoperative course was progressing as expected, although she was experiencing a great deal of postoperative pain. The nurse assigned to her care today was at morning tea and I was covering for him during his break. As I entered her hospital room Pita was moaning and clearly in some sort of distress. When I asked how I could help her, she requested pain medication. She was clutching her lower abdominal area and complaining of pain at her wound site. I assessed Pita's pain as I tried to help her to become more comfortable by repositioning her in bed. I checked her medication record, quickly reviewed her progress notes and nursing care plan and decided to offer her an injection for pain. This is what she wanted. I explained that I would get her medication and left the room to prepare it.
>
> When I returned to her room Pita was moaning more loudly than before and rolling from side to side in her bed. After administering the medication I again tried to help Pita to become more comfortable in bed. She began moaning more loudly and I noticed tears in her eyes. Although I thought I had done what I could, I felt I needed to stay with Pita a bit longer. 'What is it?' I said softly but directly into her ear. 'Tell me, please.'
>
> She began to cry and I began to become more concerned. I placed my hand on her shoulder and looked at her. She looked at me and said, through her tears, 'It's the pain. It is so awful.'

'I know,' I said 'sometimes the pain can be awful.'

I was going to explain that the injection she had just received should alleviate some of the pain but she interrupted me. 'I just got off the phone to my husband,' she blurted out. 'He told me that the hospital wants payment of my bill right away. There has been some mix up with our health insurance or something like that. I don't know what we are going to do.' With this she began to cry almost uncontrollably.

I stood there feeling more than just a bit useless. What could I, a nurse, do about her financial difficulties? 'Oh, I'm sorry,' I said. 'This must be so distressing for you, first the surgery, then the pain and now money worries.' My comment sounded a bit pathetic to me, but to my surprise she began to calm down and cry less.

She looked at me and said, 'You have no idea how worried I am. We do not have much money. My husband is out of work at the moment.' With this statement she stopped crying, wiped the tears from her eyes and looked at me.

'I cannot do anything about your money situation personally but I will find someone who can help you with it. Maybe it can be sorted out,' I told her. I could see Pita begin to relax. I thought to myself that the medication was beginning to take effect, but I realised it was not simply the medication. I knew that my being there to listen and understand was helping Pita. I told her I would get the social worker to come and discuss the financial situation with her. She looked relieved. I asked if she would like her husband to be present when the social worker came to visit.

'Yes,' she said.

'I will go and try to contact the social worker now,' I told her.

'Thank you,' she said, 'thank you so very much.' As I left her room I thought to myself, now this is holistic nursing care. Although I knew I could not directly assist with Pita's financial worries, these worries were part of her overall nursing care. And to think that all I initially did was answer her call light. Her physical pain was compounded by her emotional worry. I was glad that I had looked beyond the obvious.

Looking beyond the obvious enables nurses to see the complexity of the entire person who is the patient. What enables nurses to be able to look beyond the obvious are their skills in caring for the patient as an entire person, not merely as a clinical condition. Without the technical ability to ease Pita's physical pain, it would have been unlikely that the nurse in this situation would have had an opportunity to understand Pita's emotional distress.

Because nursing care involves management of the patient's clinical condition, the relationship between nurses and patients is often established from that base. The fact that nurses care for patients in ways that are physically comforting establishes that they are caring human beings. Physical care is often the means through which emotional care is offered. Patients come to know nurses as people who care about not only their clinical condition but also about what this condition means in a personal way.

Sometimes nurses believe that interpersonal skills are separate from other clinical skills, such as technical competence in administering medication. Just as patients cannot be separated into their component parts, neither can nursing care be split into that which is physical and that which is not. Nursing skills are as holistic as patients.

Focusing too much on tasks

Sometimes nurses neglect the interpersonal side of nursing, although physical care is offered to patients. Consider the following story, told by Charles, the relative of a patient:

I wasn't sure what to expect from the community nurse who came to visit us that day. Nerina, my wife, had already been through so much. The surgical repair to her back had gone all wrong. She contracted what seemed to me like every possible surgical complication. She responded poorly to the anaesthetic and took longer than usual to come out of it. She spent the night of surgery under constant surveillance by the nursing staff and they indicated that it was a bit 'touch and go'.

I was torn between staying with Nerina and returning home to be with my children. My mother was there at home with my children but, at age four and six, I felt that the absence of their mother in the home meant that they needed reassurance by my presence. At the same time I did not want to leave Nerina's side. So I stayed with Nerina, deciding that the children and my mum could cope without me.

Eventually Nerina came out of her anaesthetic sleep, but she went on to develop infections both in her surgical wound and her lungs. When I finally brought her home from hospital she was still very weak and ill. I felt extremely uncertain about my ability to care for Nerina at home. I helped with her care in hospital, but the nurses were always there as a back up. How was I going to care for her at home? The nurses at the hospital reassured me that the nurses in the community, who would visit us regularly, would be able to provide the necessary support to my care of Nerina. With this in mind I eagerly anticipated the initial visit from the community nurse. With this visit came the possibility of the assistance I felt I needed.

Terri, the first nurse to visit us at home, seemed in a hurry even as she arrived. She did not take time to say much to me, or Nerina for that matter, and turned down my offer of a cup of tea. She seemed rushed and wanted to proceed straight away to changing Nerina's dressing. Terri seemed to know a lot about Nerina's condition and asked questions about the antibiotic medication Nerina was taking. The questions were quick and to the point. No time to expand, I thought, even though I knew Nerina had some questions about these medications. Terri didn't seem to have the time for any questions we might have, only her own. She skilfully and efficiently proceeded to change Nerina's dressing. As she did, she reviewed quickly what she was doing and why she was doing it. She explained that I would need to learn how to handle the dressing change. Terri went through numerous details about the dressing, all of which seemed important to me.

As I watched and listened, I thought, 'How am I ever going to be able to do this?' She proceeded with such skill and speed that I hardly had time to absorb all these details. I began to feel anxious about remembering everything. There was no time to review the details or have my questions answered.

'There,' she said, as she completed the dressing, 'that's all there is to it. You'll be right now,' she said as she patted me on the back. She helped Nerina get comfortable in bed and began to pack up.

'But,' I said 'I'm not sure I can actually do that dressing.'

'Of course you can,' Terri replied. 'Just do what I did. There's nothing to it.' She repeated, 'You'll be right, don't worry,' and patted me on the back again. She told us that she would be returning to visit in two days time. She said goodbye to both of us and I showed her to the door.

'Thank you,' I mumbled, more out of politeness than sincerity. Thank you for what? I thought to myself.

Nerina was resting when I returned from seeing Terri to the door. I went away from her room, sat down and tried to recall everything Terri had said about the dressing. I began to feel a bit panicked about remembering everything and still had so many questions in my mind. I felt a bit lost. Maybe next visit…

Unfortunately, this story illustrates how easily nurses can focus on a task to the exclusion of all else. Terri's technical ability to change the dressing was without question. But her inability to relate to Charles and Nerina on an interpersonal level does raise questions. Perhaps she had an extremely heavy caseload on the day she visited them. If this was the reason for her efficient yet diminished care, she could have acknowledged this by telling them she was in a hurry. Had Terri been sensitive to what Charles was expressing, she could have offered follow up in the form of a telephone call. Anything that indicated that she was interested in what he was experiencing may have helped.

Terri's lack of acknowledgment of how Charles was experiencing the situation, his doubts about changing the dressing after such a brief and rushed explanation, indicated a lack of awareness on her part. This lack of awareness for Charles' situation could indicate a lack of concern and regard for him. Instead of acknowledging Charles' concern, Terri brushed it aside with a false reassurance of 'You'll be right.' In doing so, she not only failed to notice his concern but minimised it in a way that demonstrated that she did not care to understand.

Terri failed to appreciate that what she may take for granted, changing a dressing, was somewhat overwhelming for Charles. Her explanation was inadequate because she did not take the time to find out if he understood what she had explained. She did not even allow time for him to ask any questions.

Failing to listen

When Therese entered my hospital room that morning I had the feeling the day wasn't going to be all that pleasant. She had the manner of an army drill sergeant, moving quickly from patient to patient, not asking how our night had been or how we were feeling. She was one of those nurses who was focused on what *she* was doing, as if we, the patients in that room, were superfluous to her mission. Had she bothered to ask, or even notice the expression on my face, she would have realised how awful the previous night had been for me. I had not slept or even rested for that matter. I could not find a comfortable position in bed because the pain in my hip seemed to be getting worse.

My hip had been badly broken in an automobile accident six days ago. When the surgeons described how they repaired my hip it sounded like carpentry work to me. There were metal pins, screws and plates used to repair and strengthen what would now be a weak part of my body. The pain in my hip was excruciating. During the 21 years of my life I have not experienced anything like it. In fact, I can hardly recall ever being sick.

The nurses in hospital seem to come in two varieties, the ones who are sympathetic and understanding about my pain, and the ones who treat me like a sook when I complain. Therese seemed like the latter type. She briskly attended to the other patients in the room before coming to me. I had the feeling she was going to make a big deal about having a shower *right now*. She did. As she approached me she said, 'Now it's your turn, young man. Time to get up. Let's go.'

I tried to be pleasant when I asked her to let me have my shower after morning tea. I explained that the pain medication I had received earlier was starting to take effect and I wanted to relax and rest awhile before getting out of bed. But Therese was not open to any negotiation on the shower time. She told me that I had to get up and get going now, 'Part of the treatment,' she said. She offered no explanation about why the shower had to be now, only that *now* is what she expected. I felt angry and frustrated but knew better than to try to talk her out of her plans for me. She was in control. She did not seem to care about me.

This story illustrates what happens when nurses fail to take an individual patient's needs into account. Had Therese listened to this patient and explored his reasons for wanting to delay the shower she might have understood his request. Instead she alienated him and gave the impression of only caring about what *she* believed was best.

The importance of self-awareness

Wayne is an experienced registered nurse who has worked for many years on an inpatient, orthopaedic ward. Tom, a patient on that ward, came to symbolise one of Wayne's greatest frustrations as an orthopaedic nurse. Tom was addicted to pain medication and, although Wayne could understand intellectually that Tom became addicted as a result of medical intervention, he experienced an all too familiar sense of helpless frustration in trying to be of assistance to him.

Tom knew he needed to 'do something' about his addiction because his life had literally become his illness. When Tom's doctor suggested that he go 'cold turkey' in stopping the medication Wayne could see the panic on Tom's face. He pleaded with the doctor to 'not let that happen again' as he had previously experienced the agony of abrupt cessation of his pain medication. As Wayne stood by Tom's bedside he too began to experience familiar feelings: helplessness at his inability to assist Tom, frustration at a system that allows addiction, and anger at both Tom and his doctor. Wayne knew he would be the one to experience Tom's suffering first hand and he did not want to stand by helplessly. Part of him blamed Tom for getting himself into this predicament in the first place. After all, he was a responsible adult who should know better. All of these feelings created tension within Wayne and sparked a desire to detach from the situation.

Through reflecting on this experience Wayne began to realise that his anger was misdirected at Tom, through the interpersonal dynamic of 'blaming of the victim.' He began to recognise that his efforts to help Tom would be fruitless unless he aligned himself with him. Previously he lectured, coerced, cajoled and detached from patients who were addicted. He began to realise that such responses kept him distanced and uninvolved. He decided that this time he would get involved and began to explore how he might be a resource for him. Wayne listened with a new openness to Tom's plight and plea for help and explored the possibility of assistance from the drug and alcohol team. When Wayne approached Tom's doctor with the idea of a referral to that team, his frustration mounted as he met with resistance. Through discussions with other nurses Wayne came to realise that he could initiate the referral. He mobilised help from the drug and alcohol team in assisting Tom with his withdrawal from pain medication. He formed an alliance with Tom that was based on understanding of his situation and tolerance for his predicament.

Wayne was astonished at his change in attitude toward patients who became addicted to pain medication. No longer did he feel annoyed and frustrated; no longer could he blame patients for the situation. He developed insight into his own frustration and a sense of empowerment in his nursing role. Most importantly he grew to appreciate the importance of accepting patients as they are before trying to help them move to where they want to be. His self-awareness increased because he was willing to reflect on his own beliefs and values, and doing so benefited Tom.

Understanding Stephen

Sometimes nurses become so accustomed to the routine of health-care that they treat patients in a routine manner, asking the same questions and failing to demonstrate an appreciation that, to patients, illness and health are not only routine—they are personal and significant. When nurses demonstrate awareness of the highly personal and unique experiences of patients, they are connecting on an interpersonal level. Consider the following story, told by a patient:

> As I awaited my coronary bypass surgery I was filled with mixed emotions. I was pleased that technological advances in health-care enabled such surgery to be performed, but at the same time I was worried about the outcome. When the surgeons explained the surgical procedure they did so with a detail that I appreciated. Everything I wanted to know had been covered and they answered each of my questions with patience and complete explanations. But I could still see that to them the procedure was routine. They had successfully completed hundreds, even thousands, of these procedures and approached the explanations with a matter-of-fact manner that would be expected with such familiarity. But to me, the surgery could never be routine.
>
> After they left my hospital room the nurse who was caring for me that day, Jan, came in to see me. I had come to know and trust Jan during my stay in hospital. She had been present as the surgical team explained what was to happen during the bypass procedure. Jan also had many years of experience in caring for patients who were undergoing coronary bypass surgery.
>
> I did have a few more questions that Jan answered with knowledge and detail. She then sat down next to my bed and explained that sometimes patients need more than factual details. Sometimes they also have fears related to the surgery that cannot be allayed through information alone. She asked me if I had any fears.
>
> Because I knew and trusted Jan, I told that my greatest fear was that of becoming a cripple, unable to care for myself and function as an independent

person. Some of the possible complications that the surgeons reviewed led me to believe that this was a possibility. I was surprised at how freely the words came out, as I am not a person who discusses feelings easily, especially when these feelings are related to my fears. Obviously I had some fears and Jan's concern and interest helped me to express them. I told her that I was not afraid of dying, only afraid of living half a life following the surgery.

She understood what I was telling her. She didn't try to alleviate my fears by offering me statistics about the probability of my becoming a cripple. The surgeons had already presented the statistics. There is not much consolation in knowing that there is a 10 per cent chance of this complication or a 5 per cent chance of that complication. Although I was somewhat reassured in hearing these facts, how was I to know whether I'd be the 90 per cent or the 10 per cent?

Instead of focusing on further details, Jan just listened to me. And she demonstrated to me that she understood. When my daughter came to visit me that evening I relayed my conversation with Jan to her. I told my daughter how impressed I was with the fact that Jan initiated this discussion with me. Talking about my interaction with Jan provided an opportunity for me to discuss my fears with my daughter, who also listened and understood. Without the trigger from Jan, I'm not sure I would have discussed my feelings with my daughter. Jan demonstrated that she knew my impending surgery was more than just another statistic or a routine event. I was facing a major event in my life and she was there to understand what this event might mean to me. She was concerned about me as a person.

Nurses sometimes shy away from discussing patients' feelings because they fear that they may 'upset patients' through such discussions. Patients' feelings are part of their experiences. Bringing them out into the open demonstrates acknowledgment of the fears, it does not *create* them.

Like any interaction with patients, nurses need to approach discussion of feelings with patients with sensitivity. The patient in this story demonstrated that he was comfortable discussing his feelings. He also indicated that he trusted Jan, an essential prerequisite for the discussion of feelings. Had he responded to Jan's exploration with reluctance it would have been insensitive of her to continue.

This final point raises one of the most important aspects of interacting with patients. *There are no context-free rules about interacting with patients.* Nurses must consider a host of variables when they make contact with patients. Sometimes a discussion about feelings is suitable to the context, while at other times such discussions do not fit the context. Throughout this book, guidelines and theory about how to establish interpersonal contact with patients are presented. However, each interaction, like each patient and each nurse, will be unique and dynamic in its own right.

CHAPTER SUMMARY

This chapter contains selected stories that illustrate the importance of interpersonal connections in nursing. In the chapters that follow, further illustrations and explanations that reinforce each of the highlighted concepts—understanding, responding and listening—are presented.

Some of the stories in this chapter feature interactions with patients' family members. Throughout this book most references are to the patient. All of the principles and guidelines that are presented refer to interactions with any person for whom the nurse cares—family members, friends and patients themselves. The term 'patient' has been used for convenience, however, effective interpersonal relationships in nursing are not limited to patients. They extend to any person for whom a nurse cares.

CHAPTER 2

THE PATIENT–NURSE RELATIONSHIP

INTRODUCTION

The skills described in the following chapters offer nurses a range of alternatives when interacting with patients. The skills of listening, understanding, exploring and intervening are not ends in themselves, but useful ways to establish and build relationships between patients and nurses. Using such skills effectively increases the possibility that patients and nurses will connect and relate in meaningful ways. These skills enable nurses to establish meaningful contact with patients and to understand patients' experiences. Operating from within patients' experiences enhances the possibility that nursing care will be individualised and context-specific, as opposed to mechanical, procedural or task-oriented.

Technical proficiency in skill use holds no guarantee that skills will be used in ways that are beneficial to patients. A view that skills can be used merely as techniques, applied in a rational, objective manner, loses an essential element—that the skills only make sense when viewed within the subjective reality of a relationship between two human beings, nurse and patient. When viewed as techniques, devoid of the subjective experience of the relationship, interpersonal skills lose their most crucial quality—that they are relational and interactional.

General guidelines for the appropriate utilisation of each skill are presented in the following chapters, but these guidelines may not provide enough direction for nurses as they try to determine which skill is most fitting under a given set of circumstances. This is because the 'best' approach can be determined only within the context of the relationship between patient and nurse. No single response is ever correct in itself; no magical formula can be applied out of this context.

Nurses' personal styles; personality factors of both patient and nurse; the patient's immediate situation and their perception of it; how patients are responding to nurses; and how nurses are responding to patients are but a few of the contextual variables that need to be considered when determining the 'best' way to respond helpfully to patients. It is through direct involvement in the relationship, 'being there', that nurses can develop appropriate responses. There is no available blueprint for skill use.

Chapter overview

This chapter addresses the whole of the relationship between patient and nurse so that skills can be placed within this context. It begins with a discussion of the nature of the relationship between nurse and patient, focusing on mutual understanding and collaboration as essential features. Then specific aspects of the relationship are reviewed, including social versus professional relationships; interpersonal distance versus involvement; therapeutic superficiality versus intimacy; and mutuality and reciprocity. The various types of relationships that may develop are reviewed and the focus of skill use in each type of relationship is explored. The final section of this chapter traces how relationships progress from beginning to end by highlighting critical issues at each stage of relationship development.

THE NATURE OF THE NURSE–PATIENT RELATIONSHIP

Interpersonal relationships between patients and nurses humanise nursing care, because the relationships are the vehicles through which nurses are responsive to patients' subjective experiences. The relationship meshes the nurse's compassion and knowledge with the patient's experience. Through their relationships with patients, nurses express concern, care and commitment. In the absence of interpersonal relationships with nurses, patients can be viewed as objects, clinical conditions or a set of problems to be solved. Nursing care that is offered without a human connection is impoverished.

The connection is created by the way nurses and patients interact, and every interaction between patient and nurse is placed within the overall context of a relationship. For example, listening without judging and responding with understanding, help to create a relationship based on acceptance and respect. Each interaction helps to develop and define the relationship, but each interaction is merely a 'snapshot' of the entire moving picture that is the relationship.

The act of aligning oneself alongside another person in an attempt to help or be of assistance, in this case, to nurse, helps to distinguish that interpersonal relationship from other social relationships. How nurses relate to and are with patients exemplify how they see themselves as helpers. In this sense understanding the nature of the relationship between nurse and patient is akin to understanding the nature of nursing itself. The relationship is the vehicle through which help is offered; it is central to nursing.

There are claims that centralising the interpersonal relationship between patient and nurse is a new situation (see, for example, Barthow, 1997; Porter,

1994; May, 1992b; Ramos, 1992; Salvage, 1990). Making explicit the beneficial aspects of the interpersonal interventions (helping patients by talking and relating to them) is an attempt to move away from care that is predominantly physical and task oriented. An orientation toward the completion of tasks is associated with nurses' functional role in a health-care organisation (that is, a job). Under such a system nurses are discouraged from relating to individual patients because doing so has the potential to distract them from completing their allocated tasks (May, 1993). Likewise, work was organised in such a way to protect nurses from involvement. For the most part this system was impersonal. Often patients were regarded as sets of tasks and often nurses were regarded as sets of skills to accomplish the tasks. Encouraging patients and nurses relate as subjective beings alters such arrangements.

Movement toward an interpersonal orientation is aligned with a professional role. With this role comes a mandate for nurses to relate to patients as more than simply a set of tasks or a passive recipient of care. Acknowledging the importance of this interpersonal relationship and focusing on its uniqueness is associated with professionalism. Forming therapeutic relationships with patients became a new way to conceptualise what it means to be a professional nurse, a means by which nurses can gain and claim professional autonomy and authority.

The impetus for nurses to relate to patients has been reinforced through the use of the nursing process, a way of developing individualised care for patients. Furthermore, the introduction of primary nursing, a system of allocating nursing care responsibility of individual patients to individual nurses for an entire episode of care (for example, a hospital stay), is based on the notion that a relationship between the primary nurse and their patients will develop. Individualised patient care through primary nursing also increases professional accountability and promotes continuity of care. Relating to patients as individual people also helps to humanise the health-care environment in which increasing technology threatens to dehumanise patients. Finally, notions of holistic care, as opposed to fragmentation, are contingent on knowing more about a patient than simply a diagnostic category or an anticipated clinical pathway.

The move to relate has not been without its critics. There are suggestions that requiring nurses to relate to patients as subjective beings is a questionable form of control and surveillance (May, 1992b; Armstrong, 1983). In support of this contention, May (1992a) cautions nurses that transforming patients from objects (of physical care) to subjects (with psychosocial needs) carries with it the risk of 'inventing' living and coping problems for patients when such 'problems' are matters of daily living. Solving problems such as these through the development of therapeutic/protective relationships becomes a vehicle for nurses to legitimate their interpersonal work.

Nevertheless, the basis for relating to patients is not really new or revolutionary in nursing. It may come as no surprise that Nightingale's *Notes on Nursing* (1859) contains numerous references to the need to understand idiosyncrasies of individual patients. Nightingale iterates and reiterates both how to relieve the anxieties of sick people and also how 'not to' exacerbate their worries or concerns. She is even prescriptive about how to talk to sick people. For example, she stresses the need for eye contact through her recommendation to be seated while talking. She warns of the problems of false reassurance, referred to as 'chattering hopes', stating that there is 'scarcely a greater worry which invalids have to endure' (p 54). She admonishes friends, visitors and attendants from attempting to cheer the sick by 'making light of their danger and by exaggerating their probability of recovery' (p 54). The language of today's nursing may have changed from the time of Nightingale, but the underlying message remains the same. The patient is a unique individual with unique concerns and worries and nurses need to understand the patient's point of view.

The basis of the relationship between nurses and patients is mutual understanding—alignment that enables them to engage in mutual endeavours. By aligning themselves with patients, nurses are able to judge what is of most benefit within patients' situational contexts. While understanding is the most basic and essential quality of the relationship, there remains an unanswered question—understanding for what reason, to what end? To help patients, to counsel them, to be therapeutic, or to conduct therapy? All of these have relevance to nursing. Most nurses help patients, some counsel patients, some relationships are therapeutic and some nurses conduct therapy with patients. The question, however, is still not entirely answered.

Helping versus counselling versus psychotherapy

One way to try and uncover the answer to the question of whether the focus of the relationship is helping, counselling or psychotherapy is to differentiate helping, counselling and psychotherapy. The distinction between these three processes is often blurred, and the terms *helping*, *counselling* and *therapy* are often used interchangeably. The concepts and processes of each are similar and the considerable overlap between them creates an impression that they are equivalent. Although they share similar aspects, they are not entirely the same.

Helping

'Helping another human being is basically a process of enabling that person to grow in directions that person chooses, to solve problems and face crises' (Brammer, 1988: 5). In this sense, persons in need of help define helping. They determine whether they want help, they seek it and they select the goals to be achieved through the helping process. In essence, persons in need of help define it on their own terms. They may ask for information or seek assistance in making a decision, solving a problem, or expressing their feelings (Brammer, 1988).

Helping that is undertaken with the presumed intent of changing another person has an arrogant quality because this assumes that the person offering help is superior, more competent, or more powerful (Brammer, 1988: 5).

Counselling

'Counselling is a process concerned with assisting normal people to achieve their goals or function more effectively' (Ivey et al., 1987: 18). Sometimes counselling is provided without the person's consent, as is often the case with prisoners on parole, but as a general rule it is engaged in because the person actively seeks counselling, in order to deal with an aspect of living that has become troublesome, for example, marriage counselling. At other times, counselling is sought for assistance in making life decisions, for example, employment counselling. People who solicit the aid of a counsellor are usually able to function effectively in their daily lives but desire a higher level of satisfaction with living. In general, professionals who have specific training and education in counselling techniques, processes and theory formally conduct counselling.

The terms helping and counselling are often used interchangeably. From the descriptions, it can be seen why. Both approaches centre on providing assistance to persons who seek it, to resolve an issue that, as a rule, has become troublesome in their lives.

Psychotherapy

Of all three processes, psychotherapy has the clearest distinction. It is a 'process concerned with reconstruction of the person and...changes in personality structure' (Ivey et al., 1987: 18). As a rule, psychotherapy is restricted to those situations in which the person has an identifiable clinical condition, often an abnormal behaviour pattern, and is conducted by professionals who have specialised training and education in the field. While it is preferable that psychotherapy be employed through mutual agreement between the person in need of therapy and the therapist, it is also sometimes attempted without the active consent of the person, for example, an involuntary admission to a psychiatric inpatient service. In these instances, much effort is made to engage the person in a therapeutic alliance, that is, to obtain consent by virtue of the fact that there is agreement to participate in therapeutic interaction with the therapist.

The nursing context

The nursing literature uses the three terms, helping, counselling and psychotherapy, referring to the helping relationship and process, the counselling role of the nurse and the therapeutic patient–nurse relationship. It is clear, from the descriptions, that elements of each process are present in nurse–patient relationships, although no one description clearly captures the essence of the purpose of these relationships. This is because nurses relate to people in a variety of life situations, from people facing life crises, to those in need of standard and routine health-care, to those whose behaviour is deemed to be abnormal. Thus, the processes of helping, counselling and psychotherapy all fit the nursing context, with no singular process providing clear direction for patient–nurse relationships in general.

'Helping' is the term preferred by Benner (1984), who states that the term *therapeutic* has inherited meaning from the psychoanalytic therapy perspective (a theory of psychotherapy) in which the therapist purposefully distances self. In rejecting the terminology, Benner highlights the frequency with which the term therapeutic has been applied to relationships between patients and nurses; it is often touted as the ideal. Because of its association with therapy, the term 'therapeutic' is often replaced in the nursing literature with the terms helping and counselling. However, in the clinical specialty of mental health nursing, the term therapeutic is the most fitting, because processes based on psychotherapy clearly fit this clinical context.

In reviewing expert nurses' descriptions of their practice (Benner, 1984) in *all* clinical areas, a direction can be found. The description of the helping domain of nursing practice offers insight into the complexity of patient–nurse relationships. From these descriptions of expert nursing practice, 'helping encompasses transformative changes in meanings, and sometimes simply the courage to be with the patient, offering whatever comfort the situation allows' (Benner, 1984: 48). This description provides useful guidance in understanding the range of form and purpose patient–nurse relationships can encompass. It reinforces the notion that 'being with' a patient, fully present and involved, is helpful in itself. It also leaves open the possibility of helping patients gain new perspectives.

NURSING AS CARING

Much of what is said and written about the nurse–patient relationship rests on the assumption that the nature of the relationship is helpful, that is, patients are assisted in some way through their interpersonal interactions with nurses. One explication of the notion of 'being helpful' is found in nursing research investigating the concept of caring. Caring is often considered fundamental to nursing, that is, it is considered an essential ingredient in nursing. This raises a number of questions, not the least of which is the meaning of the word *caring*. Quite simply, caring means 'it matters' (Benner & Wrubel, 1989).

If a person cares about their automobile then what happens to the vehicle matters to them. In the process of caring *about* the vehicle they will also care *for* the automobile, for example, by keeping it tuned and running smoothly. To understand the person's care it is useful to consider why they care, that is, the motivation to care. The motivation to care may be because the machine is their sole means of transportation, or it may be because the car is a symbol that boosts the owner's sense of self and identity.

Attention to the motivation to care in nursing is also important to consider, especially in relation to the need for self-awareness. Nurses who care because it helps them to increase their self-concept run the risk of harming others by confusing their own needs with the needs of patients. This highlights the need for self-awareness, which is covered in chapter 3.

Research on caring in nursing

There are nursing leaders who have consistently asserted that caring is the most central concept to good nursing (most notably, Leininger, 1984;

Watson, 1985). As such, the assertion suggests that understanding the theoretical construct of caring is akin to understanding nursing itself. Regardless of whether the claim is accepted or rejected, caring and nursing remain intrinsically linked (Cheung, 1998).

Although claims about the centrality of caring in nursing had been expressed previously, it was not until the early to mid 1980s that extensive nursing research into caring was undertaken when researchers were attempting to explicate a meaning of caring that was unique to nursing.

Despite numerous research studies into the concept of caring throughout the 1980s, the concept remained poorly defined and there were disagreements about its meaning (Morse et al., 1990). In their analysis Morse, et al. (1990) identify, from the nursing literature, five perspectives of caring: caring as a human trait, caring as a moral imperative or ideal, caring as an affect, caring as the nurse–patient interpersonal relationship and caring as a therapeutic intervention. Authors of more recent literature reviews and analyses (Kyle, 1995; Sourial, 1997) maintain that the concept of caring remains poorly explicated in nursing literature.

Although there are numerous conceptualisations, the predominant theoretical construction of caring in nursing encompasses an emotive, intimate, interpersonal relationship (Van Hooft, 1987; Macdonald, 1993). This is reinforced by a number of studies in which nurses refer to and describe caring through expressive behaviours that promote involved and intimate interaction with patients (Larson, 1986; Wolf, 1986; Forrest, 1989; Morrison, 1991; Astrom et al., 1993; Cheung, 1998). Likewise, philosophical analyses of caring in nursing have stressed a moral commitment to and respect for a patient's unique humanness (Griffin, 1983; Gaut, 1986; Kitson, 1987; Gadow, 1988). Thus, the prevalent view of caring is described as interpersonal engagement with patients.

Nevertheless, the claim that interpersonal caring is of primary importance in nursing has met with scholarly critique. Van Hooft (1987) argues that the central concern for nurses is patients' health, and nurses should focus on health outcomes rather than on the development of involved and intimate relationships with patients. Morse (1992) contends that focusing on caring directs nurses to consider their intentions (that is, it is nurse-focused), and suggests comfort as the aim and outcome of caring, (that is, what the patient experiences, which is patient-focused). Macdonald (1993) questions whether a push for nurses to develop deep caring connections with patients is an unnecessary imposition on nurses and raises questions about nurses' freedom to 'not care'. Finally, in an analysis of caring, Sourial (1997) concludes that a better conceptual foundation for nursing is holism, as most of the literature on caring is oriented toward this philosophy.

There is ample material available on how nurses perceive and construct caring because this is how many of the studies have been directed (Benner, 1984; Larson, 1986; Wolf, 1986; Benner & Wrubel, 1989; Forrest, 1989; Morrison, 1991; Astrom et al., 1993; Cheung, 1998). Nurses' voices have dominated the construction of the concept of caring. While it is of interest to know how nurses perceive caring, what is even more illuminating are the results of research studies that compare how nurses conceptualise caring with patients' conceptualisations. Such comparisons overcome some of the difficulties with the previously cited research that focused on what nurses were doing while interacting with patients, without exploration of their intentions and consideration of the patient's perception and role in the course of interacting.

Many of the studies that do make such comparisons are easy to synthesise because the researchers used the same measure, the Care-Q instrument (developed by Larson, 1986) and similar methodologies. The results are remarkably consistent across patient populations and geographic locations (Larson, 1984; Larson, 1986; Keane et al., 1987; Mayer, 1987; Cronin & Harrison, 1988; Kormorita et al., 1991; von Essen & Sjorden, 1995). Nurses' responses in these studies reveal that they perceive the most important caring behaviours to be expressive (that is, feeling-oriented), for example, listening to the patient. The nurses' perceptions contrast with what the patients say is most important. The caring behaviour patients value most are instrumental behaviours (that is, action-oriented), for example, giving medications on time, notifying medical staff when necessary and explaining what is physically wrong with the patient. That is, patients were more concerned than nurses with behaviours that indicated technical competence as a demonstration of caring, rather than social competence.

There is no comprehensive explanation for the discrepancies between what nurses think is caring and what patients think is caring, although the studies reported what nurses thought was important to patients, not how they actually behaved while caring for them (McKenna, 1993). One explanation for the discrepancy in nurses' and patients' perceptions of caring may relate to the use of the Care-Q instrument (Larson, 1986), which includes items describing both expressive and instrumental behaviours. Nurses who placed the expressive items in priority (the Q-sort methodology) may have assumed technical competence (McKenna, 1993). In contrast, when skilled nurses related narratives of caring (Astrom et al., 1993) they focused on both expressive realities of being available and accessible to understand patients' experiences, and the instrumental acts of acute medical interventions and practical problem-solving. The nurses in Astrom et al.'s 1993 study reported that they based their caring actions on a conscious judgment of what would be best for the patient. Those judgments included both emotional distancing in order to intervene in a technical manner, and deliberately interacting on a deeper emotional level in order to intervene in a social manner.

While patients in the studies cited did not report expressive (interpersonal) behaviours as the most important caring action, the absence of respect and regard for the patient as a person, for example, being treated like an object, was viewed by patients as non-caring (Rieman, 1986). More recent studies that have explored patients' perceptions of nursing care (Appleton, 1993; Fosbinder, 1994; Webb & Hope, 1995; Hegedus, 1999) demonstrate that patients do value nurses' interpersonal skills. In these studies patients regarded psychosocial aspects of care as important. In one study that required patients to rate nursing care items (Webb & Hope, 1995), 'listening to patients' worries' was top of the list of important nursing activities, followed by 'relieving pain' and 'teaching patients'. Interpersonal aspects of nursing care included being friendly and approachable.

Being sensitive to patients' opinions about care is an important aspect of good nursing care. Fosbinder (1994) confirms that patients value the interactive style of nurses who cared for them. The main activities described by patients in her study were the acts of informing and explaining, getting to know the nurse and trusting the nurse. In Hegedus' study (1999) both patients and nurses agreed that being treated as an individual is the most important nursing caring behaviour.

In conclusion, studies exploring the nature of caring in nursing demonstrate that both instrumental and expressive nursing behaviours are needed for patients to feel cared-for. As Dunlop (1986) points out, caring cannot be understood as compassion and concern while ignoring physical aspects of nursing. Nurses in some studies emphasised interpersonal competence while patients focused on technical skills. Nevertheless, the combined results of the reviewed studies suggest that caring involves psychosocial and technical skills. This sentiment is expressed well by Roach (1985) who states: 'While competence without compassion can be brutal and inhumane, compassion without competence may be no more than meaningless, if not harmful, intrusion into the life of a person or persons needing help' (p 172).

CHARACTERISTICS OF THE RELATIONSHIP BETWEEN PATIENT AND NURSE

No single definition could possibly capture the rich and complex nature of the relationships between patients and nurses. Each relationship is distinct, because both patient and nurse are distinctive and the way they interact and relate is unique. Each participant brings particular experiences to the relationship.

Rather than imposing artificial limits by specifying a definition of the relationship, various facets of the patient–nurse relationship are described here. The facets include the characteristics of social versus professional relationships; interpersonal distance versus involvement; therapeutic superficiality versus intimacy; and mutuality and reciprocity.

Social versus professional relationships

When the suggestion is made to beginning nurses that they are 'to be professional' in their relationships with patients, they often state a preference 'to be friends' with patients. In saying this, these nurses could be revealing a desire to remain in the comfortable and familiar arena of social relationships, where the rules for relating are predictable. It may also be that an emphasis on problem-solving and goal-setting (two processes often considered to be 'professional') contributes to the preference for 'being friends'. A common distinction made between the social relationships of friendship and professional relationships is that the professional relationship is goal-directed.

Fears of 'not knowing what to do' and anxieties about 'how can I solve patients' problems?' are logical responses to being asked to set goals and solve problems.

The most likely reason for the expressed desire 'to be friends' with patients, as opposed to being professional, probably emanates from a preconceived notion that 'to be professional' is to be distant, detached, aloof and cool. This aura of the professional stance, that of the detached observer who also has the answers, involves expectations that these nurses may be unwilling to accept. Being professional is sometimes equated with denying or abandoning the personal, human side of the nurse. These beginning nurses could be saying, 'How can I leave myself behind when I interact with patients?'

Nurses do not, and cannot, leave themselves behind when they enter the health-care setting, but neither are they there to be friends with patients, in the strictest sense of the word. This is not to say that nurses cannot be friendly, sociable and personable with patients, or that professional relationships do not have similarities with friendships. Nevertheless, professional relationships are different from other types of personal relationships, such as friendship.

Some of the ways that social relationships differ from professional relationships include the following: the nurse usually initiates the professional relationship with patients; there are time and space limits to professional relationships, in that they do not go on for life; and interactions are confined to a particular setting, be it a hospital setting or a patient's home. The final, and perhaps the most significant, difference is that patient–nurse relationships are formed with a focus on one of the participants only—the patient. Nurses are expected to meet their own needs for social contact, inclusion and affection outside of their relationships with patients. This is not to say that these needs might not be met through relationships with patients, but more to emphasise that the relationships are not used as the primary source of nurses' social-need fulfilment.

Differences in focus, intensity and perspective

Gadow (1980) offers a useful analysis in differentiating personal and professional relationships by describing these differences in terms of focus, intensity and perspective.

In professional relationships, the nurse's focus of concern is away from self and toward the other, the patient. Emotions are expressed and genuine feelings of distress for the patient's situation are felt (as in social relationships), but these emotions are not expressed by nurses for the purpose of obtaining relief or attention from patients. Nurses' concern and interest remain for the patient. There is no expectation that the patient is mutually concerned about the nurse, as would be the case if nurse and patient were friends involved in a personal relationship. In friendships, there is equal concern; for the professional, concern is one-sided (Gadow, 1980).

In addition, the intensity of the situation is experienced differently in personal and professional relationships. In professional relationships, nurses may become emotionally aroused, and feel the patient's concern, distress, or sense of urgency. Therefore, nurses may experience emotional intensity along with the patient in a given situation, but in a reflective manner, rather than the immediate way that patients experience the intensity of their situations (Gadow, 1980). The reflective nature of nurses' experience of the intensity of a situation means that nurses use their experience of patients' distress as a way of considering what would be of help to patients. Nurses integrate this experience with their knowledge of how to be of help. Helping to alleviate patients' distress is *why* nurses share and experience patients' distress. In personal relationships, more value is placed on sharing experiences than helping (Gadow, 1980). Professional relationships are experienced by nurses as more purposeful than friendships (Ramos, 1992).

The final difference in Gadow's analysis is that of perspective. The professional maintains an objectivity that is impossible for friends to sustain. While objectivity does not equate with distance and lack of connection with the patient, it does relate to the one-sided nature or focus of these relationships. That is, in professional relationships, nurses remain focused on patients, rather than on their own subjective experiences. This is not to say that nurses should disregard their own subjective experiences, but rather the significance of these experiences is placed in the context of how it affects the patient and the relationship.

Gadow's analysis indicates that it is not the level of personal involvement that differentiates friendship from professional relationships, but the form and direction of the involvement. The amount of personal involvement in the two types of relationships may be equal. Both types of relationships rely on active demonstration of personal qualities, so the notion that nurses' professional relationships are devoid of their personal selves is rejected. In fact, nurses rely on their personal qualities and style of relating. This idea challenges the notion that to be professional is to maintain a distanced stance in which nurses share little of their personal selves, and brings forward the next facet of patient–nurse relationships: interpersonal distance versus involvement.

Interpersonal distance versus involvement

The very fact that a relationship exists between patient and nurse implies a degree of interpersonal involvement, yet nurses are often warned of the dangers of becoming 'involved' with patients.

Two major reasons are often presented as the basis for warning about over-involvement. First, there is a danger that too much involvement will result in a loss of objectivity, the fear that involvement will bring with it emotions that interfere with cognitive process, that is, nurses who become emotionally involved with patients will not be able to 'think clearly'. Second, nurses are advised of the dangers of involvement with patients because it is perceived that such involvement will result in an emotional draining, leaving nurses unable to cope with the sometimes harsh reality of nursing. Nurses may believe that they can protect themselves from hurt, from the emotional aspects of illness, from depletion of their own internal resources through distancing strategies that remove them from the situation emotionally and numb them from the reality of pain and suffering. Interpersonal distancing and lack of involvement has been shown to be a defensive strategy used by nurses in an effort to cope with the distress of nursing (Jourard, 1964; Menzies, 1961).

The reasons usually given for warnings about involvement are brought into question by Benner's (1984) research into expert clinical nursing practice. The experts in this study involved themselves with patients by identifying with them and imagining that they or someone they loved was in a similar predicament (Benner, 1984: 209). This strikes a concordant note with the notion that in caring one sees the other's reality as a possibility for oneself (Noddings, 1984). Identification invokes involvement in the situation, not as a passive observer but as an active participant. Through identifying with patients, nurses involve themselves in a personal way in patients' experiences. This involvement, of being close to the heart of the situation, enables nurses to notice what is significant and to notice subtle changes in patients. Rather than hampering nurses' clinical judgment, involvement has the potential to enhance it.

Additionally, not only did the expert nurses *not* become drained or depleted by their involvement with patients, but they also had the experience of feeling affirmed and stronger for it (Benner, 1984). Their involvement enabled them then to draw on resources both within themselves and the patients with whom they had been involved.

Nevertheless, there is still the risk that such identification and involvement may result in nurses becoming overwhelmed by emotional reactions. The expert nurses in Benner's study did remind themselves 'of their "otherness" whenever their identification distorted their caring' (Benner, 1984: 209).

These nurses have come to terms with what has been referred to as the 'paradox of helping' (Brammer, 1988: 47). They were able to be involved enough to participate, emotionally, spiritually and intellectually, in their relationships with patients, yet remained distanced enough to maintain control and use their involvement to assist patients.

It must be noted, however, that the nurses in Benner's study were relating clinical practice that was judged to be at an expert level. Their experience may not be similar to that of all practising nurses, especially those at a beginning level. Nevertheless, their experience does provide encouragement for nurses to relinquish an inordinate fear of involvement. These findings are supported by Lawler's study on nurses' work with the body. The nurses in this study recognised that emotional detachment does not work, and they often needed to unlearn what they had been told (Lawler, 1991: 128).

Over-involvement

While involvement is necessary, there is still a risk that the scales can tip into over-involvement. More than likely it is the danger of over-involvement that leads to the warnings about involvement in the first place. When nurses become emotionally overwhelmed, they do run the risk of over-involvement (Benner & Wrubel, 1989: 373).

When nurses are over-involved they can no longer retain a sense of 'otherness' that enables them to maintain a sense of control. Over-involved relationships become close personal friendships in which the nurse relinquishes the professional role and the patient relinquishes the patient role (Morse, 1991). The nurse functions as omnipotent rescuer and leaps in and takes over, assuming the patient's burdens and problems and failing to perceive the resourcefulness of the patient (Benner & Wrubel, 1989). In over-involved relationships, nurses over-extend themselves, often to their own personal and professional detriment (Morse, 1991). When nurses sacrifice some professional control for the bonds of friendship they feel less satsfied and less helpful to the patient (Ramos, 1992).

The following scenario is an example of an over-involved relationship, told in the first person by the nurse:

> When I heard Pat's story of how she received a gunshot wound to her spine at close range, from her husband during a domestic argument, I felt anger toward her husband and a deep sense of sympathy for Pat. There was virtually no hope that she would ever walk again as the bullet had severed her spine. She was out of intensive care, out of immediate life-threatening danger, when we met. I liked her the moment I met her and felt an affinity toward her. She was a physically beautiful woman of 35, who sustained a charm and graciousness that would be difficult for most people under the circumstances. We instantly 'hit it off', and over the next three months of her hospitalisation became quite close. The fact that I often thought about her when I was off duty did not seem remarkable to me; I often thought about patients when I was at home. But there was something different about our relationship. We came to know each other on a deeply personal basis, and I no longer thought of her as a patient. I also got to know her family very well and was treated like part of their network. Her parents, three sisters, brother-in-law and three nieces were an extremely close-knit family. They maintained a continual presence at Pat's side, supporting and caring for her in every possible way. They sensed my deep commitment to Pat, and expressed appreciation for it. Neither Pat nor her family ever spoke of Pat's husband, the person I held responsible for putting her in a wheelchair. Not surprisingly, he had not been in to see her. My anger toward him grew as I became closer to Pat. 'How could anyone have done this to her?' My sense of injustice and my firm belief in the senselessness of firearms in the home kept my anger strong. But Pat never demonstrated any anger, in fact, she never talked about 'what happened'. She accepted her situation, the complex physical problems that accompany a spinal injury, her life in a wheelchair and her altered future with equanimity and remarkable resilience. I admired her strength and supported it, for it was keeping her going against enormous odds. I began to feel I was the only one who could care for her properly. If I had been on days off and found that she had a 'set back' during that time, I would accuse my colleagues of not caring for her adequately. When her nightmares began, and the events of the shooting were vividly replayed in them, her fear and anguish started to seep through. She chose me to be the only one with whom she shared her nightmares and her feelings. Although she expressed anger and sadness, she never dwelled on these emotions. Perhaps she knew I felt the same way, perhaps it was that I always listened, quietly encouraging her to 'get it out'. She told no one else of the emotional pain, because she knew the others who

were closest to her, her family, were bearing their own anguish. She never wanted to be a burden, and this internal resource saw her through the long rehabilitation process. When she was discharged from hospital to the rehabilitation centre, I visited as often as I could, even though it was an hour-and-a-half drive from my place. I was often invited to her sister's home. Through these visits I stayed in touch with Pat and her entire family. When my own personal circumstances necessitated a relocation from the area, we lost touch with each other, even though we wrote to each other for a while. To this day, I feel pangs of guilt because it seemed I had abandoned Pat when I moved away. The rational part of me tries to assuage my guilt, but in my heart I cannot reconcile the fact that it is my fault that I am no longer part of Pat's life. It just seemed there was no way to say goodbye, or that I should have ever said goodbye. In the end, for all I did for Pat, it felt as if I had failed her.

The guilt that this nurse feels for having ended this relationship, and the fact that she questions whether it should have ended, signals over-involvement. She also expresses that she acted as a rescuer and saviour to Pat, having a special relationship that was not attained by anyone else. In a sense, she lost her objectivity because she had difficulty accepting the reality that relationships with patients are usually not lifelong. Could she, or should she, have avoided this over-involvement? In all likelihood the answer is no. It happens, and when it does, most nurses learn from the experience (Morse, 1991).

It is important for nurses to recognise when they are at risk of over-involving themselves with patients. But if it happens, it is equally important to reflect on the situation and learn from the experience. Talking it over with a trusted colleague (see chapter 11) would not only provide support, but also enhance and accelerate learning from the experience.

This story raises an interesting question. What if patients and nurses do become friends? What if there is never an appropriate time to say goodbye because patient and nurse want to maintain contact with each other? Do such possibilities imply over-involvement? Probably not, but they do suggest a level of involvement in which patient and nurse come to know each other intimately.

It does happen that patients and nurses develop into lifelong friends even though their initial meeting was not purely social in nature. However, if this becomes an everyday occurrence in a nurse's life, it does signal a need for self-reflection (see chapter 3). It could indicate that the nurse is unable to focus energy on patients. Nurses who 'make friends' with the majority of patients they meet may be treating their own needs as more important than patients' needs.

Nurses are at risk of over-involvement when they believe they are the only ones who can help a patient, when they try to rescue patients, when they cannot imagine a relationship with a patient ending and when they feel over-extended or overwhelmed by a relationship with a patient.

There is an art to knowing what can be offered without an over-extension of personal resources. Through reflective practice, nurses learn how to offer what they can, without dictating results, and with a clear recognition that they are not the only ones who contribute to patients' wellbeing (Benner & Wrubel, 1989: 376). The key to avoiding over-involved relationships is not to avoid involvement altogether, but rather to find the right kind of involvement (Benner & Wrubel, 1989). The degree of involvement varies with the type of relationship that is formed between nurses and patients, and these types of relationships are covered later in this chapter.

Issues of social versus professional relationships and distance versus involvement help in bringing forward the next facet of patient–nurse relationships: therapeutic superficiality versus intimacy. As discussed previously, the term 'therapeutic' has a different meaning in this context from its meaning in the context of psychotherapy.

Therapeutic superficiality versus intimacy

All relationships between patient and nurse begin at a level of superficiality. Relationships at this level are characterised by minimal self-disclosure and focus primarily on 'safe' (nonpersonal) content areas because there is minimal knowledge and understanding of each other, and trust has yet to be established (Coad-Chapman, 1986). Social exchanges and chitchat are common at this level.

Some nurses fail to recognise the value of such interactions, believing that they are not really benefiting patients during these interchanges (remember the focus on 'doing'). Because deep and meaningful interaction is not occurring, they fail to perceive the relevance of these superficial exchanges. Social interactions are valuable because they are a way for nurses and patients to get to know each other. Although not directly beneficial to the patient per se, these interactions serve in the development of the relationship, that is, there is relational benefit. Being friendly and informal helps to break down authoritarian barriers sometimes associated with professional roles (Hunt, 1991).

Therapeutically intimate relationships (Coad-Chapman, 1986) are characterised by a high degree of mutual involvement, trust and self-disclosure of a personal nature. Patients and nurses feel free to share their thoughts, feelings and perceptions when involved in such a relationship. Topics are of a personal nature, feelings are expressed openly and freely, and both nurse and patient are committed to the relationship.

The main differentiation between the two types of relationships is the content of the interactions, and the level of trust and self-disclosure. In both superficial and intimate relationships, nurse and patient are in the process of relating to each other, albeit at different levels.

Some relationships remain at a superficial level, with nurses providing technical care and patients being satisfied with that care (Morse, 1991). Ramos (1992) described this level as instrumental, with the nurse focusing on the task at hand. For example, a patient visiting an outpatient clinic for a routine pap smear would not expect, nor probably desire, any more than a nurse who listened, explained the procedure in understandable language, and provided privacy and comfort during the procedure. Therapeutic intimacy is not warranted.

Other relationships develop beyond this level and become profoundly moving experiences for both patient and nurse. For example, a situation in which a nurse connects with and enables a patient to face dying with dignity, meaning, peace and comfort involves a deeply meaningful, often intimate, relationship between them.

An awareness that different levels of relationships exist between themselves and patients enables nurses to feel confident in maintaining a relationship at a superficial level, and, at times, in choosing to engage in a relationship that progresses to a more intimate level. Descriptions such as 'therapeutic intimacy' imply an expectation that all relationships between nurse and patient should reach this level of involvement, or that nurses should at least attempt to have their relationships with patients reach this level. Not only is such an expectation unrealistic, and often inappropriate, it also fails to acknowledge the central characteristics of mutuality and reciprocity in the relationship.

The major difference between superficial and intimate interpersonal involvement between patients and nurses is the extent to which they are known to each other. At a superficial level very little is known beyond the formal roles of patient and nurse. At the intimate level of involvement the formalised roles fade into the background and patient and nurse become known to each other as unique beings. Not all patients will become known in this way because the clinical situation and context does not warrant this level of personal knowing.

Knowing the patient

In making clinical decisions about nursing care of patients, nurses take into account different sources of knowledge and different ways of knowing. For example, knowledge about pathophysiology assists nurses in knowing what to do when patients are recovering from abdominal surgery. In addition to knowledge such as anatomy and physiology, nurses need to take into account how individual patients are responding as they recover from abdominal surgery. In synthesising results of field studies in a variety of nursing care settings Liaschenko and Fisher (1999) have differentiated three different types of knowledge that nurses use in their work.

The first of these knowledge types is referred to by Liaschenko and Fisher as *case knowledge*. This knowledge is generalised and objective, and includes areas such as the knowledge of anatomy, physiology, physical disease processes and pharmacology. This knowledge is based on statistics and probabilities of the clinical situation. Nurses need not necessarily interact with patients in order to use this knowledge. They can understand the mechanics of a myocardial infarction without ever seeing a patient who has experienced one.

The second type of knowledge in Liaschenko and Fisher's schema is central to nursing work. Referred to as *patient knowledge*, it is the knowledge of how individual patients are responding to their clinical situations. This knowledge enables nurses to negotiate the care of patients within a health-care system. This type of knowing is based on understanding what individual patients are experiencing and therefore requires interaction between nurse and patient. That is, nurses need interpersonal skills to understand a patient's response to the clinical situation at hand.

A third type of knowledge identified by Liaschenko and Fisher involves an understanding of the unique individuality of the patient, knowing the patient's personal and private biography and understanding how that person's actions make sense for them. It is *person knowledge*.

Patient knowledge and person knowledge encompass what is currently identified in the nursing literature as the concept of 'knowing the patient' (Henderson, 1997; Liaschenko, 1997; Radwin, 1995a). Broadly speaking, the concept refers to a process whereby nurses are able to treat a patient as an individual person because they know something about them. 'Knowing the patient' is identified as a central caring behaviour (Swanson, 1993) and associated with expert clinical nursing practice (Benner et al., 1992). There is also empirical evidence that 'knowing the patient' aids clinical decision-making (Radwin, 1995b; Tanner et al., 1993; Jenks, 1993; Jenny & Logan, 1992).

Clinical decision-making involves complex processes that are cognitive and experiential. Effective decisions require multiple ways of coming to know a situation and knowing the patient is one of those ways. For example, nurses in Jenny and Logan's study (1992) used individual patient responses in determining how to wean the patient from mechanical ventilation. The physiology of respiratory functioning and the mechanics of artificial ventilation provide nurses with 'case knowledge' (Liaschenko & Fisher, 1999) based on standardised, statistical evidence, generalisable to a majority of patients. Nevertheless, nurses in this study also used knowledge of how an individual patient was responding to the gradual discontinuation of mechanical ventilation (Jenny & Logan, 1992).

'Knowing the patient' reinforces a strongly held belief in nursing that treating patients as individuals is part of professional identity and values. Some knowledge of the patient does assist in nursing care but it is not always desirable or necessary for nurses to enter into the personal and intimate aspects of a patient's life (that is, to have 'person knowledge'). Such entry may even be intrusive (May, 1992a) or coercive (Liaschenko, 1997). 'Knowing the patient' is a result of interacting with and relating to that person in some way; it does not mean that nurses have formed a long-term relationship with the patient, nor that they even have to talk to the patient. The patients whom nurses were discussing in Jenny and Logan's study (1992) could not speak during the weaning process because there were endotracheal tubes through their vocal cords! And yet nurses were able to 'know the patient' by observing their responses to nursing actions.

Mutuality and reciprocity

Interpersonal involvement between nurse and patient cannot be mandated. It needs to be mutually agreed upon by both nurse and patient (the negotiation process in which this happens is discussed later in this chapter). There must be freedom to determine how they will relate; their involvement cannot be preordained and outcomes cannot be predetermined because these remain unpredictable at the outset of the relationship. While nurses aim to understand patients' experiences, they also need to appreciate patients' desire for the relationship and felt need to connect with the nurse.

Establishing the right level of involvement is not simply a matter for nurses because relationships are mutual endeavours between patients and nurses. Each participant, nurse and patient, influences the level of involvement. This is referred to as *mutuality*. Mutuality is the mid-point between nursing care that is determined by the nurse, without reference to the patient, and care that is determined by the patient independent of the nurse. The former is paternalistic; the latter is autonomous (Henson, 1997).

Although it is more common for nurses to initiate the relationship, either participant, nurse or patient, may make the initial overtures. The other participant must respond in some way to this initiative, for example, the nurse solicits the patient's participation in the relationship by exploring the patient's experience, and the patient responds by disclosing information. Or, the patient solicits the nurse's help and the nurse responds by providing assistance. This call-and-response exchange is what is referred to as *reciprocity*. Therapeutic reciprocity is the mutual exchange of meaningful thoughts and feelings. It involves nurse self-disclosure in an effort to assist the patient (Marck, 1990). At times the mutuality needed to sustain the relationship is not present; in these situations, there is a unilateral relationship.

Mutual versus unilateral relationships

A unilateral relationship is one in which one participant is unwilling or unable to develop the relationship to the level desired by the other participant (Morse, 1991: 456). When patients' conditions warrant a quick response, nurses engage in unilateral decision-making, not taking time to take patient understanding into account (Ramos, 1992: 502). Nurses may continue their efforts to relate at a deeper level, despite the patients' unwillingness or inability to be engaged in the relationship. Likewise, patients may try to engage a nurse in a relationship even when the nurse is unwilling or unable to make an investment in the relationship (Morse, 1991).

When relationships between patients and nurses are mutual, there is a shared sense of responsibility and commitment to maintain the relationship. Mutual relationships between patients and nurses vary in their degree of intensity and involvement and this raises questions about how and why some relationships remain on a superficial level, while others progress to the level of intimacy. The process used in determining the level of involvement is one of negotiation between patient and nurse (Ramos, 1992; Morse, 1991).

Factors affecting the negotiation of mutual relationships

Through negotiation, both nurse and patient make a choice to move the relationship to deeper levels of involvement and commitment. The negotiation is based on patients' and nurses' perceptions of the situation, and of each other.

From patients' perspectives, it is the seriousness of the situation (as they perceive it), their feelings of vulnerability (perceived absence of personal resources), and their degree of dependence that affects whether they seek interpersonal connection and involvement with nurses. When patients perceive their situation as serious, rendering them dependent on nurses for care, they are likely to make overtures and efforts to find a nurse whom they feel they can trust, and on whom they can rely. In addition, when patients interpret that the demands of the situation outweigh their perceived capabilities for meeting these demands (that is, they are vulnerable) they are likely to seek involved relationships with nurses. When patients perceive their situation as minor or routine, that it does not require them to become dependent on the nurses and they feel they can cope, they expect no more than routine, technical nursing care (Morse, 1991). Patients do not seek connection and involvement under these circumstances.

Nurses base their decision about entering into a more than superficial relationship on their evaluation of the patients' needs and their available support systems, that is, their evaluation of the patient's situation. Because this evaluation may be different from the patient's interpretation, the importance of understanding (see chapter 5) is reinforced.

In addition to their evaluation of the patient's situation, nurses also base their choice about becoming involved with a particular patient on whether or not they sense a personality 'click', as well as their estimation of the patient as a person (Fosbinder, 1994; Ramos, 1992). Nurses choose to become involved with patients who touch or appeal to them on a personal or emotional level (Morse, 1991).

The negotiation process

Patients who desire a more than superficial level of involvement will try to determine if the nurse is a 'good person'. This is done by asking the nurse personal questions, aimed at having the nurse self-disclose (see chapter 7). Patients look for nurses whom they like and on whom they feel they can depend. Likewise, patients determine if the nurse is a 'good' nurse by looking for indications of kindness, empathy, enjoyment of nursing and nursing competence. They test the nurse's ability to keep a confidence by sharing a minor secret. If a nurse passes the test of dependability and trustworthiness, the patient makes friendly overtures to build the relationship (Morse, 1991).

It can be seen from this description of the negotiation process that, although patients may not be able to choose which nurses are assigned to their care, they do have a choice about nurses with whom they become involved. Depending on the health-care setting, nurses may or may not be able to influence which patients are assigned to their care, but the preceding description of the negotiation process indicates that nurses choose those patients with whom they become involved.

The depth of the relationship is determined by many factors and nurses who realise which factors are operating in a relationship are in a position to establish appropriate relationships. The goal is not to form as deep a relationship as possible, but rather to create conditions that keep possibilities open. Unaware nurses may inadvertently hinder the development of a relationship or try to deepen relationships under circumstances where this is not warranted.

Dislike between patient and nurse

Just as it is unrealistic for nurses to expect that each relationship with a patient will be deeply meaningful, it is equally unrealistic to expect that they will like every patient with whom they come into contact. The reverse side of the coin of mutually satisfying relationships is revealed whenever nurses and patients are unable to form *any* level of relationship because they dislike each other. This feeling may be unilateral or mutual.

When it is the nurse who feels antipathy toward a patient, there is often a sense of accompanying guilt. Nurses may feel they are remiss in their professional responsibility when they dislike patients. This feeling can be offset by a realisation that nurses' responsibility is to provide adequate care for patients, irrespective of whether they actually like an individual patient. If nurses allow their dislike of a particular patient to interfere with actually caring for that patient, they are failing in their 'duty of care'. More often, however, it is the relationship between them that falters when nurses and patients do not like each other, not the nursing care that is provided.

It is more than likely that a nurse who senses disaffection toward a patient will either try to ignore it or, worse, blame the patient for the difficulty. Either response has the potential to have a negative effect on the relationship between this patient and this nurse.

Nurses who sense dislike for a particular patient first need to admit the feeling to themselves and learn to accept it as a natural part of being a person. Through self-exploration (see chapter 3), nurses may be able to unravel their reasons for feeling negative about a patient. Even if they are unable to discover why they are reacting this way, nurses who engage in self-reflection are able to separate what may be 'their' problem from what is an aspect of the patient.

Talking to colleagues is another useful way to learn more about these reactions to patients. Most experienced nurses probably have encountered unpleasant feelings toward patients, and those that have may be able to offer valuable insights into how to manage the situation effectively. But for colleagues to be tapped as a resource there must be open acknowledgment that dislike of patients is an expected occurrence. When nurses accept themselves they are in a position to learn and grow (see chapter 3). In time it may happen that a nurse develops ways of coping with situations that engender dislike of patients. Unless there is recognition and acknowledgment of the difficulty, such growth is unlikely to occur.

Admitting negative feelings about particular patients to colleagues serves another potentially useful purpose. Usually there are other nurses working in the same area, with the same patients, who do not react negatively to that particular patient. What rubs against one nurse's grain may roll easily off another nurse. Often an agreement can be reached so that those nurses who do not feel disdain toward a particular patient can care for that patient.

Sometimes, however, all nurses working in a particular locality dislike the *same* patient. When this happens, it is useful for all nurses caring for this particular patient to discuss the situation with each other in an effort to develop a workable way of relating to that patient. Neither nurses nor patients should be blamed when they do not get along, because of what may be a 'personality clash'. Reflecting on the situation, talking it over with colleagues and developing ways of working with and around the potential problem are the best approaches.

TYPES OF RELATIONSHIPS

Through the process of negotiation, different types of nurse–patient relationships are developed, characterised by their level of involvement and commitment (Ramos, 1992; Morse, 1991). Ramos (1992) identifies three types of relationship: instrumental, protective and reciprocal. They bear remarkable resemblance to three of the four types of patient–nurse relationship referred to by Morse (1991): the clinical/instrumental relationship, the therapeutic/protective relationship, the connected/ reciprocal relationship and the over-involved relationship.

In all types of relationships, technical competence is assumed to be present, so this factor does not enter into the type of relationship that is negotiated between patient and nurse. The first three types of relationship outlined by Morse (1991) and Ramos (1992) are discussed here, in terms of the focus of each set of skills (listening, understanding, exploring and intervening) used in the relationship. The over-involved relationship has been reviewed previously in this chapter.

Relevance of skill focus and type of relationship

Each set of skills—listening, understanding, exploring, and intervening—is used in each type of relationship. It is not simply a matter of the type of skill used, but rather the focus of its use. In specifying a focus for skill use, there is a danger that these specifications will be used as prescriptions, hard and fast rules that require rigid adherence, but they should be used as guidelines that are fluid and open to change. These guidelines are presented in an effort to fit the skills into the particular context of the type of relationship negotiated between patient and nurse. The focus of skill use in each type of relationship is summarised in Table 2.1.

The clinical/instrumental relationship

In clinical/instrumental relationships nurses and patients interact in a routine or standard manner. Nurses perform technical care that is usual or standard for the circumstances. These relationships are characteristically short in duration, and involve a health situation that is perceived by nurse and patient to be minor and routine. The patient's vulnerability and dependence is almost nonexistent, and the nurse follows clinical protocols in a technically

Table 2.1 Focus of skill use in various levels of relationship

	Clinical/instrumental	Therapeutic/protective	Connected/reciprocal
Type of Knowing	Case knowledge	Case knowledge and patient knowledge	Case knowledge, patient knowledge and person knowledge
Listening	Content	Content and obvious feelings	Content and underlying feelings
Understanding	External view of the clinical situation	External and some internal patient response	Primarily internal, from patient experience
Exploring	Factual data, not feelings	Factual data and patient perceptions of the immediate situation	Personal meanings of both the situation and effects on patient life
Intervening	Explanations and factual information	Sharing information	Sharing own interpretations
	Reassuring presence and manner	Mobilising resources	Providing support
			Concrete and specific feedback

competent manner. There is little negotiation involved in this relationship, although there is implicit agreement to keep the relationship at this level (Ramos, 1992; Morse, 1991).

Focus of skill use in clinical/instrumental relationships

A clinical/instrumental relationship is not cold and distant, as the words technical, routine and standard might imply. Because the care is routine, that does not mean that the patient is treated as a 'number' or a 'case', reduced to an object. The nurse is concerned and interested, conveying this by being friendly and cordial. Social exchanges and chitchat are often part of the interactions in these types of relationships.

During interactions in a clinical/instrumental relationship, attending and listening skills are present, but the focus of listening remains primarily on content (see chapter 4). Unless directly stated by patients, feelings usually are not discussed or explored. Understanding is external (see chapter 5), based on the nurse's clinical knowledge, rather than internal, subjectively based understanding. Exploration (see chapter 6) is focused on factual data, although strict adherence to a prescribed form or format is potentially alienating to the patient. Intervening skills are of the stabilising type (see chapter 7), reassurance is provided through the nurse's manner and presence, and explanations and factual information are shared. The nurse's self-awareness (see chapter 3) during clinical/instrumental relationships is focused primarily on clinical knowledge of the patient's situation, although personal biases and values may impinge on the relationship, for example, nurses may believe that patients should not complain about minor, routine procedures; they may become judgmental of patients as a result.

The therapeutic/protective relationship

Therapeutic/protective relationships between patients and nurses are formed in the majority of situations (Ramos, 1992; Morse, 1991). Morse (1991) considers this level as mutual, while Ramos (1992) refers to it as unilateral because the nurse maintains most of the control. This type of relationship is usually of short or average duration, with the patient facing a situation that is perceived by the patient as neither life-threatening nor serious. The patient's internal and external resources for meeting the demands of the situation are adequate. Although the nurse's perspective is primarily that the patient *is* a patient, there is also recognition and understanding of the patient as a person.

Focus of skill use in therapeutic/protective relationships

In attending, listening and exploring, the nurse focuses on both content and feelings, when these emotions relate directly to the patient's health situation. For example, when patients are anxious prior to surgery, the nurse perceives the anxiety and explores further, in order to determine the patient's need for information and/or reassurance. Understanding skills (see chapter 5) enable nurses to focus on the patient's subjective experience of the health event, and exploration (see chapter 6) is therefore focused on both factual data and the patient's perception of the situation. Interventions are aimed primarily at maintaining and stabilising the patient's resources; nevertheless, there is the possibility that information shared by the nurse will alter the patient's perception of the situation (see types of interventions in chapter 7). Because the therapeutic/protective relationship is more involved than the clinical/instrumental relationship, nurses' self-awareness is focused on how they are affecting the patient.

Connected/reciprocal relationships

A connected/reciprocal relationship is one in which the nurse and patient become involved to the degree that they perceive each other as people first, and their roles as patient and nurse become secondary. At this level of involvement nurses understand the meaning of the clinial situation for the patient as a person (Ramos, 1992). Usually, these types of relationships take time to develop, but a degree of connection may happen in a short time when patients' situations are extreme, in terms of seriousness, vulnerability and/or dependence (the factors affecting negotiation). Both nurse and patient choose to enter connected/reciprocal relationships, and trust and commitment are deep and complete. In a connected/reciprocal relationship, nurses often choose to 'go the extra mile' for patients, and act 'above and beyond' the call of duty (Ramos, 1992; Morse, 1991). Patients describe these types of relationships as 'friendships' (Fosbinder, 1994).

A major difference between therapeutic and connected/reciprocal relationships is that the nurse functions as a source of support in the connected/reciprocal relationship, whereas in the therapeutic/protective relationship nurses are support mobilisers and enhancers. This is because in the therapeutic/protective relationship, patients' supportive resources are present, even if not immediately available. In a connected/reciprocal relationship the nurse is involved and committed, although the relationship does not necessarily extend beyond the patient's contact with the health-care setting. These relationships are memorable for both patient and nurse, and nurses in connected/reciprocal relationships feel that they have made a significant difference to the patient (Morse, 1991). Although they require a great deal of energy, nurses leave these relationships feeling energised by the strong bond (Ramos, 1992).

Focus of skill use in connected/reciprocal relationships

In connected/reciprocal relationships, nurses attend and listen to the entirety of the patient's story, and are able to perceive themes, by relating content to underlying feelings (see chapter 4). Understanding is primarily internal (see chapter 5), with the nurse developing awareness of the deeply personal, subjective experience of the patient. Exploration is focused on meanings, and exploration that is based on cue recognition and perception (see chapter 6) is frequent. Interventions are aimed at the nurse as being the source of support (see chapter 7), and the nurse's interpretation of the situation is shared with the patient, in order to assist the patient in making sense of what is happening in the situation. Self-disclosure is high, characteristic of therapeutic intimacy, and the nurse is free to share concrete and specific feedback (see chapter 7) about the relationship. There is 'you–me' talk as nurse and patient feel safe in sharing their immediate reactions about how they are experiencing each other. Self-awareness skills (see chapter 3) focus on the nurse as participant in the relationship, and both nurse and patient experience change as a result of their relationship.

Summary of skill use in various types of relationships

Each type of patient–nurse relationship is qualitatively different from the other. In each, nurses use the same skills, but the focus of skill use alters as relationships become more involved and intense. A high degree of self-disclosure on the nurse's part is inappropriate in a clinical/instrumental relationship, yet significantly helpful in the connected/reciprocal relationship. The focus of listening extends from content only in clinical/instrumental relationships to themes and meanings in connected/reciprocal relationships. Understanding is primarily external in clinical/instrumental relationships and primarily internal in connected/reciprocal relationships. Exploration moves from the safe areas of content in clinical/instrumental relationships to the intimate area of feelings and meanings in connected/reciprocal relationships. Interventions in clinical/instrumental relationships are of the stabilising type, while mobilising interventions characterise connected/reciprocal relationships.

THE PROGRESS OF THE RELATIONSHIP

It is important that nurses understand not only the various types of relationships that are formed with patients, but also how these relationships develop and progress. An ability to track the progress of development of relationships enables nurses to time their responses accordingly. For example, without trust—the major issue in beginning relationships—challenging (see chapter 7) may alienate patients and reflecting feelings (see chapter 5) could be perceived by patients as intrusive. Tracking the progress of relationships means paying careful attention to the major issues of relationship development and to how patients are responding to the efforts of the nurses.

The progress of relationships is described in terms of phases of development: prior to interacting; establishing the relationship; building the relationship; and ending the relationship. The major themes and issues that are characteristic of each phase serve as signals and signposts in the progress of relationships. These indicators are aspects for nurses to notice, to be concerned about, and to respond to with an awareness of their significance to the development of relationships.

Not all relationships pass through each phase, and not all issues will be relevant. The phases and their central themes and issues are presented as a guide to tracking the progress of the relationship. They are not definitive, but rather present a probable scenario. For this reason they should be treated with caution. Using the concept of phases of development runs the risk that they will be perceived as rigid, adhered to as dogma or, worse, applied in a procedural, step-by-step manner. Relationships between patients and nurses are fluid, flexible and dynamic. No one picture could ever capture the complexity and variety of these relationships. The phases presented here should be viewed with these qualifications in mind.

Prior to interacting

The primary issue prior to interacting with a patient is the nurse's awareness of their own current thoughts, feelings and attitudes that may affect how the patient is approached. Hearing about patients in a handover report or reading about them in their health-care records sets up certain expectations, thoughts and feelings.

When there is knowledge of a particular patient, the nurse examines what, if any, thoughts, feelings and attitudes are engendered by such knowledge. For example, there may be fear and anxiety associated with caring for a patient with a known history of mental illness. These preliminary thoughts and feelings need not be negative, for example, a nurse may enjoy caring for patients of a particular age group, gender or clinical condition.

Self-awareness skills (see chapter 3) are especially critical during this phase of relationship development. Any or all of a nurse's thoughts, feelings and attitudes, prior to interacting with a patient, may affect the relationship, for better or worse. For this reason self-awareness is where the relationship begins.

Establishing the relationship

In the initial phase of interacting, the major issue between patient and nurse revolves around trust. Both patient and nurse evaluate each other at this time, with questions such as:

- Can I be myself with this person?
- Will I be accepted?
- How trustworthy is this person?
- Will they like me?

The initial phase of the relationship is thus characterised by uncertainty and mutual exploration to decrease this uncertainty, as both patient and nurse assess each other. Nurses assess patients in terms of their current health status and their needs for nursing care (most often accomplished by a formal nursing assessment), *and* in terms of whether or not they feel they can work with the patient (Morse, 1991). Similarly, patients assess nurses in terms of deciding if they can trust the nurses and whether they can work with them. This mutual assessment provides the avenue for negotiating the relationship.

Trust

The formation of trust is essential if the relationship is to progress beyond a superficial level, because trust enables patient and nurse to place confidence in each other. Interpersonal trust means that one person in the relationship believes that the other person can be relied and depended upon. They are secure in the knowledge that acceptance, support and regard will be forthcoming. Without trust, there is minimal self-disclosure and little chance that patients will share their experiences with nurses or that nurses will come to understand patients' experiences.

Building trust is not simply a matter of the patient trusting the nurse; nurses must also be able to trust patients. It is a mutual process; it must be reciprocated. Nurses must trust patients' inherent capabilities and resources, as well as their judgments about what is best for them. Nurses demonstrate their trust in patients by treating them with respect and regard (see chapter 3), and accepting and supporting them as capable human beings.

From the patients' perspective, nurses must be perceived as trustworthy. Nurses are fortunate because their professional role is viewed as trustworthy by most patients. Patients expect that nurses will care for them, meet their physical needs and provide comfort. In fact, when nurses 'don't seem to care' patients will often express shock and dismay, feeling betrayed by an apparent failure of the nurses to fulfil their role.

Nurses can rely on patients' inherent trust in their role only to a limited extent. They must live up to patients' expectations that they are trustworthy through consistent actions, behaviours and attitudes. Patients' self-disclosure to nurses must be met with acceptance and support in order for trust to develop.

Another important aspect in developing trust is for nurses to share their thoughts and reactions to patients' self-disclosure. Without feedback from nurses, patients who are sharing information about themselves may feel naked and vulnerable. Have you ever shared something of yourself, your thoughts, feelings or reactions, with another person, only to be met with a silent, stone-faced response? Under such circumstances, it is unlikely that you felt trust in this person. Likewise, patients rely on responses from nurses, and understanding responses (see chapter 5) are the most trust-enhancing. Moralising, evaluative and judgmental responses, early in the relationship, lead to patients feeling rejected.

Another way that mutual trust is promoted is when nurses share something of themselves with patients (see chapter 7). Self-disclosure that is reciprocated builds trust. Patients often ask nurses personal questions in an attempt to establish nurses' trustworthiness. These questions, although personal in nature, are not intimate questions, but rather ones that request factual information about the nurse. Honest, nondefensive responses to such questions help patients to sense that the nurse trusts them. This is not to say that nurses should immediately share deeply personal information about themselves in an effort to promote trust. Too much personal information will frighten patients and is as counterproductive as too little information.

Mutual assessment

In this initial phase of the relationship, nurses and patients assess each other in an effort to determine if they will get along, if there is any commonality or shared interest between them (for example, both whether they are lovers of opera), and if they feel they can work together. Patients may question the nurse's motivation to nurse, ask how much nursing experience the nurse has and generally observe the nurse to determine what kind of person they are.

Patients test nurses as to their dependability and their ability to keep a confidence (Morse, 1991). All of these are strategies used to determine how far the involvement between patient and nurse will proceed. The patient bases the decision about whether to trust the nurse on what is determined during this phase. Nurses also assess patients during this initial phase in order to choose consciously whether to make an emotional investment in the patient (Morse, 1991). This personal assessment is not the same as a formal clinical assessment, which is designed to elicit information that has direct bearing on patients' nursing care.

The initial interview

Most frequently, the relationship between patient and nurse begins with an interview, during which the nurse collects pertinent data about the patient. Depending on the setting, the data that is to be collected is often specified on a formal nursing history/assessment form. Patients are usually the source of information, although if they are unable to interact, for example, if they are unconscious, family and friends are used as the source of information. The initial information received by the nurse forms the basis for nursing care planning.

Because this interview is also the time during which patient and nurse begin to get to know each other, the process of how the interview is conducted is as significant as the content. The climate established during this initial contact is crucial to the subsequent formation of the relationship. This interview sets the tone and establishes some of the ground rules on which the relationship will operate.

A rapid series of questions, asked in succession, may leave patients feeling intruded upon and bombarded by the nurse. Patients may form the impression that their role is to be obedient in providing answers. Lack of an explanation by a nurse about why the information is being collected may create confusion and uncertainty about the nurse's intentions. An initial interview conducted in an automatic, routine manner may create the impression that a nurse does not care about patients as people.

While this section cannot describe all the aspects of an initial nursing assessment (for example, observation of physical signs), it does describe ways of conducting the initial interview with the recognition that it serves to establish the relationship between nurses and patients, as much as it serves to establish an adequate nursing data base. These general guidelines for conducting the initial interview relate to its process, how it is conducted, rather than to its content.

Exploration skills (see chapter 6) will predominate during this interview, however, the skills of attending and listening (chapter 4), as well as responding with understanding (chapter 5), will also feature in the interview.

Process aspects of the initial interview

It is essential that nurses establish the interview within the context. This is done by proper introductions and explanations of the meaning of the interview. Nurses who introduce themselves and clearly describe their role in the particular health-care setting help to establish this context. While this may appear obvious, it is striking how often this is overlooked or brushed aside too quickly.

A clear description of the nurse's role in the setting includes more than a simple statement of name and title. It includes a description of how often the patient is likely to interact with and see this particular nurse. Is the interview being conducted by a student of nursing who is present in the setting for that day only? In this case, the patient will not see this nurse again, and should be informed of this fact, without having to wonder or ask. Is the interview being conducted by a permanent member of the hospital nursing staff who is about to go on days off? Again, this should be explained clearly. It is disconcerting for the patient to share information with a relative stranger, who is then not seen again, without an explanation of why this occurred.

An explanation of why the information is being sought, provided in a manner that the patient is likely to understand, also helps to set the interview within a particular context. Saying 'I need some information about you so that the nurses can care for you while you are here' is hardly adequate for a patient who is unfamiliar with the particular setting. A better way would be to explain to the patient that nurses need to know 'how a particular health situation concerns you personally, how it is affecting your day-to-day functioning and how it is likely to affect you in the future', followed by an explanation that the information is used to make nursing care specific to the particular patient.

If nurses are unsure or unclear about why they are collecting the information, other than to meet a requirement of the particular health-care agency, it is not likely that the explanation will be adequate. For this reason, nurses are encouraged to think through what they need to know about patients and why they need to know this in order to provide nursing care.

Lastly, in establishing a context for the interview, it is important to explain to patients what will be done with the information they share. The information that relates directly to the patient's nursing care will be recorded and shared with other nurses and other health-care professionals, and this practice of sharing information should be explained to patients. Not every detail of patients' stories needs to be shared, and it is best if patients are reassured that information that will be shared will be reviewed with them at the completion of the interview.

This raises an interesting point about confidentiality in the patient–nurse relationship. How can patients come to trust nurses if they believe there is little information that will be kept in confidence? In fact, one of the ways that patients test nurses' trustworthiness is by sharing a minor secret to see if it will be held in confidence (Morse, 1991). For this reason, nurses are encouraged to question the sometimes established norm of 'telling all' to other nurses.

Confidentiality is not merely keeping patient information inside the confines of a particular setting, but also considering what should be shared, through reporting and recording, with other nurses and other health-care professionals. Information that has no direct bearing on the nursing or other health-care of the patient should be considered confidential and treated as such.

Each of these aspects, introducing self, explaining the purpose of the interview and informing patients how the information will be handled, helps to set the context and climate of the interview. Once the 'stage is set' in this manner, the specific data collection, the exploration phase, can begin.

In beginning the exploration phase of the initial interview it is best to start with 'safe' topics that allow some rapport to be established, before moving into more sensitive areas. Delving into deeply subjective experiences is inappropriate as a beginning focus, when the relationship is new and possibly fragile. It is unlikely that patients will share highly personal information before trust has been established—the sharing of such information is a sign that the patient is beginning to trust the nurse, or at least wants to know if the nurse is trustworthy.

During the interview, it is important that nurses bear in mind that patients are the experts on how their health situation is affecting their lives, although the nurse may have a clinical understanding of what is most pertinent. For example, patients may not perceive the significance of a question relating to how many stairs must be negotiated in their living quarters, but for some health situations this factor is very important. Nurses rely on their clinical knowledge in directing the interview, but need to mix nurse-led with patient-led exploration (see chapter 6).

The initial interview provides an opportunity for nurses to share information with patients. This is done by asking patients what questions are on their minds, as well as correcting any misinformation or misunderstandings they may have about their current health situation. Sharing information at this time also balances the interview, establishing a climate of reciprocity.

Building the relationship

Once the relationship is established, both nurse and patient know where each other stands and have an idea of what to expect from the relationship. The uncertainty that characterises the beginning of the relationship is reduced. It is at this point that nurses often experience a different type of uncertainty, an uneasiness and sense of pressure about 'doing something' for the patient. Because they have encouraged patients to disclose and share their experiences, nurses may feel that they now must take action and do something about what the patient has shared. When nurses experience their sense of responsibility in this manner, this may lead to taking on and assuming patients' burdens. Under such circumstances, nurses run the risk of feeling helpless, powerless and out of control. Taking on patients' burdens is also one of the warning signals of over-involvement. These highlight the two central issues in building the relationship: control and power.

Control

An attitude that it is the nurses' responsibility to solve patients' problems for them reflects issues of control. Indicators that nurses may be too controlling in their interactions include:

- Talking more than listening
- Evaluating more than understanding
- Leading more than following
- Advising more than informing

In order to manage effectively the issue of control, nurses must remind themselves that their role in the relationship is not that of rescuer, but rather that of facilitator, one who eases burdens by enabling patients to increase their access to their own resources. Through facilitating, nurses focus less on having the answers and more on enabling patients to maintain control and develop their own answers. In believing their role is a facilitating one, nurses do not relinquish their responsibility to patients, but assume their responsibility in a collaborative manner. In doing so, nurses operate from a position of partner in care, as distinct from the position of a provider of care.

This is not to say that every patient will want or need to be in control, or will be able to develop their own resources. Some patients prefer nurses to provide answers and offer solutions. In some clinical situations it is appropriate for nurses to assume control because of the patient's clinical condition, desire and orientation, or a combination of these factors.

In building the relationship, the major focus is to develop a congruence between what the patient wants in the way of help and assistance and what the nurse offers. There could be difficulties experienced in the relationship if nurse and patient are operating from incongruent perspectives. For this reason, nurses are encouraged to reflect on how the patient is approaching the relationship in relation to how they are approaching it. The models of helping, (see figure 3.2) are useful when considering congruence between how the patient desires to be helped and how the nurse offers help. It is pointless to force patients into collaboration if they believe that nurses are experts with the solutions to their problems. Likewise, to take over and exclude patients from decision-making when they want this level of influence is equally pointless.

Power

Another issue in building the relationship is power. Chapter 7 includes a discussion of power, in terms of how nurses influence patients, that places emphasis on enabling rather than controlling power. Nurses should remain conscious of the fact that they have legitimate authority, by virtue of their position. Nevertheless, the issue of power in building the relationship refers to the power that is developed through meaningful connection with patients. Nurses who are trusted and regarded favourably by patients have power to influence these patients.

Appropriate use of nurses' influencing power in their relationships with patients is an empowering process. Empowering means relating to patients in such a way that they feel capable and competent. Benner (1984) refers to the concept of caring power, which is used to empower patients, rather than dominate, control or coerce them. Nurses have the potential power to:

- transform patients' views of their situations
- reintegrate patients with their social world
- remove obstacles or stand alongside and support and enable patients
- solicit patients' resources
- bring hope, confidence and trust
- affirm the human capacity to cope

All of these processes are powerful in their own right. Nurses engaged in these processes are not operating from a traditional view of 'power over' but rather the empowerment that comes from belief in, regard for and strengthening of patients. In this sense, empowerment is similar to the characteristic of respect (see chapter 3).

Ending the relationship

One of the major factors differentiating social relationships from professional ones is that professional relationships between patients and nurses are usually time-limited. Most patients and nurses are aware that, at some point in time, each will disengage from the relationship. Relationships between patients and nurses end for a variety of reasons: patients recover and are discharged from the health-care setting; they are referred to another setting for follow-up care; nurses may depart from the clinical setting; and sometimes relationships end with the death of the patient. Whatever the reason for ending the relationship, there is a need to disengage and bring a sense of closure to it. The central issues involved in ending the relationship are emotionality and review.

Emotionality

Frequently, emotions are aroused during the disengagement process, and it is at this stage that both patients and nurses are most likely to express emotions about each other and the relationship. Emotions may range from sadness and frustration to satisfaction and happiness. Most often there is a mixture of emotions. Nurses experience satisfaction when patients recover, especially if they have played a role in that recovery. While there may be a degree of sadness in saying goodbye, this is frequently offset by the feeling of satisfaction and happiness for the patient.

Depending on the type of relationship that has developed and the degree of connection and commitment between patient and nurse, the emotionality that often accompanies saying goodbye may or may not be present. In clinical/instrumental relationships, there may be no emotions involved, except perhaps feelings of gratitude expressed by the patient. In connected/reciprocal relationships, emotions may run high as both patient and nurse have come to know each other intimately.

Handling these emotions is a matter of bringing them into awareness (see chapter 3) and expressing them openly. Nurses who are able to express their feelings about the relationship that has developed are behaving in an authentic, congruent manner (see chapter 3). In an effort to encourage the patient to reciprocate in expressing emotions, nurses may choose to reflect feelings (see chapter 5).

Review

Regardless of whether there is any emotionality in saying goodbye, the ending of the relationship is most satisfying when there is a review of what happened during the relationship. Various scenes may be relived and shared, or it may be a simple matter of reassuring the patient that all is now well. Reviewing what happened during their relationship does not mean that nurses and patients should relive every interaction, but rather briefly recount significant events. Such a review brings a sense of closure to the relationship.

At times, there is no opportunity to say goodbye to patients. If nurses feel unsettled when this happens, it is often helpful to share this experience with a colleague who also knew the patient (see chapter 11). Vicariously reliving the relationship with colleagues may help to bring a sense of closure to the relationship.

CHAPTER SUMMARY

The essential nature of relationships between patients and nurses is that of mutual understanding. In developing relationships with patients, nurses not only focus on understanding patients' experiences, but also on understanding the level of involvement desired by patients. Relationships that develop between patients and nurses differ in their level of involvement, and nurses are encouraged to establish a level of involvement that is appropriate to the circumstances. Regardless of the level of involvement, all the skills presented in the following chapters are used in nurse–patient relationships, but the focus of their use alters depending on the type of relationship formed. With an appropriate focus, skills are employed within the context of the relationship between patient and nurse.

Critical issues emerge at various phases of development of relationships, and awareness of these issues enables nurses to address them. The issues of self-awareness, trust, mutual assessment, control, power, emotionality and review have been presented with an emphasis on the need for collaborative efforts between patient and nurse. All skills included in this book are presented from this point of view.

REFERENCES

Appleton, C. (1993). The art of nursing: the experience of patients and nurses. *Journal of advanced nursing*, 18, 892–899.

Armstrong, D. (1983). The fabrication of the nurse–patient relationship. *Social science and medicine*, 17, 457–460.

Astrom, G., Norberg, A., Hallberg, I.R. & Jansson, L. (1993). Experienced and skilled nurses' narratives of situations where caring action made a difference to the patient. *Scholarly inquiry for nursing practice: an international journal*, 7 (3), 183–193.

Barthow, C. (1997). Negotiating realistic and mutually sustaining nurse-patient relationships in palliative care. *International journal of nursing practice*, 3, 206–210.

Benner, P. & Wrubel, J. (1989). *The primacy of caring: stress and coping in health and illness*. Addison-Wesley, Menlo Park CA.

Benner, P. (1984). *From novice to expert: excellence and power in clinical nursing practice*. Addison-Wesley, Menlo Park CA.

Benner, P., Tanner, C. & Chesla, C. (1992). From beginner to expert: gaining a differentiated clinical world in critical care nursing. *Advances in nursing science*, 14 (3), 13–28.

Brammer, L.M. (1988) *The helping relationship: process and skills*, 4th edn. Prentice-Hall, Englewood Cliffs NJ.

Cheung, J. (1998). Caring as the ontological and epistemological foundations of nursing: a view of caring from the perspectives of Australian nurses. *International journal of nursing practice*, 4, 225–233.

Coad-Chapman, A. (1986) Therapeutic superficiality and intimacy. In: D.C. Longo & R.A. Williams (eds). *Clinical practice in psychosocial nursing: assessment and intervention*. Appleton-Century Crofts, East Norwaek CT.

Cronin, S.N. & Harrison, B. (1988). Importance of nurse caring behaviours as perceived by patients after myocardial infarction. *Heart & Lung*, 17 (4), 374–380.

Dunlop, M. (1986). Is a science of caring possible? *Journal of advanced nursing*, 11, 661–670.

Forrest, D. (1989). The experience of caring. *Journal of advanced nursing*, 14, 815–823.

Fosbinder, D. (1994). Patient perceptions of nursing care: an emerging theory of interpersonal competence. *Journal of advanced nursing*, 20, 1085–1093.

Gadow, S. (1980). Existential advocacy: philosophical foundation of nursing. In S.F. Spiker & S. Gadow (eds). *Nursing: images and ideals* (pp 79–101). Springer New York.

Gadow, S. (1988). Covenant with cure: letting and holding on in chronic illness. In J. Watson & M. Ray (eds). *The ethics of care and the ethics of cure: synthesis in chronicity* (pp 5–14). National League for Nursing, New York.

Gaut, D.A. (1986). Evaluating caring competencies in nursing practice. *Topics in clinical nursing*, 8 (2), 77–83.

Griffin. A.P. (1983). A philosophical analysis of caring in nursing. *Journal of advanced nursing*, 8, 289–295.

Hegedus, K.S. (1999). Providers' and consumers' perspectives of nurses' caring behaviours. *Journal of advanced nursing*, 30, 1090–1096.

Henderson, S. (1997). Knowing the patient and the impact on patient participation: a grounded theory study. *International journal of nursing practice*, 3, 111–118.

Henson, R.H. (1997). Analysis of the concept of mutuality. *Image: the journal of nursing scholarship*, 29, 77–81.

Hunt, M. (1991). Being friendly and informal: reflected in nurses' terminally ill patients' and relatives' conversations at home. *Journal of advanced nursing*, 16, pp 929–938.

Ivey, A.E., Ivey, M.B., Simek-Downing, L. (1987). *Counselling and psychotherapy: integrating skill, theory, and practice*, 2nd edn. Prentice-Hall, Englewood Cliffs NJ.

Jenks, J.M. (1993). The pattern of personal knowing in nurses' clinical decision making. *Journal of nursing education*, 32 (9), 399–415.

Jenny, J. & Logan, J. (1992). Knowing the patient: one aspect of clinical knowledge. *Image: journal of nursing scholarship*, 24 (4), 254–258.

Jourard, S.M. (1964). *The transparent self.* Van Nostrand, Princeton NJ.

Keane, S.M., Chastain, B. & Rudisill, K. (1987). Caring: nurse patient perceptions. *Rehabilitation nursing*, 12 (4), 182–184.

Kitson, A.L. (1987). A comparative analysis of lay-caring and professional (nursing) caring relationships. *International journal of nursing studies*, 24 (2), 155–165.

Kormorita, N.I., Doehring, K.M. & Hirchert, K. (1991). Perceptions of caring by nurse educators. *Journal of nursing education*, 30 (1), 23–29.

Kyle, T.V. (1995). The concept of caring: a review of the literature. *Journal of advanced nursing* 21, 506–514.

Larson, P.J. (1984). Important nurse caring behaviours perceived by patients with cancer. *Oncology nursing forum*, 11 (6), 46–50.

Larson, P.J. (1986). Cancer nurses' perceptions of caring. *Cancer nursing*, 9 (2), 86–91.

Lawler, J. (1991). *Behind the screens: nursing, somology, and the problem of the body.* Churchill Livingstone, Melbourne.

Leininger, M. (ed.) (1994). *Care: the essence of nursing and health.* Charles B Slack, Thorofare, NJ.

Liaschenko, J. & Fisher, A. (1999). Theorizing the knowledge that nurses use in the conduct of their work. *Scholarly inquiry for nursing practice: an international journal,* 13 (1), 29–41.

Liaschenko, J. (1997). Knowing the patient? In S.E. Thorne & V.E. Hayes (eds). *Nursing praxis: knowledge and action* (pp 23–38). Sage, Thousand Oaks CA.

Macdonald, J. (1993). The caring imperative: a must? *Australian journal of advanced nursing,* 11 (1), 26–30.

McKenna, G. (1993). Caring is the essence of nursing practice. *British journal of nursing,* 2 (1), 72–76.

Marck, P. (1990). Therapeutic reciprocity: a caring phenomenon. *Advances in nursing science,* 13 (1), 49–59.

May, C. (1992a). Individual care? Power and subjectivity in therapeutic relationships. *Sociology,* 26 (4), 589–602.

May, C. (1992b). Nursing work, nurses' knowledge, and the subjectification of the patient. *Sociology of health and illness,* 14 (4), 472–487.

May, C. (1993). Subjectivity and culpability in the constitution of nurse–patient relationships. *International journal of nursing studies,* 30 (2), 181–192.

Mayer, D.K. (1987). Oncology nurses' versus cancer patients' perceptions of nurse caring behaviors: a replication study. *Oncology nursing forum,* 14 (3), 49–52.

Menzies, I. (1961). A case study of the functioning of social systems as a defence against anxiety. *Human relations,* 13 (2), 95–123.

Morrison, P. (1991). The caring attitude in nursing practice: a repertory grid study of trained nurses' perceptions. *Nurse education today,* 11 (1), 3–12.

Morse, J.M. (1991). Negotiating commitment and involvement in the nurse–patient relationship. *Journal of advanced nursing,* 16, 455–468.

Morse, J.M. (1992). Comfort: the refocusing of nursing care. *Clinical nursing research,* 1 (1), 91–106.

Morse, J.M., Solberg, S.M., Neaner, W.L., Bottoroff, J.L. & Johnson J.L. (1990). Concepts of caring and caring as a concept. *Advances in nursing science,* 13, 1–14.

Nightingale, F. (1859). *Notes on nursing: what it is and what it is not.* Reprinted 1992, Lippincott, Philadelphia PA, originally published by Harrison & Son, London.

Noddings, N. (1984). *Caring: a feminine approach to ethics and moral education.* University of California Press, Berkeley CA.

Porter, S. (1994). New nursing: the road to freedom? *Journal of advanced nursing,* 20, 269–274.

Radwin, L.E. (1995a). Knowing the patient: a process model for individualized interventions. *Nursing research,* 44 (6), 364–370.

Radwin, L.E. (1995b). 'Knowing the patient': a review of research on an emerging concept. *Journal of advanced nursing,* 23, 1142–1146.

Ramos, M.C. (1992). The nurse–patient relationship: theme and variations. *Journal of advanced nursing*, 17, 496–506.

Rieman, D. J. (1986). Noncaring and caring in the clinical setting: patients' descriptions. *Topics in clinical nursing*, 8 (2), 30–36.

Roach, S. M. (1985). A foundation for nursing ethics. In A. Carmi & S. Schneider (eds). *Nursing law and ethics* (pp 170–177). Springer-Verlag, Berlin.

Salvage, J. (1990). The theory and practice of the 'new nursing'. *Nursing Times*, 86 (4), 42–45.

Sourial, S. (1997). An analysis of caring. *Journal of Advanced Nursing*, 26, 1189–1192.

Swanson, K. (1993). Nursing as informed caring for the well-being of others. *Image: the journal of nursing scholarship*, 25, 352–357.

Tanner, C., Benner, P., Chesla, C., Gordon, D.R. (1993). The phenomenology of knowing the patient. *Image: journal of nursing scholarship*, 25 (4), 273–280.

Van Hooft, S. (1987). Caring and professional commitment. *Australian journal of advanced nursing*, 4 (4), 29–38.

von Essen, L. & Sjorden, P. (1995). Perceived occurrence and importance of caring behaviours among patients and staff in psychiatric, medical and surgical care. *Journal of advanced nursing*, 21, 266–276.

Watson, J. (1985). *Nursing, human science and human care: a theory of nursing*. Appleton-Century-Crofts, East Norwaek CT.

Webb, C. & Hope, K. (1995). What kind of nurses do patients want? *Journal of clinical nursing*, 4 (2), 101–108.

Wilkinson, S. (1991). Factors which influence how nurses communicate with cancer patients. *Journal of advanced nursing*, 16, 677–688.

Wolf, Z.R. (1986). The caring concept and nurse identified caring behaviours. *Topics in clinical nursing*, 8 (2), 84–93.

Part II

THE SKILLS

This part of the book explores specific interpersonal skills that nurses must develop in order to interact with patients effectively. Descriptions of these skills begin with nurses' self-awareness in chapter 3, then progresses throughout chapters 4–6 to focus on the individual skill sets of listening, understanding and exploring. While there are numerous references to how each relates to other sets, separating them, chapter-by-chapter, enables readers to develop skills within manageable learning segments. chapter 7 offers insight and guidance to nurses as they move from understanding patients' situations to taking meaningful action when relating to patients. The numerous learning activities that appear throughout these chapters serve to deepen readers' understanding of the skills and how to use them effectively.

CHAPTER 3

KNOWING SELF: SELF-AWARENESS

INTRODUCTION

Nurses do not leave themselves behind when they enter a nursing practice setting. When caring for patients they use not only knowledge and procedural know-how but also what they think and feel, what they believe and value, and how they perceive themselves. These aspects of personality have direct bearing on nurses' interactions and relationships with patients.

In developing interpersonal effectiveness nurses need a wide and varied repertoire of skills and an understanding of their use as well as a practical know-how. In addition to knowledge and practical ability nurses need to develop an awareness of how effectively they are using their skills because such awareness enables them to evaluate their own performance. Nurses who are able to evaluate their own performance are in a position to learn, grow and become more skilled and effective in their interactions with patients.

Traditionally, nurses are taught to focus their attention on patients and to try to ignore their subjectivity. This may be interpreted to mean that nurses should disregard or forget themselves whenever they engage in nursing care. By focusing on patients, at the exclusion of themselves, nurses run the risk of failing to recognise the significance of how *they* are affecting patients and how patients are affecting *them*. In the process, nurses may fail to attend to their own reactions and responses, erroneously perceiving these personal experiences to be superfluous or irrelevant to patient care.

The skills presented in the following chapters of this book can be learnt, developed and refined. Nevertheless, the skills are only as effective as the person using them. Each nurse employs the skills in a unique way. Effectively relating to patients involves more than simply using the right skill, at the right time, with the right patient. *What matters and makes a difference are not the skills themselves, but the nurse who is using the skills.* Each nurse develops a style of relating to patients that is 'right' for that particular nurse.

A nurse who focuses solely on the skills without awareness of their own personality runs the risk of contrived performance that lacks spontaneity and a personal touch. For these reasons, the initial focus of interpersonal skill development is placed on self-awareness, self-exploration and self-understanding.

Chapter overview

This chapter begins with a discussion of the importance of self-awareness, particularly in light of the concept of the 'use of self' in nursing. A brief overview of reflection and reflective practice is presented in the next section, as such processes are an effective means of increasing self-awareness. Reflective processes involved in developing self-awareness are then reviewed, with an emphasis on the interactive nature of these processes. The processes for developing greater self-awareness include introspection, feedback from others and self-sharing. The following section provides an overview of the facets of the self that are of critical significance in patient–nurse relationships. The qualities and traits of effective helpers are also reviewed because self-awareness enhances the development of these. Challenges frequently encountered when learning interpersonal skills are then discussed. The final section, self-assessment of interpersonal skills, provides useful guidelines for evaluation of present skill level and suggested directions for further skill development.

THE IMPORTANCE OF SELF-AWARENESS

An awareness of self in relation to patients assists nurses in attending to the mutual relationship, not simply the patient in the relationship. A failure to take into account the effects nurses themselves have on patients, and their relationships with them, can lead to mistaken assumptions and judgments about what patients are experiencing.

Self-awareness is developed for the purpose of becoming authentic, congruent and open with patients. If nurses are authentic with patients, they are sincere and genuine, not only as people who care what happens to patients, but also as people who are unafraid to show that they are human. The more nurses are aware of themselves, the more likely it is that their interpersonal skills will be used in an authentic and natural manner. Self-awareness enables nurses to act in ways that are in harmony with who they are, congruent with and true to their unique nature and style. Openness with patients is the ability to accept patients as they are, rather than how nurses may want them to be.

Consider the following story:

> Sylvia is an experienced registered nurse who prides herself on her ability to care for seriously injured and impaired victims of brain damage. Peter had become one of those patients whom all the nurses on Sylvia's ward had come to dislike. He was labelled as uncooperative and difficult. Because some

alleged his injuries had been self-inflicted he engendered little sympathy from the nursing staff. They did not like caring for Peter and often complained bitterly to each other about their negative feelings toward him.

One day during change-of-shift report, Sylvia began to listen to her colleagues' complaints and negative judgments about Peter. She had been thinking about how some patients are labelled as difficult because of a journal article that she read. She came to realise that Peter had fallen into this unfortunate category. To her colleagues' relief and surprise she asked to be assigned to care for Peter. Little did they realise that Sylvia was challenging herself to try and understand Peter as a person rather than a label.

That day when she entered his room she noticed, for the first time, the frightened and uncomfortable look on this young man's face. His primary manner of communication was through blinking his eyes as he had sustained an unstable neck injury. His hands were restrained because he was in the habit of pulling at tubes and equipment. Sylvia stood there for a moment, noticing and absorbing his situation.

Without even thinking she suddenly realised the cool temperature of the room and noticed that Peter had nothing more than a light sheet draped over his naked body. She looked at him and said 'I bet you are cold'. His eyes blinked furiously in the affirmative. She immediately went to get him a warm blanket. The look of relief on his face was incredible. Throughout the entire time no one had noticed that Peter was cold. They did not notice because they had failed to perceive him as a person.

Sylvia no longer could say 'no' to the 'personhood' of Peter by thinking of him as a label. She began to question the dynamics that had led the nursing staff to label Peter and dismiss him as troublesome and difficult. Through reflection Sylvia had become more self-aware. Her awareness allowed her to put aside the labels used about Peter and to attend to his comfort needs.

This story highlights the importance of self-awareness: through active reflection and open acknowledgment Sylvia was able to take corrective action. Sometimes nurses try to deny the existence of negative patient labels, claiming that such evaluations are unprofessional and therefore unacceptable. They do so in the erroneous belief that nurses, by virtue of being professional people, can rise above their natural human tendency to judge, or that at least nurses can put such judgments aside so that they do not interfere with their nursing care. Such denial is unfortunate because it diminishes self-awareness. Furthermore, there is empirical evidence that nurses' judgments about patients can and do influence patient care.

A recent study by Olsen (1997) found that nurses' sense of caring and concern for patients was influenced by whether they thought the patient was responsible for the clinical situation. Nurses expressed less concern and sense of caring toward hypothetical patients who were seen to be responsible for their illness. Nevertheless, participants in the study did indicate they would make an effort to mitigate patient responsibility as a means of establishing a connection with the patient. In another study investigating actual behaviour of nurses and patients in their care Carveth (1995) found nurses to be less supportive of patients who were labelled 'difficult', although the amount of time nurses actually spent with difficult patients was equal to the time spent with patients considered to be 'ideal'. Like the nurses in Olsen's 1997 study, nurses in Carveth's 1995 study tried to mitigate patient behaviour through the use of persuasion or coercion to change behaviour seen by the nurses as deviant.

The results of these two studies echo earlier studies that demonstrate how nurses' attitudes and interpersonal behaviour toward patients are affected by judgments made about patients. The judgments were based on patient characteristics such as: the nature of the patient's disease, similarity of patient's and nurse's values, social skills, ability to communicate and gratitude for care (Grief & Elliott, 1994; Forrest, 1989; Baer & Lowery, 1987; Drew, 1986; Armstrong-Esther & Browne, 1986; Sayler & Stuart, 1985; Kelly & May, 1982). Similarly, Johnson and Webb (1995a) found that nurses do judge the social worth of patients and that such judgments do have moral consequences. Nevertheless, their findings from a field study of nursing indicate that social evaluations of patients are not simply tied to personal characteristics of patients and their individual circumstances (for example, bearing responsibility for their illness). Referring to the process as 'social judgement' Johnson and Webb (1995a, 1995b) describe a complex and dynamic system whereby evaluations of patients' social worth is negotiated and renegotiated throughout their interactions with nurses. That is, nurses' evaluations of patients can and do change over time.

The evidence suggests that it is more useful to encourage nurses to actively reflect on their evaluative perceptions of patients rather than deny or ignore that their judgments can and do affect patient care. Once negative evaluations are brought in to conscious awareness, nurses can explore their meaning, and, like Sylvia in the story, take corrective action if necessary. Reflection won't prevent negative evaluations, but it will assist nurses in challenging or altering them.

The more nurses know about themselves, the more it is likely that they will come to accept themselves. The more nurses understand about themselves, the easier it becomes for them to understand patients. The more tolerant nurses are of themselves, the more tolerant they can be of patients. The more comfortable nurses are with themselves, the more comfortable they can be with patients. It is through coming to accept and understand their own perspective that nurses can come to accept and understand patients' perspectives. As nurses come to know their own experiences as human beings they are better able to relate to the person who is the patient.

Self-awareness helps nurses to build a healthy self-concept, both as people and nurses. Self-awareness can lead to comfort with the self, and genuine liking of the self. This is no easy task to achieve. It often takes a long time and a person's relationship with themselves is dynamic, not static.

Liking oneself is not the same as thinking one is all-good, without faults or failings. Liking oneself is about knowing one's strengths and areas for improvement, putting these together and concluding that what exists is acceptable. When nurses know, understand and like themselves, they are less likely to hide behind their professional role, and more likely to make contact with patients on a genuinely human level.

The relationship between self-awareness and professional growth

Nurses need to be able to evaluate how effectively they are relating to patients and self-awareness is essential in this assessment. Evaluation of performance in the use of the skills presented in the following chapters is best achieved through the process of self-assessment. In assessing their performance, nurses begin with an awareness of how they are interacting with patients. Through consideration of their *intentions, actions, responses* and *reactions*, nurses are able to evaluate their own performance in the interest of learning how to be more effective. Self-awareness is not simply a matter of perceiving the self as is; it is also a process of encouraging self-growth to become more effective in relating to patients. It would be irresponsible for nurses simply to accept themselves and not challenge themselves to change and grow through their nursing experiences. Through challenge comes change, and nurses willing to challenge themselves are open to personal and professional growth.

Use of self

When relating to patients, nurses are effective when they bring as much of themselves as possible into the relationship. In doing so, they are deliberately using themselves for the benefit of patients. This is the conscious use of self as a therapeutic agent, meaning that the principal tool used is the self. This requires that the tool be in good working order.

When nurses use themselves for the benefit of patients they have a sense of agency, they have influence and control. In developing this sense of agency nurses need to become aware of what they have to offer patients, for example, they need to know their personal strengths and their personal areas for improvement. Self-awareness enables nurses to view themselves as human beings, with failures, faults, successes and strengths, as people who have something to offer patients.

ACTIVITY 3.1   ➡ **316**

WHAT DO I HAVE TO OFFER TO PATIENTS ?

 Process

1. Divide a blank piece of paper into two columns. In the first column record a description of those aspects of yourself that you think are positive, ones you like about yourself. In the second column describe those aspects of yourself that you would prefer to change, ones you do not always like about yourself. You do not need to share this list with anybody else—be as honest as possible with yourself.

2. From your list of positive aspects, in the first column of your paper, reflect on how you could put these aspects to use in caring for and relating to patients.

3. From your list of negative aspects, in the second column of your paper, reflect on how these may affect your relationships with patients, for better or for worse.

4. Write a brief summary of how you could use your personal self in developing your professional self.

Discussion

1. Which was easier: describing positive aspects of yourself or negative ones?

2. Which column contains more information?

3. Frequently, when completing activities such as this, it is difficult to separate the 'you' that you want to be (ideal self), from the 'you' that exists (real self). How true was this for you in completing the activity?

Self-awareness versus self-consciousness

Completing activity 3.1 often engenders feelings of self-consciousness and discomfort in people. This is because focusing on the self, especially the positive aspects, is usually a private affair, and 'seeing yourself on paper', even when it is not shared with anyone else, brings the private into the open, which often creates a sense of self-exposure and anxiety.

In bringing the self into awareness, even through an activity such as this, there is a danger of becoming preoccupied with self and uncomfortably self-conscious. Self-awareness is not the same as self-consciousness. There needs to be a balance between the self-consciousness that is experienced through focusing too much on self, and the lack of self-awareness that leads to alienation from the self. Achieving this balance is important for nurses because the risks of focusing too much on themselves are as great as the dangers of failing to take themselves into account at all.

Egan (1994) refers to the need to be 'productively self-conscious' when engaged in helping relationships. Productive self-consciousness has positive effects because it is the ability to be absorbed in an interaction, while simultaneously being aware of internal reactions and perceptions. It is the ability to raise self-awareness to a level that enhances reflection on the self, while not becoming so preoccupied with the self that there is a lack of ability to focus on the person being helped.

REFLECTION AND REFLECTIVE PRACTICE

Reflection is an active exploration of personal experiences, consciously employed for the purpose of making sense of those experiences. Some people naturally engage in reflective processes, thinking deeply on life and their experiences of it. Other people may need guidance and assistance to be reflective. Professional nurses often are encouraged to engage in reflection because nursing knowledge is embedded in practical experience.

A spirit of inquiry sparks reflective nurses to think about their actions as they are engaged in clinical practice. In this sense reflection is a way of functioning; it involves a here-and-now pursuit to make sense of the everyday world of nursing practice as it is unfolds. This is reflection that 'looks on'. Reflection also involves thinking about experiences after they have occurred; this involves a there-and-then thinking process in order to use experience for the purpose of learning. This is reflection that 'looks back'. Reflection is also important prior to experience (Greenwood, 1993) as nurses consider their intentions and plans for patient care. This is reflection that 'looks forward'.

Regardless of whether it occurs before, during or after clinical practice, reflection is a process for understanding and appreciating experiences (Clarke et al., 1996). This is especially true when experiences are novel and/or formidable. More importantly, reflection is a way of challenging and changing perspectives (Atkins & Murphy, 1993), the purpose of which is to improve practice. Such improvements are aided and enhanced by linking reflections to theory. In this sense reflective processes accompany learning, encouraging nurses to develop theoretical understandings that will serve as guides for future action.

Nurses can reflect on various aspects of practice: the technical (for example, treatment regimes), the practical (for example, routines in care), the social and political (for example, how health-care resources are expended) and the personal (for example, knowledge of the self) (Clarke et al., 1996). 'The focus of reflection is *the self* within the context of the specific practice situation' (Johns, 1999: 242). In this respect the processes of reflection are closely related to increasing self-awareness. Nevertheless, a certain amount of self-awareness is required for reflection to occur in the first place (Atkins & Murphy, 1993).

Processes for reflection

Effective reflection requires active strategies to support the process (Wilkinson, 1999; Johns, 1995). This means that most successful reflection is accompanied by structured activities such as keeping a professional diary or completing the activities in this book. Unless there is some means of tracking an individual nurse's reflections over a period of time, sustainable professional growth through reflection may be difficult to ascertain.

In a recent study with first-year nursing students, Davies (1995) reports how students' changed their views of their clinical nursing experience over the course of the year. Tracking these changes was possible through the use of reflective processes. What is most interesting from this study is that the client emerged as the central focus of care for students, shifting from their initial focus on themselves.

With increasing frequency clinical supervision is considered by many as an ideal method to encourage and support reflective practice (Kim, 1999; Fowler, 1998). Clinical supervision, whether conducted individually or in groups of nurses, is aimed at using reflective processes for the purpose of improving the quality of nursing care. It has been shown to be useful in the development of interpersonal skills (Tichen & Binnie, 1995) and in increasing self-awareness (Begat et al., 1997).

Pitfalls in reflection

Despite its obvious benefits, reflection does have its potential pitfalls. It is important to remember that effective reflection will inevitably lead to anxiety (Haddock & Bassett, 1997) because the process of reflecting involves change and challenge. It requires nurses to show a willingness to be challenged to view experiences in different lights and to reconsider what may be long-held and cherished beliefs. The anxiety and discomfort that accompanies effective reflection points to the need for support systems to be in place, for example, colleagues who serve as skilled facilitators and mentors (Foster & Greenwood, 1998; Carr, 1996).

Another pitfall relates to the difficulty of reflecting after an event has taken place. This difficulty is called 'hindsight bias' (Jones, 1995), a term that describes the way that people recall events that fit with the known outcome. For example, if a nurse were to interact with a patient who seemed distressed about a forthcoming procedure, only to discover that the distress involved another life event, then it would be difficult in retrospect for the nurse to recall that she initially associated the patient distress with the procedure. Her recall of events would match what she now understands, not what she originally thought.

Taylor (1997) cautions nurses in the wholehearted embrace of reflection as a way of changing practice through empowerment and emancipation of nurses. The structural arrangements that are required for such emancipation may not be easy to attain, and reflection alone does not guarantee success in making such structural changes. In fact, reflective practices may result in nurses feeling less empowered by systems of health-care delivery. Incorporating reflection on the sociopolitical structures in which nursing care is embedded may help to offset this potential pitfall. Greenwood (1998) refers to this as 'double loop learning', which results in the construction of more socially desirable realities for nursing practice.

A final pitfall in the use of reflection is perhaps the most challenging of all in relation to beginning practitioners and students of nursing. It is that a nurse may need to be clinically experienced in order to benefit from reflection (Fowler, 1998). This implies that the nurses who most need to learn in terms of clinical experience may be least able to benefit from the process of reflection. Nevertheless, structured reflection, especially under the guidance of a more experienced nurse, is a useful way for beginning nurses to assess their own interpersonal skills and to improve self-awareness.

PROCESSES IN DEVELOPING SELF-AWARENESS

It is unlikely that nurses, or anyone else for that matter, will ever fully know and appreciate all facets of themselves. Nevertheless, nurses can develop their capabilities to engage in self-reflection, to perceive and accept input from others, and to openly disclose themselves to others to increase their self-awareness.

Introspection

When considering how to increase self-awareness, the process of introspection, or self-reflection, often comes to mind. This often begins with noticing what elicits a personal response. 'Why did I react negatively when that patient told me he wanted to die? Why did I want to leave the room? Was it that I felt helpless, or unsure about how to respond? Do I believe that self-destructive thoughts are unacceptable? Have *I* ever felt this way before? Why did I find it so hard to listen to what he was saying?' Often when something or somebody spurs a response, the tendency is to look to that person or thing rather than to reflect on the self. Noticing and reflecting on thoughts about oneself involves introspection, one of the principal ways that self-awareness develops.

Paying attention to such thoughts and feelings, (that is, allowing them to enter into, rather than forcing them out of, awareness) encourages nurses to discover more about themselves. Introspection, listening to oneself, means trusting oneself, being honest with oneself, accepting oneself and sometimes challenging oneself. Nevertheless, introspection is only effective in increasing self-awareness when personal thoughts and feelings are used for the purpose of discovering more about oneself.

ACTIVITY 3.2

PERSONAL REACTIONS TO OTHER PEOPLE

 Process

1. Recall a time when you reacted strongly to another person, either negatively or positively. On a separate piece of paper, record the circumstances and your reactions.

2. Reflect on why you think you reacted this way, and record this, by completing the following sentence: 'I think I reacted this way because I...'

Discussion

1. How did your reactions affect the way you related to this person?

2. What do you think and feel about the way you reacted?

3. What did you learn about yourself?

This activity may have uncovered emotional reactions to patients because feelings are bound to be a part of nurses' responses to patients. Personal emotions are aspects of self-awareness that may pose dilemmas for nurses because they are often taught, implicitly or explicitly, to keep their emotions under control. Nurses who allow emotions *to reach conscious awareness and focus on them* run the risk of losing control. Emotions that are allowed to surface may go rampant.

Many nurses interpret the need to maintain control over their emotions to mean that they should be void of emotions. While a lack of emotional display in some situations assists nurses in managing such situations, a total lack of emotions prevents nurses from establishing interpersonal contact with patients (Lawler, 1991).

Rather than deny their emotional responses, it is better for nurses to be aware of and reflect on such reactions. Without awareness, it is likely that these emotions will be expressed inadvertently to patients. Nurses who keep in tune with their emotional responses have a greater chance of maintaining true control than those who try to control emotions by ignoring them.

More importantly, nurses' feelings and reactions to patients serve a purpose—they provide useful information in measuring how the relationship with a patient is progressing. For example, anger and frustration toward a patient, when left unexamined, may lead to labelling that patient. It could be that the feelings of anger and frustration are a result of the nurse's inability to understand what the patient is experiencing. Perhaps the patient is not conforming to the nurse's expectations of a 'good patient'. A host of other possibilities exist. Self-reflection enables nurses to discover what their emotional reactions might be revealing about *their* relationships with patients. Personal thoughts and feelings triggered through interaction with patients are useful sources of information about oneself.

Input from others/interactive reflection

There are limits to how far self-awareness can progress and develop through the use of introspection alone. Natural 'blind spots', the ease with which self-reflective thoughts can be ignored, dismissed and defended, along with the tendency to protect the self through self-deception pose barriers in the use of the introspective process.

Other people provide useful information through the way they react and respond. For this reason, another effective way to complement, not replace, self-reflection occurs when nurses attend to feedback from others, be it solicited or unsolicited. Feedback from good friends is useful and can be solicited. Feedback from patients is another useful source of information, although nurses usually do not solicit it.

Input from patients

Patients are not only expressing information about themselves when they interact with nurses, they also are expressing information about how they perceive the nurse. Patients reveal how they feel and what they think about the nurses who are interacting with them by the manner in which they behave. What they choose to discuss, how freely they disclose information and how comfortable they seem during an interaction are examples of input that patients provide about how they see the nurse. The cues that indicate the effect nurses are having on them automatically surface throughout interactions. Nurses need to be receptive to such input from patients because this feedback informs them about themselves. In this regard, nurses need not actively solicit patient feedback.

Perceiving such input from patients begins with an awareness and understanding of its relevance. Next, nurses need to be open to receiving the information. Asking themselves questions such as 'What is it about me that enables patients to openly express their feelings?', 'Why is this patient telling *me* this?' and 'Have *I* inadvertently communicated that I do not wish to hear what this patient is saying?' enables nurses to become open to input from patients.

ACTIVITY 3.3

PERCEIVING FEEDBACK FROM PATIENTS

Process

1. Reflect on a recent interaction with a patient. Record what happened between you and the patient.

2. Describe how this patient responded to you.

3. Through reflection about how this patient responded, try to determine what this patient was 'telling' you, about how they perceived you.

4. Discuss the situation and your experience with another participant.

Discussion

1. What are the various ways that participants interpreted how patients responded to them? What cues indicated these responses?

2. At the time of the interaction with the patient, how aware were participants that patients were actually revealing how they perceived the nurse?

3. How many participants described negative/ineffective interactions? How many described positive/effective ones? What does this say?

It is natural for nurses to ignore or reject input and feedback about themselves when this information lacks congruence with personal images (what nurses believe they are or want to be). Nurses who are feeling inept may not notice when patients reveal that they *are* quite effective. For this reason, feedback and input from others, especially patients, may challenge nurses to reconsider their current perspectives.

Self-sharing

Another process that is effective in increasing self-awareness arises out of a combination of self-reflection (introspection) and interactive reflection (input and feedback from others). It is the process of self-sharing—the disclosure of personal thoughts, feelings, perceptions and interpretations by openly expressing them to others.

How self-sharing increases self-awareness

Self-sharing enhances self-awareness because it triggers (and therefore solicits) feedback from others, and also because it intensifies self-reflection. When internal thoughts, feelings and attitudes are made external through open discussion, they are often internally clarified, expanded and accepted. Sometimes self-sharing internally persuades nurses to challenge and alter their thoughts, feelings and attitudes. In this sense, self-sharing often transforms into a process of 'thinking aloud', and then having a dialogue with the self while using the other person as a sounding board.

At other times self-sharing enables nurses to test the validity of their current thoughts, feelings and attitudes. In 'testing' their internal responses nurses are asking others what they think or feel about these responses. This often leads nurses to reconsider their responses in light of what others think and feel.

The relationship between self-sharing and self-awareness is a circular one (see figure 3.1). While a certain degree of self-awareness is helpful to begin self-sharing, it is not vital. Through self-sharing, further input is received,

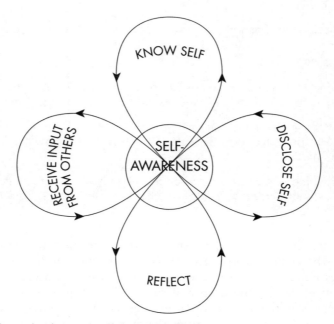

Figure 3.1 Relationship between self-sharing and self-awareness.

both from others and from the self, which is then useful in increasing self-awareness.

Risks of self-sharing

Despite its potential value for increasing self-awareness, disclosing oneself to others is not always easy to do. There are many reasons for keeping oneself to oneself, choosing not to disclose. The following activity is designed to uncover some of the reasons why self-sharing may be difficult.

ACTIVITY 3.4

DIFFICULTIES IN SELF-SHARING

 Process

1. Working on your own, rank each of the following topics from 1–12, according to what is easiest for you to disclose about yourself (1) to what is hardest to disclose (12). Place these topics in the context of interacting with someone you do not know very well.

    a. Talking about my fears

    b. Sharing my hopes and dreams

    c. Discussing my family life

    d. Describing my previous health problems

    e. Stating what I dislike about other people

    f. Complaining about a mark on an assignment

    g. Expressing my political views

    h. Stating what I want or need

    i. Expressing confusion or uncertainty

    j. Describing how I like to be treated by others

    k. Complaining about being treated unfairly

    l. Telling others that I am not pleased about something they have done.

2. Review your answers to step 1 and reflect on those items that you determined as easy to discuss (those ranked 1–5). Record your reasons for evaluating these items as easy to disclose.

3. Review your answers to step 1 and reflect on those items you determined as difficult to disclose (those ranked 8–12). Record your reasons for evaluating these items as difficult to disclose.

4. Compare your responses with two other participants. Discuss your responses to steps 2 and 3. Summarise what is easy to disclose and what is hard to disclose, focusing on your reasons why this is so.

5. This step lists some of the reasons for lack of self-disclosure. Working individually, rate each of these reasons in terms of how often it is true for you. Use the following descriptions:

   - Often
   - Sometimes
   - Rarely

   If I tell others what I think and feel ...

   a. I may hurt them.

   b. They may take advantage of me.

   c. I may appear weak.

   d. I may become emotional.

   e. They may hurt me.

   f. They may talk to others about me.

   g. I may discover something about myself that I'd rather not know.

   h. They may use what I've said against me.

   i. I may discover problems I never knew I had.

6. Working in the same groups of three as for step 4, discuss those items that you rated as 'Often' and 'Sometimes'. What similarities are there in your responses? What differences are there?

Discussion

1. What are the major reasons for reluctance to self-disclose?

2. What are the major disadvantages in self-disclosure? What are the major advantages?

3. How does self-disclosure promote self-awareness?

The major difficulty in disclosing self is the exposure that it brings. Once people are exposed, they often feel vulnerable, especially if the disclosure has been about problem areas or negative thoughts, feelings and perceptions. There are risks of being rejected, being hurt and being challenged by others. This sense of vulnerability is not necessarily destructive to nurses because of its potential to increase feelings of empathy with patients, who often feel exposed and vulnerable when they disclose themselves to nurses. While there are obvious risks in exposing self, these are offset by its potential benefits.

The climate conducive to self-sharing

Because of the exposure and vulnerability that self-sharing can bring, it needs to take place in an atmosphere of trust and respect—trust in the sense that the disclosure will not be met with rejection and respect in the sense that disclosed information will be regarded, not dismissed or ridiculed.

As a general rule, there is ease and comfort with disclosure when it is likely that personal thoughts, feelings and attitudes will be understood and appreciated by the other person. This is more likely to happen when the other person shares similar experiences. For this reason, nurses often benefit by disclosing themselves to other nurses (see chapter 11). Through the process of self-sharing, nurses can be supported by other nurses. They also may be challenged at times to reconsider their perceptions, thoughts and feelings.

Self-disclosure with patients

Self-disclosure with patients (see chapters 5, 6 and 7) is different from self-sharing. Self-disclosure with patients is employed as a therapeutic skill, and is therefore for the benefit of the patient, not the nurse. Although self-disclosure with patients may result in increased self-awareness for the nurse, this is not its primary focus. The intent of self-disclosing with patients is to promote interaction and increase interpersonal involvement with patients. The primary intent of self-sharing with people other than patients is increased self-awareness in the nurse.

AREAS OF SELF-EXPLORATION

It is important that nurses not only understand the processes for promoting greater self-awareness but also that they recognise those areas of themselves that are most relevant to the nursing-care context. There are many facets of each nurse's personal self that are woven together to create the essence of the person who is the nurse. While many aspects of the self can be considered, those addressed in activity 3.5 have a potential to affect the way that nurses approach helping patients.

Personal philosophy about health

Personal value systems, the 'shoulds' and 'ought tos' that direct individual behaviour, are part of all people's lives. These values and beliefs, which are personal and unique to the individual, assist a person in making choices and decisions about living. They provide direction about what is important, what matters, what is seen as significant and what is worthwhile. These values and beliefs are not static; they are altered, revised and adapted through life experiences. Nurses often find that their beliefs and values alter throughout their professional lives.

One aspect of personal value systems that is of particular relevance for nurses is their beliefs about health and helping. For example, nurses may feel less inclined to care for patients that they believe are responsible for their health problems (Olsen, 1997).

ACTIVITY 3.5 316

BELIEFS ABOUT HELPING IN NURSING PRACTICE

 Process

1. For each of the following statements, record on a separate sheet of paper the response that most closely identifies your personal beliefs and attitudes. Use the following scale:

    3   Basically, I *agree* with this statement
    2   I am *undecided* in my opinion about this statement
    1   For the most part, I *disagree* with this statement

    a. Patients should be encouraged to accept that they have contributed to their own health problems.

    b. What happens in nurse–patient relationships is more the nurse's responsibility than the patient's.

    c. People are masters of their own destinies; solutions to whatever problems they have are in their own hands.

    d. There are many social factors contributing to health problems that are beyond individual control.

    e. Whether they realise it or not, people engage in behaviours that cause health problems.

    f. Effective health education could prevent major health problems.

    g. Patients should be encouraged to find solutions and take action on their own behalf when dealing with health problems.

    h. It irritates me when I hear somebody say that patients caused their own health problems; most of the time people can't help it.

    i. Providing advice to patients is an essential aspect of effective health-care.

    j. In my view of human nature, people are responsible for creating their problems.

    k. People should be presented with options for health-care so that they can choose what suits them best.

l.   In recovering from an illness, it is essential that patients heed the advice of health-care professionals.

m.   Patients' health problems are most often of their own making.

n.   Most people could change their problematic health habits if they really wanted to.

o.   Patients cannot be held responsible for causing their own health problems.

p.   Patients should determine their own goals when working with health-care professionals.

q.   Most health problems are the result of the personal choices people make in conducting their lives.

r.   I don't have much time for patients who won't follow the advice of knowledgeable health-care experts.

s.   Diseases and illnesses are largely a result of biological and genetic factors, which are usually beyond individual control.

t.   Patients should place themselves in the hands of qualified health professionals who know best what to do about health problems.

Discussion

1.   Reflect on your responses and consider whether you tend to hold people responsible for their health problems.

2.   Consider your responses in light of whether you tend to think that people should take responsibility for their own health-care.

3.   In general, what do your responses reflect about your beliefs about health and health-care?

Activity 3.5 is designed to make participants think about how they would approach helping other people on the basis of two central issues: *blame* and *control* (Brickman et al., 1982). Blame is the degree to which people are held responsible for causing their problems and control is the degree to which they are held responsible for solutions to their problems. Both involve questions of personal responsibility, and assumptions about personal responsibility have direct effects on the type of help offered.

Brickman et al. (1982) developed four models of helping based on the issues of blame and control (see figure 3.2). The view from within the Medical model is that people are neither responsible for creating their problems, nor are they responsible for solutions to their problems. The Compensatory model operates from beliefs that people cannot be blamed for their problems, but are held responsible for doing something about them. Beliefs within the Enlightenment model are that people are responsible for

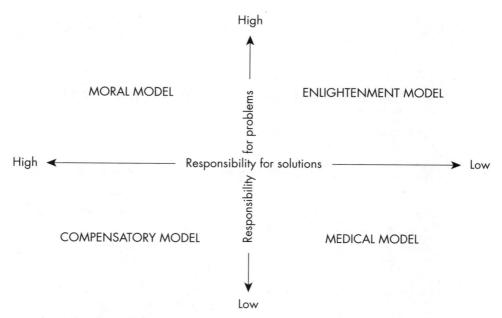

Figure 3.2 Models of helping (based on Brickman et al., 1982).

creating their problems, but need to rely on others in solving these problems. The Moral model holds people responsible for both creating their problems and developing their own solutions.

Each stance results in an orientation to how to be of help to patients. The Medical model relies on expert advice and treats patients as passive recipients of assistance. Patients are expected to seek and heed such advice and assistance. While people are not blamed for their problems, they may be blamed if they fail to cooperate with the solutions offered. Helping in the Compensatory model centres on the mobilisation of needed resources, providing opportunities to compensate for what are seen as failures and weaknesses that are outside individual control. Acceptance of personal blame and a reliance on an external authority is the helping approach used in the Enlightenment model. The Moral model focuses helping on motivating people to change through persuasion, appeal, reprimand and reproach (Brickman et al., 1982; Cronenwett, 1983; Corey et al., 1988).

In nursing practice there is likely to be a mixed application of these models, as illustrated in the following examples. Nurses might hold active smokers responsible for problems such as lung cancer, while lung cancer acquired from passive smoking usually does not bring such blame. In both of these situations people would not be held responsible for the possible solutions/treatment for the lung cancer. Nursing care would be provided to the active smokers (Enlightenment model), although some nurses may question the use of health-care resources on this population (Moral model). The victims of passive smoking might be approached using the Medical model, in which case they would not be held responsible for the cause or the solutions. A person with diabetes mellitus may not be held responsible for acquiring the disease, but will be expected to be actively involved in its control (Compensatory model). An actively suicidal person may be blamed for the problem and expected to find solutions, through effort and willpower (Moral model).

Help may not be effective if the person desiring help and the person offering help are operating from a different set of assumptions about personal responsibility (Brickman et al., 1982). For this reason, it is important that nurses not only realise their own orientation to helping and its underlying assumptions, but also that they are aware of and understand patients' orientations to helping.

Effects of personal values and beliefs

Nurses' personal values and beliefs directly affect their interactions with patients. They have the potential to restrict effective relationships with patients, however, they can also enhance these relationships.

One way that nurses' values and personal beliefs may hinder effective relationships with patients stems from the fact that these values and beliefs often function as perceptual filters. Perceptual filters allow some aspects of patients' stories to be accepted, while others are rejected. When values and personal beliefs function as filters, the skills of listening (see chapter 4) are most affected. Cultural stereotypes (see chapter 9), another possible hindrance in relating effectively with patients, often stem from values and personal beliefs.

Another way that personal values create interference occurs when nurses impose or project them onto patients, rather than keeping them in abeyance. When values and beliefs are imposed on patients, they are used as yardsticks for measuring patients. Whenever nurses make judgments about what patients 'should' or 'should not' be, there is a chance that they are evaluating patients in terms of their own value system. For this reason, nurses are encouraged to reflect on these types of judgments.

On the other hand, certain values and personal beliefs enhance and strengthen nurses' ability to relate to patients. For example, a personal belief that people are capable, worthwhile and dependable works in favour of establishing effective relationships with patients. Such beliefs help to create a climate of respect and regard for patients.

When relating to patients, nurses cannot be expected to abandon their values and personal beliefs, however they need to be able to distinguish their own philosophical stance from that of a patient. The more aware nurses are of their own values and personal beliefs, the less likely it is that interference will occur, and the more likely it is that the values that enhance effective relationships will be strengthened.

Expectations of nursing

Most nurses enter nursing with some goal in mind. It might be to secure a job with the promise of sustained demand. It could be that part-time work is appealing. An advertisement in the local newspaper might have sparked interest in nursing in a 'Why not, I'm not doing anything else with my life?' fashion. Assuming there were options available, nursing is usually chosen because of an interest in people. In all likelihood this interest in people is directly related to a desire to be of help to them.

ACTIVITY 3.6

EXPECTATIONS OF NURSING

 Process

1. Think of all the reasons why you chose nursing as a career. Record these on a sheet of paper. Do not place any identifying information about yourself on the paper.

2. Now complete the following sentences, recording your answers on the same sheet of paper.

    a. If I could do anything as a nurse it would be to ...

    b. In my role as a nurse I see myself as ...

    c. Nurses help others because they ...

    d. My greatest disappointment as a nurse would be if I ...

3. Collect all the sheets of paper and distribute them among all participants.

4. Record, on a sheet of paper visible to all participants, all the reasons identified by the participants for choosing nursing. If a reason is given by more than one participant, record how many times it is stated.

Discussion

1. Discuss the responses to each of the items in step 2 of the process. Remember, you are not discussing your own responses, but rather the ones of the anonymous participant who authored the paper you received.

2. Do motivations to nurse and expectations of nursing focus exclusively on helping others or are there references to personal gains and benefits?

This activity probably highlighted a common myth about nursing, the belief that all benefits in nursing are for the patient, never the nurse. By focusing solely on their desire to help and to assist others, nurses fail to acknowledge the potential benefits of nursing for themselves.

ACTIVITY 3.7

PERSONAL BENEFITS OF NURSING

 Process

1. On a sheet of paper that only you will see, answer the following questions:

    a. What does nursing do for you?

    b. What do you personally gain through nursing?

    c. What benefits are there for you in nursing?

    d. How does nursing satisfy you?

2. From your answers and personal reflection, list personal needs that are met through nursing.

Discussion

1. How difficult was it for you to answer these questions?

2. What feelings did you experience while completing the activity?

3. Why is it important for nurses to realise that there are personal gains in nursing?

Activity 3.7 challenges the notion that nurses nurse solely because they are meeting the needs of patients. The 'ideal' nurse is often perceived as self-sacrificing, and so 'other-oriented' that there is a denial of self. Such an ideal does not exist in reality.

Personal needs

Forming meaningful relationships with patients and assisting them with health issues and problems often has benefits for nurses as well as patients. For example, nurses derive satisfaction in seeing patients recover from illnesses, especially when they know that they made a difference to the recovery. Does this mean that nurses meet their own needs through their nursing relationships? A recognition and acknowledgment of the personal benefits of nursing results in an affirmative answer to such a question. Nevertheless, there are obvious risks involved because nurses' personal needs may interfere whenever relationships with patients are used as the *primary* source of meeting these needs. For example, relying on patients to satisfy the nurse's need for personal recognition, appreciation and validation is fraught with danger. For this reason, nurses need to develop awareness of potential trouble spots, those personal needs that may interfere in their relationships with patients.

ACTIVITY 3.8

PERSONAL NEEDS THAT MAY INTERFERE

Process

1. Use one of the following descriptions to rate questions a–j:

   ▪ Hardly ever
   ▪ Sometimes
   ▪ Most of the time

   How often do I ...

   a. let people take advantage of me because I am afraid to say no to their requests?

   b. focus on problems and negative aspects of a situation, so I fail to take into account the positive side of people and their strengths?

   c. feel as if I must 'do something' to make other people feel better, to rescue them?

   d. think I need to have all the answers when other people discuss problems with me?

   e. worry about whether or not other people like me?

   f. feel the need to be needed?

   g. need to be in control of situations?

   h. want other people to take care of me?

   i. feel controlled by other people?

   j. act as openly with other people as I want them to be with me?

2. Review your answers. If the majority of your answers are 'Sometimes', go back and change them to either 'Hardly ever' or 'Most of the time'. All of the items will be true for most people *some* of the time!

3. Identify the items that are 'Hardly ever' and 'Most of the time'. Reflect on these in terms of how these aspects of yourself may affect your relationships with patients.

Discussion

1. The items included in this self-assessment relate to three general areas of basic human needs: the need to feel attached to other people (included); the need to be in control; and the need for

affection and affirmation from other people. Which one of these general areas of personal needs is predominant for you?

2.   Discuss each of the three basic human needs and how, if they are predominant in a nurse, interactions and relationships with patients may be affected, for better or worse.

PERSONAL QUALITIES AND TRAITS

The focus of the preceding sections of this chapter has been on increasing self-awareness because self-awareness leads to self-understanding, self-challenge and eventual acceptance of aspects that characterise each nurse. Other than considering how these aspects of the self potentially affect relationships with patients, no effort has been made to evaluate them (or the nurse they characterise) in terms of right/wrong, good/bad or desirable/undesirable. No evaluation has been attempted because nurses must first develop awareness of 'what is' before considering 'what should be'. Understanding 'what is' provides a starting point, a reference from which to work toward 'what should be'.

There are certain characteristics, personal beliefs, values and orientations toward helping that enhance nurses' abilities to relate effectively to patients. In this regard, they are the 'what should bes'. When they are present in the nurse these characteristics help to facilitate interpersonal connections with patients because they help to create the necessary interpersonal climate for the development of patient–nurse relationships. The presence of this climate enables nurses to effectively use the skills and processes described in this book. If the facilitative climate is absent, the use of the skills may become hollow, mechanical and artificial.

ACTIVITY 3.9

CHARACTERISTICS OF EFFECTIVE HELPERS

 Process

1.   Think of someone in your life that you think is a helpful person to you, the person you go to for understanding, assistance and guidance.

2.   Think about what this person is like. What personal characteristics do they possess? Focus on specific characteristics that are helpful to you. Describe these on a sheet of paper.

3.   Now think about what this person does that you find helpful. What specific things does this person do? Describe these on your sheet of paper. Do not be concerned if there are similarities between answers to steps 2 and 3. In some instances they may be exactly the same.

4. Review what you have written. Briefly summarise what, in your opinion, enables this person to be effective in helping you.

5. Compare your descriptions with all other participants by compiling an overall description of a person who is helpful. Record this in a place visible to all participants.

6. Select key words from the description and record them.

Discussion

1. What are the similarities in participants' individual descriptions? What are the differences?

2. Focusing on the key words identified in step 6 of the process, describe personal characteristics that are essential in being a helpful person.

3. Is there anything you would add to this list of personal characteristics?

From activity 3.9 you may have discovered that people perceived to be helpful embody certain characteristics (what they are), demonstrate certain skills (what they do) and possess a degree of understanding about people (what they know). It is the personal characteristics associated with helpful people that are discussed here.

Characteristics that enhance the ability to be helpful include:

- Authenticity and congruence
- Respect and warmth
- Confidence and assertiveness

Self-awareness enables these characteristics to be fully realised and developed by nurses.

Authenticity and congruence

To be authentic means that nurses behave in ways that are reflective of their true selves. Authenticity means not hiding behind the role of nurse, but rather enacting the role in a manner that expresses the uniqueness of each nurse.

Frequently, when nurses try to use the skills described in this book, feelings of awkwardness and lack of authenticity accompany their first attempts. This is especially true if the skill being tried is unfamiliar and foreign to the nurse's current repertoire of skills. While a skill may be unfamiliar, the personal values from which it emerges may not be. For example, a nurse may be unaccustomed to reflecting feelings (see chapter 5) because of being raised in an environment where feelings were hardly ever expressed and never discussed openly. Unless this nurse believes that patients' feelings are important to understand and comes to realise that, for some patients, feelings are the most significant facet of their experience, the nurse may fail to try to use feeling reflections with patients. This nurse must tap into their authentic desire to help patients in order to overcome feelings of reluctance and awkwardness. That is, a genuine desire to be of help spurs the nurse to express concern and regard for patients through the use of (the skill of) reflecting feelings.

Congruence is related to authenticity because with congruence comes consistency between what nurses believe, how they feel and what they do. The skills described in this book are only effective if they are used in conjunction with an attitude that matches their intent. There is little point in pretending to listen through appropriate attending behaviour (see chapter 4) if a nurse is not currently interested in what a patient is expressing. A listening posture without an attitude of genuine interest lacks congruence. Attempting to understand (see chapter 5) without an open attitude to the uniqueness of each patient's experience also lacks congruence. A congruent manner is one in which the nurse's intent and related action are in harmony with each other.

The nurse's self-awareness is the key to demonstrating both authenticity and congruence. Without awareness of who they are and how they are feeling at a given moment, and an examination of personal motives and intentions, nurses are at risk of losing touch with themselves. Authenticity and congruence cannot be demonstrated under such circumstances.

Respect and warmth

With respect comes a deep concern for patients' individual experiences, an acceptance of their perspective and feelings. Respect emerges from the value that each human being has inherent worth and dignity. Under conditions of respect, patients are more likely to feel free in expressing who they are and what they are experiencing. When they are respected, patients are free to be themselves; they need not fear that they will be placed against a standard of what they 'should' be experiencing.

Holding personal judgments in abeyance (see chapter 4) is one of the most striking ways nurses convey respect to patients. This highlights and reinforces the need for self-awareness. Unless nurses are cognisant of their personal values and beliefs, they may inadvertently judge patients against a personal value system.

Respect operates from an attitude of being 'for' patients. To be respectful is to assume the patient's goodwill (Egan, 1994), to believe that patients are doing their best to cope, to adapt, to change. Respect upholds an inherent belief in patients' capabilities and resources. An attitude that is suspicious of patients' motives and behaviours lacks respect if suspicion is the nurse's first reaction.

This is not to say that nurses cannot or should not challenge patients to transform their view of a situation (see chapter 7). Respect means not starting from the point of challenging, but rather developing an understanding of the situation (see chapter 5), then intervening to promote change if this is required.

Warmth is a feeling and is conveyed primarily through nonverbal behaviour that demonstrates an active interest in and regard for patients. It is designed to put patients at ease with nurses because, through the expression of warmth, nurses convey friendliness, approachability and interest. In this way warmth is an active demonstration of respect because it conveys active concern. Warmth is not emotionally effusive or overly friendly behaviour. It cannot be feigned through insincere over-concern for patients; it requires authenticity and congruence in order to be effective.

Too much warmth creates a sense of false solicitude, lacking genuineness. Patients might become frightened at the prospect of a nurse whose concern seems extreme, especially if this occurs early in the course of the relationship. Too little warmth distances patients because this gives an impression of lack of concern and regard. Judging the 'right' degree of warmth, especially in the beginning of a relationship with a patient, can only be achieved by paying careful attention to how the patient responds to the nurse's demonstration of concern through warmth.

Confidence and assertiveness

Even when nurses are congruent and authentic, and able to convey respect and warmth, unless they also have an ability to express themselves confidently and assertively they may not be able to make interpersonal contact with patients. Knowing what to say and how to say it becomes inconsequential if nurses fail to use interpersonal skills because they are apprehensive and hesitant. Being confident and assertive is as important as being skilled and aware. High-level awareness and excellent technical ability are meaningless unless they are actually used when called for (Egan, 1994). For example, nurses need to be assertive when they share perceptions and take the lead in exploring (see chapter 6), and challenge patients to reframe their perceptions (see chapter 7).

Assertiveness is most often presented as a means of resolving conflict, defending individual rights if they have been violated. However, conflict is not the specific focus here. In the general context of patient–nurse relationships, being assertive and confident means that nurses are able to take advantage of opportunities to make interpersonal contact with patients.

While nurses often recognise the need to be assertive when advocating *for* patients (for example, when another health professional is disregarding a patient's request), they often express concerns about being assertive *with* patients. Whenever nurses think 'I can't say *that* to a patient' they are experiencing concerns about what will happen. These concerns include a fear of upsetting patients, a discomfort with the expression of feelings, a perception that it is intrusive to ask personal questions and a reticence about delving into the subjective experiences of patients. Apprehensions such as these often inhibit nurses and may even restrict them from meeting their professional responsibilities to patients. For example, if a nurse is reluctant to explore a patient's apparent distress (out of fear of compounding that distress), vital information about the patient's experience may be missed or overlooked.

The concerns that inhibit nurses are often based on faulty assumptions such as 'patients will become *more* upset if asked to discuss their distress', 'nurses should be passive and obedient' and 'it is impolite to discuss sensitive and personal matters with a relative stranger'. In becoming assertive with patients nurses need to overcome these concerns by challenging these assumptions.

Firstly, nurses do not have the 'power' to 'make' patients more upset simply on the basis of bringing patients' distress into the open (although this is different from abuse of power, which is discussed in chapter 7). When patients are distressed they are often relieved to share their emotional pain with an interested and understanding nurse. Rather than compounding their tension, open discussion can actually provide comfort. Secondly, while it would be impolite to discuss highly personal matters with a stranger in a social situation, patient–nurse interactions are different from usual social interactions. In caring for patients nurses need to discuss personal matters with patients because this is part of their professional responsibility.

There is more to assertiveness than just being able to bring up sensitive and sometimes troubling subjects. At times being assertive translates into making the decision 'not' to discuss something. For example, when a patient is coping by maintaining their emotions within manageable limits a nurse can make an active decision *not* to explore or focus on feelings. Additionally, the discussion of feelings requires trust between patient and nurse (see chapter 5), and a nurse may choose to delay such discussion until trust is established. As long as the decision not to say something is based on an assessment of the situation, rather than the nurse's internal fear, assertiveness is present. Being assertive in relating to patients means that nurses have both the courage to say something and the wisdom to remain silent.

Personal style

Authenticity, congruence, respect, warmth and assertiveness are desirable characteristics that each nurse demonstrates in a unique manner. Although these characteristics help to create an interpersonal climate that enhances meaningful connections, they should not be construed as personality prescriptions for nurses. Each nurse develops personal capabilities for relating to patients.

There are skills useful in establishing these relationships that can be learnt and developed. There are certain conditions, such as respect and warmth, that enable nurses to use the skills most effectively. These conditions can be enhanced and developed. There are approaches to helping patients that can be employed, for example, challenging patients to reframe their experiences (see chapter 7). These approaches can be understood and developed.

Each nurse finds a way to use the skills, to express the necessary characteristics and to integrate a variety of approaches in a unique expression of that nurse's personality. Some nurses are good at challenging patients, and do so quite effectively and naturally, while other nurses find this approach difficult and are frustrated when they attempt to use it.

In developing a personal style, nurses must learn how to blend the skills and characteristics with their own personalities and to discover how their personal selves merge into their professional selves. A concerted effort to understand, practise and employ the skills results in this blending. Engaging in the processes of self-awareness accelerates the development of a personal style in relating to patients. Nevertheless, some unique challenges arise when nurses attempt to learn and develop the skills of interacting in a manner that is unique to them.

Developing a personal style of relating to patients poses certain learning challenges because beginning nurses have developed a characteristic style of communicating and relating to other people prior to entering nursing practice. Although these familiar patterns of interacting may be comfortable for the individual nurse as a person, they may not be suitable within the nursing context. In learning the skills and developing them for the nursing context, nurses are often challenged to alter or change their customary and usual patterns of interaction. In meeting this challenge a total transformation of a nurse's particular manner is not necessary because such transformation may not reflect the nurse's personality. Nevertheless, alterations to existing patterns of interacting are often necessary in order to develop a personal style that is both authentic to an individual nurse and appropriate to the context of nursing care. While the person who is the nurse has not changed, the nursing-care context signals the need for a change in approach.

LEARNING THE SKILLS

The following chapters contain descriptions of a range of skills that enable nurses to interact effectively with patients. While theoretical understanding of the skills is a vital aspect of learning, understanding not accompanied by technical know-how in the use of the skills is insufficient. For this reason, learning the skills of interacting with patients is achieved most effectively through the performance of the skills.

Each nurse is encouraged to attempt each of the skills, see how they fit the particular nursing context and determine what alterations can be made to help them fit better. Some of the skills will be familiar and using them will come naturally because they already exist in the nurse's repertoire. Other skills will be foreign and nurses may feel awkward and unnatural when initially attempting to use these skills. Selecting some of the skills because they are comfortable to use and ignoring others because 'they don't feel right' limits practical learning opportunities and potential.

The need to 'unlearn'

More than likely, the skills presented in the following chapters will be recognisable as everyday activities. For example listening (see chapter 4) is a process that people engage in daily, whether it be effective or ineffective. This familiarity with some skills, however, presents a specific dilemma to nurses as they approach learning how to fit skills into a nursing-care context as well as blending the skills with their personality.

Because nurses have been interacting with other people all of their lives they may believe that they already know how to talk to patients, and they may be disconcerted to find out there is more to learn. But these familiar patterns of interacting may not be effective within the nursing-care context. As a result, some nurses may fail to recognise and appreciate the alterations that may be needed to make their interactions with patients more effective.

Learning how to use interpersonal skills within the nursing-care context is often a matter of 'letting go' of habitual and automatic ways of interacting, ways that have become comfortable. For example, offering advice and giving solutions is a common response to someone who presents a problem. In chapter 5 this way of responding is shown to be less effective than a response that demonstrates understanding. If offering advice and giving solutions is their customary way of responding to those in need, nurses are challenged to refrain from their usual way of responding. The necessity of letting go of familiar patterns and 'unlearning' ways that may have become entrenched presents a major hurdle in learning and developing effective interactive skills with patients.

Departing from the comfortable zone of usual and customary patterns of interacting and attempting new and unfamiliar ways initially results in feelings of being untrue to oneself. Nurses may become confused by this apparent lack of authenticity, which has been discussed as a core condition for effective interactions. Nurses may feel inept, clumsy and overly self-conscious as they struggle to let go of the familiar and to meet the demands of learning new ways of interacting.

Such feelings are often unavoidable during initial attempts in using any new skill and this highlights the need for continuous self-awareness. Through self-awareness, nurses come to appreciate what they are attempting in their interactions with patients, why they are attempting this and how it is affecting patients. Nurses are encouraged to promote their own growth as people and as nurses, and to challenge growth within themselves by trying various ways of interacting with patients, even when these ways initially feel awkward. With continuing practice, self-awareness and patience with the learning process, the skills will eventually become natural. At this point a personal style emerges.

Reactions to learning the skills

Some nurses fail to perceive and appreciate the significance of learning interpersonal skills simply because they *have* been interacting with other people all their lives. These nurses view the skills of interacting with patients as little more than commonsense and 'doing what comes naturally'. Because the skills used when interacting with patients are not exclusive to nursing, these nurses fail to perceive the importance of spending time learning them or recognising how the nursing-care context necessitates an alteration in interaction patterns.

Such reactions fail to take into account the fact that commonsense is not inborn, but learned behaviour. Toddlers do not have the commonsense to recognise the dangers of running onto a street full of moving vehicles. While the commonsense that nurses have developed throughout their lives could assist them in learning the skills, there is also a danger that this commonsense approach may inhibit learning. For example, commonsense may dictate that patients should not be worried or alarmed by what the nurse perceives to be a minor situation. Under such circumstances, the commonsense approach may be to try and talk patients out of their 'needless' worrying through the use of platitudes and clichès. While such an approach seems to have a rational, objective basis, and it fails to acknowledge the reality of patients' experiences, and is therefore less effective than approaching patients by trying to understand their experiences.

In believing that interacting with patients is nothing more than commonsense, nurses may fail to develop the self-awareness necessary to recognise when their approach is not effective. They may fail to reconsider habitual and automatic responses and attitudes and to realise that the context indicates a need for a change in these usual approaches. In simply 'doing what comes naturally', nurses fail to learn how to develop skills specific to the nursing context.

At the opposite end of the spectrum are those nurses who accept the importance of learning how to interact with patients and immerse themselves in learning the skills. For these nurses, a different type of learning challenge may present itself. In attempting to learn the skills, these nurses may become reticent about saying anything to a patient out of fear of making a mistake and saying the wrong thing. If they do attempt to employ the skills, these nurses may have a stilted manner.

Most often this reaction is a result of a common misconception that talking to patients is somehow dramatically different from talking to people who are not patients. The nurses who become almost paralysed when trying to use the skills, or who use the skills in a stilted manner, often are stifled by a belief that 'being therapeutic' means being completely different from usual. The major consequence of this belief is that it retards development of a personal style.

The nurses who are resistant to learning new ways of interacting, because they believe that interacting with patients is nothing more than commonsense, assume that relationships with patients have no special features. The nurses who are reticent to interact with patients, out of fear of making a mistake, assume that relationships with patients are entirely different from other types of human interactions and that a common ground cannot be established. Both groups are misguided and are acting on false assumptions. The first response reflects a rejection of the professional self ('I'll just be myself'), while the second response fails to recognise the use of personal self ('I no longer *can* be myself').

While relationships with patients have characteristics that are different from social relationships such as friendship (see chapter 2), the person who is the nurse remains the same. Nurses must come to realise that their professional self emerges from their personal self (Leddy & Pepper, 1998); neither is a separate entity.

These reactions to learning the skills of interacting within the nursing context highlight the need for continuous self-appraisal and self-challenge.

By focusing their efforts on becoming more aware, nurses who react to learning the skills in the ways described in the preceding paragraphs are able to meet the challenges posed by these reactions. By reflecting on their responses, nurses not only become aware of their faulty perspectives (if any exist) on interactions with patients, but are challenged to review and revise these perspectives. The essential aim in developing such an awareness when interacting with patients is to be able to assess and evaluate how current perspectives and interpretations could be affecting the development of effective interpersonal skills.

SELF-ASSESSMENT OF INTERPERSONAL SKILLS

Active and ongoing self-assessment is an active strategy for reflection and is one of the most effective ways to increase interpersonal effectiveness as a nurse. Self-assessment draws on all of the processes for developing self-awareness that are described in this chapter. Nurses need to develop the ability to observe themselves as they participate in interactions with patients. This requires nurses to develop abilities to stand apart from themselves temporarily, and to tune their senses to recognise effective and ineffective interaction patterns. Observing feedback and input from patients, which indicates how patients are responding to the nurse's attempts to interact, adds to this self-evaluation. Discussion with other nurses about relationships with patients offers opportunities to be both reassured and challenged. Finally, the sharing of motives, intentions, thoughts and feelings, both with self and other nurses, offers further opportunities for growth in interpersonal effectiveness with patients.

Advantages of self-assessment

Self-assessment is a useful way to approach the development of skills for a variety of reasons. Firstly, focusing on assessing self, especially when initially attempting to use the skills, helps to release nurses from the fear of saying the wrong thing. Through the process of self-assessment, 'mistakes', when made, are viewed as indicators for further growth and development, rather than outright failures. Nurses who can recognise when they either miss the point or could be handling an interaction more effectively have an opportunity to recover and move the interaction back on track. When awareness is lacking errors and omissions go unrecognised, and future learning opportunities are missed.

Secondly, self-assessment has the advantage of using the nurse's firsthand experience in the interaction. Nurses who have participated in an interaction know best what happened. In this sense, 'being there' provides essential input. Nurses who 'were there' understand their own intentions during the interaction and can therefore evaluate an interaction in light of these intentions. In this regard, evaluation of performance is placed within the context of actual interactions, as opposed to employing rules that are context-free. This approach takes into account the specific factors relevant to a given interaction and places evaluation within the light of these factors.

Finally, and perhaps most importantly, developing the ability to assess self enables nurses to engage in continual learning. Through awareness and self-assessment, nurses come to understand their personal strengths and areas for improvement, and performance is evaluated in terms of these personal aspects. When every interaction is viewed as an opportunity for learning, nurses engage in continuous professional growth. In this respect, self-assessment, the evaluation of one's own performance, is considered an essential ability, even a skill in its own right.

Self-assessment is useful in evaluating interpersonal effectiveness after an interaction has occurred, and this is the most common way in which it is initially developed. When developed to its fullest, self-assessment also enables nurses to determine how best to approach a given situation *during* an interaction.

During interactions with patients, nurses have a range of skill options to employ, assuming their repertoire of skills is extensive. For example, the choice to encourage a patient through attending and listening (see chapter 4), through the use of exploration (see chapter 6) or through the use of empathy expression (see chapter 5) depends on nurses' ability to evaluate their own performance in the immediate situation and to track the progress of the relationship (see chapter 2). Through maintaining an orientation towards self-assessment, the choices that are made have a sounder basis than those made by using either a trial-and-error approach or a standard textbook description.

Approaches to self-assessment

Beginning and experienced nurses are encouraged to begin their self-evaluation with an assessment of how they are currently functioning with their interpersonal skills. Activity 3.10 is designed to increase awareness of current interaction patterns. It relies on the process of introspection, discussed earlier in this chapter, and is therefore an activity that should be completed in solitude.

ACTIVITY 3.10

ASSESSMENT OF CURRENT SKILLS

 Process

1.   Observe your interactions for approximately ten days. Focus on situations in which you are aware of how you are interacting. These situations should contain interactions during which you felt you were effectively interacting with the other persons, and those that you felt were not as effective. These should be situations that illustrate how you typically communicate and interact with other people. Some examples of the type of situations you may observe include:

- introducing yourself to a stranger
- needing to clarify something that you have not understood
- asking another person about themself
- speaking in a group
- asking someone for a favour
- wanting to say 'no' to a request
- giving or seeking information
- receiving negative feedback about yourself
- explaining why you did or said something
- disagreeing with someone
- seeking assistance from someone
- expressing concern for someone else
- wanting to help someone else
- demonstrating to someone that you care about them

2. Record these situations as soon as possible after they occur. Include a description of what happened, what you thought about what happened and how you felt about what happened.

3. After you have recorded these situations for about ten days, review them in order to determine your major strengths when interacting with other people and those areas that you think you could improve.

Discussion

Write a brief summary of your interactions, using the following as a guide:

- what you observed about your interpersonal interactions (for example, 'I notice that I don't always listen when I am worried about what I am going to say')
- your strengths and areas for improvement (for example, 'I am good at starting conversations with people I do not know')
- your personal goals for improving your ability to interact and relate to others (for example, 'I would like to be able to seek clarification so that I'm sure I understand')

In addition to reflecting on 'everyday' interactions, it is essential that nurses reflect on their interactions with patients. Interactions with patients are different from everyday interactions in the sense that nurses are often focused on being of help to patients. While helping others does occur during everyday interactions, this is not always the primary intent of such interactions.

In order to determine how best to approach situations with patients, nurses must be able to observe and reflect on the interaction while simultaneously participating in the interaction. The complexity of self-assessment is often overwhelming as a result of these demands. Because the ability to become a participant–observer during interactions can be quite cumbersome to manage all at once, it is often useful to sort the process of self-assessment into manageable units. Although the ultimate aim is to combine all units, first mastering smaller units helps develop the art of self-assessment. The following approaches and activities focus on these smaller units: observing, perceiving, reflecting, evaluating and making alterations on the basis of the evaluation.

Reflection after interactions with patients

An effective approach to assessing performance, and one of the most commonly used approaches, is a reflective evaluation of an interaction after it has occurred. This approach to self-assessment is used after nurses have spontaneously participated in an interaction with a patient. Through reflection, nurses are able to identify skills that were used, assess the effects of these skills and, using patient responses and theoretical concepts as a guide, construct a probable explanation of why the skills were effective or ineffective.

Activity 3.11 is presented as a useful way for nurses to reflect personally on interactions with patients, be they positive or negative experiences.

ACTIVITY 3.11

GUIDE TO SELF-REFLECTION

 Process

1. Describe (either through speaking or writing) an interaction in terms of what happened. Do not think about why it happened, just what happened between you and the patient.

2. Answer the following questions:

   a. What did you say that was helpful to the patient?

   b. What was your intent in saying this?

   c. How did you know it was helpful?

   d. What did you say/do that was not helpful to the patient?

   e. What was your intent in saying this?

   f. How did you know it was not helpful?

   g. What could you have said that would have been more helpful?

   h. What were you feeling during this interaction?

   i. What do you think the patient was feeling during the interaction?

   j. How would you have changed this interaction if you could do it again?

Nurses may fall into the trap of being overly critical of themselves whenever they reflect on their interactions with patients, because they place pressure on themselves to 'do it right'. Rather than viewing interactions as opportunities for growth, nurses who want to 'do it right' perceive interactions as tests of effective performance. This view often stifles personal and professional development.

Whenever nurses are asked to reflect on their interactions, there is a danger that they will recall only those interactions during which they felt ineffective. For this reason it is important that nurses focus on positive, fulfilling and beneficial interactions, as well as those interactions that could have been more effective. Satisfying and successful interactions are as informative as those that are not.

Focus on specific skills during an interaction

At times nurses will want to develop a specific skill or related set of skills because they perceive these skills as difficult, uncomfortable to use or hard to understand. Under these circumstances an effective way to self-assess is to focus on these skills during an interaction.

ACTIVITY 3.12 317

SELF-ASSESSMENT OF SPECIFIC SKILLS

 Process

1. Identify which skill or set of skills is particularly difficult to understand or seems too uncomfortable to use.

2. Review the section of this book that covers this particular skill or set of skills.

3. During interactions with patients, look for opportunities when this skill or set of skills is appropriate to use or notice each time you use the skill or set of skills during an interaction with patients.

Discussion

Each time you use the skill or set of skills:

1. Evaluate its effects on interaction with the patient.

2. Observe how the patient responds.

3. Reflect on how you felt and responded.

4. Make a note of the circumstances and immediate situation.

Maintaining an ongoing record

The previously described self-assessment methods are most effective whenever nurses keep track of a number of patient interactions. Such a record is sometimes referred to as a 'journal' or 'diary'. In maintaining such a record, nurses are able to develop their understanding and use of interpersonal skills by referring to a variety of situations and circumstances. When a variety of situations are evaluated, comparisons and contrasts can be made and patterns begin to emerge. Keeping track of various patient situations, and various ways of interacting in these situations, enables nurses to formulate a more complete understanding than simply focusing on isolated events or isolated skills.

Soliciting help from other nurses

In addition to the introspection that the previous approaches encourage, it is useful for nurses to solicit feedback from other nurses about how they are interacting with patients. The questions in activity 3.11 can be used to prompt information from other nurses. The questions are exploratory. They refrain from passing judgment and encourage other nurses to reflect and determine how they are interacting.

This approach to helping other nurses is preferable to providing solutions and offering advice. When solutions and advice are given, nurses are not encouraged to generate their own solutions. Also, it is only the nurse who 'was there' during a given interaction who knows exactly what happened. Nurses who were not present, yet receive a reported account of what happened, are relying on the nurse giving the account and are processing the information through their own filters. It is preferable for the nurse who 'was there' to process the interaction through their own perceptual filters because this approach has the greatest possibility for promoting self-awareness. Other nurses may offer alternative perspectives, thus encouraging a reappraisal of the situation, but it is best to begin with attempting to understand.

Pitfalls in self-assessment

The tendency to judge or evaluate their performance is often automatic, even natural for nurses. Nevertheless, a negative evaluation can be quite troublesome when the perceived stakes are great. In evaluating their interactions with patients, the stakes are often high for nurses because of a need to maintain a positive professional image. Most nurses will want to be effective in their interactions with patients, and performance judged as ineffective may threaten a nurse's professional image and professional esteem. For example, when nurses recognise that they have blocked or inhibited an interaction with a patient, they may find this behaviour unacceptable in a professional sense. In order to preserve and maintain an image as effective professionals, they may overlook, diminish, justify or even reject flaws and mistakes in their performance.

Overcoming this potential pitfall is best achieved through recognition and continuous awareness that self-assessment is done for the purpose of professional growth and development. Continual reflection and evaluation of performance enables nurses to build on their experiences and learn from them. Through self-assessment nurses determine what was right or wrong, effective or ineffective about their interaction skills and patterns. Nevertheless, this evaluation is not the end point of self-assessment. Self-assessment is employed primarily for the purpose of seeking ways to improve. Thus, it is not simply an evaluative process but a learning process. A commitment to continual learning is an essential aspect of professionalism.

Another potential pitfall in using self-assessment is a tendency to gloss over performance, perceiving it globally as either all good or all bad. Focusing exclusively on positive aspects is as much a pitfall as focusing exclusively on negative aspects of performance. Nurses who can focus only on mistakes or flaws in their interactions with patients are being too harsh in their self-evaluation. Nurses who can focus only on positive aspects of their performance are failing to recognise areas for improvement and learning, which exist in the majority of situations.

The tendency to view performance globally as either all good or all bad is kept in check through the realisation that most interactions will contain a mixture of positive and negative aspects. Whenever nurses can perceive only one type or the other, their self-assessment lacks accuracy and completeness. If this happens, nurses are encouraged to reflect further in order to develop a balanced view of evaluation.

A final potential pitfall in using one's self as the assessor of performance emerges whenever nurses lack understanding of the criteria on which to base their evaluations. A lack of understanding of how and why interpersonal skills are used is addressed through further reading and discussion about the theory of effective interactions in nursing. Additionally, nurses may need to solicit assistance from an external authority, for example, an experienced nurse or an educator, in developing appropriate criteria on which to base their self-assessment.

CHAPTER SUMMARY

Nurses need to develop acute self-awareness whenever they engage in interactions and relationships with patients, because the primary tool they are using in these circumstances is themselves. Without self-awareness, nurses run the risk of imposing their values and views onto patients. *Values that serve the nurse may be detrimental or useless to patients.* There is a danger that without self-awareness, nurses may confuse their own values with those of their patients. Although connected through the relationship, nurses need to maintain an identity that remains separate from the patient.

More than any other parts of nursing, interpersonal relationships with patients are likely to engender feelings within nurses. The processes of self-reflection provide assistance in handling such reactions to patients.

This chapter has reviewed three processes for developing self-awareness:

- Introspection
- Input from others
- Self-sharing

Nurses are encouraged to use these processes in their day-to-day encounters with patients. Reflection, both in solitude and through interaction with others, as well as self-sharing enable nurses to meet the challenges of self-growth.

Self-awareness is the primary means through which nurses are able to evaluate their effectiveness in relating to patients. Through self-awareness, nurses remain in touch with what they are doing, and how this is affecting patients for whom they care.

REFERENCES

Armstrong-Esther, C.A. & Browne, K.D. (1986). The influence of elderly patients' mental impairment on nurse-patient interaction. *Journal of advanced nursing*, 11, 379–387.

Atkins, S. & Murphy, K. (1993). Reflection: a review of the literature. *Journal of advanced nursing*, 18, 1188–1192.

Baer, E. & Lowery, B. J. (1987). Patient and situational factors that affect nursing students' like or dislike of caring for patients. *Nursing Research*, 36 (5), 298–302.

Begat, I., Severinsson, E., & Berggren, I. (1997). Implementation of clinical supervision in a medical department: nurses' views of the effects. *Journal of clinical nursing*, 6 (5), 389–394.

Brickman, P., Rabinowitz, V.C., Karuza, J., Coates, D., Cohn, E. & Kidder, L. (1982). Models of helping and coping. *American psychologist*, 37 (4), 368–384.

Carr, C.J. (1996). Reflecting on clinical practice: hectoring talk or reality? *Journal of clinical nursing*, 5, 289–295.

Carveth, J. A. (1995). Perceived patient deviance and avoidance by nurses. *Nursing research*, 44 (3), 173–178.

Clarke, B., James, C. & Kelly, J. (1996). Reflective practice: reviewing the issues and refocusing the debate. *International journal of nursing studies*, 33 (2), 171–180.

Corey, G., Coreu, M.S. & Callahan, P. (1988). *Issues and ethics in the helping professions*, 3rd edn. Brooks/Cole, Belmont CA.

Cronenwett, L.R. (1983). When and how people help: theoretical issues and evidence. In P.L. Chinn (ed.). *Advances in nursing theory development* (pp 251–270). Aspen, Rockville MD.

Davies, E. (1995). Reflective practice: a focus for caring. *Journal of nursing education*, 43 (4), 167–174.

Drew, N. (1986). Exclusion and confirmation: phenomenology of patients' experiences with caregivers. *Image: journal of nursing scholarship*, 18, 39–43.

Egan, G. (1994). *The skilled helper*, 5th edn. Brooks/Cole, Monterey CA.

Forrest, D. (1989). The experience of caring. *Journal of advanced nursing*, 14, 815–823.

Foster, J. & Greenwood, J. (1998). Reflection: a challenging innovation for nurses. *Contemporary nurse*, 7, 165–172.

Fowler, J. (1998). Evaluating the efficacy of reflective practice within the context of clinical supervision. *Journal of advanced nursing*, 27, 379–382.

Greenwood, J. (1993). Reflective practice: a critique of the work of Argyris and Schon. *Journal of advanced nursing*, 18, 1183–1187.

Greenwood, J. (1998). The role of reflection in single and double loop learning, *Journal of advanced nursing*, 27, 1048–1053.

Grief, C.L. & Elliot, R. (1994). Emergency nurses' moral evaluation of patients. *Journal of emergency nursing*, 20 (4), 275–279.

Haddock, J. & Bassett, C. (1997). Nurses' perceptions of reflective practice. *Nursing standard*, 11 (32), 39–41.

Johns, C. (1995). The value of reflective practice for nursing. *Journal of clinical nursing*, 4 (1), 23–30.

Johns, C. (1999). Reflection as empowerment? *Nursing Inquiry*, 6, 241–249.

Johnson, M. & Webb, C. (1995a). Rediscovering unpopular patients: The concept of social judgement. *Journal of advanced nursing*, 21, 455–466.

Johnson, M. & Webb, C. (1995b). The power of social judgement: Struggle and negotiation in the nursing process. *Nurse education today*, 15, 83–89.

Jones, P.R. (1995). Hindsight bias in reflective practice: an empirical investigation. *Journal of advanced nursing*, 21, 783–788.

Kelly, M.P. & May, D. (1982). Good and bad patients: a review of the literature and a theoretical critique. *Journal of advanced nursing*, 7, 147–156.

Kim, H.S. (1999) Critical reflective inquiry for knowledge development in nursing practice. *Journal of advanced nursing*, 29, 1205–1212.

Lawler, J. (1991). Behind the screens: nursing, somology, and the problem of the body. Churchill Livingstone, Melbourne.

Leddy, S. & Pepper J. M. (1998). *Conceptual bases of professional nursing*, 4th edn. J B Lippincot, Philadelphia PA.

Olsen, D. (1997). When the patient causes the problem: the effect of patient responsibility on the nurse-patient relationship. *Journal of advanced nursing*, 26, 515–522.

Sayler, J. & Stuart, B.J. (1985). Nurse-patient interaction in the intensive care unit. *Heart & Lung*, 14, 20–24.

Taylor, B. (1997). Big battles for small gains: a cautionary note for teaching reflective processes in nursing and midwifery practice. *Nursing inquiry*, 4, 19–26.

Tichen, A., & Binnie, A. (1995). The art of clinical supervision. *Journal of clinical nursing*, 4 (5), 327–334.

Wilkinson, J. (1999). Implementing reflective practice. *Nursing standard*, 13 (21), 36–40.

CHAPTER 4

ENCOURAGING INTERACTION: LISTENING

INTRODUCTION

'It wasn't much, I mean, I really didn't do anything to help. All I did was listen.' Comments such as these, especially when expressed by nurses, fail to acknowledge or demonstrate an appreciation for the complexity and power of effective listening. 'Just listening' seems so simple, as if no effort is required, no expertise needed. Listening is powerful because it encourages patients to share their experiences; it validates patients as people with something to say; it promotes understanding between nurse and patient; and it provides the nurse with information on which to act. It is not nearly as 'simple' as it sounds on the surface. Quite a lot is happening when nurses 'just' listen. When nurses listen, *just* listen, they pay careful attention to what they hear and observe, they focus on what is explicitly expressed by the patient and they try to determine what the patient is meaning. Effective listening requires receptivity, sustained concentration and astute observation. All of this can hardly be summed up as 'not doing anything'.

Nursing care is based on an understanding of patients' personal experiences of health and their responses to illness. In order to reach this level of understanding, nurses must first listen to patients' stories. The skills of listening are fundamental and crucial to patient–nurse relationships. Listening permeates the entire relationship; if meaningful interpersonal connections are to occur, listening must be engaged in throughout every interaction.

Listening actively demonstrates nurses' presence with and interest in patients. Through listening, nurses orient themselves towards patients as people who 'are there'. Listening encourages patients to express themselves, because it provides the necessary time and space for such expressions. Listening enables patients to experience being heard and accepted by nurses. Listening enables nurses to understand and appreciate patients' experiences. As such, it sets the stage for effective helping. Nurses base their responses to patients on what is perceived through listening. Once the stage is set, the players can enact their roles (the one helping and the one helped), but it is vital that the stage remains set throughout the relationship.

Chapter overview

This chapter begins with a description of the process of effective listening, highlighting its complexity. Then the benefits of listening within the context of patient–nurse relationships are discussed. Because nurses need to listen with 'nursing ears', listening goals within the nursing-care context are explored next. The following section on mental preparation, the readiness to listen, focuses on how to become more receptive to patients by reducing potential interferences and distractions. A discussion of the skills of listening follows. These include attending, observing, perceiving, interpreting and recalling. The chapter concludes with a description of how to evaluate whether listening has been effective.

THE LISTENING PROCESS

Listening is a complex process that encompasses the skills of reception, perception and interpretation of input. The process begins with input. Sights, sounds, smells, tastes and tactile sensations are received through the sensory organs. The initial step in the listening process is the reception of this input, predominantly through the eyes and ears. The ability to receive the input is dependent upon the listener's state of readiness, when receivers are 'turned on' and 'tuned in'. Next, the received input must be noticed as important; it must be actively perceived. During this stage of the process, external and internal distractions often interfere with accurate perception and create filters, which partially or completely block the input. Almost as soon as the input is perceived, the listener attaches meaning to it—an interpretation is made.

The meaning attached to a particular piece of sensory input is connected to the listener's memory, previous experience, expectations, desires, wants, needs and current thoughts and feelings. For example, nurses working in a hospital unit know when they hear a particular buzz and see a light over a doorway to a patient's room (sensory input received and perceived) that the patient in that room has turned on the call light, requesting assistance (interpretation). To an outsider, the sound and sight of the call light activation may be received and noticed, but no particular meaning is derived unless there is a familiarity with how hospital units are equipped. If they are busy nurses who notice the call light may interpret the patient's request for assistance as a nuisance (interpretation based on needs). Likewise, a nurse may decide that the patient requesting assistance is not in immediate need if this particular patient turns on the call light for minor reasons (interpretation based on experience and expectations).

Effective listening encompasses not only receiving sensory input, but also perceiving it and interpreting its meaning. When nurses correctly interpret what patients are expressing, listening has been effective.

Hearing and listening

Listening and hearing are not the same. Any person with the apparatus for detecting audible tones can hear, but may or may not be capable of listening. People without hearing capabilities may be able to listen, while those with hearing capabilities may fail to listen. Listening involves paying active attention to what is being said; it is more than simply receiving sensory input.

Active and passive listening

Effective listening, the active process of taking in, absorbing and eventually understanding what is being expressed, requires energy and concentration on the part of the listener. Have you ever been in a conversation with somebody who claimed to be listening to you but was attending to another matter, for example, watching television or reading? No matter how much this person may try to convince you that they are is listening, it is not likely you will believe it, because they are not offering their full attention.

Hearing, without fully concentrating and attending, is passive listening. Active listening is listening for the purpose of understanding. Not only does it require the reception of sensory input, but also astute observation, undivided attention and the processing or interpretation of what is heard. While some people may be capable of listening to background music while reading or studying, this type of passive reception does not serve listeners well during engaged interpersonal interaction. Effective listening is only achieved in an active and involved manner. It cannot be done passively.

BENEFITS OF LISTENING

It is important that nurses understand the benefits of effective listening in order to more fully appreciate its power and helpfulness. The benefits are described as those for the patient, those for the nurse and those for the relationship between them.

For the patient

Effective listening is consistent with the concept that nurses care about patients. When nurses take and make time to listen to what patients are expressing, they demonstrate genuine interest in and regard for patients. Listening is one of the clearest ways for nurses to convey respect for and acceptance of patients. By listening, nurses actively demonstrate to patients that what they have to say matters, that patients matter. Nurses give of themselves when they listen. Patients feel worthwhile because they have been given the nurse's time, energy and attention. Listening reinforces the inherent worth of patients and, as a result, patients feel comforted because they are valued, acknowledged and validated. Patients do report that listening is an important aspect of what they want in a nurse (Webb & Hope, 1995).

For the nurse

Any verbal response that nurses make is based on what is perceived through listening to the patient. Listening to patients enables nurses to receive information about patients, collect data on which to base nursing-care activities and reach deeper levels of understanding with patients. Being fully present with a patient, as would be evidenced through listening, has been linked to effective clinical decision-making in nursing (Doona et al., 1997).

Theoretical understanding of a particular clinical situation offers possibilities and probabilities, but listening to an individual patient's experience offers concrete, personally unique data on which to base responsive nursing care. For example, chronic illness often affects a patient's sense of self-worth (a theoretical possibility). But by listening to an individual patient's experience of and reactions to chronic illness, the nurse comes to understand concretely and specifically how this particular patient's sense of self-worth is, or is not, affected by the experience. Listening encourages patients to open up and tell their stories and, as a result, nurses are in a better position to understand patients more personally.

For the relationship

Listening encourages further interaction between patient and nurse. It is a catalyst in promoting trust in their relationship, because patients will come to know that they can rely on the nurse to 'be there'.

At times, listening with understanding is all that is needed in an interaction; it is an end in itself. For example, listening to a patient's expression of sadness in response to a loss may be just what the nurse needs to do in order to be of help. At other times, listening is a means to another end, a responsive nursing action based on understanding that is achieved through listening. For example, as a result of listening to a patient express a lack of understanding about a current medication regime, the nurse can explain why it is important, for example, to take medication prior to eating.

LISTENING WITH NURSING EARS

The general benefits of listening in the nursing-care context are important to appreciate, however, the benefits refer primarily to how meaningful interaction between patient and nurse is enhanced. What about the content of listening in the nursing-care context? When nurses listen, they need to listen for aspects of the patient's experience that are significant in the context of nursing care. What should be the focus when listening to patients? What kinds of meanings and understandings are specific to the clinical practice of nursing? What particular aspects of patients' experiences are most relevant to nurses? Listening with 'nursing ears' is listening for specific nursing-related meanings, and an understanding of these meanings forms the basis of listening goals within the nursing context.

ACTIVITY 4.1

LISTENING GOALS IN NURSING

 Process

1. Form small groups of about five participants.

2. Discuss the answers to the following questions:

   a. 'What do I need to know and understand about patients in order to care effectively for them?'

   b. 'When I am listening to patients, what is most significant for me to notice about what they are expressing?'

3. Record and compare your answers with other small groups.

Discussion

1. Do the answers to the questions provide any focus for listening in nursing? If so, what is the focus?

2. Are there aspects of patients' experiences that are more significant to nursing than other aspects? What are these?

3. What are the major goals of listening in the nursing context? List them.

4. Listening with nursing ears means focusing on goals. Compare your list in step 3 with the following goals (presented in question form):

   a. What effects do patients' current health status have on their daily living?

   b. How do patients interpret their health status?

   c. How are patients reacting to the health-care they are receiving?

   d. How are they reacting to your nursing approach in particular?

   e. How much do patients understand about their health status and health-care? How much do they want to understand?

   f. Who or what is most important to patients? What do they value the most in life?

   g. What is worrying patients the most about their health status and health-care?

Activity 4.1 poses challenges, because it suggests that certain limitations can be imposed on listening. Does listening with 'nursing ears' mean that nurses should ignore, avoid or filter out aspects that are not directly related to nursing concerns? Hardly, because this implies partial listening. While it is important for nurses to recognise what concerns them *as* nurses, there is potential danger when listening goals are overemphasised. When this occurs, goals for listening become barriers.

Rather than perceiving these goals as limitations, it is better to think of them as focusing lenses through which to view patients. To take the analogy further, imagine looking through the lens of a camera and focusing on a particular subject within a scene. While the entire landscape is in view, the camera lens brings some aspects of the picture into sharper focus than others. Such is the case when using listening goals in the nursing context. While the entire 'picture', that is the patient, is in view (received), some aspects are brought more sharply in focus (perceived), because these aspects have direct relevance to nursing care.

Another way to employ listening goals in nursing is to use them as orienting and guiding frameworks during the interpretation of received messages. Attention needs to be paid to the patient's entire message, however, the message is interpreted in light of the goals of listening. The message is perceived as is, but the meaning is interpreted using a nursing framework. This framework, or orientation to listening, is then viewed as enhancing rather than limiting because it provides direction to the nurse's listening.

> When he first met James Nott, Matthew, an experienced cardiac nurse, was completing the usual admission procedure onto the cardiac surgical ward. He had to complete all the necessary observations of James' physical condition but, more importantly, he needed to get to know James as a person. As Matthew listened to his story of a lifelong problem with his mitral valve, he realised that James understood the implications of his scheduled valve replacement surgery. James told Matthew that he knew that the surgery would need to be done someday. Naturally, James was concerned about the surgery itself, but he reassured himself in the knowledge that he was in the capable hands of an experienced cardiac surgery team. As he listened, Matthew began to realise the potential impact of the surgery on James' life. He was employed as a night-shift supervisor of a large coal preparation plant, a position he worked hard to obtain and an achievement of which he was proud. Nevertheless, his job involved a great deal of walking around the plant and James noted his increasing inability 'to get around like I used to'. He was afraid that he might become disabled after the surgery, unable to continue in a job he obviously enjoyed. He understood the details of the surgery, recognised that it was necessary, and accepted it. Yet he was worried about what it might mean to his future. In focusing on James' concern about the potential impact of the surgery, of what it might mean in terms of his daily life, Matthew was listening with 'nursing ears'.

READINESS TO LISTEN

Effective listening requires a certain amount of mental preparation in order to achieve a state of readiness. A nurse's 'readiness to listen' is as important as the act of perceiving actively and fully what a patient is expressing. Even before messages are received, the conditions necessary for the reception of input must be realised. Firstly, nurses must have the intent and desire to listen to patients. Positive intentions and desires alone, however, are not enough; they need to be conveyed to the patient. All too often nurses appear 'too busy', and therefore not ready to listen to patients. Scurrying around tending to the myriad of tasks that occupy a nurse's day communicates to patients that there is really no time to stop and listen. Focusing on tasks reflects a value that the tasks are more important than the people who are the patients. Patients are left with the feeling that the nurse's time is too precious to interrupt.

ACTIVITY 4.2

INDICATORS OF LISTENING

 Process

1. Think of someone in your life who really listens to you. Visualise this person. Reflect on your reasons for choosing this person. Why do you think of this person as one who listens? What does this person do, that leads you to believe that they listen?

2. Record your thoughts and reflections about this person.

3. Now think of someone in your life who does not seem to listen to you. Visualise this person. Reflect on your reasons for choosing this person. Why do you think of this person as one who does not listen to you? What does this person do, that leads you to believe that they do not listen?

4. Record your thoughts and reflections about this person.

Discussion

1. Compare your recordings of each person, the listener and the non-listener. What differences do you note?

2. Summarise the major differences between people who listen and people who do not.

3. If working in a group, compare your summary with the summaries of other participants.

Activity 4.2 highlights characteristics of effective listeners, namely:

* availability to interact
* having the time to listen
* not interrupting the speaker

- not judging, evaluating, advising or imposing their own ideas on the speaker
- not merely listening for what they want to hear
- openness to whatever is being expressed

Effective listeners demonstrate the readiness to listen.

Receptivity

In order for a television set to receive a signal or transmission, the set has to be tuned into the correct frequency, so the signal can be processed. This analogy is useful in understanding the readiness to listen. Nurses must 'tune into' patients' signals and adjust their receivers so that the messages are not only audible, but also comprehensible. This involves the mental preparation of focusing concentration on a patient's messages and developing antennae to notice what a patient is expressing.

Tuning in to a patient's message is hard work. Some signals are easier to receive than others. At times, there is so much interference that the signal cannot be received at all.

ACTIVITY 4.3

EASY OR HARD TO LISTEN TO

 Process

1. In small groups of about five to six participants, think about the subjects, topics, feelings and experiences that patients bring up with nurses. Consider as many as possible. List these.

2. Review the list and discuss whether the item is easy to listen to or hard to listen to, and mark each accordingly.

3. In small groups compare lists, and discuss similarities and differences.

Discussion

1. Were there any general areas which were assessed as difficult? as easy? What are they?

2. On what basis were assessments of easy or hard made?

3. Are there any general trends and themes present? What are these themes? Divide these into easy and hard categories.

4. How might this assessment of easy and hard enhance or interfere with effective listening?

Reducing interference

Interference stems from distractions that draw attention away from the patient and prevent clear reception of a message. Such distractions originate internally (from within the nurse) and externally (from outside of the nurse).

External interference

It is important to pay careful attention to the external environment when attempting to listen. For example, the sights and sounds of a busy, bustling hospital setting often present many potential sources of external interference. The ringing of telephones, a variety of health-care personnel coming and going and patients being transported from one area to another are potential distractions. When nurses visit patients in their home setting, distractions such as the playful noise of small children and a radio or television may be sources of interference. It is not always possible to eliminate external sights, sounds and other stimuli, but attempts should be made to reduce them as much as possible when listening to patients.

In a hospital setting, drawing the curtains around a patient's bed not only provides a degree of privacy, but also decreases the number of external distractions and potential interferences. This simple act is effective in reducing the amount of visual distractions, but may not reduce the audible ones. Also, it sends a clear message to others that a meaningful activity is occurring.

Interruptions from other staff members can be particularly distracting— even the fear of being interrupted is a potential distraction. Nurses working together in a clinical setting need to be mindful of this; they should assess the need to distract another nurse who is engaged in an interaction with a patient.

Sometimes there are aspects of patients themselves that are sources of external interference. Examples of this kind of interference include: patients who speak in accents that are distracting to a nurse; patients who express themselves in a disjointed, rambling manner; and patients whose speech is barely audible and halting. In these instances, nurses can reduce the interference by attempting to put aside the distractions and concentrating carefully on what the patient is expressing.

In general, the reduction of external interference occurs whenever attempts are made to exclude the outside world. This is done by placing barriers between the outside world and the patient and nurse, or by consciously tuning out external noise.

Internal interference

When nurses are ready to listen, they are able to forget themselves for the moment. They allow themselves to be engrossed in the interaction with a patient and to notice and perceive what the patient is expressing. Internal interference, the nurse's own thoughts, feelings, preoccupations or value judgments, are often more difficult to control than external interference. A noisy television set (an external interference) can simply be switched off in order to eliminate it as a source of distraction. Internal interferences cannot simply be switched off.

Thoughts as internal interference

One common preoccupation, which interferes with listening, is the worry a nurse often feels about how to respond to the patient. 'What am I going to say to this patient?' 'What am I going to do for this patient?' Thoughts such as these are often related to a self-expectation that nurses must 'do something' in order to help patients. As a result, nurses become so preoccupied with their own anxieties that they fail to listen and perceive what the patient is expressing. An internal reminder that something is being done—'I am listening to what this patient is expressing'—can help to draw nurses' focus away from their own thoughts and onto the patient. If something else can be done it will become evident *after* the nurse listens, with understanding, to what the patient is expressing.

Other thoughts that potentially interfere with listening include any preoccupations that a nurse may have at any given moment. These range from 'Have I remembered to defrost something to eat for dinner tonight?' to 'There is a waiting room full of mothers and babies and I am not going to have time to see each of them' to 'Ms Holmes will need pre-op medications soon. I wonder how long this conversation is going to last. How can I bring it to a close?' Sometimes these thoughts can be excluded from conscious awareness, while at other times they signal the need to attend to another matter, then return to the interaction at hand. At yet other times, such thoughts are impossible to exclude from conscious awareness, but nurses pretend to be listening. It is far better to cease the interaction until such time that undivided attention can be given to a patient than to feign listening.

Value judgment as internal interference

The natural tendency to judge what is heard as right or wrong, good or bad, interesting or boring is one of the greatest sources of internal interference when attempting to listen. This tendency is considered natural because it happens automatically, often without conscious awareness. 'That is a stupid way to react.' 'Mr Lyons should not be feeling this way.' 'What's she going on about—it's really nothing.' Such thoughts are judgmental, because they channel the patient's message through the nurse's personal interpretive filter. They interfere with listening because they close off possibilities that do not match the nurse's internal frame of reference.

What is heard may be evaluated negatively and rejected outright as unacceptable. Even if what is heard is evaluated in a positive light, it interferes with a nurse's ability to fully appreciate and understand the uniqueness of a patient's experience, because the nurse is still relying on a personal frame of reference.

While it is almost impossible to prevent valuative thoughts, an aware nurse recognises them as stemming from a personal value system, and therefore is able to separate their own value system from the patient's value system.

Personal judgments, once separated, can then be held in suspense, deferred and kept peripheral to the patient. Being non-judgmental is a near impossible goal to achieve, however, keeping one's value system separate and suspended is achievable. The most critical aspect of suspending judgment is the nurse's self-awareness (see chapter 3).

Feelings as internal interference

Sometimes internal interference stems from a nurse's lack of ability to cope with what the patient is expressing, for example, a feeling of despondency might overwhelm a nurse listening to the sorrow of a young mother dying of cancer. Nurses may fail to listen because of their own anxieties, and they may, unwittingly or unknowingly, either change the subject or avoid interacting with the patient altogether. There are times when nurses' own circumstances create a sense of vulnerability that prevents them from being fully present with a patient. But, the majority of times, nurses fail to listen to patients' stories that are distressing out of fear of not knowing what to say or how to respond. Not listening or even avoiding a patient for these reasons potentially compounds the patient's distress because it isolates and distances a patient from the nurse.

Nurses must remind themselves that listening to a patient's distress, no matter how disturbing, is comforting simply because it shows they are fully present and genuinely interested in the patient. Words spoken by nurses in an attempt to comfort may actually intrude. Listening is 'being there' with these patients. Often, patients do not want or need words in these extreme situations. The caring presence of another human being is more than adequate.

When nurses become overwhelmed, and perhaps paralysed, by their own feelings as a result of what patients are expressing and experiencing, seeking support from other nurses is preferable to avoiding or emotionally abandoning the patient (see chapter 11).

Once the state of readiness to listen is achieved, a nurse is available to be fully present during an interaction with a patient. Attention is focused and undivided, perceptual filters are open, antennae are up and interference is reduced. This state of readiness, when maintained throughout the interaction, not only enables nurses to listen, but also encourages further interaction.

THE SKILLS OF LISTENING

The groundwork involved in achieving the readiness to listen is an inward process initiated by nurses as they prepare both themselves and the environment. Readiness alone, however, is not sufficient for effective listening because two-way communication with a patient has not yet begun. This section explores the interactive nature of listening because the skills of listening are enacted through interchange with another person. The skills of listening are divided into five areas: attending, observing, perceiving, interpreting and recalling.

Attending

Attending behaviour is the outward, physical manifestation of a nurse's readiness to listen. It communicates to the patient that the nurse is available to listen and accessible to interact. The outward behaviour of attending conveys the message, 'Go ahead, you have my attention, I'm here with you now'.

The messages of attending are sent through nonverbal channels, predominantly body posture and eye contact. For example, a nurse checking the patency of an intravenous drip line (no matter how casually), while attempting to listen, is not fully communicating their intent because they are not demonstrating attending behaviour to the patient.

ACTIVITY 4.4 **317**

PHYSICAL ATTENDING

 Process

1. Divide the large group into three groups. Designate one of the three groups as As, one as Bs and one as Cs.

2. Distribute instructions to As, Bs and Cs. (These instructions can be found in the appendix.) Do not share the instructions with participants who are not in the same group.

3. As and Bs should seat themselves according to the instructions. Allow enough room between each B so that they will not disturb other groups during the activity.

4. Cs should stand around the edge of the room and act as observers during the activity. Cs should follow the guidelines for observing as outlined in their instructions.

5. As and Bs now have a quiet conversation, following the instructions.

6. After five minutes, As and Bs stop the conversation and show each other their instructions.

7. Cs report their observations.

Discussion

1. How did the Bs' nonverbal behaviour change during the conversation?

2. What did the Cs notice about the change in the Bs' nonverbal behaviour, about two minutes into conversation?

3. What did the As notice about the Bs' nonverbal behaviour during the conversation?

4. What did the Bs notice about their own nonverbal behaviour during the conversation?

Attending behaviour has two key elements: the spatial position of the nurse in relation to the patient and the maintenance of eye contact. During activity 4.4, the Bs probably altered their nonverbal behaviour by leaning forward and looking directly at the As when the conversation became more 'interesting'. They assumed the posture of attending.

While attending, nurses physically place themselves in a manner that promotes interaction between them and the patient. Attending behaviour demonstrates active interest in the patient. Egan (1994) presents general guidelines for attending, using the acronym SOLER, which stands for:

S   Squarely facing the person in a front-on presentation
O   Open posture, conveying an acceptance and openness to the other person
L   Leaning forward, demonstrating active interest
E   Eye contact maintained, including being at the same eye level as the other person
R   Relaxed posture, demonstrating an ease with self, the other and the situation.

Attending promotes active engagement between nurses and patient, and encourages patients to continue expressing themselves.

ACTIVITY 4.5   ➡ 317

ATTENDING AND NON-ATTENDING

Process

1. Divide into pairs and designate one person as A and the other as B.

Instructions to A

2. Tell a story to B about something exciting or interesting that has happened to you. Talk for about five minutes on the subject.

Instructions to B

3. Begin the interaction by assuming the attending posture, that is, face A, maintain eye contact, lean forward and remain relaxed and open. After about a minute or two, start to lean back, fold your arms and look away from A. Focus on something other than what A is saying, for example, stare out the window, clean your nails, flip through a book. Do anything to violate the rules of attending. Remain silent, do not interrupt or change the subject, but do try to keep listening.

4. Stop the conversation after about five minutes.

Discussion

1. How did A feel during the interaction? What happened to A when B began non-attending?

2. How did B feel during the interaction? What happened to B when they began non-attending?

3. How did the conversation change when B no longer appeared interested?

Attending encourages further interaction between patient and nurse, while non-attending is discouraging. In activity 4.5, person A probably did not wish to continue the conversation after person B began non-attending. No matter how intent a nurse may be on listening, without attending a patient will not be encouraged to continue.

Some words of caution about attending

The intensity of attending is not always appropriate, because it is not always warranted by the topic at hand. Try assuming the posture during a conversation about the weather. You will note that intense attending feels awkward when the subject of the conversation is of little consequence. A discussion about the weather, unless there has recently been a significant event related to the weather, does not warrant such an intense listening response. This is important for nurses to bear in mind. There are times when patients discuss subjects that do not require the intensity of attending and for a nurse to assume the posture is not only awkward, but inappropriate.

The attending guideline about maintaining eye contact is another area that presents some difficulty, and caution needs to be exercised when applying this guideline. Unbroken eye contact is unnatural, awkward and even threatening because of the discomfort it creates. The head-on position of attending is criticised (Shea, 1988) because it forces eye contact that is then difficult to break. When nurses are attending, it is important to bear in mind that occasional breaks in eye contact are not only natural, but also desirable in maintaining comfort and ease during the interaction.

Finally, an attending posture, which focuses on eye contact as one of its central aspects, may not be appropriate in some cultures. Maintaining eye contact can be a sign of disrespect when there are cultural norms about status. Looking directly into the eyes of a person who is of a higher status is unacceptable when these cultural norms are operating. Likewise, eye contact may vary with age and gender. Nurses need to be sensitive to how patients are responding to their attempts to encourage interaction through attending behaviour and a large part of this sensitivity is awareness of age-related and cultural variances (see chapters 8 and 9).

Attending within the clinical nursing context

In nursing, it is sometimes difficult to assume the classic attending posture. Nurses must learn to adapt the attending posture to the realities of their particular clinical setting. It is not always possible to face the patient squarely.

In a hospital situation, when patients are lying in bed and the nurse is standing nearby, the attending mandate of squarely facing the other may be impossible to achieve. How can attending be demonstrated under these circumstances? Nurses need to physically situate themselves in such a manner to establish eye contact, maintain a relaxed stance and be close enough to interact in a meaningful manner, but far enough away to maintain comfort.

Standing at the side of the bed is preferable to standing at the foot of the bed. Although the foot position would allow a nurse to squarely face a patient, it may actually discourage interaction because it creates too much distance between patient and nurse, and places the nurse in an authoritarian stance. By placing themselves at the side of the bed, nurses are almost facing the same direction as the patient. Shea (1988) believes this position is actually preferable to the 'squarely facing' one, because it demonstrates that a nurse is attempting to view the world *with* the patient, sharing a common perspective.

While standing at the side of the bed, nurses are faced with the challenge of lowering themselves to the eye level of the patient, unless the height of the bed is at a level that places the patient at the same eye level as the nurse. Having a seat is the most logical way to meet this challenge. This also sends the message to the patient that the nurse intends to remain there, to interact. While seated, nurses are obviously accessible and available to patients.

Awareness that being seated is preferable can pose a dilemma for nurses. There may be a shortage of chairs. If they seat themselves, they may be reprimanded or frowned upon by other nurses for not working hard enough. The hard work of listening to patients is often unrecognised and unacknowledged, especially in the hospital setting where so much 'other work' needs to be accomplished.

Silence

Obviously, when nurses are attending and listening to patients, they are silent. Silence plays a major part in effective listening and its value is important to recognise. To be silent and not interrupt a patient who is expressing themselves is a sign of respect and interest.

Silence can also go further in its helpfulness. Both patient and nurse may be silent for short periods of time. Silent moments are useful because they allow patient and nurse time to collect their thoughts and reflect on what has been expressed; they provide an opportunity for either patient or nurse to change the direction of the conversation; and they slow the pace of the interaction. Nevertheless, nurses frequently experience difficulty in remaining silent because of a felt need to say or do something.

There are times when silently being with a patient, fully attending and being fully present, is quite helpful. Patients who are in severe physical pain may not wish to talk or be spoken to, but would like to have a nurse present. Patients who are psychologically depressed may feel pressured to interact, and would benefit from a nurse's silent, undemanding presence. These two situations provide examples of contexts in which the silent presence of nurses is appropriate and helpful.

During a verbal interaction, it is important to ascertain when to allow the silence to proceed and when it is better to break the silence with speech or action. Nurses can employ some general guidelines when they are faced with the decision. First and foremost, silence should not be used as a substitute or excuse for not knowing how to respond or what to say. When used in this way silence could be interpreted by the patient as rejection or lack of interest on the part of the nurse. It is better for nurses to admit to feeling 'at a loss for words' under these circumstances. Silence is also ineffective if the patient expects or wants a verbal response from the nurse. Careful attention to the flow and direction of the interaction allows nurses to 'check its pulse', and perceive patient cues that indicate discomfort with the silence.

Silent periods also have limitations if they last longer than about 10–15 seconds (Cormier et al., 1986). When silence progresses beyond these time limits, the flow of the interaction may be stifled, rather than enhanced. Try this experiment the next time you are interacting with a patient: when a silent period ensues, check your watch and time it. You may be surprised how lengthy a 10–15-second period of silence actually feels. Next, evaluate whether or not the silence is of benefit to the interaction. Repeated experiments of this kind enable nurses to judge the length and usefulness of silent moments during interactions with patients.

Observing skills

Effective listening includes astute observation of the patient. A large part of listening is not only paying careful attention to what is expressed, but also how it is expressed. During listening, nurses have a good opportunity to observe the nonverbal aspects of the patient's expressions. Subtle and obvious cues about patients' experiences are better understood when nurses perceive patients' nonverbal behaviour. Nonverbal cues often shed light on the feeling aspects of a patient's experience. Feelings are most often expressed through facial expression, eye contact, body posture and movements, and other nonverbal behaviour. Such patient cues are signals for further exploration (see chapter 6), but the nurse must first notice the cues. The noticing of cues and their initial interpretation occur in the context of listening.

ACTIVITY 4.6

NONVERBAL EXPRESSIONS OF FEELINGS

 Process

1. Form groups of five to six participants and decide on a topic for discussion. The chosen topic can be of any nature, but it needs to be one about which participants *can* express emotions. Controversial topics are most effective for example, euthanasia, abortion, IVF, rights of smokers.

2. Participants should reflect on their feelings or emotions in relation to the selected topic. Each participant records this feeling or emotion on a slip of paper. These slips of paper are not shared with other participants.

3. Participants should reflect on how they usually express their chosen emotion nonverbally.

4. In small groups now discuss the chosen topic. Throughout the discussion, each participant expresses their chosen feeling through nonverbal means only. Participants are not to express their chosen feeling in a verbal manner, that is, they cannot *say* how they feel.

5. Stop the discussion after about ten minutes.

6. Each member of a small group should record what feeling they believe was being expressed by each other member, as well as the nonverbal behaviour that led to this conclusion. Participants do not consult with any other members at this point.

7. Each group member takes a turn asking other members what feeling they thought they were expressing. After each states their conclusion, the member whose feeling was being discussed shows the other members the feeling recorded during step 2. Continue around the small group until each member's feeling expression is discussed.

Discussion

1. On what basis did participants determine what feeling was being expressed? Would this differ between cultural groups, age groups or gender groups?

2. How accurate were the guesses about what feeling was being expressed? What discrepancies existed between what others interpreted and what the participant intended to convey? Why?

3. What does this say about the valid interpretation of nonverbal messages?

No doubt, participants in this activity experienced a heightened awareness of the nonverbal indicators of feelings, because they were asked to determine what feelings other participants were expressing. Their perceptual antennae were ready for the reception of nonverbal input. It is beneficial for nurses to develop and maintain this degree of heightened perceptual awareness when interacting with patients. Heightened perceptual awareness enables nurses to be more astute in their observations. It makes them notice the way in which a patient is relaying messages.

The inherent difficulty in accurately interpreting nonverbal messages is also demonstrated in activity 4.6. This highlights and reinforces the need for nurses to check their perceptions through exploration (see chapter 6). Noticing and observing nonverbal cues of patients is significant in the context of listening. The cues must then be validated by the patient as to their correct meaning because listening enables nurses to observe them, but not necessarily to interpret them accurately.

Perceiving messages

Attending demonstrates nurses' interest in listening to the patient and observing enables nurses to notice nonverbal cues presented by patients. Patients are now encouraged and free to tell their story to an actively interested nurse, and the nurse is in a position to receive the patient's messages.

There are many facets to patients' stories, including the actual content of the story, the related feelings and the general theme of the story. Each facet comes together to create a picture of the patient, the whole story. While it is vital that the nurse receives the entire story, knowledge of the various facets of messages guides a nurse's perception throughout the listening process.

The following story, related by a female resident of a nursing home, serves as an example of the various facets of a story:

> Michael, the diversional therapist, never pushes you to participate in his activities. He takes one look at you and knows whether you feel like participating that day. He'll say, 'Come along, and just watch today, okay?' He always has so many activities going, but you really don't have to do anything you don't feel like doing. That is what's so good about this place.

The content of this story revolves around the activities conducted by the diversional therapist. The feelings expressed are of contentment and satisfaction at not being forced to participate in these activities. The resident uses her discussion of the diversional therapy program as an illustration of the general manner in which residents of the nursing home are treated. The general theme is one of feeling respected by the way she is treated at the nursing home. The content (the diversional therapy activities) and its related feelings (happy and satisfied) come together to form the theme, the importance of having her wishes respected by others.

Notice how the resident speaks of herself in the second person, using the personal pronoun 'you' to indicate herself. When listening to patients it is important that nurses recognise use of the pronoun 'you' in patients' direct reference to themselves. In doing so, they are relating information about themselves, not another person. Perceptive nurses, who are in tune with patients' expressions, notice this use of language and can more fully understand the themes of patients' stories as a result.

At times, patients directly express the content, feeling and thematic facets of their stories, as in the example about the diversional therapist. At other times, however, any or all of the facets are expressed indirectly, through implications, hints and cues. Either way, the various facets of the patient's story must be received and perceived by the nurse who is listening.

Perceiving content

The content of a message contains the objective, factual data about the topic being discussed and includes what is being discussed, who it involves, and when and where an event occurred. The content of a message is the story line. The following example, related by a female patient on an orthopaedic ward of a hospital, serves as an illustration.

> I had these pains in my Achilles tendon. I think it had something to do with playing tennis every day. At first I tried to ignore the pain, but it became so bad that I knew I had to do something. When I saw my local GP, he suggested cortisone injections, so I took the advice and had the injections. That was when the real trouble started. First my right leg started to give way, buckling on me. I fell a few times, and then the final time I fell, I really hurt myself. Now I'm told the right tendon has snapped, and here I am, needing to have it repaired. The whole thing has been going on for about six months now.

The content of this patient's story includes: pain, falling, the local GP, cortisone injections, injured Achilles tendon, the need to have the tendon repaired and a time frame of the past six months.

ACTIVITY 4.7 ➡ 317

LISTENING FOR CONTENT

(Adapted from Carkhuff, 1983)

 Process

1. This activity lists six patient's stories, as told by them. Read each one *once* only. Then cover it up and try to recall the content of the story. If possible, have someone else read the stories to you aloud (once only).

2. Record as much of the content of the message that you can recall. In recalling content, think about the following: 'who' is being discussed, 'what' is being discussed, 'when' and 'where' did the 'what' occur, and 'why' it is being discussed. Record the content on a piece of paper using the headings who, what, when, where and why.

Patient story I

I felt something really strange in my hip when I stood up yesterday. It began to really hurt and I was having trouble walking properly. Because it was Sunday afternoon I didn't want to bother anybody. So I took some aspirin, took it easy and went to bed early. The next morning when I woke up I rang my doctor. She said to go and have the hip X-rayed before I do anything else.

Patient story II

The day started off as usual. I fed him breakfast, and got him ready to go to kindy. I was getting ready to go to work, when he suddenly began rolling on the floor, clutching his stomach and writhing in pain. It took me a while to work out what was happening, and I felt panicked inside, although I didn't let on. I knew it was something major, but had no idea what was happening. I rang my GP's surgery, and the receptionist said to come in straight away. I got into the car immediately and drove there.

Patient story III

I was outside doing the gardening when I suddenly realised I could not move my left arm. I looked at it, saw it was still there, but could not make it move an inch. My beautiful left arm was just hanging there. I walked toward the house, not knowing exactly what I was going to do. I sat down on the sofa to think, when I realised that I could move my arm again. Then I really didn't know what to do.

Patient story IV

I have been really worried about him. He hasn't been himself for months. When he comes home from work, he has dinner and then just sits in front of the television. I can tell he is not really paying attention to it because he just stares. He doesn't even laugh at the funny bits of his favourite show. When I ask what's wrong, he just shrugs his shoulders.

Patient story V

I know I should have regular pap smears but I never seem to find the time. What with the kids, my job and everything I can't fit in a trip to my GP. Anyway, there is not cancer in my family. Maybe doing all those tests is just a way for the doctors to make money.

Patient story VI

All that chemo and radiotherapy really takes it out of me. I try so hard not to give in to feeling so tired. I go to my room and think, 'Oh, I'll just go close my eyes for a few minutes', and the next thing you know I have been asleep for a few hours. It's not fair on my kids because they need me to be there for them.

(*Note*: Suggested answers to this activity can be found at the end of this chapter.)

Discussion

1. In each story, which part of the content was easiest to recall? Which was most difficult? What difficulties did you experience in recalling the content of the stories?

2. How accurate was your recall of content, when you compare your results with those provided at the end of the chapter? (Do not become overly concerned if your answers do not match exactly the ones provided.)

3. Did you discover you 'read into' the stories, and added content that was not originally there? Were there aspects of the content that you deleted? or distorted?

4. What methods did you find yourself using as you attempted to recall the content of the stories?

Activity 4.7 highlights some of the difficulties inherent in listening. Firstly, there is a tendency for the listener to add elements that are not directly stated. For example, the assumption is often made that the person speaking in story II is the mother of the child. It could be a primary care-giver of any relationship.

When nurses are listening, there is a tendency to make assumptions about what the patient is discussing. Sometimes these assumptions are accepted and even acted upon as if they were fact. When listening, it is important that nurses keep this tendency under check and recognise that further interaction is necessary to validate these initial assumptions (see chapter 5).

Perceiving feelings

When listening, the nurse must perceive the feeling aspects of the patient's story, the emotional reactions and subjective responses that accompany the content. Patients often have strong emotional reactions to their health status and health-care. The connection of feelings to content begins to complete the picture that is the patient's experience. At times, patients express their feelings directly. For example:

- 'I'm really worried about the operation.'
- 'I am so pleased with the results of that test.'
- 'I'm feeling a bit down and blue today.'

When expressed in a straightforward manner, patients' feelings are easy to perceive, as long as nurses are ready to listen and receive input. More often, feelings are not expressed so openly and directly. Feeling expression follows a more circuitous route, unlike content, which is often expressed in a straightforward manner. Feelings are often hinted at, implied, inferred and talked around, rather than talked about. It could be that patients are reluctant to share their feelings because of uncertainty about how the nurse will react. This is especially true when trust has not yet been established between them. It could be that patients are unaware of, and out of touch with, their feelings. These are possible explanations for why feelings are expressed indirectly.

A more probable reason is that adults often try to conceal emotions, because they have learnt, through socialisation, which emotions are appropriate to express in various situations (Nelson-Jones, 1988). It may be that patients believe that feelings are not appropriate to share with nurses. But, no matter how much patients try to disguise or hide their feelings, their indirect expression is received by nurses whose perceptual antennae are ready to receive feeling messages.

There is, however, a word of caution about focusing on feelings. Research demonstrates that when nurses were perceptive to patients' feelings, the patients' distress increased (Reid-Ponte, 1992). This could be because patients were encouraged to express emotions to nurses who were good listeners. There is evidence that nurses tend to overestimate the degree of emotional distress patients are experiencing, when compared to what patients report (Hegedus, 1999; Farrell, 1991). That is, patients often do not perceive that their feelings are as significant as nurses think they are. The interpersonal dynamics at play are important to bear in mind when listening for feelings.

In listening for feelings, it is vital for nurses to suspend their personal judgments about what is acceptable and appropriate. Feelings, by their very nature, are often irrational, illogical and difficult to control. In order for nurses to be open to the perception of patients' feelings, they must hold the view that feelings are acceptable.

Open perception of feeling messages poses a challenge to nurses, not only because of the natural tendency to judge them, but also because of the way in which they are indirectly expressed. As described in the section on observing, feelings are often expressed nonverbally, and an observant nurse will pick up these nonverbal cues. Feelings are also expressed indirectly, through verbal means, and the perceptive nurse will notice them.

ACTIVITY 4.8

LISTENING FOR FEELINGS

 Process

1. Participants in a group take turns reading each patient statement aloud. Before each participant reads the statement they should think about a feeling to be conveyed along with the statement and then read it with the nonverbal cues that depict that feeling. Each participant records what they think the person reading the statement is feeling.

   a. 'I'm dying, aren't I?'

   b. 'Are you sure you know what you are doing?'

   c. 'That right leg won't ever be as strong as it used to be, no matter how hard I try.'

   d. 'I just wish I could be like I was before.'

   e. 'I've had enough. I just want to die.'

   f. 'Why can't anybody show me how to get out of this bed without pain?'

g. 'I don't think my back will ever stop aching.'

h. 'You have to be tough to be a nurse, don't you?'

i. 'The labour didn't go the way I expected.'

j. 'Have you ever done this procedure before?'

k. 'I'm not sure I should be taking all those tablets.'

l. 'I should have known better than to leave the cleaning liquid sitting out on the bench top. Now look what's happened.'

(*Note*: The answers to this activity can be found at the end of this chapter.)

Discussion

1. Refer to the end of the chapter and compare your answers with those provided. Reflect on the differences between your answers and the ones provided.

2. If you are working in a group, compare your answers with other participants', following the reading of each patient statement. Discuss any differences in perception of feelings and try and determine why they are different.

While there is a tendency to jump to conclusions and make assumptions when listening for content, there is an even greater danger of this when listening for feelings. Listeners tend to project their own opinions about what feelings are being expressed. This is partly because feelings are subjective by nature. The tendency is for the listener to perceive feelings on the basis of what they would feel, given a similar set of circumstances. As with suspending judgment, nurses need to rely on their self-awareness in order to keep this tendency in check.

Interpreting: listening for themes

The content of a patient's story and its accompanying feelings come together to form the general theme. Themes are the general point of the story, the consequences and implications of the content and feelings. It could be said that an understanding of the theme is the ultimate goal of listening, for once the point of each story is understood, the patient's entire experience comes into sharper focus. Nurses come to understand the theme of a patient's story by asking the following questions:

- What is the significance of the content and feelings?
- Why is the patient bringing this up at this time?
- How is this affecting the patient at the moment?

- What are the consequences of what the patient is expressing?
- What are the implications for the patient?

Understanding themes requires interpretation. This is always tentative at first and needs to be validated with the patient. After nurses have listened and attempted to understand, they are ready to respond. Perhaps the nurse's current understanding, achieved through listening, needs to be clarified, explored, and/or reflected back to the patient through paraphrasing. The skills needed to achieve any of these are covered in chapters 5 and 6.

ACTIVITY 4.9   ➡ 318

LISTENING FOR THEMES

 Process

1. Form pairs for this activity. Each member of a pair is to relate a story of something that has recently happened in their life. The story need not be earth shattering, but it should be meaningful to the person telling the story.

2. The other person is to listen, attend and say little during the telling of the story. At the completion, the listener states what they think is the theme. The person telling the story then validates (or invalidates) what the listener has interpreted as the theme.

3. Discuss any differences in interpretation.

Discussion

1. How accurate were the interpretations of the theme? What accounted for any inaccuracies?

2. What interfered with listening? What enhanced it?

During this activity, it was probably easier for the listener to identify the theme if they had had a similar experience, that is, when the story had a sense of familiarity about it. Repeated listening and identification of themes enables nurses to attain a sense of familiarity with common patient themes. Listening with understanding becomes a valuable learning experience in accurately perceiving patients' stories.

Recalling messages

Sometimes the greatest challenge in listening is the recall of what patients have said. Accurate recall is important if understanding is to occur. Themes often become apparent only after numerous interactions with a patient. Nurses must rely on their ability to recall previous interactions and put them together with current ones.

ACTIVITY 4.10

RECALLING MESSAGES

 Process

1. Four volunteers are needed for this activity. They will participate in the relating of an incident that occurred during the night shift at a hospital. The details of the incident are provided below.

2. Two of the volunteers are to leave the room. The other two are to seat themselves in a place where all other participants can hear their conversation.

3. All other participants act as observers. They are to make notes of what is added, deleted and distorted each time the incident is reported.

4. The two volunteers who are in the room are to pretend they are in a handover report at the end of a night shift. One of them relates the following incident to the other by reading it aloud:

    At about 2 a.m., Mr Smithers became confused and agitated. He got out of bed, went into the next room, over to Mrs Blue's bed and began to tell her about how to grow azaleas. Mrs Blue became frightened, rang her husband on the phone, and asked him to come in immediately. She was so loud on the phone that all the other patients in the room were awakened. There was a recently admitted patient in bed 18. She reacted to Mrs Blue, tried to get out of bed and fell to the floor. In the meantime, Mr Smithers made his way off the ward and was heading toward the lift. Fortunately, another nurse was getting out of the lift and escorted him back to the ward. We contacted the RMO to come and see the new admission and Mr Smithers. He ordered X-rays for the new admission and a sedative for Mr Smithers. Now everybody is settled and back in bed. There were no major injuries, but it was a real circus here for a while. In the midst of all of the chaos, Mr Blue arrived, in response to his wife's request. We let him visit with her for about twenty minutes and now he's returned home. The incident report was completed and sent.

5. One of the volunteers, who is out of the room, is now called back in. The volunteer who received the report relates the incident to the volunteer who has come into the room, by retelling the story without reading it. No assistance is offered to the volunteer who is relating the story; they must rely on memory to recount the incident.

6. The remaining volunteer (who is still outside of the room) is brought back into the room, and the previous volunteer relates the incident to them by retelling the story. Again, no assistance is offered to this volunteer in retelling the story.

7. Each time the incident is retold, the observers are to record any additions, deletions and distortions made to the original story.

8. The incident report is now read aloud, as it was told originally.

Discussion

1. The participants who observed the activity should now relate what was added to the original story. What was deleted? What was distorted when the story was retold?

2. What accounted for the alterations that were made to the original story?

3. Volunteers should report their reactions to having to retell such a complex story.

Patients' stories are usually not as complicated as the one told in activity 4.10. Nevertheless, this activity does highlight how easily stories become diminished, embellished and/or distorted. Recalling patients stories takes concentration and effort. If nurses find themselves asking patients to retell their stories many times, patients may not believe that they have listened in the first place. When nurses listen and remember what they have heard, patients are comforted to know that somebody has taken the time to understand them.

EVALUATION OF LISTENING

In the final analysis, nurses listen in order to respond in a manner that matches the patient's experience. Listening is considered effective when the nurse's response reflects understanding of what the patient is expressing. This is not to say that initial understanding (achieved through listening) will be entirely accurate. The nurse's interpretation is always tentative, awaiting correction, validation or further explication from the patient. Responses that shift the focus, change the subject or miss the point entirely, do not indicate active listening.

ACTIVITY 4.11   ➡ **318**

RESPONSES THAT INDICATE LISTENING

Process

1. Each of the following patient statements has a variety of possible responses. Evaluate each response in terms of whether it indicates that the nurse making the response has listened. Record on a piece

of paper a YES or NO on the basis of your evaluation. Do not evaluate how good or bad the response seems to you, or base your decision on whether or not you would actually make the response. Judge the response *only* in terms of listening, by asking yourself, 'Does the listener response indicate that the listener has heard the patient?' 'Does the response indicate an understanding of what the patient has expressed?'

a.

Patient

I don't think I'm going to make it. Am I going to die?

Responses

i.   The power of positive thinking can really help a lot. Many people in your situation have survived because they refused to give up. Keep fighting. Where there is life, there is hope.

ii.   What has happened to make you worried about it?

iii. I can't really say. You'll have to ask your doctor this question.

iv.   We are all going to die sometime, but it's a frightening prospect when it stares us in the face.

b.

Patient

Why is my blood pressure being taken so often?

Responses

i.   We have to check your blood pressure frequently.

ii.   It's doctor's orders.

iii. It is a general observation to keep a check on your vital signs.

iv.   Is it worrying you?

c.

Patient

How long will I be in here?

Responses

i.   As long as we think you need to be.

ii.   Let's discuss it with the doctor. If you think you're ready to go home, and the doctor is happy for you to go, then you can be discharged.

iii. People who have the operation you are having usually stay in hospital about three days. That's the usual routine, if there are no complications.

iv.   What has your doctor said about this?

d.

Patient

Why me? Why do I have to be the one that suffers like this?

Responses

i.   It is the part of the usual course of this disease. If you tell me when you feel worse and better, I can help with the pain.

ii.   We all suffer some kind of pain during our lifetime.

iii. It is just a bit of misfortune. You'll have better luck next time, I'm sure.

iv.   I wish I could answer that question. I'm not sure there always is a reason.

e.

Patient

I have contemplated suicide because I've hit rock bottom.

Responses

i.   Are you thinking about suicide right now?

ii.   Things can't be that bad.

iii. What's happened to you that you have hit rock bottom?

iv.   What exactly have you contemplated?

f.

Patient

What's going to happen when I come out of the operation?

Responses

i.   We will look after you.

ii.   There's nothing to worry about. You will feel better than you did before.

iii.   Have you had a general anaesthetic before?

iv.   You'll be drowsy for a few hours, and depending on your level of pain, you will receive regular pain relief.

g.

Patient

I'm not sick, and yet I have to take all of these tablets every day.

Responses

i.   It does seem a bit silly, doesn't it?

ii.   It could be that you don't feel sick because you *are* taking the tablets.

iii.   Which tablets are you taking?

iv.   How long have you been taking the tablets?

2.   Now review each response for which you recorded a YES. Evaluate each in terms of the major goal of listening, that is, the encouragement of patients to continue expressing their experiences. How encouraging is each?

3.   Compare your answers with the ones provided at the end of the chapter.

(*Note*: The answers to this activity can be found at the end of this chapter.)

CHAPTER SUMMARY

Meanings are derived, and initial understanding is achieved through active listening. Listening enables nurses to perceive the patient's reality, the world as the patient is experiencing it. After listening effectively, nurses are in a position to respond according to what is perceived. Listening engages both the nurse and patient. It is an essential and fundamental process in establishing effective relationships in nursing practice.

ANSWERS TO ACTIVITIES

ACTIVITY 4.7: LISTENING FOR CONTENT

Patient story I

WHO: self (speaker), doctor
WHAT: something happened to hip, difficulty walking

WHEN: Sunday afternoon
WHERE: not stated
WHY: reason for having the X-ray

Patient story II

WHO: speaker, child, GP's receptionist
WHAT: serious stomach pain, rang GP, drove to GP's surgery
WHEN: beginning of a day
WHERE: GP's surgery
WHY: explain the story, but not entirely clear

Patient story III

WHO: speaker
WHAT: unable to move left arm
WHEN: not stated
WHERE: garden, then house
WHY: don't know what to do

Patient story IV

WHO: speaker, 'him'
WHAT: he is not himself
WHEN: 'for months'
WHERE: home, in front of television
WHY: worried about 'him'

Patient story V

WHO: speaker, GP
WHAT: no time to have regular pap smears
WHEN: not stated
WHERE: not stated
WHY: questioning whether regular pap smears are necessary

Patient story VI

WHO: speaker
WHAT: chemo and radiotherapy, feeling tired
WHEN: now
WHERE: speaker's room
WHY: can't attend to children

ACTIVITY 4.8: LISTENING FOR FEELINGS

1. a. fear, anxiety, worry
   b. fear, anxiety, worry
   c. frustration, anger, resignation

d.　sadness, anger, frustration

e.　sadness, anger, resignation

f.　anger, frustration

g.　sadness, anger

h.　fear, anxiety, apprehension

i.　disappointment, frustration

j.　apprehension, anxiety, fear

k.　uncertainty

l.　regret, guilt

ACTIVITY 4.11: RESPONSES THAT INDICATE LISTENING

Note: The answer NO indicates that the nurse responding has not understood/acknowledged what the patient is saying, while the answer YES indicates active reception of what the patient has said.

1. a. *Patient:* I don't think I'm going to make it. Am I going to die?

    i.　NO The power of positive thinking can really help a lot. Many people in your situation have survived because they refused to give up. Keep fighting. Where there is life, there is hope.

    ii.　YES What has happened to make you worried about it?

    iii.　NO I can't really say. You'll have to ask your doctor this question.

    iv.　YES We are all going to die sometime, but its a frightening prospect when it stares us in the face.

   b. *Patient:* Why is my blood pressure being taken so often?

    i.　NO We have to check your blood pressure frequently.

    ii.　NO It's doctor's orders.

    iii.　YES It is a general observation to keep a check on your vital signs.

    iv.　YES Is it worrying you?

   c. *Patient:* How long will I be in here?

    i.　NO As long as we think.

    ii.　YES Let's discuss it with doctor. You need to decide if you think you're ready to go home. If the doctor is happy for you to go then, you can be discharged.

    iii.　YES People who have the operation you are having usually stay in hospital about 10 days. That's the usual routine, if there are no complications.

    iv.　YES What has your doctor said about this?

   d. *Patient:* Why me? Why do I have to be the one that suffers like this?

    i.　NO It is the part of the usual course of this disease. If you tell me when you feel worse and better, I can help with the pain.

    ii.　NO Everyone suffers some kind of pain during their lifetime.

    iii.　NO It is just a bit of misfortune. You'll have better luck next time, I'm sure.

    iv.　YES I wish I could answer that question. I'm not sure there always is a reason.

e. *Patient*: I have contemplated suicide because I've hit rock bottom.

    i.   YES Are you thinking about suicide right now?

    ii.   NO Things can't be that bad.

    iii. YES What's happened to you that you have hit rock bottom?

    iv. YES What exactly have you contemplated?

f. *Patient*: What's going to happen when I come out of the operation?

    i.   NO We will look after you.

    ii.   NO There's nothing to worry about. You will feel better than you did before.

    iii. NO Have you had a general anaesthetic before?

    iv. YES You'll be drowsy for a few hours, and depending on your level of pain, you will receive regular pain relief.

g. *Patient*: I'm not sick, and yet I have to take all of these tablets every day.

    i.   NO It does seem a bit silly, doesn't it?

    ii.   NO It could be that you don't feel sick because you *are* taking the tablets.

    iii. YES Which tablets are you taking?

    iv. YES How long have you been taking the tablets?

REFERENCES

Carkhuff, R.R. (1983). *The student workbook for the art of helping*, (2nd edn). Human Resource Press, Amherst MA.

Cormier, L. S., Cormier, W. H. & Weisser, R. J. (1986). *Interviewing and helping skills for health professionals*. Jones and Bartlett, Boston MA.

Doona, M.E., Haggerty, L. A. & Chase, S. K. (1997). Nursing presence: an existential exploration of the concept. *Scholarly inquiry for nursing practice: an international journal*, 11 (1), 3–16.

Egan, G. (1994). *The skilled helper*, (5th edn). Brooks/Cole, Pacific Grove CA.

Farrell, G.A. (1991). How accurately do nurses perceive patients' needs? A comparison of general and psychiatric settings. *Journal of advanced nursing*, 16, 1062–1070.

Hegedus, K.S. (1999). Providers' and consumers' perspectives of nurses' caring behaviours. *Journal of advanced nursing*, 30, 1090–1096.

Nelson-Jones, R. (1988) *Practical counselling and helping skills*, (2nd edn). Holt, Rinehart and Winston, Sydney.

Reid-Ponte, P. (1992). Distress in cancer patients and primary nurses' empathy skills. *Cancer nursing*, 15 (4), 283–292.

Shea, S. C. (1988). *Psychiatric interviewing: the art of understanding*. Saunders, Philadelphia PA.

Webb, C. & Hope, K. (1995). What kind of nurses do patients want? *Journal of clinical nursing*, 4 (2), 101–108

CHAPTER 5

BUILDING MEANING: UNDERSTANDING

INTRODUCTION

Understanding a patient's experience, that is, viewing the world from the patient's perspective, is one of the most central aspects of interacting and building relationships in nursing. Mutual understanding is the basis of meaningful interaction, and, in the patient–nurse relationship, it is the nurse's responsibility to facilitate this understanding. Mutual understanding requires time, effort, commitment and skill. It is challenging for one person to understand and appreciate another person's reality.

Effective attending and listening opens doors and aids the nurse's entry into the patient's world. The stage is set for a meaningful relationship, because interpersonal contact has been established. Listening enables the nurse to develop an initial understanding of the patient's experience. It is important to recognise that this understanding remains tentative, until it is either validated or corrected and altered through further interaction with the patient. The impressions formed in the process of listening are often partial, inaccurate and superficial. The nurse who acts immediately, without further interaction to check the accuracy of these impressions, risks attempting to build a relationship that lacks mutual understanding and providing help that is not necessarily congruent with the patient's needs. Taking time to understand a patient's experiences enables nurses to ground nursing care within the patient's reality.

Listening is largely an absorptive activity, as nurses take in and process patients' stories. But at some point during an interaction, verbal responses must be uttered; the nurse usually has to say something. A variety of verbal responses are possible, however a response that promotes greater understanding between patient and nurse is most beneficial, especially in the early stages of the relationship. Responses that promote understanding not only demonstrate that the nurse has listened, they also convey a desire to comprehend the patient's experience more fully. Effective listening demonstrates open acceptance of the patient, and encourages the patient to interact. Effective understanding encourages further interaction because it openly acknowledges the patient's experience, confirming its reality. Understanding responses check how effectively the nurse's perceptions and interpretations correspond to the patient's meaning. Because they build meaning, understanding responses deepen the relationship between patient and nurse.

Chapter overview

This chapter begins with an overview of the ways in which nurses can verbally respond to patients. The various ways of responding are explained in depth, in order to demonstrate how they differ in intent and impact on the patient–nurse relationship. Understanding is shown to be the most appropriate way to respond when building this relationship. Understanding is viewed as the basis of the relationship, and the importance of understanding between patient and nurse is highlighted. The skills of understanding are covered next in the discussion. The skill of paraphrasing is the major skill of understanding, and therefore is treated more extensively than the other skills. The other skills include: seeking clarification, reflecting feelings, connecting and summarising. Empathy is presented as a central concept in understanding. The concept of empathy is explained, and how this concept is integrated into nursing practice is delineated. An analysis of how emapathy is conceptualised in nursing assists in the comparision of empathy with other related concepts such as sympathy.

VERBAL RESPONDING

After actively listening to a patient and forming an initial impression, it is natural for a nurse to respond verbally. While it is important that responses be spontaneous and sincere, it is equally important that they be thoughtful, developed with intention and skilfully employed. The nurse's initial verbal responses set the direction for further interaction. Because there are a variety of possible ways to respond, nurses must ensure that their verbal responses move the relationship in a desired and intended direction. Choice of a response is based on insight into how it may affect the patient, the interaction and the relationship. A nurse who has this insight and awareness is in the best position to respond in a manner that both matches the current situation and realises the response's desired intent. In regard to intent, nurses should consider what they need to know about patients and why they need to know it.

The initial phase of the relationship between patient and nurse is a particularly sensitive and critical time for responding, because, more than likely, the trust required for full patient disclosure is not yet firmly established. Responses that work best at this time are those that validate patients by acknowledging their experiences. Validating and acknowledging responses convey the nurse's willingness to understand the patient. Patients will come to trust those nurses who can be relied on to understand.

Inadvertently, nurses may respond in a manner that suggests a lack of desire to understand. The following response, which denies the patient's experience, is an example:

Patient: I'm worried about how my family is going to manage without me.

Nurse: No need to worry, they'll survive without you. It'll do them good to realise how much you do for them.

While the nurse may have wished to encourage the patient with this response, it is likely that the response indicates a rejection of the patient's perception of the situation. By failing to acknowledge the patient's reality, responses such as these engender the feeling that the nurse does not want to understand. Compare the preceding example with the following:

Patient: I'm worried about how my family is going to manage without me.

Nurse: What is worrying you most about how they will manage?

Here the nurse provides acknowledgment and confirmation of the patient's reality. Responses such as this deepen interpersonal engagement and promote understanding between patient and nurse; as such, they build trust.

Most nurses develop habitual, routine and even stylised ways of responding to patients. The intent is usually to be of help or assistance to patients, but this intent may not be fully realised if nurses overuse one type of response and/or lack awareness of the impact of their responses. Goodwill and desire alone are not sufficient in the absence of awareness and direction.

ACTIVITY 5.1

YOUR USUAL STYLE OF RESPONDING I

 Process

1.   For each following statement or question (a–o), write a response. Do not spend too much time pondering your response, but do try to be helpful to the person speaking. Record a response that is typical of how you would usually respond.

    a.   A resident of a nursing home: 'I miss my wife. I don't know where she is. Where is she? Can you tell me?'

    b.   A relative of an unconscious patient hospitalised in intensive care: 'Mum is really going to be upset when she wakes up. She is going to kill us for letting her be in here.'

    c.   An adolescent patient during a routine health checkup: 'My folks keep pressuring me about the future. I don't have a clue about what I want to do.'

d. A first-time mother about to be discharged from a postnatal unit: 'How am I ever going to be able to manage this baby on my own?'

e. A client to a community nurse during a home visit: 'I am so glad to see you. I have not been at all well lately.'

f. A patient, a young man, who is having regular haemodialysis: 'My girlfriend left me because she's afraid she might catch something and my best mate doesn't visit me any more because he hates the sight of blood.'

g. A resident of a hostel for the elderly: 'It's really boring in here. The days are so long and there's no one to talk to except the nurses, and they are always so busy.'

h. A mother during a routine visit at an early childhood centre: 'My husband left and I am having so much trouble managing on my own.'

i. A resident of a nursing home: 'It's hard when you grow old and your friends and family start to die. My children are great, but they have their own lives.'

j. A patient, a woman, during an outpatient clinic visit for a routine pap smear: 'I am not really sure about having any more children. I'm 39 now and reckon I've pushed my luck far enough. I have two healthy children. Perhaps I should just leave it at that.'

k. A patient during a postoperative clinic visit: 'You know, I just take one day at a time. It's been two months since my surgery and I'm still not sure if I'll ever feel like my old self again.'

l. A patient during an admission interview in hospital: 'I've lived with arthritis for years, but lately I'm having more trouble than usual. I can hardly get out of bed in the morning and the pain is becoming unbearable.'

m. A resident of a hostel for the elderly: 'You can't possibly understand what it feels like. You never had this problem. How would you understand?'

n. A client, a pregnant woman, during an antenatal visit: 'People are kind and concerned, but no one really knows what it is like to lose a child. It's the most painful experience imaginable. You never get over it.'

o. A patient, a man hospitalised for a myocardial infarction: 'I'm really worried about how my family will cope without my help. I have three small children, my wife works and we share all the household chores. Now that I've had this heart attack, I'm not sure how much assistance I can offer.'

2. Reflect on each of your responses:

   ■ What is your intention?
   ■ What do you hope to achieve by responding in this way?
   ■ How do you hope the patient will react to your response?

3. If you are working in groups, form pairs. One person now reads the statement or question and the other person reads their recorded response. The 'patient' reflects after each response:

   ■ What is your impression of the nurse? and of the response?
   ■ How has the response affected you?
   ■ How encouraged are you to continue the interaction?
   ■ How much do you think the nurse understands your situation?

   The 'patient' then shares these reflections with the 'nurse'.

4. The 'nurse' now shares their intention (step 2 of the process) with the 'patient'. Make a note of the following:

   ■ How congruent is the nurse's intention with the effect on the 'patient'?

5. Continue to read each statement or question followed by its response and share the reflections.

6. Switch roles and complete steps 3, 4 and 5.

Discussion

1. What differences are there between the 'nurses'' intentions and the 'patients'' impressions of the responses? How do you account for this?

2. Were there some responses that were more encouraging than others? Which ones were encouraging? and discouraging?

3. Which responses resulted in a negative impression on the 'patient', for example, 'the nurse does not understand', 'does not really care' or 'does not wish to discuss the topic'?

WAYS OF RESPONDING

This section explores the various types of responses nurses might have to patients, based on categories developed by Johnson (2000). In this scheme, responses are categorised according to their intent, what they are designed to do or their purpose. On this basis, the majority of responses fit into one of the following categories:

■ Advising and evaluating
■ Analysing and interpreting

- Reassuring and supporting
- Questioning and probing
- Paraphrasing and understanding

The categories include those responses that are significant—ones with the potential to have a critical impact on the interaction and the relationship. There are other possible responses that would not fit into any of these categories, for example, small talk about the weather. They are not included because they are of less consequence to the overall relationship.

Each way of responding may be helpful in its own right, and can be effectively employed within the context of the patient–nurse relationship. Nevertheless, each has a different intent, suggests a different type of relationship between patient and nurse and therefore has a different impact on their interactions, especially in the sensitive early stages. Some responses facilitate interaction better than others, so timing and an awareness of each type of response are crucial.

Advising and evaluating

This category includes responses that offer an opinion or advice, ranging from a mild suggestion to a directive about what the patient should do. Such responses are based on the nurse's opinions and ideas and therefore have an evaluative edge. Examples in this category include:

- 'It's best not to dwell too much on such things.'
- 'Try to relax and stop worrying so much, it doesn't really help.'
- 'Ask the doctor these questions.'
- 'Just tell your mother it's your life and you'll do with it what you want.'

Responses such as these are among the most common made by people who are trying to help. When nurses use this type of response they convey the message that they 'know best' and are in a position that is superior to the patient (Johnson, 2000). Advice and evaluation carry the implication that patients are unable to know what to do, thus increasing their sense of vulnerability. For this reason, advising and evaluating responses run the risk of being met with a defensive reaction or a rejection of the advice. Have you ever told a friend what you think they should do to resolve a problem, only to be met with 'Yes, but...', or 'That's easy for you to say', or 'I already tried that and it didn't work'. When given as an initial response, advice rarely works because of its potential to produce a sense of inadequacy in the patient and the patient's need to defend against this feeling.

Responses that advise offer solutions about what ought to be done. As a general rule, it is better to reach a sound understanding of a patient's situation before launching into solutions. An advising response gives the impression that a patient's difficulties and problems are easily solved, that there is a 'quick fix'. Some situations are easily resolved but, more often than not, further elaboration is needed before answers are found (if any *can* be found). Advice giving is better left until the nurse fully understands the patient's experience.

Just as it is difficult to listen without judging, it is equally difficult to curtail the tendency to evaluate and advise. The tendency of nurses to give advice reflects how many nurses perceive their role, as possessing knowledge and expertise. This perception often leads nurses to attempt to help patients by telling them what to do and providing answers.

While there are times when nurses offer expert advice to the patient, it is important that the patient's need and desire for such advice is established beforehand. Likewise, if advice is to be effective, it must be based on a clear understanding of the patient's experience. For example, explaining the usual course of events following anaesthesia and advising how to cope with 'waking up' is advice based on understanding of the situation. This is an objective, 'case knowledge' (see chapter 2), which does not necessarily require interaction with the patient. In a more subjective situation, such as anxiety about impending surgery, telling a patient to relax is of little use unless the nurse takes the time to understand the nature of the patient's worry. Advice given without understanding runs the risk of being ill timed or irrelevant.

Advising versus sharing information

Giving advice is sometimes confused with sharing information. While they are similar, sharing information is not the same as telling patients what to do. When they share information (see chapter 7) nurses provide knowledge, alternatives and facts. When they offer advice, nurses provide specific actions to perform. Advice also involves reliance on the nurse's personal value judgments, while sharing information is free of such judgments.

Analysing and interpreting

A response that analyses and interprets reaches beyond what the patient has expressed into a deeper level of meaning. An interpretive response reads into patients' messages, giving the impression that the nurse knows how patients *really* feel or what they *really* think. Interpretations imply that a nurse knows more about patients than they know themselves (Johnson, 2000). Examples of analysing and interpreting responses include:

- 'You really don't want to assume responsibility for your own health.'
- 'You are acting like most new mothers, worrying too much and being overprotective of your baby.'
- 'You are afraid that if you tell the surgeon how you feel about the operation, he will reject you entirely and drop you as a patient.'

Responses such as these delve beneath the surface and open up areas that the patient has not expressed directly. As with advising, interpreting may have a legitimate place, but as an initial response it is often too threatening to be effective in building the relationship. An interpretation, regardless of its accuracy, can be threatening because it confronts patients with another reality, one that they may not be willing or able to face. Because such interpretations have a confronting edge, they are better left until the relationship has been established and the nurse has 'earned the right' to challenge in this way (see chapter 7).

Patients are more likely to accept interpretations from a nurse who has taken the time to fully understand their situation. It is unlikely that a nurse would know a patient well enough to make interpretations early in the course of their relationship. As an initial response, interpretations are intrusive and invasive and may impede the development of trust.

Reassuring and supporting

There is a definite place for realistic reassurance and support (see chapter 7) in the course of patient–nurse relationships, and a nurse's approach needs to convey an overall attitude of support whenever interacting with patients. Nevertheless, a falsely reassuring response (the type discussed here) is one that glosses over and minimises the importance of the patient's experience, before that experience is entirely acknowledged and understood. In this respect, a falsely reassuring response is one that attempts to smooth the patient's discomfort, by making everything sound 'all right', regardless of the objective or subjective reality of the situation. It may convey a patronising attitude or present the patient with a sense of unrealistic assurance. Examples of responses that falsely reassure and support include:

- 'A good night's sleep will do wonders for you.'
- 'There is nothing to worry about. It is only a minor procedure.'
- 'Don't be silly, Mrs Jones, nothing will go wrong.'
- 'You'll feel better after the operation and will get well soon.'

False reassurance may sound good on the surface but, more often than not, it is dismissive of the patient's reality; it lacks understanding. Reflect for a moment on how you feel whenever someone tells you not to worry about something that is causing you concern. Do you have an impression that this person is genuinely interested? Does this person demonstrate a desire to understand your concern?

The use of clichés is another example of responses that attempt to support and reassure. Some examples include:

- 'It's always darkest just before a storm.'
- 'Every cloud has a silver lining.'

Responses such as these, often said whenever patients express anxieties and concerns, fail to acknowledge the subjective reality of patients' experiences. They carry an implied judgment that patients' concerns are unfounded, even foolish. Because they discount the validity and significance of patients' feelings and perceptions, falsely reassuring responses sound as if the nurse is not really interested. Like premature advice, reassuring responses and clichés attempt to 'fix things' before they are fully clarified and understood.

Questioning and probing

A response that questions and probes is one which attempts to gather more information and explore the situation further. It indicates a need for elaboration and may ultimately lead to greater understanding. Examples of this type of response include:

- 'What is worrying you most about the operation?'
- 'Where is your pain?'
- 'What have you tried to get to sleep?'
- 'What do you think?'

Responses that question and probe indicate that nurses are trying to understand, but need more information to do so. Early in the course of the relationship, the nurse frequently employs questions in an effort to get to know the patient. Throughout the course of the relationship, questions are further employed to develop an even greater understanding of the patient's experience. Unless they are overused, responses that question and probe are quite useful if they are stated correctly and timed appropriately. There are other ways to explore aside from questioning and probing, and effective exploration involves the use of a variety of skills (see chapter 6).

Paraphrasing and understanding

When nurses paraphrase, they share their understanding with patients by rephrasing what patients have expressed, using their own words instead of patients' words. Responses, which paraphrase what the patient has expressed, demonstrate that the nurse's intention is to understand the patient more fully. Examples in this category include:

- 'You are unable to sleep because of your uncertainty about the future.'
- 'You are feeling more relaxed now that you are in your own home.'
- 'It seems strange to you that you should have to keep asking the same questions over and over again.'

Responses that demonstrate understanding confirm and validate what patients have expressed, thus communicating nurses' genuine interest in and acceptance of patients. Through the use of the paraphrase, nurses share their understanding of patients' messages, in order to ensure this understanding is correct. Paraphrasing and understanding responses demonstrate that the nurse wants to follow the patient's meaning and will check to ensure this happens. They convey the message 'I won't assume I know what you mean or what you need until I am certain I know—and only you can tell me'. Early in the course of the relationship, this type of response is especially effective, because it places patient and nurse on equal footing and helps to build trust.

All other categories of responses, except questioning and probing, are based on an assumption that nurses know what patients are experiencing and what is best for them. An understanding response attempts to validate or invalidate these assumptions. The meaning a nurse constructs from what a patient has expressed may not be what the patient actually meant. An understanding response is of value in preventing such lack of congruency; it addresses one of the most common problems in communication, which occurs when people don't realise there is sometimes a difference between what is meant and what is said and consequently misunderstanding what is meant.

ACTIVITY 5.2 ➥ 318

RECOGNITION OF THE TYPES OF RESPONSES

 Process

1. For each statement (a–l) in step 2 there are five possible responses. Read all five responses to the statement and decide on the response that most closely matches what you would say under the circumstances.

2. For each set of five responses, determine which of the following categories best represents each response (record your answer on a separate sheet of paper):

   E   Advising and evaluating

   I   Analysing and interpreting

   S   Reassuring and supporting

   P   Questioning and probing

   U   Paraphrasing and understanding

   There is a response from each category in each set.

   a.   'I'm just so fed up with being sick and in pain. I'm tired of having to rely on the nurses all the time.'

      Responses

      i.   'It's okay to rely on us. That's why we are here.'

      ii.   'You are an independent type of person who prefers to do things for yourself.'

      iii. 'All of this is really starting to get you down.'

      iv.   'Just relax and let us help you.'

      v.   'What is bothering you the most?'

   b.   'I never really looked after myself. Now look how I am suffering.'

      Responses

      i.   'I don't know what you mean.'

      ii.   'Lots of people say the same thing.'

      iii. 'Well, you would have looked after yourself if it mattered to you.'

      iv.   'It's hard to look back with regrets, isn't it?'

      v.   'Sounds as if you're angry at yourself.'

c.   'Don't bother with me. I am going to die anyway.'

Responses

i.   'That sounds sad and depressing.'

ii.   'Don't talk like that. You are not going to die.'

iii.   'What makes you say that?'

iv.   'It's not a bother to look after you. I am here because I want to help you.'

v.   'You have given up hope because you are getting on in age.'

d.   'I'm in so much pain all the time. I manage to get through the day all right, because I keep busy, but my backache prevents me from getting a good night's sleep. So I keep busy during the day, end up really tired, but then can't get the rest that I need. I'm getting more and more tired all the time.'

Responses

i.   'Why don't you try some relaxation exercises to get to sleep?'

ii.   'How often do you have a bad night?'

iii.   'Keeping busy during the day helps with the pain, but getting enough sleep at night is more of a worry for you right now.'

iv.   'Sounds as if you are letting the pain control your life.'

v.   'I'm sure you'll be able to work something out once you become accustomed to living with the pain.'

e.   'People think they want to live a long time, but I'm telling you, don't ever grow old. You'll end up in a place like this. It's boring and depressing. Look at everybody here, do they look happy to you?'

Responses

i.   'Everybody feels a bit blue sometimes. Things will get better—you'll see.'

ii.   'Come on, let's go for a walk. It's a beautiful day today.'

iii.   'What's so boring and depressing about this place?'

iv.   'You are approaching things with a negative attitude so, naturally, the whole world looks grim.'

v.   'You're really not happy about being here, are you?'

f. 'My wife died recently. I don't want to talk about it.'

Responses

    i. 'It does help to talk about these things.'

    ii. 'What *do* you want to talk about?'

    iii. 'You'll get over it in time, I am sure.'

    iv. 'Maybe you are the type of person who has difficulty letting people help you.'

    v. 'You don't feel like talking to me?'

g. 'I know I should change my diet and alter my lifestyle. The doctor said I am a high risk for a heart attack. I've always been a bit of a go-getter, take after Dad in that respect. He had a heart attack at 50, so I guess I should do something—but I really don't know where to start.'

Responses

    i. 'Sounds as if you have been avoiding the inevitable. You know what to do, but don't want to face it. You could change if you really wanted to.'

    ii. 'Just try a bit harder to slow down and eat the right foods.'

    iii. 'You have an idea about what you should do, but are having trouble getting started.'

    iv. 'What do you think you should change first?'

    v. 'Worrying about it will only make things worse. I'm sure you can change.'

h. 'I get so tired looking after David day after day. There is all the physical care, but I think the mental strain is the worst. I worry constantly about where he is and what he is doing. I think he gets a bit annoyed with my constant hovering over him. The worst thing is that I get no relief—it's so constant.'

Responses

    i. 'The constant worry is really getting to you and wearing you down. You just can't seem to get away from it.'

    ii. 'People in your situation often feel this way. It's a difficult problem to come to terms with.'

    iii. 'Try and put the worry out of your mind at least once each day. Make yourself a cup of tea, sit down and just relax.'

iv. 'Is there ever an opportunity for you to get away?'

v. 'There may be a bit of guilt in what you are saying. You probably keep thinking about the times in the past when you could have been more understanding and supportive toward David.'

i. 'The least they could have done was warn me that Dad was going to be sedated. Those doctors didn't even tell me beforehand so I could have a quick visit with him. Now I need to leave the hospital without even speaking to Dad.'

Responses

i. 'You sound like one of those people who likes to be in control.'

ii. 'The doctors were really busy. Otherwise I am sure they would have told you.'

iii. 'I can see you are frustrated and angry about not getting to talk to your Dad.'

iv. 'If this happens again, I would say something if I were you.'

v. 'What exactly did they tell you?'

j. 'Mum was always there to look after us when we needed something. Now that she's sick, I guess it's our turn to look after her. It feels so strange and I'm not sure she will even let us do much for her.'

Responses

i. 'Because you always had her to look after you, you wonder if she will let you look after her.'

ii. 'Of course she will. Your mother is a sensible woman.'

iii. 'You feel scared that you won't be able to switch roles with your Mum.'

iv. 'Tell me more about it.'

v. 'Just tell her she needs you now and she will have to let you take care of her.'

k. 'What will happen to me if John dies. I don't know what I would do. I couldn't go on without him.'

Responses

i. 'No need to worry about things before they happen.'

ii. 'You're scared because you have allowed yourself to become too dependent on John and can't see how you'll make it on your own.'

iii. 'What makes you think he won't make it?'

iv. 'I suppose it's frightening to think you can't survive without John.'

v. 'There is plenty of help around. You can join a social club in your area.'

l. 'That surgeon explained everything about the operation, but I could not understand what was being said. I didn't even know what to ask.'

Responses

i. 'You're scared to ask questions of the doctors because they are so powerful.'

ii. 'So the surgeon's explanation was not quite enough for you to understand.'

iii. 'What questions do you still have?'

iv. 'The next time you see the surgeon, tell him you want some answers.'

v. 'Don't worry too much, most people don't really understand the technical aspects of surgery.'

(*Note*: The answers to this activity can be found at the end of the chapter.)

Discussion

1. Compare your answers with those provided at the end of the chapter. Are there any types of responses that were difficult to recognise? Which are they? Review the section of the text that pertains to these.

2. In groups of five to six participants, discuss your answers. Are there any types of responses that other members had difficulty recognising? Which are they? Discuss these until understanding of each type of response is achieved.

3. Review your responses to step 1 of the process and determine whether there are some types of response you seem to provide naturally. Compare these results with the other participants in the group.

4. Discuss the reason(s) you tend to provide some types of response more than others.

ACTIVITY 5.3

YOUR USUAL STYLE OF RESPONDING II

 Process

1. Refer to the responses that you recorded for activity 5.1: *Your usual style of responding I.*

2. For each of your responses, determine which type of response you used (that is, advising and evaluating; analysing and interpreting; reassuring and supporting; questioning and probing; or paraphrasing and understanding) and mark each accordingly. You may have used more than one category in a given response. If this is the case, include all categories used.

3. Tally the total number of times you used each type of response. Is there one type you used more than others? Reflect on the reasons for your apparent preference.

4. Have someone else determine which types of responses you used. Discuss any discrepancies and make a final determination of which type of response was used.

Discussion

1. Compare your tally with other participants. Is there a type of response that was preferred by a majority of participants? Discuss the results.

2. Which ways of responding seem to fit the perceived role of the nurse? Which do not?

3. How frequently was the paraphrasing and understanding response used? Discuss why this is the case.

The advising and evaluating type of response is one of the most frequently used when people are trying to be helpful (Johnson, 2000). This is probably due to people's natural tendency to make judgments and offer opinions, especially when they are trying to be of help. There are times when being directive and prescriptive will be of help to patients, but there are risks if this approach is used exclusively or too extensively. When using advising and evaluating responses, nurses place themselves in the position of expert and fail to acknowledge patients' expertise and capabilities in managing their own lives. Patients are not encouraged to seek solutions that fit their unique experience but rather are offered solutions and answers.

Nurses often show a strong preference for the reassuring and supporting type of response. This is understandable because nursing care is best given in a reassuring and supportive atmosphere. Nevertheless, a truly reassuring and supportive manner differs from glossing over the patient's experience with a reassuring cliché. Falsely reassuring statements may negate the reality of patients' experiences. Because of their failure to acknowledge and affirm the patient, such responses interfere with effective interaction between patient and nurse.

Two recent studies demonstrate how nurses respond to patient anxiety. The most common responses tried to cheer the patient up (reassuring and supporting) or offered an explanation about the symptoms (advising and evaluating). The least frequent responses demonstrated understanding (Motyka et al., 1997; Whyte et al., 1997). For more detail on these studies, see chapter 7, page 201, *Ways of responding revisited*.

It is important to recognise that none of the categories is inherently good or bad. Each is appropriate at different times in the relationship and under different circumstances. The ultimate aim is for each nurse to develop as wide a repertoire as possible, and to use each type of response with awareness of its appropriateness and consequence. (Subsequent chapters cover the various types of responses, except the understanding type, which is the subject of this chapter.)

Understanding responses are most appropriate for building a relationship based on mutual meaning. They are effective in the early stages of the relationship and are also used throughout, as a natural reaction to active listening (see chapter 4). Regardless of how effectively a nurse has suspended judgment during listening, the patient's messages still are processed through personal, interpretative filters. In processing patients' messages, nurses form impressions and reach conclusions about what patients are expressing and experiencing. These interpretations may not be entirely correct. If a nurse's interpretation of what a patient is saying is not shared actively and openly with the patient, potential misunderstandings are likely to go unchecked. In giving an understanding response nurses share their interpretations so that they can be validated or corrected. Such responses enable nurses to build meaning that is congruent with a patient's experience.

THE IMPORTANCE OF UNDERSTANDING

In order to be of help to patients, it is best if nurses operate from a vantage point within patients' experiences. When responding with understanding, nurses attempt to view the world from the patient's point of view. Nurses reach for meaning by asking. 'What is this patient experiencing?' 'What is the meaning of the experience for the patient?' 'Am I following…do I get the drift?' Understanding responses check the answers to such questions. The following scenario serves as an illustration:

Patient: It doesn't seem right that I am still in so much pain. My hip surgery was six weeks ago, and I still can't seem to get comfortable. Is it just me? I asked my doctor and she said 'No, this is not unusual, so don't worry.' But I really don't know.

Nurse: It doesn't seem right to you that you are still in so much pain six weeks after the surgery.

Patient:	Yes and no, because I really didn't know exactly what to expect.
Nurse:	So, it's more that you don't know the usual course of events following hip surgery.
Patient:	Yes, I mean all the doctor said was this is not *unusual*, so I'm still in the dark. I think I'm getting a bit neurotic about the whole thing.
Nurse:	So, what you really want to know is how much pain is reasonable and to be expected six weeks after the surgery.
Patient:	Yes, if I knew for sure that this is expected I wouldn't be so worried. What do you think?

Because understanding is achieved, the nurse can now proceed to act. The nurse can provide the patient with concrete information (see chapter 7) about recovery after hip surgery. Exploration (see chapter 6) into the exact nature of the patient's pain also may be warranted. Perhaps support (see chapter 7) in pain management can be provided. The key is that the nurse is guided by the understanding that, for *this* patient, fear of the unknown is the central meaning in the expression.

Notice how the nurse's initial understanding response was not entirely accurate. The patient took the opportunity to clarify the meaning because the nurse's response indicated a desire to understand. The patient's final question, 'What do you think?' is indicative of their beginning trust in the nurse. The patient feels able to rely on this nurse because the nurse has taken the time to understand the situation.

Because each patient's experience is unique, another patient may have expressed similar thoughts for an entirely different reason. Here is a similar scenario, with a different patient:

Patient:	It doesn't seem right that I am still in so much pain. My hip surgery was six weeks ago, and I still can't seem to get comfortable. Is it just me? I asked my doctor and she said 'No, this is not unusual, so don't worry.' But I really don't know.
Nurse:	It doesn't seem right to you that you are still in so much pain six weeks after the surgery.
Patient:	It's not the pain so much, but the amount of medication I'm taking.
Nurse:	You think it might be too much.
Patient:	Well, yes, I take those tablets every four hours. Could I be taking too many?

As with the first scenario, the nurse may need to explore this situation further, or offer concrete information about the likelihood of taking too much pain medication. The illustrations show how different patients experience the same event. These scenarios exemplify the importance of achieving understanding, which is based on the patient's view of the situation. While the situation is similar, each patient's experience of it is different. In each scenario, the nurse listens to the patient's view, comes to understand it and is then able to operate from a vantage point within the patient's experience. The nurse can now offer help, in the form of advice, information or reassurance, that is specific to the patient.

Internal and external understanding

The understanding that is emphasised here is termed internal because it is grounded in the patient's subjective world and personal view of a situation. External understanding, on the other hand, is an objective view of a situation. In nursing, these external understandings are based on clinical information that is devoid of any specific patient (for example, a textbook case, referred to as case knowledge, see chapter 2).

Nurses often become so focused on having the answers that they rely exclusively on an external understanding of the situation. An over-concern with 'What can I do?' often prevents nurses from asking 'What is this like for this patient?' This keeps nurses externally focused. There is a danger that nursing care based solely on external understanding will be misguided, and will not take into account the uniqueness of the patient. In the scenarios given earlier, the nurse could have relied on an informed understanding of recovery following hip surgery, and not taken the time to understand *this* patient's experience of recovery.

Focusing externally can lead to premature and automatic solutions, which look to results and outcomes. Focusing internally meets patients where they are and offers a way of operating from within their experiences, before moving to solutions and outcomes. Advising, evaluating, interpreting and falsely reassuring, in the absence of internal understanding, usually arise from externally focused approach. Both external and internal understandings are necessary. They can be combined to provide guidance in appreciating what is appropriate in caring for a particular patient.

Barriers to understanding

Many potential barriers exist when nurses are trying to understand a patient's perspective and frame of reference. The interferences that affect listening (see chapter 4) are still active. The natural tendency to judge and evaluate must still be kept in abeyance. An even greater barrier that exists is the tendency to jump to conclusions about what the patient is experiencing. Unless the patient validates these conclusions, they remain assumptions. Unshared assumptions lead to unshared meaning.

THE SKILLS OF UNDERSTANDING

An interpersonal capability to build meaning through skilled interaction is as significant as an awareness of the importance of understanding. The skills of understanding are presented here in a particular order. Paraphrasing, seeking clarification and reflecting feelings are used prior to connecting and summarising. The final skill, expressing empathy, is viewed as the sum total of all other understanding skills (see figure 5.1). The point at which the nurse can accurately express empathy is the point at which mutual understanding is achieved.

Paraphrasing

Paraphrasing is the backbone of understanding skills. When nurses paraphrase they restate what the patient has expressed, but instead of using the patient's words, nurses rephrase the patient's message in their own words and mode of expression. A paraphrase is a translation from the patient's language and manner of expression into the nurse's. Through the use of the paraphrase, nurses share their understanding of what patients have expressed.

Paraphrases acknowledge what the patient has said and demonstrate that the nurse has listened. They encourage further patient expression because they are confirming and accepting. Paraphrases, although statements, contain an implied question, 'Is my understanding of what you are saying the same as what you mean to say?' They often begin with phrases such as:

- 'So, what you are saying is...'
- 'Would I be correct in saying that you...'
- 'In other words...'
- 'Let me see if I understand correctly...'

Beginning a paraphrase with phrases such as these brings the implied question into the open. However, it is not essential that paraphrases begin in this manner. A nurse may simply rephrase what the patient has expressed.

The value of the paraphrase is its ability to check the accuracy of the nurse's understanding of what the patient means against the patient's intended meaning. Use of the paraphrase is an effective way to prevent misunderstandings. Because patients hear the nurse's interpretation, they are afforded an opportunity to confirm or deny its accuracy.

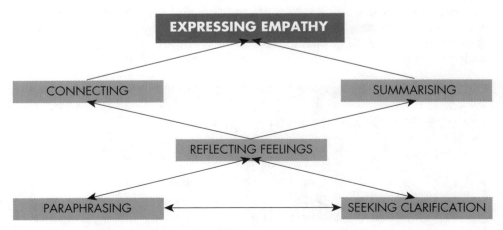

Figure 5.1 Hierarchy of understanding skills

Interchangeable responses

When paraphrasing, the nurse attempts to produce a response that is interchangeable with what the patient has expressed. An effective paraphrase neither adds to (additive response), nor detracts from (detractive response) what the patient has said.

Additive responses include comments on, explanations of, and opinions about what the patient is expressing. Analysing and interpreting responses are examples of additive responses. Although quite helpful when the goal is to increase the patient's awareness, additive responses do not necessarily facilitate the nurse's understanding.

Responses that detract are ones which shift the focus away from the patient or focus only on what the *nurse* thinks is important. Offering premature solutions and advice are examples of detractive responses. Paraphrases neither add nor detract; they are interchangeable with what the patient has expressed, and do not attempt to alter the meaning of that expression.

Accuracy in paraphrasing

Even though nurses attempt to make paraphrases interchangeable, there is still no guarantee that they will be entirely accurate. The meaning a nurse derives from the patient's expression may not be what the patient intended. This does not signal failure, because an inaccurate paraphrase allows the patient to correct the nurse's misinterpretation before progressing further in the interaction. In responding to a paraphrase, the patient has an opportunity to restate the meaning of an expression, amplify it or reiterate what was originally expressed. As long as nurses do not detract completely from the meaning, understanding can still be achieved through further interaction.

For this reason, it is important to state a paraphrase in a tentative manner, and closely observe the patient's response to it. Even when it is inaccurate, a paraphrase still conveys the nurse's desire to understand and willingness to engage in interactions that build meaning. The ultimate aim is to achieve congruence between what the patient means and what the nurse understands the patient to mean. This requires effort, time and the use of responses that work toward this aim. Mutual understanding must be negotiated between patient and nurse. The paraphrase works toward the goal of mutual understanding, because it enables meaning to be negotiated.

ACTIVITY 5.4 ➥ 319

PARAPHRASING—HAVE I GOT IT RIGHT?

 Process

1. Form pairs for this activity, and designate one person as A and the other as B.

2. A makes a statement about a recent interaction with a patient that was significant.

3. B responds with a paraphrase and begins with, 'So, in other words, what you are saying is...' B is not to advise, judge, evaluate or probe. At the end of the paraphrase, B asks, 'Have I got it right?'

4. A confirms or denies B's paraphrase and then continues to discuss the situation. B continues to paraphrase each of A's statements, asking each time, 'Have I got it right?' This process continues until A is able to say to B, 'Yes, you have got it right, that's exactly what I mean.'

5. Reverse roles, with B relating a story and A paraphrasing.

Discussion

1. How accurate were the initial paraphrases? What was the response to an inaccurate paraphrase? How long did it take to achieve accuracy?

2. What were the effects of the use of the paraphrase on the interaction? How did each participant feel during the interaction?

3. How was listening affected when you knew you had to paraphrase?

The paraphrase is effective in building meaning and, when used to this end, it results in greater understanding between patient and nurse. As with any skill, nurses must pay careful attention to how patients respond to paraphrasing. When the paraphrase encourages patients to elaborate on their experiences, thus enabling nurses to understand these experiences more fully, it is working toward its desired end.

Overuse of the paraphrase

Overuse of the paraphrase, in the absence of other skills, can be frustrating for a patient because the interaction may seem to be going in circles, with little forward progress. Continuous rephrasing of what the patient has said gives the impression that the interaction is 'going nowhere'. To prevent this, paraphrases need to be used with a mixture of other skills.

The aim and intention of the paraphrase must be borne in mind. An accurate paraphrase is a direct acknowledgment of what a patient has expressed. It serves as confirmation of the patient's reality. It conveys that the nurse is willing and able to view the patient's experience from the patient's frame of reference. All of this is done in order to deepen the relationship and encourage further interaction. When paraphrases stifle interaction, they do not meet their intended aim.

Reluctance to use paraphrasing

Despite the value of the paraphrase in building and negotiating meaning, there is sometimes a lack of appreciation of its use. Nurses are sometimes reluctant to employ the paraphrase out of a fear of appearing inept or poorly informed. They often think they 'should' automatically understand what patients are experiencing, and may feel foolish in not knowing. It is virtually impossible for nurses to fully appreciate what patients are experiencing, until an effort is made to understand. Each patient's experience is unique, and subjective. To believe there is an objective reality that is applicable to all patients is unrealistic.

At other times, reluctance to employ the paraphrase stems from a fear of reinforcing a patient's negative state. For example, when patients express unpleasant emotions or self-destructive thoughts, nurses may fear that restating such negative experiences elevates them, giving them more status than they deserve. Nurses may believe that it is better to deny or dismiss them, avoid further discussion of them or try to talk the patient out of them. But avoidance alienates patients, giving the impression that nurses do not really care.

The paraphrase acknowledges the patient's reality, demonstrates acceptance of it and conveys the nurse's desire to understand that reality. This is not the same as agreement and reinforcement; eventually a nurse may challenge a patient and encourage the adoption of an alternative perspective (see chapter 7). Another perspective cannot be introduced until the nurse shares the patient's current perspective and paraphrases work toward this shared understanding.

Seeking clarification

The skills of clarification are used whenever nurses are uncertain or unsure about what patients are saying. Under these circumstances, paraphrasing is not possible, because the nurse is unable to get an adequate sense of what the patient means. Through clarification, nurses convey that they are trying to understand, and will not proceed until they are able to do so. Statements that clarify could begin with:

- 'I'm not sure I follow you...'
- 'That's not clear to me...'
- 'Run that by me again...'
- 'I'm not certain what you mean...'
- 'I don't follow what you are saying...'
- 'I'm having difficulty understanding that...'
- 'I'm a bit confused about...'

Notice how the nurse takes responsibility for the lack of clarity and understanding. The intent and effect would be very different if statements such as 'You're not expressing yourself clearly' or 'That's not clear' were made. A properly phrased clarification is focused on a desire to receive a clearer message from the patient, a rephrase, an illustration and/or amplification. It should not put patients on the defensive or lead to discomfort by creating the feeling that they have to justify themselves or provide rational explanations to nurses.

Clarification through questioning

Clarification is often achieved through the use of probing skills (see chapter 6), however, the intention is not focused as much on exploration as it is on clearing up an area of confusion or ambiguity. An open question, such as 'What do you mean?' is a direct clarification. Nurses must use such a question with care and caution because of its potential to sound critical and accusatory (it could imply, 'You are not making sense'). Intonation and other nonverbal aspects make the difference.

Restatement

At times a restatement of what a patient has said is an effective means of clarifying. The nurse simply parrots the patient's exact words, usually switching from the first person to the second person. The accompanying nonverbal intonation should indicate that the restatement is really a prompt, which is aimed at further amplification. Restatement is similar to one-word or phrase accents (see chapter 6), except that in restatement, the entire message is reiterated. An example of a restatement is:

Patient: I can't move my right arm.

Nurse: You can't move your right arm?

Sometimes nurses overuse restatement because they do not know what else to say. Overuse of parroting can lead to frustration on the part of the patient, so its use should be kept to a minimum. It should be used with the intention of reaching greater clarity and understanding, not as a substitute for lack of words.

Clarification through self-disclosure

At times, nurses clarify what a patient has said by sharing how they might feel, think and perceive the situation if they were the patient. An example is: 'I'm not sure I entirely follow what it's like for you, but if I were you I'd be...' Care must be exercised when using self-disclosure, because of the potential to shift the focus from the patient to the nurse. In using self-disclosure in this manner the nurse is attempting to clear an area of confusion, not detract from what the patient is expressing.

Reflecting feelings

Reflection is the mirroring of feelings expressed by patients. Because feelings are often expressed indirectly, nurses translate the feeling aspects of a patient's message into other words. In this sense, reflecting feelings is similar to the paraphrase. Instead of rephrasing the actual words of the patient, the nurse rephrases an indirectly expressed emotion. An example of reflecting feelings is:

Patient: This darn leg won't get any stronger, despite all the physio.

Nurse: That leg is frustrating you, isn't it?

Reflecting feelings is useful because it conveys the nurse's recognition of feelings and confirms the existence of emotions. More than any other area of the patient's experience, feelings must be accepted as valid and real. Like the paraphrase, the reflection of feelings must be stated tentatively, awaiting feedback from the patient, which either confirms or denies the accuracy of the nurse's perception.

Reflecting feelings is verbalising what a patient has implied, but this is not the same as interpreting the patient's feelings. An interpretation involves adding to the patient's expression, rather than bringing into the open what was expressed indirectly. The nurse is still working with what the patient has communicated, not providing an explanation of, or judgment about, the patient's feelings.

In reflecting feelings, as in paraphrasing, nurses attempt to respond interchangeably with what patients have expressed. An interchangeable feeling reflection matches both the type of feeling and its intensity. Frustration is different from anger; feeling a bit blue is not the same as feeling despondent; happiness is not equivalent to elation. Making the distinction between different emotions and feelings requires an extensive vocabulary. A major difficulty in reflecting feelings is a limitation of the language the nurse possesses for describing feelings. The following activity is designed to increase your feeling word vocabulary.

ACTIVITY 5.5

BUILDING A FEELING-WORD VOCABULARY

(Adapted from Carkhuff, 1983)

 Process

1. Divide a blank piece of paper into seven vertical columns. Place the following 'feeling' categories at the top of each column:

   Happy Sad Angry Confused Scared Weak Strong

2. In each column record as many words as you can that express the emotion. Phrases such as 'over the moon' can also be used.

3. Form groups of five to six participants and compare lists. Add words from other participants' lists that you have not already recorded.

4. Evaluate each feeling word on the list according to its intensity. Label each as *high, medium* or *low* intensity. For example: elated = high; happy = medium; pleased = low.

Discussion

1. In which feeling category(ies) was it easy to develop words and phrases? Which were difficult? Why are some categories easier to describe than others?

2. Which feeling category has the most words and phrases? Which the least? What do you make of this?

3. Compare the feeling categories that were hard and easy with the ones that have the most and least words and phrases. Is there any relationship? Explain.

4. Look at the language used in each of the categories. Are some feeling words and phrases more appropriate with patients in different age groups and from different cultural backgrounds?

5. What role does culture play in the evaluation of feeling word intensity?

6. Are there some words and phrases that you would not personally use under certain circumstances? What are they and why would you not use them?

When nurses are reflecting feelings, they must firstly identify the appropriate feeling category. Most feelings will fit into one of the categories used in activity 5.5. Secondly, the intensity of the feeling expressed must be determined. Once the correct feeling and its intensity have been decided, a word or phrase that accurately describes the feeling is selected. The choice of words must suit the age and cultural background of the patient (see chapters 8 and 9).

A nurse's feeling word vocabulary can be further built through interactions with patients by paying careful attention to the language used when patients express various emotions and feelings.

ACTIVITY 5.6

REFLECTING FEELINGS

 Process

1. Refer to patient statements from activity 4.8: *Listening for feelings*. For each statement, develop a response that reflects the expressed feeling. Refer to the list of words and phrases developed in activity 5.5: *Building a feeling word vocabulary*.

Discussion

1. Which feelings were easy to reflect? Which were difficult? What do you make of this?

2. Are there any feeling reflections you would find personally difficult to express? Why?

Because feelings are often expressed indirectly, through nonverbal means, inference and innuendo, nurses may first need to check their perceptions (see chapter 6) of how a patient is feeling before attempting to reflect the feeling accurately. Frequently it is better to check perceptions of feelings before proceeding to reflect them.

A word of caution about reflecting feelings

Some patients are more comfortable than others in discussing their feelings. Additionally, a discussion of feelings may enhance a patient's sense of vulnerability, because feelings are difficult to control and contain. When a patient is working hard at containing emotions, and prefers to keep doing so, it is insensitive for a nurse to proceed into a discussion that uncovers these feelings and focuses on them. Nurses must pay careful attention to a patient's reaction to the discussion of feelings.

Likewise, discussion of feelings should be left until trust has formed between patient and nurse. The extent to which a patient is relaxed and at ease with a discussion of feelings demonstrates the degree of trust that has been established. The nurse can use a feeling discussion as a means of determining how much trust has been established. This requires acute awareness and sensitivity to the patient's response.

Connecting thoughts and feelings

Chapter 4, on listening, differentiated listening for content and listening for feelings. In this chapter, the skill of paraphrasing is used predominantly to respond to content, while reflecting feelings responds to emotional states. While it is possible to perceive them separately, and even respond to them separately, patients' experiences include both content and feelings. Initially, nurses may choose to focus on one or the other when responding. Eventually, thoughts (content) and feelings (emotion) must be put together. Connecting skills are used for this purpose. When connecting, nurses can use the following format:

■ 'You feel...when...'

Connecting thoughts and feelings adds depth to the nurse's understanding and moves the interaction in a forward direction. Through this response a nurse is moving into the area of fully understanding a patient's experience. Listening attentively and clarifying enables nurses to make the connection between patients' thoughts and their feelings. Again, it is necessary for the nurse to await feedback from the patient, which confirms, denies or expands on the nurse's understanding.

ACTIVITY 5.7 **319**

CONNECTING THOUGHTS AND FEELINGS

Process

1. Refer to each patient statement in activity 5.2: *Recognition of the types of responses*. Ignore the responses that are provided and

develop one of your own that connects the patients' expressed thoughts to their feelings. Use the format: 'You feel...when...' as a guide. Refer to your *feeling word vocabulary*, developed in activity 5.5, for ways to describe feelings.

2. Compare your responses with other participants.

Discussion

1. What differences are there in responses developed by various participants? Were there some responses that were the same?

2. In comparing connecting responses, how similar are the feeling portions? How different are they?

3. In comparing the connections between feelings and content, did some participants focus on content that was different from that of other participants?

Summarising

Summarising is the skill of responding in a way that reviews what has been discussed between patient and nurse. It is a brief, concise collection of paraphrases and feeling reflections that are accurately connected. Like other skills of understanding, a summary allows the nurse to check understanding by verbalising it, then awaiting feedback from the patient. Summaries often begin with:

- 'So, to sum it up...'
- 'We have discussed so much, let me see if I can pull it together...'
- 'Overall, I get the picture that...'

Summarising is used most often to bring closure to an interaction, and serves as a final check of the nurse's understanding. When nurses use summarising to bring closure to an interaction, it is important that they allow adequate time for patients to respond. As with other understanding skills, the patient needs an opportunity to clarify, expand on an idea or correct the nurse's misinterpretation.

There is an even more important reason for allowing adequate time following a summary. Frequently, patients present the most significant aspect of their experience just as the time draws near to close an interaction. In this case, the patient perceives the nurse's summary as a signal that time is of the essence, and uses the remaining time as a final opportunity for expression. This is not at all uncommon during patient–nurse interactions. An aware nurse recognises and accepts this interpersonal dynamic, and allows time for its occurrence.

While closure is the most common reason to summarise, a summary is also effectively used either in the middle or the beginning of an interaction. When used in the middle of an interaction, a summary serves to open new areas of discussion, by clearing the way for new ideas (Brammer & MacDonald, 1996). When it is used at this point, summarising serves as an exploration skill, that encourages patients to bring forward new thoughts and feelings. When it is used at the beginning of an interaction, summarising serves to orient both patient and nurse to the current interaction by reviewing previous interactions.

EXPRESSION OF UNDERSTANDING

When nurses employ the skills of understanding (paraphrasing, seeking clarification, reflecting feelings, connecting and summarising), in conjunction with effective exploration (see chapter 6), they are in a position to know what a patient is experiencing from the personal perspective of the patient. This inside understanding involves knowing what is happening to that person, and even knowing what it is like to be that person. Knowing through vicarious experiences such as these is often referred to as empathy.

Empathy is the ability to perceive the world from another person's view, and take on the perspective of another, while not losing one's own perspective. It relies on a strong sense of self, for without awareness of one's own perspective, attempts to enter another person's world may result in becoming lost in the world of the other. Empathy is the process that enables nurses to know the patient (see *Knowing the patient* in chapter 2).

Empathy in nursing

Nurses have embraced the process of empathy as essential to caring practices (Pike, 1990; Olsen, 1991; Wiseman, 1996; White, 1997). As a result of being empathic, the nurse comes to know and understand the patient's experience. This absorption of the patient's reality is one way that empathy is realised in nursing. Some of the first nursing theorists to discuss empathy (Triplett, 1969; Zderad, 1969; Travelbee, 1971) emphasised the purpose of empathy as the promotion of rapport between patient and nurse. Rapport is built through mutual understanding and it is important that the patient feels understood by the nurse. Therefore nursing theorists who first discussed empathy also stressed the importance of the nurse communicating their understanding to the patient (Zderad, 1969; Kalisch, 1973; Gagan, 1983).

Effects of empathy on the relationship

When communicating empathy, nurses respond with a direct, clear and accurate statement that reflects the core of the patient's experience. Expressing empathy is a skill that involves nurses' sharing openly with patients that they understand their perspectives. Expressing empathy communicates this understanding, conveying both acceptance and confirmation of the reality of the patient's experience.

Empathic statements capture the essence of the patient's experience and move the relationship into a more intimate zone (Shea, 1988). For this reason, empathy expression, especially in relation to patients' feelings, can be intrusive and prematurely intimate. Yet empathy expression in nursing is often equated with emotions. For example, White (1997) and Wiseman (1996) consider critical attributes of empathy to be recognition and understanding of the patient's feelings. Nevertheless, knowing the patient (see chapter 2) in such an intimate way may not be appropriate or desirable.

An empathic statement exposes patients, laying their reality in the open. It can expose areas of weakness, uncertainty and vulnerability. A patient may not want this exposure, and sensitivity to the patient's reaction to an empathic statement is needed. If the patient wants to appear strong or maintain control, the nurse who is sensitive will accept this and move out of the intimacy that empathy can bring.

This move into intimacy is one reason that there are cautions in the nursing literature against a wholehearted, unquestioning embrace of empathy. Gould (1990) warns that it may be unrealistic and idealistic to expect nurses to be empathic with all patients. Diers (1990) says that empathy may not be always appropriate to the patient's situation. Gordon (1987) cautions against a danger in nurses projecting their own perceptions onto patients in an effort to be empathic.

It is for these reasons that timing is crucial when expressing empathy. If a nurse moves too quickly into empathic expression, a patient may feel invaded and inhibited. For these reasons, all the other skills of understanding should be used first, in order to establish understanding and build the relationship. When the patient demonstrates comfort with discussing feelings, has validated the nurse's paraphrases, confirms the connections made between thoughts and feelings and agrees with the summary, then the relationship is ready to move into the intimate zone of empathy. The point at which a nurse truly understands is the time to express empathy.

Another purpose of empathy

In addition to the promotion of rapport and understanding, empathy in nursing is considered a means of promoting personal change and growth within the patient (Pike, 1990). This purpose of empathy relies on the nurse's objective analysis of the patient's experience and is based on a counselling model of helping (see chapter 2 for a definition of counselling), which promotes more effective ways of living.

The counselling view of empathy in the nursing literature is based primarily on the work of Carl Rogers (Gould, 1990; Morse et al., Exploring empathy, 1992; Thompson, 1996). Rogers, a psychologist who pioneered client-centred therapy, considered empathy to be an essential feature of the therapeutic counselling relationship (Rogers, 1957; 1961). The humanistic philosophy that underpins Rogers' theory of counselling is consistent with patient-centred nursing care and the development of a therapeutic patient–nurse relationship. Therefore, it is understandable that nurses who first conceptualised the therapeutic nature of the patient–nurse relationship were influenced by the work of Carl Rogers.

Nevertheless, there is growing awareness and mounting criticism that a conceptualisation of empathy in nursing that is based on theory borrowed from and developed for another discipline is inappropriate (Gould, 1990; Morse et al., Exploring empathy, 1992; Baille, 1996). A counselling view of empathy, with its focus on encouraging a patient's personal growth, may not always be appropriate in a nursing situation unless the nurse is also a psychotherapist. Although nurses often interact with people who are experiencing change and transition, not all patients are in the process of personal growth. Nurses need to understand a patient's personal experience of illness (one purpose of empathy), but not necessarily focus on encouraging psychological growth and personality change (another purpose of empathy).

Description of empathy in nursing literature

In addition to empathy being recommended for different purposes, many authors claim empathy is poorly described in the nursing literature (White, 1997; Wiseman, 1996; Morse et al., Beyond empathy, 1992; Gould, 1990). The result is a weak theoretical understanding. Part of the difficulty lies in the fact that empathy is a complex concept. It 'may be seen as an ability, a communication style, a trait, a response, a skill, a process, or an experience' (Wheeler & Barnett, 1994: 234).

In their review of the nursing literature on empathy, Morse et al. (Exploring empathy, 1992) identify four components of empathy. First is emotional empathy, which involves the subjective sharing of feelings. Next is cognitive empathy, which involves the ability to comprehend another's feelings from an objective stance. Third is moral empathy, or the inherent motivation to comprehend the experience of another. Fourth is behavioural empathy, which involves conveying understanding of another's perspective through communicating.

The four aspects of empathy that were identified by Morse et al. (Exploring empathy, 1992) can be compared to those described in Aligood's (1992) analysis of empathy. Aligood identifies two types of empathy: basic and trained. Basic empathy is an innate capacity to apprehend another's perspective, and can be likened to the emotional and moral components of empathy. Unlike basic empathy, trained empathy is learned. Trained empathy involves the cognitive and behavioural aspects of empathy, which is standing back and analysing the patient's situation and communicating that understanding to the patient.

Empathy that is considered to be therapeutic most often includes the cognitive and behavioural components (Morse et al., Beyond empathy, 1992), that is, trained empathy (Aligood, 1992). Although empathy is a skill that can be taught (Wheeler & Barrett, 1994), there is evidence that 'trained empathy', that is, the learnt skills of reflecting understanding to a patient, is not really sustained over time (Evans et al., 1998). While the communicative aspects of empathy can be taught, basic empathy is inherent. Nurses need self-awareness of their innate capacity for empathy so that they can build on their basic empathy and learn to express it through a personal style rather than a textbook formula.

Empathy and sympathy

Often a distinction is made between empathy and sympathy. Sympathy is viewed as 'feeling for' another person and empathy as 'feeling with' the other.

Sympathy is often considered less desirable because nurses need to put their own concerns to one side and focus on the patient (Kalisch, 1973; Pike, 1990); these authors consider sympathetic responses to be focused on the nurse. In contrast Morse et al. (Beyond empathy, 1992) assert that because a sympathetic response is focused on the other (that is, the patient), responses such as sympathy and pity may be as comforting for patients as empathy. Florence Nightingale encouraged nurses to be sympathetic; so did Travelbee (1971). Still, nurses are encouraged to be empathetic, not sympathetic. What is the difference between sympathy and empathy?

Wispé's (1986) analysis of the distinction between empathy and sympathy may assist in answering this question. She asserts that in empathy we consider what it would be like *if* we were the other person; in sympathy we automatically (reflexively) know what it would be like *to be* the other person. In empathy we 'reach out' to that person; in sympathy we are 'moved by' the other. Sympathy urges action to alleviate the suffering of the other; empathy urges efforts to comprehend the consciousness of the other. Sympathy is a way of relating, while empathy is a way of knowing. We can send a sympathy card as an action; we do not send empathy cards.

Despite the useful analysis, the attempt to differentiate sympathy and empathy remains troublesome. The results of Baille's (1996) research into empathy has been criticised as confusing empathy with sympathy (Yegdich, 1999), because the nurses in Baille's 1996 study described empathy as familiarity with the patient's situation because they had similar experiences. Perhaps what is at issue is not delineating one from the other but recognising that both sympathy and empathy have a place in nursing. Just because they can be distinguished from each other does not mean one is more beneficial to patients than the other. In nursing empathy is often touted as more beneficial even though it has not been fully researched as to its effects on patient outcome. There is evidence that empathy decreases patient distress (Reid-Ponte, 1992; Olson, 1995) but other responses such as commiseration, pity and consolation serve to comfort patients (Morse et al., Beyond empathy, 1992). More importantly, such responses are more engaging of the patient than the learned response of behavioural and cognitive styles of empathy that rely on objective analysis.

In their analysis Morse et al. (Beyond empathy, 1992) use the criteria of engagement with the patient and focus on the patient as a way of determining what type of nursing response is of comfort to the patient. In a way, this approach sidesteps the sympathy–empathy distinction, but offers a useful way of determining the purpose of responses intended to be helpful and understanding. Those responses that engage patients and focus on them (as compared to responses that focus on the nurse and disengage the patient) are considered to be helpful because they are comforting.

Therefore, both sympathy and empathy can be employed for the purposes of helping and comforting patients. Sympathy will compel the nurse to act, while empathy will compel the nurse to understand. A sympathetic response to a patient's physical pain, followed by action to relieve the pain, is more appropriate than an empathic response, which merely confirms understanding that the patient is indeed in pain.

Expressing empathy

The purpose of expressing empathy should be borne in mind. Empathy is used to encourage the patient to continue expression, to provide direction to the nurse, to decrease the patient's sense of isolation and to bond the patient and nurse in understanding. Often support and reassurance, direct aid and assistance, or advice or challenge follows the expression of empathy. At other times, empathy expression is an end in itself; it offers comfort and solace to patients—they know they are not alone because they are understood. See chapter 7, page 204, *Comforting* for further discussion of emapthy.

The frequency of empathy expression is also crucial. Short, precise empathic statements should be employed whenever nurses think understanding has been achieved. Too much empathy expression, especially early in the relationship, can sound paternalistic and superficial (Shea, 1988). Lack of empathy expression leaves patients with a sense of isolation, as if nurses do not care to receive their world.

The most congruent and compelling goal of empathy in nursing, that is, for nurses to come to understand a patient's experience, is that nurses' actions are based on their understanding of the patient's situation. In nursing there is an obligation to act, not simply to understand, and acting without understanding may result in actions that are not helpful to patients. This is one possible explanation about why more experienced nurses in Reid-Ponte's (1992) study were less empathic than their less experienced colleagues. Clinical experience provides the knowledge to act, therefore experienced nurses may need to spend less time being verbally empathic in order to understand patient needs.

As a moral position, empathy demonstrates a commitment to understanding patients. In this regard its benefits are without question. What is questionable is whether cognitive and behavioural aspects of empathy should be given more credence because they are considered 'therapeutic'. They also have the potential to create more intimacy than is warranted by the patient situation (for example, the clinical/instrumental relationship described in chapter 2), or disengage the patient because they are mechanical and objective when empathy is expressed in a formulaic manner such as 'I hear what you are saying'. Beginning nurses should bear these considerations in mind when employing the skills of understanding.

Reluctance to express empathy

At first, it feels awkward for nurses to express to patients what patients are experiencing. The awkwardness is based on a false notion that it is presumptuous and arrogant, if not downright impolite, to openly state what another person is experiencing. When empathy is expressed with an attitude of 'let me tell you what you are experiencing', its basic nature has been violated. When employed in this manner, attempts at empathy expression will be met with defensiveness on the patient's part and will work against an effective relationship. Empathy expression is a confirmation, not an accusation. The nurse must remain sensitive and open to correction. When stated with too much certainty, empathy expression alienates rather than engages the patient.

ACTIVITY 5.8

EXPRESSING EMPATHY

 Process

1. Refer to activity 5.1: *Your usual style of responding I.*

2. For each statement or question, develop a response that expresses empathy with the 'patient's' experience. Assume you have validated your understanding and have accurately understood the patient.

3. Compare these responses with the ones you originally developed when completing activity 5.1.

Discussion

1. What differences are there between the responses you originally developed and the ones you have now developed?

2. Which took more time to develop?

3. What risks are there in expressing empathy to patients?

4. What benefits are there in expressing empathy?

CHAPTER SUMMARY

Understanding responses are used after nurses have received meaningful input from patients, during the process of listening. Once initial impressions are formed, understanding responses are employed to build meaning between patients and nurses. The skills of understanding are used to bring nurses in touch with patients' private and personal worlds. They allow nurses to be 'in tune' with patients.

Attending and listening to patients' reactions to understanding responses is essential, and highlights the need for constant listening. Patients may react to an understanding response by validating it, denying it, altering it or expanding on it. Each of these patient reactions provides an opportunity for nurses to deepen their level of understanding.

It requires time and effort to truly understand another's reality. Nurses need to allow themselves time to think and reflect on how effectively they are understanding patients' experiences. They need to allow themselves enough time to respond with understanding to patients. This may also involve 'letting go' of familiar ways of responding, in favour of responses that reflect understanding.

ANSWERS TO ACTIVITIES

ACTIVITY 5.2: RECOGNITION OF THE TYPES OF RESPONSES

2. a. i.   S (reassuring and supporting)
       ii. I (analysing and interpreting)
       iii. U (paraphrasing and understanding)
       iv. E (advising and evaluating)
       v.   P (questioning and probing)

    b. i.   P (questioning and probing)
       ii. S (reassuring and supporting)
       iii. E (advising and evaluating)
       iv. U (paraphrasing and understanding)
       v.   I (analysing and interpreting)

    c. i.   U (paraphrasing and understanding)
       ii. E (advising and evaluating)
       iii. P (questioning and probing)
       iv. S (reassuring and supporting)
       v.   I (analysing and interpreting)

    d. i.   E (advising and evaluating)
       ii. P (questioning and probing)
       iii. U (paraphrasing and understanding)
       iv. I (analysing and interpreting)
       v.   S (reassuring and supporting)

    e. i.   S (reassuring and supporting)
       ii. E (advising and evaluating)
       iii. P (questioning and probing)
       iv. I (analysing and interpreting)
       v.   U (paraphrasing and understanding)

    f. i.   E (advising and evaluating)
       ii. P (questioning and probing)
       iii. S (reassuring and supporting)
       iv. I (analysing and interpreting)
       v.   U (paraphrasing and understanding)

    g. i.   I (analysing and interpreting)
       ii. E (advising and evaluating)
       iii. U (paraphrasing and understanding)
       iv. P (questioning and probing)
       v.   S (reassuring and supporting)

    h. i.   U (paraphrasing and understanding)
       ii. S (reassuring and supporting)
       iii. E (advising and evaluating)
       iv. P (questioning and probing)
       v.   I (analysing and interpreting)

    i. i.   I (analysing and interpreting)
       ii. S (reassuring and supporting)
       iii. U (paraphrasing and understanding)
       iv. E (advising and evaluating)
       v.   P (questioning and probing)

    j. i.   U (paraphrasing and understanding)
       ii. S (reassuring and supporting)
       iii. I (analysing and interpreting)
       iv. P (questioning and probing)
       v.   E (advising and evaluating)

    k. i.   S (reassuring and supporting)
       ii. I (analysing and interpreting)

iii.	P (questioning and probing)	ii.	U (paraphrasing and understanding)
iv.	U (paraphrasing and understanding)	iii.	P (questioning and probing)
v.	E (advising and evaluating)	iv.	E (advising and evaluating)
I. i.	I (analysing and interpreting)	v.	S (reassuring and supporting)

REFERENCES

Aligood, M.R. (1992). Empathy: the importance of recognising two types. *Journal of psychosocial nursing*, 30 (3), 14–17.

Baille, L. (1996). A phenomenological study of the nature of empathy. *Journal of advanced nursing*, 24, 1300–1308.

Brammer, L.M. & MacDonald, G. (1996). *The helping relations: process and skills*, (6th edn). Allyn and Bacon, Boston MA.

Carkhuff, R.R. (1983). *The student workbook for the art of helping*, (2nd edn). Human Resource Press, Amherst MA.

Diers, D. (1990). Response to 'On the nature and place of empathy in clinical nursing practice'. *Journal of professional nursing*, 6 (4), 240–241.

Evans, G.W., Wilt, D.L., Aligood, M.R. & O'Neil, M. (1998). Empathy: a study of two types. *Issues in mental health nursing*, 19, 453–461.

Gagan, J. M. (1983). Methodological notes on empathy. *Advances in nursing science*, 5 (2), 65–72.

Gordon, M. (1987). *Nursing diagnosis: process and application*, (2nd edn). McGraw-Hill, New York.

Gould, D. (1990). Empathy: a review of the literature with suggestions for an alternative research strategy. *Journal of advanced nursing*, 15, 1167–1174.

Johnson, D. W. (2000). *Reaching out: interpersonal effectiveness and self actualization*, (7th edn). Allyn and Bacon, Boston MA.

Kalisch, B.J. (1973). What is empathy? *American journal of nursing*, 73, 1548–1552.

Morse, J.M., Anderson, G., Bottoroff, J.L., Younge, O., O'Brien, B., Solberg, M. & Mellveen, K.H. (1992). Exploring empathy: a conceptual fit for nursing practice? *Image: journal of nursing scholarship*, 24, (4), 273–280.

Morse, J.M., Bottoroff, J., Anderson, G., O'Brien, B. & Solberg, S. (1992). Beyond empathy: expanding expressions of caring. *Journal of advanced nursing*, 17, 809–821.

Motyka, M., Motyka, H. & Wsolek, R. (1997). Elements of psychological support in nursing care. *Journal of advanced nursing*, 26, 909–912.

Olsen, D.P. (1991). Empathy as an ethical and philosophical basis for nursing. *Advances in nursing science*, 14 (1), 65–75.

Olson, J. K. (1995). Relationship between nurse-expressed empathy and patient-perceived empathy and patient distress. *Image: the journal of nursing scholarship*, 27 (4), 317–322.

Pike, A.W. (1990). On the nature and place of empathy in clinical nursing practice. *Journal of professional nursing*, 6 (4), 235–340.

Reid-Ponte, P. (1992). Distress in cancer patients and primary nurses' empathy skills. *Cancer nursing*, 15 (4), 283–292.

Rogers, C. (1957). The necessary and sufficient conditions of therapeutic personality change. *Journal of consulting psychology*, 21, 91–105.

Rogers, C. (1961). *On becoming a person*. Houghton Mifflin, Boston MA.

Shea, S. C. (1988). *Psychiatric interviewing: the art of understanding*. W. B. Saunders, Philadelphia PA.

Thompson, S. (1996). Empathy: towards a clearer meaning for nursing. *Nursing praxis in New Zealand*, 11 (1), 19–26.

Travelbee, J. (1971). *Interpersonal aspects of nursing*. F.A. Davis, Philadelphia PA.

Triplett, J.L. (1969). Empathy is... *Nursing clinics of North America*, 4, 673–681.

Wheeler, K. & Barrett, E.A.M. (1994). Review and synthesis of selected nursing studies on teaching empathy and implication for nursing research and education. *Nursing outlook*, 42 (5), 230–236.

White, S.J. (1997). Empathy: a literature review and concept analysis. *Journal of clinical nursing*, 6, 253–257.

Whyte, L., Motyka, M., Motyka, H., Wsolek, R. & Tune, M. (1997). Polish and British nurses responses to patient need. *Nursing standard*, 11, (38), 34–37.

Wiseman, T. (1996). A concept analysis of empathy. *Journal of advanced nursing*, 23, 1162–1167.

Wispé, L. (1986). The distinction between sympathy and empathy: to call forth a concept, a word is needed. *Journal of personality and social psychology*, 50, 314–421.

Yegdich, T. (1999). On the phenomenology of empathy in nursing: empathy or sympathy. *Journal of advanced nursing*, 30, 83–93.

Zderad, L.T. (1969). Empathic nursing: realisation of a human capacity. *Nursing clinics of North America*, 4, 655–662.

CHAPTER 6

COLLECTING INFORMATION: EXPLORING

INTRODUCTION

The skills covered in chapters 4 and 5—attending, listening and understanding—lay the foundation for effective interaction between patient and nurse because their use enables nurses to hear, perceive and reflect back what patients are expressing. Exploration, the subject of this chapter, moves the interaction beyond absorption and reiteration of patients' messages. Exploration opens new areas, focuses on selected areas and delves more deeply into a patient's total experience.

The process of exploration is one of searching, carried out for the purpose of discovery, detection, recognition and identification. Successful exploration results in greater understanding between patient and nurse; it can be directed toward something in particular or it can be open-ended, leading to the discovery of something unexpected, which is the case with interpersonal exploration carried out in the context of patient–nurse relationships. Collecting specific information from patients, the directed type of exploration, is necessary. Is Mr Green allergic to any medications? How long did Ms Geraghty sleep last night? Does Mr Nelson understand his special low-fat diet? Answers to such questions help guide nursing approaches and actions, and nurses need to know how to collect pertinent information from patients. Nevertheless, effective exploration in the nursing context involves more than merely the collection of specific facts from patients. Open-ended, spontaneous inquiry, the other type of exploration, is also needed because it is the means by which a nurse can come to understand how a patient interprets health and illness. What are Mr Green's expectations about his pending surgery? What is interfering with Ms Geraghty's sleep? How different is Mr Nelson's special diet from his usual one? Exploration into areas such as these is aimed at discovering ideas, thoughts, perceptions, feelings and reactions experienced by patients. It is important that nurses come to understand patients' responses to health and illness and effective exploration assists in this understanding.

Consider the following story.

> Martin Johnson spent his entire life in a rural part of the country. He felt very much at home 'on the land'. He disliked city life and avoided 'the big smoke' at all possible costs. Martin also had another aversion: visiting the doctor. He always put that off as long as he could. However, the obvious problems he was experiencing with his throat made it impossible to ignore his need of medical attention.
>
> When he finally was admitted to a large metropolitan hospital for major surgery, Martin felt very much out of place. However, coping with being in the city seemed minor in comparison to his worry about being ill and in hospital. He did not ask many questions of the surgeons when they came to explain his surgery, which included possible removal of his larynx (voice box). Martin listened as the surgeons explained what they would do, but did not think too much about what it meant. Being a man of few words, he did not ask for clarification.
>
> The night before his surgery, Lucille was the nurse caring for Martin. She felt an instant rapport with him, despite his quiet nature and the paucity of words between them. As she explained to Martin what he could expect following the surgery, she slowly came to the alarming realisation that he did not understand that the surgery would affect his ability to speak. In fact, if the surgeons performed the laryngectomy he would not speak again. Although he had consented to the surgical procedure, he did not seem to appreciate the potential consequences for his life. Through exploring his understanding and desires, Lucille discovered that Martin preferred a shorter life with the ability to speak in favour of a longer life and the inability to speak. As a result of her exploration and understanding, Martin's surgery was cancelled and other treatment options were explored.

This story raises questions as to whether Martin's consent to the surgery was adequately informed and highlights the importance of coming to understand the patient's point of view. And understanding the patient's point of view is contingent on effective exploration of patient perceptions and interpretation.

Chapter overview

This chapter reviews the skills of exploration within the context of patient–nurse interaction. It distinguishes directed exploration, such as a formal interview, from the less formal, spontaneous exploration, which occurs as a result of a trigger or cue from the patient. Both types of exploration rely on the use of the same skills, and these skills are divided into the broad areas of prompting and probing. Prompting techniques include minimal encouragement; one-word/phrase accents; gentle commands; open-ended statements; finishing the sentence; and self-disclosure. The section on probing techniques covers open-ended questions and closed questions and includes a discussion of when to use each type. The final sections review two processes of exploration: focused exploration and patient-cue exploration.

ACTIVITY 6.1

DEVELOPING EXPLORATORY RESPONSES I

 Process

Record how you would respond to each of the following patient statements. Do not concern yourself with how 'right' or 'wrong' your responses are, but do try to make them helpful to the patient. Assume that all statements are made to you, the nurse caring for the patient making the statement.

1. A hospitalised 65-year-old woman, who has recently undergone a total hip replacement: 'How am I ever going to manage on my own when I return home?'

2. A hospitalised patient speaking to a first-year nursing student: 'Do you know what you are doing? How much experience have you had?'

3. A twenty-year-old woman who is undergoing diagnostic tests on an outpatient basis: 'The doctor keeps evading my questions. What is really going on?'

4. A mother of a five-week-old baby during a routine visit to an early childhood centre: 'I wish I could get a decent night's sleep like I used to.'

5. A long-term resident of a nursing home: 'I can't stand being here. There's nothing to do and no one ever comes to visit me.'

6. A twenty-year-old man who is hospitalised with a fractured femur, following a motor vehicle accident: 'Why do these things always have to happen to me? All the bad things like this happen to me.'

7. A hospitalised patient, during medication rounds in hospital: 'I think all of these tablets are really making me sleepy.'

8. A hospitalised patient during morning care: 'I have asked the doctors how long they think I have to live, but they keep avoiding the question. Will you tell me, please?'

9. A hospitalised patient during morning nursing rounds: 'I'm so glad to see you. Those nurses on the night shift just don't help me.'

10. A 70-year-old man in an outpatient clinic, following consultation with the doctor: 'If what the doctor says is true, I don't see the point in going on and suffering...better to just end it now.'

Discussion

1. Each of the statements presented in the process section indicates a situation that requires further exploration by the nurse—more information, clarification and/or elaboration is required. Review

your responses and decide which of your responses *do* explore the patient's statement. Mark these with a tick.

2.   Write a new response for those not marked. Try to make this revised response an exploratory one.

(*Note*: This activity will be further developed in Activity 6.10: *Developing exploratory responses II*.)

PLANNED VERSUS SPONTANEOUS EXPLORATION

Planned exploration is directive, that is, the nurse controls the interaction by directing the flow and content of the patient's response. A good example of planned exploration is a formal interview conducted for the purpose of health assessment. Spontaneous exploration is responsive, that is, the nurse responds to something the patient has said or done. In planned exploration, nurses assume the lead and introduce the topics; in spontaneous exploration, nurses follow patients' leads. The distinction between planned exploration and spontaneous exploration is somewhat artificial because similar skills and techniques are used for both types of exploration. The distinction is drawn to highlight the different contexts in which nurses use exploration skills and techniques.

A common context in which nurses use exploration skills is when they conduct a health assessment. Most often nurses conduct health assessments when they encounter a patient for the first time, for example, on admission to hospital. Brown (1995) urges nurses to clarify the purpose of health assessments. If the purpose is to collect data about the patient's health status, then planned interviewing is appropriate. If the purpose of the health assessment is also to explore personal meaning of a patient's health status, then a less formalised, spontaneous exploration is appropriate. In nursing, both purposes are relevant. Nurses need to collect factual data about a patient's health as well as understanding the meaning of the health experience for patient. As a result, exploration is most effective when it is both planned and spontaneous. Brown refers to this style of exploration as 'conversational interviewing', which closely mirrors the balanced give and take of everyday conversations, as compared to the one-way, controlled structure of a formal interview in which 'questions impose an obligation to answer' (1995: 340).

Planned exploration

During planned exploration, the nurse directs and leads the search for information regarding pertinent aspects of a patient's 'health story' and current needs for nursing care. Specific data collection is the primary purpose of planned exploration, and topic areas are introduced and explored on the basis of what the nurse needs to know in order to care for the patient. Nurses direct and often control this type of exploration.

Structured, planned exploration occurs in the beginning phase of the patient–nurse relationship, usually upon initial contact between patient and nurse. The manner in which exploration occurs during these initial contacts sets the stage for subsequent interactions and further development of the relationship, by establishing the conditions for trust and openness. A nurse whose approach is authoritarian and rigid may convey a message to the patient that the nurse is in control, and obedience in answering the questions is expected. This might happen when the nurse becomes so focused on filling out a nursing history form that patients are left with the impression that completion of the record is more important than them as people. Likewise, an over-concern with the techniques of exploration may interfere with a nurse's ability to fully attend and listen to patients' replies.

Spontaneous exploration

This type of exploration occurs when nurses pick up and follow through in exploring a patient cue. Patients often express their needs to nurses in indirect, disguised ways (Macleod Clark, 1984), not because they want to keep the nurse guessing, but because patients perceive that an indirect message poses less of a threat to nurses. How nurses respond to these messages, or cues from patients, helps to shape the direction of their continuing relationship. This type of exploration tends to be patient-controlled and patient-led. The nurse follows the patient's lead instead of the patient following the nurse's lead.

Spontaneous exploration is important to the continuing relationship between patient and nurse, because it affirms that the nurse is attending and listening to the patient. It deepens the relationship and communicates the nurse's continued interest in the patient's welfare, because it is a concrete demonstration of the nurse's ongoing concern for the patient.

The difference between planned and spontaneous exploration

In both types of exploration, information is collected and greater depth of understanding is achieved, but the process is different because the roles of leader and follower are reversed. In the real world of patient care, this distinction in the types of exploration may not be obvious because there is give and take between nurse and patient. The roles of leader and follower are continuously shifting.

Whether leading or following, nurses utilise similar skills and techniques, although the type and frequency of skills used may be different, for example, more questioning techniques are employed in planned exploration than in spontaneous exploration. Planned exploration, such as the formal interview, often follows a prescribed format, even if the sequence is altered; spontaneous exploration has no set format. Planned exploration aims to solicit fairly standard information, while spontaneous exploration is more a search for meaning and for a patient–nurse relationship in which more information and feelings can be shared. The differences are highlighted in table 6.1.

Table 6.1 Planned versus spontaneous exploration

Planned exploration	Spontaneous exploration
Directive	Responsive
Nurse-led	Patient-led
Prescribed format, usually	No prescribed format
Information solicited	Meaning sought
Topic areas determined by the nurse	Topic areas introduced by the patient
More questioning techniques (probes) used	More exploratory statements (prompts) used

ACTIVITY 6.2 ➥ 319

WAYS OF EXPLORING: QUESTIONS VERSUS STATEMENTS

 Process

1. Form pairs for this activity. The participants in a pair should not be well-known to each other. Designate one person as the interviewer and the other as the interviewee. If the number of participants is uneven, form a group of three, with the third person acting as an observer.

Interview I

2. The interviewer is to find out as much as possible about the interviewee by asking questions *only*. The interviewer is not to make any statements during the interview. This interview is to last five minutes.

3. After the interview, each of the participants records a summary of the information discussed, as well as the reactions and feelings experienced during the interview. Observers (if used) record what type of information (for example, factual, opinions, feelings) the interviewer actively solicited, as well as general impressions about the comfort level of participants in the interview.

Interview II

4. Interviewer and interviewee now reverse roles. Conduct a second interview, only this time the ground rule is that *no* questions are to be asked during the interview. The interviewer is to learn as much as possible about the interviewee by making statements only. This interview is to last five minutes. The observer records the specific strategies used by the interviewer during the interaction.

5. After the interview, each of the participants records a summary of the information discussed, as well as reactions and feelings during the interview. Observers (if used) record the type of information that was

solicited during the interview, as well as general impressions about the comfort level of participants in the interview.

6.   Before proceeding to the discussion section, participant pairs should discuss their reactions to the activity with each other.

Discussion

On a board visible to all participants, record the answers to the following discussion questions, using the grid (figure 6.1) as a format.

	Interview I: all questions	**Interview II:** no questions
Interviewer reactions		
Interviewee reactions		
Type of information		
Strategies used		

Figure 6.1 Grid for Activity 6.2

Discussion questions for interview I

1.   What were the reactions of the interviewer to the first interview?

2.   What were the reactions of the interviewee to the first interview?

3.   What kind of information was discussed during the interview? How much was learnt about the interviewee during this interview?

4.   Observers (if used) report their general impressions of interview I.

Discussion questions for interview II

5.   What were the reactions of the interviewee to the second interview?

6.   What were the reactions of the interviewer to the second interview?

7.   What kind of information was discussed during the interview? How much was learnt about the interviewee during the interview?

8.   Observers (if used) report their general impressions of interview II.

The summary of this activity will most likely show that the second interview (with no questions used) created more anxiety. The interviewer in these circumstances often feels uncomfortable and sometimes even selfish. Nevertheless, the type of information obtained when no questions are asked often is more personal, focused and meaningful in getting to know the interviewee. Asking no questions usually results in more reciprocal sharing during the interview and this eventually leads the interviewer to a greater understanding of the interviewee on a personal level. The first interview usually collects a lot of facts about the interviewee, but does not really uncover subjective opinions and ideas. The first interview usually covers more breadth, while the second one covers more depth.

Questions tend to focus on the collection of information and are associated with formal interviews. Exploratory statements tend to focus more on reciprocal sharing of ideas, opinions, beliefs and feelings and reflect a conversational style of interacting. Each type of exploration yields different types of information: *how* information is collected affects *what* information is gleaned.

THE SKILLS OF EXPLORATION

As demonstrated in activity 6.2, exploration can be accomplished with or without the use of questions. This section divides the skills of exploration into two major categories: *prompting* and *probing*. Prompting skills are exploration techniques that are statements; probing skills are exploration techniques that are questions.

Prompting skills

Verbal prompts are a means of instigating further interaction and serve to assist the patient in elaboration and expansion of partially expressed ideas. Prompting skills include:

- minimal encouragement
- one-word/phrase accents
- gentle commands
- open-ended statements
- finishing the sentence
- self-disclosure

Minimal encouragement

Minimal encouragement is expressed by verbal responses such as, 'uh huh', 'mm hum' and 'yes'. Often they are utterances that are not really classified as words, yet convey messages such as, 'I'm with you', 'I'm following what you are saying' and 'I want to hear more'. They are signals that acknowledge the patient's verbalisation and encourage further elaboration. Visualise a person on the telephone who keeps repeating 'Yes' and 'uh huh'. Although you cannot hear the person on the other end of the line, you can ascertain that the person on this end is encouraging the other person to carry on the conversation. A person talking on the telephone uses minimal encouragement extensively because nonverbal messages are limited. In face-to-face communication, minimal encouragement reinforces attentive listening, but is not really a substitute for it. Attentive and active listening (see chapter 4) is, in itself, an effective prompt because it conveys messages similar to those of minimal encouragement.

Sometimes minimal encouragement is used without conscious awareness, even when active listening is absent. If this is the case, the verbal and nonverbal messages are incongruent. Because of this incongruence, minimal encouragement, without attentive listening, probably would not prompt further interaction. Try it in a conversation. Keep uttering 'uh huh' while not really attending and listening to the other person. Eventually the person speaking to you either gives up or tells you, 'Hey, you're not listening to me!'.

Minimal encouragement works best when patients are willing and able to continue the interaction. When patients are having difficulty verbalising their experiences, more explicit prompting and probing techniques need to be employed.

One-word/phrase accents

One-word/phrase accents are the repetition of key words or phrases, and are an effective way to both extend and focus the interaction. The choice of which word or phrase to repeat is important because it determines the direction of the exploration; it becomes the focus. It is best to repeat words or phrases that are judged to be the most central or critical. The following example illustrates the uses of accents:

Patient: My son won't be visiting me while I'm here in hospital.

Nurse: *Won't* be visiting?

Patient: Yes, he says he can't stand the sight and smells of the hospital.

Notice how the accent encourages the patient to expand the initial comment. Nurses effectively use the accent to explore what they perceive to be the most significant part of the patient's statement. Had the nurse repeated the words 'your son?' the interaction may have taken a different direction. In this regard, one-word/phrase accents are controlled by the nurse, although they are always in response to what the patient has said. If a patient does not elaborate a nurse should follow the patient's lead and end the discussion.

Gentle commands

Gentle commands (Shea, 1988) are explicit requests for information or elaboration. Although specific topics are often introduced with gentle commands, they are open-ended because they allow the patient to determine the direction and flow of the response. Examples of gentle commands include:

- 'Tell me about your family.'
- 'Can you describe that in more detail?'
- 'Tell me more.'
- 'Let's talk about that further.'

- 'Tell me what it's like for you to be in hospital.'
- 'Go on, say what's on your mind.'

In response to the first example, 'Tell me about your family', patients can choose whatever they wish to share about their family. One patient could say how many children she has, while another may focus on relationships with his extended family. The gentle command is directive in one sense yet allows the patient to control the direction in another sense.

Gentle commands should always be said in a way that allows patients to maintain a sense of control; they should not be demands. Although the idea of commanding patients to tell the nurse something sounds a bit harsh, the qualifier 'gentle' must not be forgotten. 'Gentle' means that the command is stated as an interested request for more information, rather than an order to speak. The qualifying phrase 'Can you?' is often placed before the command for this reason. 'Can you tell me about your family?' sounds less harsh than, 'Tell me about your family'. Technically, the addition of 'Can you' turns the statement into a closed question, and a patient can simply respond 'Yes' or 'No' without any further elaboration. In general, this does not happen because the underlying message that the nurse wants to hear more than a simple 'Yes' or 'No' is usually understood.

The gentleness of the command is conveyed primarily through nonverbal messages. Practise a few of the examples cited, using a variety of vocal tones and facial expressions and include the qualifier 'Can you?' at the beginning of the statement. Note that the words can sound harsh if said in a controlling, demanding manner. Nevertheless, if gentleness is put into the tone and facial expression, such commands are quite effective in exploring patients' experiences.

Open-ended statements

Open-ended statements provide a broad introduction to topics for discussion and are sometimes referred to as 'indirect questions' (Benjamin, 1969). They indicate to a patient that the nurse would like to hear more about something and provide an open invitation for the patient to speak about a topic. Examples of open-ended statements include:

- 'So, this is the first time you are having surgery.'
- 'I wonder how it is being sick when you've been so healthy all of your life.'
- 'I hear from your family that you are quite the athlete.'
- 'You've been giving yourself insulin injections for a few years now.'

It is clear from these examples that the nurse making the statement is interested in hearing more about the topic that is introduced, and desires the discussion to proceed further. Open-ended statements are invitations to patients to say more, if they choose to accept the invitation. In this way open-ended statements are similar to gentle commands, because they allow the patient to determine the direction and depth of the interaction. Open-ended statements are often a good way to begin an interaction, because they introduce a topic, but still allow the interaction to take various directions. While they introduce a topic, they do not control the direction of the conversation.

Finishing the sentence

This exploration technique is similar to open-ended statements. Instead of completing a sentence the nurse begins it, then trails off with an expectation that the patient will finish the sentence (Carnevali, 1983). Examples of finishing the sentence include:

- 'So you're most worried about...'
- 'And when you are in pain you usually...'
- 'Today has been...'
- 'What you really would like to know is...'

To be effective, finishing the sentence relies heavily on an inquisitive, anticipatory facial expression, which lets the patient know that the nurse has not had a lapse in memory or become preoccupied with other thoughts or activities. The nonverbal message, conveyed through facial expression and body posture, communicates that the nurse is awaiting completion of the sentence by the patient.

Self-disclosure

Sometimes the most effective way to encourage patients to explore their experiences with nurses is for nurses to share their own thoughts with a patient. Through self-disclosure, nurses open an area for exploration by stating their own reactions, feelings or thoughts. Self-disclosure must always be honest. There is little point in nurses fabricating information about themselves in an attempt to make patients open up. Self-disclosure is not the same as giving an opinion or a valuative judgment. Examples of self-disclosure as an exploration technique include:

- 'If I were in your place, I'd be angry.'
- 'I don't handle pain all that well.'
- 'I think I'd be wondering, what is wrong with me.'

Self-disclosure lets the patient know that the nurse is not afraid to be open. When used in the context of exploration it serves as a trigger for the patient to expand and elaborate, because it creates a climate of safety. It works well as an exploration technique with patients who seem reluctant to reveal themselves. While self-disclosures is utilised here as a means of encouraging exploration, a complete discussion of it can be found in chapter 7.

Probing skills

The techniques of asking questions are probing skills. Carefully worded and well-timed questions frequently provide the backbone of effective exploration and interviewing. Questions come in different varieties, yielding different responses and taking the interaction in different directions, depending on the type used. Both planned and spontaneous exploration combine the various types of questions. There are two major types of probing skills: *open-ended questions* and *closed questions*. Closed questions have two subtypes, which are particularly relevant to exploration within the nursing context: *focused* and *multiple-choice* questions.

Open-ended questions

Open-ended questions are those that require more than a one-word response, such as 'Yes' or 'No', thereby encouraging more elaboration in the answer. Examples of open-ended questions include:

- 'How did you sleep last night?'
- 'What concerns you most about the surgery?'
- 'What types of food do you enjoy eating?'
- 'How was your visit to the outpatient department?'

Open-ended questions begin with interrogative words such as who, what, when, where, why and how. Not all questions beginning with these words are open-ended, for example, 'Where do you live?' is a closed question, while 'Where do you see yourself in five years time?' is an open-ended question. Questions that are open-ended often yield more information than closed questions because their replies include more detailed expansion and elaboration. Additionally, open-ended questions allow more flexibility in response than closed questions. In answering open-ended questions, patients can highlight what is most relevant to their experience and therefore retain a sense of control in the interaction. Nevertheless, an open-ended question, no matter how well-stated, can pressure patients to disclose personal matters before they feel trusting enough to share their inner experiences. Because open-ended questions often probe more deeply than closed ones, nurses need to be mindful about the level of trust established before delving too deeply into the patient's experience.

Closed questions

Closed questions are those that are usually answered with a simple 'Yes', 'No' or other one-word response. They control the direction of the conversation and limit the amount of information that is shared or obtained. If closed questions are overused, an interaction begins to resemble an interrogation and can result in a patient feeling put on the spot because, short of refusing to answer or lying, the patient often feels obliged to answer direct questions posed by a nurse. Examples of closed questions include:

- 'Have you been in hospital before?'
- 'Do you wear glasses?'
- 'Is your wife coming to visit you tonight?'
- 'Do you have any children?'
- 'When did you last have something to eat?'

Focused, closed questions

At times, it is necessary for nurses to ask closed questions that are focused and directed at obtaining information about a specific clinical situation. These questions are based on the nurse's clinical knowledge and experience. Without them, important and even vital information may be missed (Shea, 1988). Examples of focused, closed questions include:

- 'Are you feeling nauseous?' (to a patient recovering from anaesthesia)
- 'Do you ever feel dizzy when you get out of bed quickly?' (to a patient whose blood pressure is low)
- 'Is your mouth dry?' (to a patient taking medication that produces a dry mouth as a side effect)

Each of these examples is a closed, focused question that is appropriate under the circumstances. The trigger for these closed questions is the nurse's awareness and understanding of what is pertinent to explore in a given clinical situation. Patients may not recognise the significance of their clinical symptoms and therefore feel reassured by such questions. An open-ended question may not yield the information needed or reveal progress in a particular direction.

Multiple-choice questions

Multiple-choice questions are another form of specific, closed questioning that is based on the nurse's understanding of a particular clinical phenomenon. In multiple-choice questions, the nurse provides options to the patient in an attempt to obtain an answer to the question, 'Which of these is correct?' A good example is when a nurse tries to obtain a complete description of a patient's pain. An open-ended question such as, 'How does the pain feel?' or even 'How would you describe the pain?' is often met with responses such as 'It feels like pain, it hurts' or 'I don't know, pain just feels like pain'. A multiple-choice question is helpful under such circumstances. In posing a multiple-choice question, the nurse asks, 'Is the pain burning, grabbing, crushing, pinpoint, dull or sharp?' This type of questioning about pain yields specific information about the nature of the patient's pain. In the example provided, the nurse uses knowledge of the various types of pain to focus and direct the exploration.

ACTIVITY 6.3 ➡ 319

CONVERTING PROBES INTO PROMPTS

 Process

Questions (probes) are often overused as a means of exploration. This activity challenges participants to turn closed questions into exploratory statements (prompts). Table 6.2 demonstrates how this is accomplished.

Table 6.2 Converting probes into prompts

Closed question	Open-ended question	Exploratory statement (prompt)
Are you feeling all right?	How are you feeling?	Tell me how you are feeling.
Will it help to make you more comfortable if I rearrange your pillows?	What would help you to be more comfortable in the bed?	Perhaps if I rearrange your pillow, you'll be more comfortable.
Did that medication help to relieve your pain?	How did that medication help in relieving your pain?	You had your pain medication 30 minutes ago, I see.
Do you want your sponge now?	When would you like your sponge?	You can have your sponge now or later.
Would it help if I stayed with you a while?	How would you feel if I stayed with you a while?	Perhaps if I stayed with you a while, it would help.

1. Make a list of closed questions pertinent to the nursing context. Divide a piece of paper into three columns and place the closed questions down the left column.

2. Convert each of these questions into an exploratory statement by first making the closed question into an open-ended one. Place these in the middle column of the page.

3. Now convert the open-ended question into an exploratory statement, a probe. Place these in the right column of the page.

Discussion

1. Which of your closed questions were easy to convert to exploratory statements? Which were difficult? Were there any that you found impossible to convert?

2. Review each of the exploratory statements and discuss how making a statement instead of asking a question would alter the interaction between nurse and patient.

3. Would you obtain different information from an exploratory statement? If so, is the information obtained more relevant?

4. Which of the exploratory statements seem appropriate to the topic being discussed? Do any seem inappropriate or foolish?

5. Can you imagine yourself using the exploratory statements? Why? Why not?

ACTIVITY 6.4

QUESTIONS AND STATEMENTS FOR CONDUCTING A NURSING HISTORY

 Process

Each of the topic areas in step 1 is an aspect of a standard nursing history, completed on admission to hospital. During the gathering of information for a nursing history, the nurse explores specific areas in order to collect data about the patient's functioning and experiences. The manner in which the data are collected depends on the nurse's ability to explore effectively. The wording of the questions and exploratory statements affects not only the type of information collected, but also the amount and quality of that information.

1. For each of the following topic areas, develop and write an open-ended question. The first one is completed to provide an example of how to undertake this activity.

Topic area	*Open-ended question*
Perception of hospitalisation:	▪ What do you anticipate will happen while you are in hospital?
	▪ What are your expectations of this hospital stay?

    Understanding of current
      health status:

    Social/living situation:

    Activities of daily living:

    Nutrition/eating habits:

    Sleep and rest patterns:

    Elimination patterns:

2. Now develop an exploratory statement for each of the topic areas.

Discussion

1. Which way of exploring—questioning (probing) or making statements (prompting)—seems more effective in collecting information in each of the identified topic areas?

2. Do some topic areas lend themselves more to exploratory statements than others?

Open-ended versus closed questions

As a general rule, open-ended questions are more effective as exploration techniques than closed questions, because responses to open questions are more elaborate and encourage expansion of ideas through the addition of subjective opinions and beliefs. They also allow the patient to direct the interaction and therefore the nurse who asks an open-ended question is likely to hear what is most significant to the patient at the time.

Does this mean that closed questions should be avoided? Not necessarily, because closed questions have a legitimate place in the context of patient–nurse interaction. The choice between open-ended and closed questions depends on what information is being sought, by whom, with whom, in which context and to what end. In making the decision to use one type or the other, nurses must consider their relationship with the patient as well as the need for specific information. For example, when a nurse wants to know whether a patient can tolerate aspirin, they might begin by asking, 'Have you ever used aspirin?' Then, if the answer is affirmative, questions such as 'How much?', 'How often?', 'For what reason?' and 'What effects were noted?' may follow. Asking open-ended questions such as 'How do you experience aspirin?' or 'What do you think about aspirin?' are nonsensical, and inappropriate to the content being explored and the information required. On the other hand, a question such as 'How was your first pregnancy?' is appropriate in exploring an experience as personal and unique as pregnancy. Nevertheless, questions such as 'How do you feel about being pregnant?' probe too deeply if patient and nurse have not established a trusting relationship. Questions need to probe at a depth that is appropriate to the level of trust between patient and nurse.

The decision about which type of question to use should be based on an understanding of each type of questioning. Table 6.3 compares the two types of question and provides useful guidelines for the selection.

If the open-ended type is selected as more suitable, the next choice is which open-ended question is best, given the circumstances. In most instances, questions beginning with 'Who', 'What', 'Where', and 'When' yield factual, objective data; while questions beginning with 'How' yield more personal, subjective information. For example, 'What surgery did you have in 1978?' will yield a factual answer such as 'I had my appendix

Table 6.3 Comparison of open-ended and closed questions

Open-ended questions	Closed questions
Yield information and facilitate elaboration	Yield information and limit elaboration
Allow patient to determine the direction of the interactions	Focus the patient in one direction
May not be useful when specific information is required	Are useful in obtaining specific information
Probe subjective experiences and may threaten patient if trust is not established	Maintain interpersonal safety by keeping the interaction on a less personal level

removed'. If this is followed by a question such as 'And how was that surgery?', exploration of the patient's subjective experience of the surgery is achieved. This general guideline is not a hard and fast rule, for example, 'What were your feelings about the surgery?' is a question that probes on a personal level. The focus of the question is as important as its type.

The most effective exploration will include a combination of both open and closed questions, as illustrated in the following interaction:

Nurse: Have you ever had surgery before? [Closed]

Patient: Yes, once before.

Nurse: What happened that you needed surgery? [Open]

Patient: I had my appendix removed when I was ten years old.

Nurse: Were you in hospital? [Closed]

Patient: Yes.

Nurse: How was that hospitalisation? [Open]

Patient: Fine, the nurses were great, my Mum was with me the whole time and I don't remember being in any pain.

Nurse: So, you have good memories of that? [Closed]

Patient: Yes.

Nurse: What do you expect will happen this time in hospital? [Open]

Patient: Well, I am a lot older, so my Mum won't be here the whole time. I am a bit worried about the pain.

Nurse: What worries you most? [Open]

Patient: That nobody will be able to help me with the pain...I am a bit of a baby.

Nurse: The nurses are here to make sure you are not in pain. You do realise that. [Closed]

Patient: Yes, I guess...but I don't know what you will do to help.

Notice how, in this interview, the nurse moves between closed and open-ended questioning and each question is appropriate to the content and the purpose of the interview. During the interaction, the nurse gathers objective data (previous experience with surgery) as well as subjective data (the patient's personal experience of the surgery). Open and closed questions are not inherently good or bad, because their 'goodness' or 'badness' depends on what information is being sought, and for what reason.

Pitfalls in the use of probing skills

Despite the fact that questions are neither good nor bad within themselves, there are some common pitfalls in the use of questioning, including some types of question that are best avoided altogether. Common pitfalls include overuse of questions, continuous multiple questions, the 'why' question and the leading question.

Overuse of questioning

The most common pitfall in probing is the overuse of questioning. Asking too many questions during an interaction can interrupt and confuse the patient (Benjamin, 1969). Overuse of questioning runs the risk of continually shifting the focus of the interaction. Additionally, it has the potential to convey the message that the nurse is in an overbearing position of authority. In order to be effective, questions need to be mixed with exploratory, prompting statements.

Continuous multiple questions

Another pitfall in questioning is the use of multiple questions, asked in succession, without allowing time for a reply from the patient, for example, 'How did you sleep last night? Did the sleeping tablet help? Was there too much noise?' While this manner of questioning sounds a bit ridiculous, it does occur in patient–nurse interactions (Macleod Clark, 1984). Asking multiple questions in succession is counterproductive to the exploration process. If a question is asked, the nurse needs to ensure that enough time is allowed for the patient to respond before proceeding.

The 'why?' question

The 'why?' question is a tricky one because often in the nursing context the answer to why needs to be sought. 'Why does Mr Kendall experience so much pain, even after maximum pain relief is administered?' 'Why is Ms Holmes having so much difficulty breastfeeding her baby?' While it is important to uncover the reasons for such occurrences, asking the question 'Why?' directly of patients can have a negative impact, and may not be the most effective way to find the answer. This is partly due to the fact that the question 'Why?' often creates anxiety and a defensive reaction. It implies that patients have to justify and explain their actions and feelings, *or* that something is not right about their actions and feelings. Imagine you are about to administer a medication to a patient and another nurse approaches you and asks, 'Why are you giving that medication now?' Your internal reaction may range from, 'What's it to you?' to 'Oh no, maybe I've made a mistake!' Perhaps your colleague just wants to know if the patient receiving the medication is still experiencing pain. Somehow, your reaction to the 'why?' question does not acknowledge such a well-intentioned motive on your colleague's behalf. Instead, you become defensive or anxious.

ACTIVITY 6.5   ➡ **319**

EFFECTS OF 'WHY?' QUESTIONS

Process

1. Form pairs for this activity. Designate one person as A and the other as B.

2. A discusses an experience that produced a strong feeling reaction.

3. B listens attentively but keeps asking 'Why?' whenever A brings up a feeling. B is to embark 'on a mission' to uncover the reasons behind A's feelings and reactions.

Discussion

1. A reports their response to the interaction by answering the question, 'How did it feel to be constantly asked why?'

2. B reports their response to the interaction by answering the question, 'How did it feel to keep asking why?' What did B notice about A's reactions?

The reaction to 'Why?' is often defensive because the question has a way of sounding like a negative evaluation. This may be due to experiences in childhood such as when Mum asked, 'Why did you spill the milk on the floor?' as she stands there, hands on hips, looking and sounding quite cross. It quickly becomes apparent to the child that Mum is not the least bit interested in *why* the milk was spilt. (Does she want an explanation about gravitational force?) The message conveyed by the 'why?' question in this instance is, 'Don't do it again, I get cross when milk is spilt'. This possible socialisation as to the interpretation of the 'why?' question, and the potential defensiveness produced by it, are reasons for avoiding its use in patient–nurse interaction.

Frequently the 'why?' question is asked in an attempt to explore feelings, for example, 'Why do you feel sad, Kate?' The use of the 'why' question in this instance assumes that Kate *knows* why she feels sad, and that these feelings have a rational basis. Patients often do not know why they feel a certain way, but may think they need to justify or rationally explain their feelings when asked, 'Why?' Again, the reaction may be a defensive one, a justification of feelings. In general, it is best to avoid the 'why?' question altogether. It is often counterproductive to exploration because of its potential to close off further interaction.

ACTIVITY 6.6

ALTERNATIVES TO 'WHY'?

Process

The following patient statements have the potential to elicit a 'why?' question from nurses. Read each and record an alternative to 'Why?'.

1. Patient (who has been on renal dialysis for a long time and is awaiting a renal transplant): 'I want to stop dialysis.'

2. Patient (who is awaiting results of diagnostic tests): 'I had a really bad night's sleep because I'm so worried.'

3. Patient (who is a recently arrived resident of a nursing home): 'How would you like being stuck in here? I hate this place and just want to die.'

4. Patient (who has recently undergone coronary artery bypass surgery): 'I really thought I was going to die this morning.'

5. Patient (who has been told she should have a hysterectomy): 'I can't possibly spare the time to have this operation.'

Discussion

1. Did you find you were tempted to ask 'Why?' in response to each statement?

2. Review your alternatives to the 'why?' question. Are any of them 'Why?' in disguise, for example, 'How come?' or 'What makes you feel that way?'

3. What type of exploratory response did you develop? Are any of the responses exploratory statements?

4. Compare your responses with those of other participants. How much variety exists between the responses?

5. Try to use some of your responses with other participants playing the role of patient. Ask the person who is playing the role of patient to describe the effects of each response.

The leading question

Another type of question to avoid is the 'leading' question. Leading questions are not exploratory but rhetorical, because they have an implied answer and are often designed to confirm what nurses think they already know. Examples of leading questions include:

- 'You're all right, aren't you?'
- 'Why don't you just cooperate with us?'
- 'Are you really going to ring the doctor at this hour of the night?'
- 'Is your anger really justified?'
- 'What's making you so hard to get along with?'
- 'You really don't want any more medication, do you?'

Leading questions are not really questions at all. They are statements in disguise, 'dressed up' to look like questions. Like the 'why' question, they have a tendency to put the other person on the defensive because they usually contain a value judgment. It is far better to make a statement than to pretend to want an answer to a question that does not really have one. Review the previous examples of leading questions, turn them into statements and note the difference.

ACTIVITY 6.7 ➡ 319

RECOGNISING TYPES OF QUESTIONS

 Process

Classify each question according to its type, using the following key:

A   closed question
B   open-ended question
C   leading question
D   disguised 'why?' question

1.   What makes you feel scared?

2.   How are you feeling today?

3.   What is your doctor's name?

4.   Do you really enjoy drinking heavily?

5.   When does your pain get worse?

6.   Are you interested in seeing a volunteer from Alcoholics Anonymous?

7.   What are your reasons for refusing your medication?

8.   What kind of nurse do you think I am?

9.   You really don't want any more pain medication, do you?

10. What did the doctor say?

11. Did that medication help with the nausea?

12. How do you like your breakfast tray to be arranged?

13. How did you go with physiotherapy today?

14. What makes you say that?

15. How old are your children?

16. How was the visit with your family last night?

17. Did you sleep well after having the sleeping tablet?

18. When are you going to stop bothering the other patients?

19. Are you worried about having sexual relations after your heart surgery?

20. Don't you think you had better try to stick to your diet this time?

21. How do you usually manage your diabetic diet?

22. Are you still hurting your baby by smoking while you are pregnant?

23. What would help you to be more comfortable?

Note: The answers to this activity can be found at the end of this chapter.

FOCUSED EXPLORATION

The skills of exploration can be employed effectively in the process of focusing an interaction between patient and nurse. The process of focused exploration deepens the nurse's general understanding of the patient's experience by concentrating on a specific aspect. This process of focusing is sometimes referred to as 'funnelling' (Burnard, 1989), because of the way in which it continues to narrow the topic being explored. Any of the various exploration skills identified can be employed in the process of focusing. The following interaction, from a postpartum maternity ward, is an illustration of focusing:

Nurse: How are you today? [Open question]

Patient: Okay, I guess.

Nurse: You guess? [One-word accent]

Patient: I didn't sleep very well last night.

Nurse: Couldn't sleep, huh? [Closed question]

Patient: No, I kept worrying about my baby.

Nurse: What, in particular, was worrying you? [Open question]

Patient: The paediatrician was here last night to examine him and he noticed his high-pitched cry.

Nurse: And? [Minimal encouragement]

Patient: Well, the doctor said it was probably nothing to worry about because it was most likely due to some swelling in my son's brain as a result of the labour. I was in second stage for a long time, you know.

Nurse: Yes, it might clear up in a few days. I have seen babies with that cry before, and it was due to temporary swelling that went away after a few days. But, it doesn't really stop the worry, just because you know it *might* be nothing. [Open-ended statement]

Patient: What is most worrying is that the doctor said it could be a sign of brain damage.

Nurse: And that's what has you most worried? [Closed question]

Patient: Yes. I kept asking the doctor what else besides temporary swelling could be causing the cry. Now I'm sorry I asked. I might have been better off not knowing. There's nothing I can do now but worry and wait.

Notice how the nurse in this interaction begins broadly then keeps focusing and narrowing the conversation. This is accomplished through the use of a variety of exploration skills. The nurse chose to focus on what they perceived to be the most significant aspect of the patient's messages. The focusing process serves to highlight and elaborate on a particular topic.

PATIENT-CUE EXPLORATION

Patients frequently communicate their needs, desires and feelings through indirect messages, indicating what they are experiencing by hints, suggestions and implied questions (Macleod Clark, 1984). Indirectly, patients are requesting a response from the nurse by presenting these communication cues.

Cues are small units of information, which are part of a larger, more complex phenomenon (Carnevali, 1983). They indicate a need for further exploration into the phenomenon. They signal the need for exploration much like a green light at a traffic intersection signals drivers to proceed. Effective exploration of patient cues, like all exploration, leads to further data collection and greater understanding between patient and nurse. Sadly, nurses frequently either fail to acknowledge patient cues or even actively discourage further exploration of them (Macleod Clark, 1984).

ACTIVITY 6.8

EXPLORING PATIENT CUES

Process

1. Think of an instance, real or imagined, in which a patient presents a cue, indicating the need for further exploration and/or elaboration (for example, a facial grimace, possibly indicating pain). Record this patient cue on a slip of paper, providing any information that would be of assistance in understanding the situation (the setting and circumstances).

2. Collect the slips of paper and redistribute them to other participants in the activity.

3. The contents of the slips of paper are then read aloud to all participants. Each participant develops and records an exploratory response, using any type of exploration technique.

4. Form groups of five to six participants and share exploratory responses in this group. Each small group discusses the various exploratory responses and selects the one that is most appropriate as an exploration technique. These are then read aloud to the rest of the participants.

Discussion

Discuss each patient cue and responses selected by the small groups. During the discussion, use the following questions to evaluate the responses, bearing in mind that the purpose of the response is to explore the cue presented by the patient.

1. Which exploration technique was used?

2. How effective is the response in exploring the cue?

3. In which context would this response be most appropriate?

4. What purpose does the exploration serve? Is it helpful? How?

5. Could you actually say this to a patient? If not, why?

Cues and inferences

A cue is a unit of sensory input, a sight, sound, smell, taste or touch, which is perceived as important to be noticed. For example, during an interaction, the nurse notices that the patient keeps fidgeting with the bed clothes. By noticing this piece of information, the nurse has perceived a cue.

Almost without awareness, meanings are assigned to perceived cues, as a way of making sense of what is experienced. The meanings attached to cues are inferences, conclusions drawn from the cues. Inferences are based on knowledge, previous experience, expectations and needs. For example, fidgeting with the bed clothes may be interpreted as a sign of general anxiety or discomfort with the interaction. Nevertheless, inferences are usually formed on the basis of more than one cue. The combination of fidgeting with the bed clothes, startling easily, pressured speech, nonstop talking and foot tapping are patient cues that may lead to an inference that a patient is anxious.

It is impossible *not* to make such interpretations about what is perceived; inferences are automatic. What is possible is to differentiate a cue (concrete data), from an inference (the interpretation of the data).

ACTIVITY 6.9 ➥ 319

CUES AND INFERENCES

 Process

Determine whether each of the following statements is a cue or an inference.

1. Answered interview questions completely.

2. Uninterested in the interview.

3. Changed the topic when asked about her family.

4. An open person.

5. Sleeping quietly.

6. Shallow, rapid respirations.

7. Doesn't understand prescribed medications.

8. Keeps asking questions about diagnostic tests.

9. No eye contact during the interview.

10. Speech is pressured.

11. Puzzled expression on her face when I asked her about the surgery.

12. Doesn't know what to expect.

13. No visible signs of distress.

Note: The answers to this activity can be found at the end of this chapter.

Discussion

1. Compare your answers with those of other class participants. Are there any differences in the answers?

> 2. If differences exist, discuss the item(s) and decide what makes them inferences or what makes them cues.
>
> 3. Compare your answers with those provided at the end of this chapter.

Once inferences are recognised by the nurse, they need to be validated with the patient, in order to determine if they are correct. In the example of fidgeting with the bed clothes, if the patient admits to feeling anxious, the inference is validated. It is important not to jump too quickly to a conclusion about patient cues. Further exploration is usually the most appropriate initial response to a patient cue.

Communication cues

When nurses prompt and probe during the process of exploration, many verbal and nonverbal cues are elicited because the exploration itself triggers the cues. A straightforward, closed question such as 'Have you ever been in hospital before?' may elicit numerous cues about the patient's experience in hospital. The patient's tone of voice may change, their rate of speech may accelerate, they may disclose feelings and reactions to previous hospitalisations. In this instance, the exploration triggered the cues and the cue is a trigger for further exploration. This spiralling effect is common in effective exploration.

Patient questions as cues

Often patient cues come in the form of questions asked of the nurse. Patient questions that are difficult to answer, yet require a response from the nurse, are examples of cues needing further exploration. For example:

- 'Am I going to die?'
- 'Is Dr Nelson a good surgeon?'
- 'What would you do if you were in my place?'

Questions such as these, which put nurses on the spot, are difficult to answer, but are equally difficult to ignore. Perceiving patient questions as cues for exploration is useful, because this enables nurses to respond effectively. Further exploration helps to uncover what is really on the patient's mind. The first example, 'Am I going to die?' can be explored by stating, 'That's difficult for me to answer, but I am curious about the question'. This open-ended statement indicates the nurse's willingness to hear more about what the patient is experiencing. Think 'exploration' whenever patients pose questions that either have no answer or are difficult to answer. It is preferable to do this rather than ignoring the question or changing the subject, which could happen when nurses feel put on the spot and uncomfortable.

Cue perception

Patient cues must be noticed and perceived if they are to be of use in exploration. Complete attending and active listening keep nurses open and receptive to cue recognition. Observing how a patient reacts and responds to the environment, and the situation at hand, is a skill in itself (see chapter 4).

Often, nurses perceive subtle communication cues from patients on the basis of a 'gut' feeling, hunch or intuition that the patient is trying to tell them something. Cue perception involves not only noticing how the patient is responding, but also trusting such 'gut' reaction about what might be going on. In the following situation, a nursing student relates such a hunch in discussing her observations of a young man, close to her own age, who had recently become a paraplegic:

> He kept joking around all morning about the MRI that was scheduled that day. I was quite comfortable with the banter because I like to joke around a lot too. He kept asking me, in a silly, almost childlike way, if I would be coming with him to 'hold his hand' when he had the procedure. Although I joked back about him being a 'big boy' now and stuff like that, I had the feeling he might have been scared about the test. I wondered how much he really understood about what was going to happen. I guess I am especially sensitive to this because, as I said, I often joke around especially about things that are really upsetting me.

A hunch such as this is often an indication of a need, however well disguised it is by a patient. The nursing student perceived the possibility that this patient was trying to express a need by interpreting the cues that he was presenting. She identified an opportunity for further exploration.

Cue exploration: sharing perceptions

Patient cues can be explored using any of the skills described in this chapter, but one of the most effective ways to explore cues is through an open-ended statement, in which nurses state their own perceptions. Open-ended statements allow nurses to validate their observations and interpretations of the cue, by sharing them with the patient. In the preceding scenario, an effective way for the nursing student to explore her hunch would be to say, 'Hey, all joking aside, I get the feeling you may be a bit uptight about the MRI'. This open-ended statement shares the student's perception with the patient, attempts to validate the perception, and therefore opens the interaction to exploration of the cues. Open-ended exploratory statements, which share the nurse's perceptions, usually begin with:

- 'I notice that...'
- 'I get the feeling that...'
- 'I'm wondering if...'

These sentences are then completed by a concrete description of what the nurse has observed, perceived and/or interpreted from the patient's messages. This is an effective way to validate a cue and explore it further, because it acknowledges the patient's message, encourages further discussion of the patient's experience and demonstrates the nurse's willingness to listen.

A word of caution about sharing perceptions

The danger in exploring in this manner is that the nurse may fall into the trap of being a pseudo psychoanalyst, always looking for hidden meanings and motives. Patients present cues in an attempt to communicate to nurses, so the question nurses must ask themselves is, 'Do I get the feeling this patient is trying to tell me something?' rather than, 'What's *really* behind this patient's behaviour?' It is a subtle yet important distinction.

ACTIVITY 6.10

DEVELOPING EXPLORATORY RESPONSES II

 Process

1. Refer to your responses in activity 6.1: *Developing exploratory responses I*. Label each of your responses according to the skills outlined in this chapter. You may have used more than one type of exploratory response.

2. Determine if you have a tendency to use one type of exploratory response in preference to the other types.

3. If you tend to ask closed questions, make these open-ended.

4. Do any of your questions begin with 'Why'? If so, find an alternative.

5. Turn your exploratory questions into exploratory statements. What possible effects would these changes have on the interaction with the patient in the situation?

ACTIVITY 6.11 320

PATIENT INTERVIEW

 Process

1. Each participant is to obtain a blank nursing history form from a health-care agency. Review the form and determine the most appropriate way to explore each area with a patient.

2. Form groups of three and designate one person as A, another as B and the third as C.

3. A conducts a nursing history interview with B acting in the role of patient. C acts as observer. A informs B about the setting and the

circumstances of the patient interview. C records the types of exploratory skills used by A during the interview by keeping a record of the name of each skill used.

4. C now interviews A, who plays the role of patient. B is now the observer. Continue as per instructions in step 3.

5. B now interviews person C, who plays the role of patient. C is now the observer. Continue as per instructions in step 3.

Discussion

1. What types of exploratory skills were used during the interviews? Were some types used more frequently than others?

2. Were there areas of the nursing history that lent themselves to the use of a certain skill more than other areas? If so, what are these areas? Which skills seemed most appropriate for these areas?

3. How did it feel when you were in the role of patient? Did you think you had enough opportunity to tell your story? Did you think the nurse got to know you as a person during the interview?

4. When you were the nurse, what was easy to explore? What was difficult? Were there any areas you thought were not covered adequately? How well did you come to understand the patient during the interview? What would you change in the interview, if you had the opportunity?

5. What generalisations can be made from the activity, in terms of conducting interviews between patients and nurses?

NURSES' CONTROL IN EXPLORATION

Previously in this chapter planned exploration was differentiated from spontaneous exploration. In planned exploration the nurse leads and takes charge of the direction and focus of an interaction. In spontaneous exploration the nurse follows the patient's lead, usually through the clarifying and probing patient cues. The same skills are used in both type of exploration, although not to the same extent. For example, closed questions may be more prevalent when the nurse is leading and one-word/phrase accents may be more prevalent when the nurse is following.

At the heart of the difference between spontaneous and planned exploration is the notion of who is in control. Control in the context of patient–nurse interaction refers to who dominates in determining the flow of information exchange (Kristjanson & Chalmers, 1990). When the patient is in control they dominate. The reverse is true when the nurse controls the interaction.

Ideally, a balance is achieved when both patient and nurse share control of interactions. Nevertheless, is there any evidence to support the ideal? Answers to this question can be found in research studies in which verbal communication between nurses and patients as they interact in clinical settings is analysed (for example, Macleod Clark, 1984; Wilkinson, 1991; Hewison, 1995). Analyses of patient–nurse interactions in studies such as these reveal that nurses 'block' and 'control' interactions through a variety of strategies. Some of these strategies included focusing on tasks, exerting power over patients, spending little time actually talking to patients and even avoiding interaction with patients. In community-based settings, Kristjanson & Chalmers (1990) found that interactions were either nurse-controlled or jointly controlled by patient and nurse, but no interactions were controlled by patients.

Although the results of the studies cited in the previous paragraph suggest that nurses do not pick up patient cues and that they control interactions, other studies suggest that when nurses are expert they are alert to patient cues (Johnson, 1993) and offered opportunities for patients to introduce issues that were affecting their lives (Brown, 1994).

While the evidence on whether nurses control interactions is inconclusive, there are helpful guidelines that can be ascertained. These guidelines include the need for nurses to be alert to the cues of patients and to be able to follow that patient lead. Likewise, nurses will at times control the interaction when they are obtaining specific information. Self-aware nurses who reflect on their interactions will notice whether they tend to be controlling in their interactions.

CHAPTER SUMMARY

The process of exploration is one of the most important aspects of patient–nurse interaction, because it not only provides the means by which information is obtained, but demonstrates the nurse's active regard for understanding the patient's experience. During planned exploration, nurses focus on what is most significant for them to know about patients. During spontaneous exploration, nurses focus on what is most significant to the patient at the time. Both types of exploration require the use of effective questioning (probes) and exploratory statements (prompts). When used in conjunction with other interpersonal skills, exploration helps to shape effective and facilitative patient–nurse interaction and leads to greater understanding.

ANSWERS TO ACTIVITIES

ACTIVITY 6.7: RECOGNISING TYPES OF QUESTIONS

Key: A closed question
B open-ended question
C leading question
D a disguised 'why?' question

1. D   What makes you feel scared?
2. B   How are you feeling today?
3. A   What is your doctor's name?
4. C   Do you really enjoy drinking heavily?
5. B   When does your pain get worse?
6. A   Are you interested in seeing a volunteer from Alcoholics Anonymous?
7. D   What are your reasons for refusing your medication?
8. C   What kind of nurse do you think I am?
9. C   You really don't want any more pain medication, do you?
10. B   What did the doctor say?
11. A   Did that medication help with the nausea?
12. B   How do you like your breakfast tray to be arranged?
13. B   How did you go with physiotherapy today?
14. D   What makes you say that?
15. A   How old are your children?
16. B   How was the visit with your family last night?
17. A   Did you sleep well after having the sleeping tablet?
18. C   When are you going to stop bothering the other patients?
19. A   Are you worried about having sexual relations after your heart surgery?
20. C   Don't you think you had better try to stick to your diet this time?
21. B   How do you usually manage your diabetic diet?
22. C   Are you still hurting your baby by smoking while you are pregnant?
23. B   What would help you to be more comfortable?

ACTIVITY 6.9: CUES AND INFERENCES

1. Cue Answered interview questions completely.
2. Inference Uninterested in the interview.
3. Cue Changed the topic when asked about her family.
4. Inference An open person.
5. Cue Sleeping quietly.
6. Cue Shallow, rapid respirations.
7. Inference Doesn't understand prescribed medications.
8. Cue Keeps asking questions about diagnostic tests.
9. Cue No eye contact during the interview.
10. Cue Speech is pressured.
11. Cue Puzzled expression on her face when I asked her about the surgery.
12. Inference Doesn't know what to expect.
13. Cue No visible signs of distress.

REFERENCES

Benjamin, A. (1969). *The helping interview.* Houghton Mifflin, Boston MA.

Brown, S.J. (1994). Communication strategies used by an expert nurse. *Clinical nursing research*, 3 (1), 43–56.

Brown, S.J. (1995). An interviewing style for nursing assessment. *Journal of advanced nursing*, 21, 340–342.

Burnard, P. (1989). *Teaching interpersonal skills: a handbook of experiential learning activities for health professionals.* Chapman and Hall, London.

Carnevali, D. (1983). *Nursing care planning: diagnosis and management*, (3rd edn). J B Lippincott, Philadelphia PA.

Hewison, A.L. (1995). Nurses' power in interactions with patients. *Journal of advanced nursing*, 21, 75–82.

Johnson, R. (1993). Nurse practitioner-patient discourse: uncovering the voice of nursing inprimary care practice. *Scholarly inquiry for nursing practice: an international journal*, 7, 143–163.

Kristjanson, L. & Chalmers, K. (1990). Nurse-client interactions in community-based practice: creating common ground. *Public health nursing*, 7 (4), 215–223.

Macleod Clark, J. (1984). Verbal communication in nursing. In A. Faulkner (ed.). *Communication* (pp 52–73). Churchill Livingstone, Edinburgh.

Shea, S. C. (1988). *Psychiatric interviewing: the art of understanding.* WB Saunders, Philadelphia PA.

Wilkinson, S. (1991). Factors which influence how nurses communicate with cancer patients. *Journal of advanced nursing*, 16, 677–688.

CHAPTER 7

COMFORTING, SUPPORTING AND ENABLING

INTRODUCTION

The material in the previous chapters has laid a theoretical foundation and a practical framework for establishing effective patient–nurse relationships. Through knowing self, listening to patients' stories, understanding patients' experiences and exploring patients' personal meanings of health and illness, nurses are able to interact with patients in ways that are helpful. Helpful interactions build relationships that are of assistance to patients and the patient–nurse relationship becomes a vehicle through which nursing actions come to life. The skills of listening, understanding and exploring are fundamental to the development of this relationship and their use must be continuous for the relationship's maintenance and further development.

Thus far, this book has alluded to how nurses take direct action in helping patients, but active intervention has not been fully explained. In fact, moving too quickly into action has been shown to be inappropriate in the absence of a relationship based on understanding. Focusing prematurely on action, intervention and outcome has the potential to stifle the nurse's understanding and appreciation of the patient's current experience.

There is inherent danger in taking action without first understanding the patient's unique orientation to the world. Interventions cannot be applied in a context-free manner, selected from a list of options as one selects a recipe from a cookbook. Such nonspecific, potentially hit and miss approaches can actually do more harm than good. For example, enabling patients to participate in their care by sharing information is most effective if nurses first determine how much information a patient wants and can use. Some patients want to know every minute detail about their nursing care, while others prefer to know the bare essentials only. It is inappropriate, even potentially harmful, to burden a patient with too much detailed information when the information is not wanted or cannot be put to some use.

This suggestion, to initially curtail direct intervention, may prove frustrating to some nurses, because a felt need to do something often overrides the need to understand the patient's experience from the patient's perspective. Time is a precious commodity in nursing practice, and the time spent in coming to understand patients' experiences may be perceived as a luxury. Nevertheless, the time and effort expended in coming to understand the patient's frame of reference are well spent, because actions, which direct and influence patients, are then based on such understandings.

These actions include: comforting patients through interpersonal interaction, supporting patients in the use of resources, enabling them to participate in their health-care by sharing information and encouraging patients to reframe their perspective through challenging and self sharing.

Chapter overview

This chapter presents skills that provide the means for nurses to take action beyond listening, exploring and understanding. These actions are psychosocial in nature, that is, they are interpersonally oriented and enacted through the nurse–patient relationship. Swanson's theory (1993) of nursing as informed caring is presented as a way of situating the skills in this chapter within the context of material in previous chapters. Ways of responding (first introduced in chapter 5) are revisited in order to emphasise when psychosocial actions are appropriate. These psychosocial nursing actions are grouped into three major areas: comforting, supporting and enabling. The primary comforting action is the skill of reassuring patients. Supporting actions, described next, promote patients' use of resources. Enabling focuses on actions that are aimed at encouraging patients to actively participate in their own care. The major enabling action described is that of sharing information and providing explanations to patients. The final skills of challenging and self-disclosure are two further examples of enabling actions.

PSYCHOSOCIAL ACTIONS THAT COMFORT, SUPPORT AND ENABLE

Often nursing actions are aimed at physical care and treatment of a disease, for example, administration of medication to provide physical relief from pain and technical competence is perceived by patients as caring (see chapter 2). But nursing actions are also psychosocial in nature. Psychosocial actions are aimed at promoting psychological ease and relief of distress, for example, through explanations that orient patients to what is happening around them.

Physical actions and psychosocial actions are inextricably linked in nursing practice. For example, hospitalised patients in Cameron's (1993) study indicated that focusing on physical care left them concerned about how they would be able to integrate illness into their lives, while focusing on psychosocial care resulted in worries about their physical care. Despite the artificiality of the separation of physical actions from psychosocial actions, this chapter focuses on psychosocial nursing actions that promote health and healing in patients and are accomplished through the patient–nurse relationship.

Swanson's theory of nursing as 'informed caring' provides a useful model for situating the interpersonal skills necessary for psychosocial actions within the context of the skills outlined in previous chapters. Five processes of caring are explicated in the theory of 'informed caring' (Swanson, 1993). The first of these is a philosophical grounding of nursing in an inherent belief in people and a conviction in personal meanings that are attached to health events (such a philosophy is enhanced through self-awareness, see chapter 3). Once 'grounded' in this philosophical stance, nurses 'anchor' their caring through striving to understand the meaning that patients attach to health events. This second process is achieved by 'knowing the patient' (see chapter 2), and is brought to life through the interpersonal skills of listening, understanding and exploring (see chapters 4, 5 and 6). The third process in the theory of informed caring is enacted by nurses when they are fully present and available to patients. Referred to by Swanson (1993) as 'being with' patients, this process was reviewed in chapter 4 in the form of attending and listening skills.

Once they are with 'with' patients, nurses express their caring through actions that pertain to the final two processes in Swanson's theory, termed 'doing for' patients and 'enabling' patients to do for themselves. Although not rigid in the sense that the processes are passed through as stages and phases, there is a sequential manner to them. For example, 'doing for' requires nurses to understand what must be done, that is, to understand a patient's frame of reference before attempting to provide psychosocial help.

As seen in table 7.1, the interpersonal skills for the first three processes of informed caring have been developed in previous chapters. This chapter focuses on the final two processes, 'doing for' and 'enabling'. Although the process of 'doing for' is predominantly expressed through physical care and skilled clinical performance of nursing care, 'doing for' also includes comforting measures that are achieved through interacting with and relating to patients. Comforting measures such as reassurance are discussed in this chapter. Supporting actions are also considered in the process of 'doing for' patients. Swanson's process (1993) of 'enabling' includes having patients participate in their health-care. Such participation is contingent on patients'

Table 7.1 Processes of informed caring and related interpersonal skills

Processes of informed caring (Swanson, 1993)	Interpersonal skills
Maintaining belief in people	Self-awareness (chapter 3)
Appreciating personal meanings of health events	Understanding (chapter 5)
Being with patients	Listening and exploring (chapters 4 and 6)
Doing for patients	Comforting and supporting (chapter 7)
Enabling patients	Encouraging participation by sharing information and challenging (chapter 7)

knowledge and understanding of their health status and care. The interpersonal skills needed to inform and assist patients in obtaining this knowledge are also reviewed in this chapter.

Indications of the need for psychosocial action

When listening and understanding, nurses are guided by patients. When taking psychosocial action, nurses assume a more active role in guiding patients. This does not mean that a nurse takes charge and control of a patient's life, but rather intervenes in a way that encourages the patient to assume as much control as possible. For example, when an understanding is reached that a patient is facing a decision, the nurse takes action in order to help the patient make the decision, rather than taking over and making the decision for the patient. Actions that are psychosocial in nature are liberating, not restrictive, and they always work from within the patient's experience.

Taking action is based on indications that it is needed. The following list includes examples of patient situations that indicate a need to intervene directly:

Psychosocial action may be required when patients are:

- in need of more information
- emotionally distressed, for example, feeling overwhelmed
- facing a health-related decision
- learning new skills
- lacking in available resources
- inadequately using existing resources
- experiencing difficulties in coping, adjusting and adapting

Patient outcomes

Psychosocial nursing actions of comforting, supporting and enabling are focused on outcomes and resources. When nurses employ these actions they do so with the deliberate intention of producing positive changes or reinforcing adaptive ones in patients. While the desired outcome may not always be directly observable and measurable, action is taken for a focused purpose. Some examples of desired outcomes include helping patients to:

- adjust and adapt to changes in living imposed by illness
- maintain self-esteem
- find meaning in illness
- feel secure and in control
- contain and control emotional distress within manageable limits
- make decisions about health-care
- access and use helpful resources

Outcomes are based on the indication of need for action. For example, the indication that a patient is emotionally distressed calls for an outcome of containing and controlling that distress within manageable limits. Not only is it important for nurses to relate desired outcome to patient need, but more importantly nurses must work with patients in determining needs and outcomes from the patients' perspective.

Patient resources

Psychosocial nursing actions are most effective when nurses work with patients' natural resources, their capabilities and means for coming to terms with health- and illness-related issues in their lives. Some actions work with the patients' existing resources, while others focus on the identification, development and use of new or unused resources. It is important for nurses to understand the patient's resources. Examples of resources include the patient's knowledge, will, desire, strength, courage; their family members and friends, other patients, self-help groups, and health services and providers (Carnevali, 1983). Possible resources are endless for some patients and quite limited for others. Essential to the use of patient resources is the recognition and acknowledgment that nurses themselves are but one, usually temporary, resource in helping patients. Nurses must look to longer term patient resources, basing their outlook on the belief that patients are themselves resourceful and capable.

WAYS OF RESPONDING REVISITED

The various ways of responding (presented in chapter 5) include the action-oriented, influencing responses of advising and evaluating, reassuring and supporting, and analysing and interpreting. These responses were rejected as initial responses in favour of understanding responses. The major reason these action-oriented responses were deemed inappropriate early in the course of the relationship between patient and nurse is because the nurse who employs them at this time is exerting too much control and influence on the patient. For example, an interpretation challenges patients to view their situations in a different light, which is based on the nurse's perceptions, rather than the patient's. There is a danger of alienating the patient if a nurse is too directive early in the course of the relationship.

The tendency for nurses to be directive in the face of patient problems was demonstrated in two recent studies (Motyka et al., 1997; Whyte et al., 1997). In these studies nurses were asked to write a verbal response to a patient complaint (tightness in the throat and difficulty swallowing). Of the 150 nurses who participated, the majority responded by directives such as 'Don't worry', 'Don't be upset' and 'I'll tell the doctor and you will be fine'. Only 2 per cent demonstrated an understanding response. When two groups of nurses were compared using the same research methods (Whyte et al., 1997), British nurses more frequently responded by collecting information about the patient complaint than did Polish nurses. Nevertheless, the majority of responses of nurses in both studies indicated that they operated from a position of authority and were directive in their responses. That is, the majority of responses indicated that the nurse assumed control rather than working with the patient to explore the meaning of the complaint further or to respond with understanding of the patient's discomfort.

Each way of responding is appropriate at various levels and stages in the development of the patient–nurse relationship. Nevertheless, the findings of the studies do indicate that nurses may tend to respond in habitual and automatic ways. The skills presented throughout this book, and especially those in this chapter, offer a range of possible alternatives. Nurses are encouraged to reflect and consider which type of response is appropriate at the time and under the circumstances. The importance of timing is highlighted as nurses consider what skills to use when. Early in the relationship the patient directs the interactions. As the relationship progresses, the nurse can exert more direct influence through direct action.

COMFORTING

Of the five ways of responding (see chapter 5) a response that attempts to comfort and reassure is used most often by people who are trying to be of help (Johnson, 2000). Nurses are no different in this respect. In the studies by Motyka et al. (1997) and Whyte et al. (1997), nurses most often tried to cheer patients with reassurance and consolation. Although participants' intentions were not investigated in these studies, the majority of their responses were most likely meant to comfort patients.

Caring and comforting

Comforting is associated with soothing distress, relieving pain and easing grief. To be comfortable is associated with being relaxed, contented and free from pain and anxiety. It is understandable that nurses attempt to comfort. In fact, Morse (1992) has urged nurses to reconsider this claim and refocus nursing care on the concept of comfort. She argues that caring focuses on the nurse, while comfort focuses on the patient. Caring is process oriented and is the motivation for nursing actions. Comfort is outcome oriented and is the aim of nursing actions. Caring is *why* nurses act; comforting is *how* they act (Morse, 1992).

Morse's argument is compelling in the sense that it offers nurses a focus of care that can be described through practices that comfort patients. Caring is more nebulous in the sense that it offers little in the way of clear guidelines for clinical performance, especially for beginning nurses. Because comfort focuses on outcomes rather than process it offers a framework for nursing action.

Patients' view of comforting

The meaning of comfort in nursing requires careful consideration, especially in relation to the patients' point of view. In a study exploring patients' views of comfort Cameron (1993) interviewed and observed a small sample (ten) of hospitalised patients. Results of the study indicate that patients' are not passive in their view of comfort, that is, patients did not wait in hope of receiving comfort. Rather, they sought it out by, for example, gathering information about their condition and treatment from caregivers and other patients. These patients also vigilantly monitored nurses' responses to them in an effort to find reassurance that all was well. Patients in this study also delved into themselves as a way of integrating their illness experience into the whole of their lives. These patients' views indicate that comfort is an active process that energises. This view of comfort as enlivening, although part of its original meaning, contrasts to current conceptualisation of comforting as soothing, easing or consoling (Cameron, 1993).

In another study of comfort, patients gave an account of an illness in which they experienced agonising pain, trauma or life-threatening conditions. In their analysis of the patients' stories Morse et al. (1994) concluded that comfort measures by nurses included taking control, reassuring, protecting, connecting, distracting (refocusing), acknowledging and supporting. Comfort measures enabled patients to retreat from discomfort and provided the opportunity for patients to regain strength and energy (Morse et al., 1994). The enlivening aspects of comfort echo Cameron's findings (1993).

In their analysis of patient biographies of illness Morse et al. (1992) describe a number of actions that promote comfort. These actions include pity (expressing regret), sympathy (conveying sorrow), compassion (sensitively sharing the distress of another), consolation (encouragement that things are not as bad as they could be), commiseration (sharing mutual situations), compassion (sharing feelings) and reflexive reassurance (appearing optimistic in order to counteract negative emotions). Each response has the potential to promote comfort because the response confirms negative emotions (pity), legitimises the patients' response (sympathy), recognises and shares feelings (compassion), reduces patients' distress (consolation), confirms universality of feelings (commiseration) and counteracts anxiety (reflexive reassurance) (Morse et al., 1992).

Each of these comforting responses focuses on the patient. More importantly, responses such as consolation and compassion interpersonally engage the patient by confirming their experience. In a similar vein, patients in Drew's (1986) study reported that they felt comforted and confident when they experienced confirming responses that were both cognitive and affective. When nurses' responses were confirming they expressed a sense of concern for the patient, demonstrated through being unhurried, making eye contact and using a soothing tone of voice. Comfort and confirmation go hand in hand.

Nurses' expression of comforting

The measures described by patients in the studies cited in the previous section indicate that spontaneous (reflexive) responses promote engagement and involvement because they express identification with the patient's pain and distress. These responses are natural and naturally human, thus promoting a sense of connection between nurse and patient.

Sometimes nurses are taught to stifle these spontaneous responses in favour of 'professional' responses that are learnt (Morse et al., 1992). Traditionally nurses are taught to provide comfort by therapeutic empathic responses (see chapter 5). Therapeutic empathy de-emphasises the emotional involvement of reflexive empathy. Emotional empathy, which is developed through experience, enables nurses to implicitly know what to do when patients are distressed (Morse et al., 1992). Informative reassurance, which provides explanation and information, is another learnt response. While intended to promote comfort, learnt responses are not as engaging as the spontaneous responses (Morse et al., 1992).

Results of studies that explicate comforting strategies (Bottorff et al., 1995; Proctor et al., 1996) include nursing actions of talking to patients in ways that help them to hold on, especially when they are in pain. Examples of 'holding on' strategies included supporting, praising and affirming the patient. Other comforting behaviours included providing information, explaining what is happening, being informal and friendly and expressing concern. Offering choices in care is another way that nurses helped patients stay in control and feel comforted.

All the skills in this chapter could be subsumed under the umbrella of the comforting strategies that have been explicated through research; this reinforces the centrality of comforting in nursing. Nevertheless, for the purpose of simplicity and clarity, reassurance is the main skill that is fully developed as a comforting action. Supporting is another comforting action, which is described in a separate section. Other skills, such as informing and challenging are developed under the umbrella of enabling patients to participate in care.

Reassuring skills

Reassuring the patient is a common nursing activity, often cited as a planned, purposeful intervention in nursing care. But how is reassurance actually offered and provided by nurses? Under what circumstances is it indicated? How can reassurance be engaging and not dismissive of patients? Unless the answers to these questions are clearly thought through and understood, there is a danger that reassurance will be oversimplified as nothing more than a natural human response.

While the responses analysed by Morse et al. (1992) as naturally comforting are spontaneous, that is they are not learnt, they are culturally conditioned. Sometimes cultural conditioning will result in a reassuring action that is not focused on the patient, but rather protective of the nurse. This is false reassurance.

False reassurance

In everyday, social situations, reassurance is frequently offered in the form of trite, trivial clichés and platitudes, repeated so often that they have lost their meaning. Ready-made comments such as 'Everything will work out', 'Don't worry' and 'It will be all right' are uttered in an almost automatic, stereotypical manner. These types of 'reassuring' response were presented in chapter 5 as examples of false reassurance. They do little to ease discomfort in the person being offered them. When reassurance is offered in this way, the effect is often opposite to its intention.

In saying to patients 'Everything will be all right', nurses may believe they have been truly reassuring, however, patients often feel dismissed by such an expression. Not only have nurses failed to meet patients in their world, but they have actually denied its existence or diminished its importance.

False reassurance distances the patient from the nurse, and may be used by nurses to distance themselves from unpleasant or difficult aspects of nursing (Faulkner & Maguire, 1984: 135). Telling a patient not to worry may make the nurse feel better but, as a general rule, unless the patient receives concrete reassuring evidence, this alone does little to calm the patient who is concerned and distressed.

Unless they are careful and thoughtful, nurses may inadvertently find themselves slipping into this automatic mode of falsely reassuring patients. Because years of socialisation are difficult to change, it is likely that a platitude or cliché will 'slip out' before a nurse realises it. When this happens, the realisation that such responses are not truly reassuring, and even potentially alienating to patients, may produce a sense of failure in the nurse.

Nevertheless, a nurse who inadvertently utters a trite cliché can recover by following the cliché with a comment that indicates awareness and sensitivity. Here are some examples of how to recover:

- '(Everything will be all right), *but my saying so won't necessarily make it so.*'
- '(Don't worry). *That's easy for me to say, isn't it?*'
- (Things have a way of working out), *but that thought may not help you to feel any better.*'
- '(Some good will come out of all of this). *That doesn't really help you, though, does it?*'

Recovering comments, such as these, demonstrate the nurse's awareness, and usually result in the interaction proceeding, rather than generating feelings of alienation and rejection in the patient. After recovering, the nurse is now free to proceed with a more realistic reassuring response.

Comforting reassurance

If effective reassurance is not about presenting such falsely reassuring responses, then what does it involve? To reassure is to restore confidence and to promote a sense of safety, control, hope and certainty. Reassurance calms the anxious, abates the uneasiness of the worried and decreases concern in the uncertain. Reassurance is concrete and directly related to the patient situation, rather than global and non-specific, as clichés are. Realistic reassurance is novel, imaginative, unique and, most importantly, specific to the patient.

The desired outcome in providing reassurance is a restored sense of confidence and feelings of safety within the patient. To reassure literally means to assure again. In this sense reassurance is restorative. By supporting their inherent power and ability, effective reassurance enables patients to face situations with equanimity. Reassurance may not 'make everything all right' (sometimes this is not possible), but the patient who is reassured can face experiences with confidence, hope and courage.

Reassurance is often associated with patient coping (Fareed, 1994). Like the previous analysis of caring and comforting, reassuring is what the nurse does, that is, it is nurse-focused, and coping is the desired patient outcome. Nevertheless, the provision of reassurance does not guarantee that the patient will feel more certain and confident, and therefore cope better. This lack of guarantee, however, should not stifle attempts to reassure patients.

Patients' need for reassurance

As with all intervening skills, the recognition of the patient's need for reassurance, and an understanding of the patient's experience in relation to this need, precedes action. Nurses must understand and appreciate the concrete, specific nature of a patient's worry. The following situation serves as an illustration of the importance of assessing a patient's need for reassurance:

> James Carroll is scheduled for an above-the-knee amputation of his right leg. He has diabetes, which has been difficult to control and manage. Prior to surgery he expresses concern by making statements such as 'I don't know how this is all going to turn out' and 'It's a bit of a worry'. The nurse caring for him avoids saying, 'Oh, don't worry, everything will be all right', appreciating the futility and potential harm of such a statement. Instead, the nurse explores what, specifically, is worrying Mr Carroll. Perhaps he fears pain postoperatively; he could be worried about how he will manage to get around after the surgery; perhaps he is concerned about loss of income (he is self-employed) during and after hospitalisation; perhaps he fears not being able to return to his usual occupation. Perhaps...perhaps...the list is almost endless. Unless the nurse responding to him understands what exactly is worrying him, any attempts to reassure him may be misguided. Through the use of exploration and understanding skills, the nurse comes to know that the fear of postoperative pain is worrying him most. Now that the specific focus of his concern is identified, the nurse can reassure Mr Carroll, with specific information, about how much pain he can expect, and, more importantly, what will be done to alleviate and control his pain.

In nursing practice there are common patient situations that indicate the need for reassurance. Awareness of these general situations, however, does not replace the necessity of exploring and understanding each patient's experience in relation to the need for reassurance.

ACTIVITY 7.1

SITUATIONS REQUIRING REASSURANCE

 Process

1. Working individually, record a patient situation that you have experienced or can imagine that indicates the patient's need for reassurance. Ask yourself, 'What made me think the patient needed reassurance?' Describe the situation as fully as possible.

2. Form groups of five to six participants and distribute the recorded situations randomly among the members.

3. Have each member review the situation and write a key word or phrase, from the recorded situation, that indicates the need for reassurance. Make a list of patient cues, from the recorded situation, that expressed the need for reassurance.

4. Record all key words and phrases, including those that are repetitive, on a sheet of paper visible to all participants.

5. On a separate sheet of paper, visible to all participants, record the identified patient cues.

Discussion

1. What themes are expressed in the key words and phrases?

2. How much variation is there in the list of patient cues?

3. What generalisations can be made about patient situations that indicate a need for reassurance?

The need for reassurance arises out of situations in which patients are apprehensive, doubtful, uncertain, worried, anxious, full of misgivings or lacking confidence. In nursing practice, there are myriad circumstances that result in patients experiencing such feelings and perceptions.

Some examples include:

- unclear/unknown medical diagnosis
- facing unfamiliar situations
- facing an uncertain outcome/future
- painful procedures

The common theme in situations indicating a need for reassurance is uncertainty (Boyd & Munhall, 1989). The need for reassurance arises out of situations that are unfamiliar, unknown, unsettling, threatening and confusing. Patients facing such situations often experience a loss of control, and need to have their confidence restored (Teasdale, 1989). They are in need of something on which, or someone on whom, they can rely to decrease their uncertainty. The intention in reassurance is then to decrease uncertainty and restore a sense of control.

Patient cues indicating uncertainty

Because of their uniqueness, patients will express uncertainty in a variety of ways. Return to the list of patient cues indicating a need for reassurance, developed in activity 7.1. Some examples of patient cues indicating feelings of uncertainty, and therefore the potential need for reassurance, include:

- openly stating fears and anxieties
- asking numerous questions
- continuous activity
- being quiet and withdrawn
- crying
- numerous requests and demands

The perceptive nurse will notice such cues, place them within the context of the patient's current situation, integrate them with an understanding of this patient's experience, and explore and validate the presence of uncertainty and need for reassurance. A general discussion of how to explore patient cues is found in chapter 6. Having established the presence of a need for reassurance, nurses now can proceed to provide it in a variety of ways.

ACTIVITY 7.2

WAYS NURSES REASSURE PATIENTS

 Process

1. Recall a time in your life when you were filled with uncertainty about something that was happening, or about to happen, to you.

2. Reflect on the situation and circumstances surrounding it.

3. What, if anything, would have allayed or did allay your uncertainty? Describe, on a piece of paper, how you were/might have been reassured.

4. Form groups of five to six participants and discuss both the described situations, and the ways of reassuring.

5. List the identified ways of reassuring.

6. Compare each small group's list, developed in step 5.

7. Prepare a list that combines each small group's list.

Discussion

1. Of the identified ways of reassuring, which are appropriate within the nursing context?

2. How might a nurse reassure patients?

3. What hinders nurses in their attempts to reassure patients? What helps?

Nurses reassure patients in a variety of ways, not just through verbal responses. They provide reassurance to patients through their presence and manner, as well as through reassuring actions and verbal responses.

Reassuring presence of the nurse

Patients are reassured by the knowledge that the nurse will be there, as the presence of another human being is reassuring in itself, especially during times of disquiet. Being present involves more than simply a physical presence; it involves the emotional presence of a nurse who is fully attending and listening. Hospitalised patients in Fareed's study (1996) described reassuring presence as 'being with […me]' and 'being there […for me]'. In fact, accessibility of the nurse was the key factor in these patients' sense of feeling reassured. Chapter 4 describes this presence, with specific reference to the comforting presence of the nurse whose entire focus is on the patient.

In addition, patients are reassured in knowing that the nurse will remain present, and will not abandon them, no matter how difficult, painful or overwhelming circumstances are for them. This vigilant, constant and reliable presence of the nurse promotes confidence within patients, thus providing reassurance.

Reassuring manner of the nurse

When a nurse conveys, primarily through nonverbal means, calmness and confidence, patients are reassured (Fareed, 1996). This highlights the need for self-awareness (see chapter 3), because nurses may unconsciously (nonverbal behaviour is largely unconscious) communicate a sense of uneasiness to the patient. A nurse's uneasiness may or may not have reference to the immediate patient, but it will compound the worry of an already worried patient. A nurse who appears unsure or uncertain can contribute to the patient's uneasiness and uncertainty.

The nurse's reassuring presence and manner maintain meaningful human contact between patient and nurse. Other nonverbal forms of communication, including touching, holding hands, massaging and ministering, are examples of physically comforting, reassuring acts (Boyd & Munhall, 1989; Fareed, 1996). Cultural and age variations in relation to the use of touch are important to understand. These are discussed in chapters 8 and 9.

Reassuring actions

In addition to the reassuring presence and manner of nurses, there are a number of actions that reassure patients. These include:

- optimistic assertion (Teasdale, 1989)
- concrete and specific feedback
- explanations and factual information

These skills are considered facilitative because they encourage patients to reinterpret their situations, in light of different or new information. They are especially helpful when a patient's current interpretation of a situation is threatening, for example, the new mother who believes that her blue feelings after birth are a sign that she is 'losing her mind'.

Optimistic assertion

An optimistic assertion is a pledge, promise or guarantee made with the intention of reassuring the patient (Teasdale, 1989). Examples of optimistic assertions include:

- 'The pain medication that we will give you routinely after your surgery is quite effective. I think you'll find it really helps.'
- 'This wound is going to heal nicely, because you are a fit, healthy person.'
- 'I will visit your family every two weeks. Most families find this sufficient, but if you need to contact me in between visits you can reach me on this number.'

Notice how making an optimistic assertion is similar to sharing information (covered later in this chapter). While sharing information is related to optimistic assertion, it is not exactly the same. An optimistic assertion usually contains an interpretation, which the patient is asked to accept without analysis (Teasdale, 1989). Information may be added to strengthen an optimistic assertion, but information itself does not provide an interpretation.

Optimistic assertions are similar to false reassurance, although they should not be empty promises or false guarantees. Termed reflexive reassurance by Morse et al. (1992) an optimistic assertion is encouragement to maintain an optimistic outlook, even in the face of dire circumstances. Patients in Fareed's study (1996) felt reassured when they were encouraged to remain optimistic, even when nurses used clichés such as 'Don't worry' or 'I'm sure this will get better for you'.

The difference between false reassurance and an optimistic assertion is the nurse's focus. When a cliché or platitude is focused on protecting the nurse and hiding distress it is not reassuring. When it is focused on the patient such a comment, genuinely and spontaneously stated, can result in comfort and reassurance.

Concrete and specific feedback

Feedback about how the nurse perceives a situation can be reassuring to patients. In order to be helpful in providing reassurance, feedback needs to be concrete and specific to the patient. Simply saying to a patient, 'I think you are progressing just fine' is not concrete enough to fully reassure the patient. Examples of helpful feedback include:

- 'I can tell that you are getting a little stronger each day, because yesterday you could only walk to the edge of the bed. Today you made it to the shower on your own.'
- 'You have been through a lot with your father's illness. It's no wonder you are feeling a bit drained.'
- 'Last month you weren't sure what you were going to do about the tumour. This month, I see a different person.'

Like optimistic assertion, feedback provides the patient with a new interpretation of the situation. This interpretation is based on the nurse's view of the situation, which is usually informed and knowledgeable. It is based on the nurse's view, but helpful feedback is neither a judgment, an evaluation, nor an analysis of the patient's situation.

In order that feedback be truly reassuring, it is essential that the nurse establishes first that the patient wants it and can use it. In addition, feedback, which focuses on the patient's strengths and resources, is more helpful than that which highlights weaknesses and shortcomings.

Providing explanations and factual information

Sharing information, especially about what is usual/expected under the circumstances, is reassuring to patients, particularly to those patients whose interpretation is based on faulty or misguided information. For example, a patient who is nil by mouth, and receiving intravenous fluids, may fear that he or she will literally 'starve to death', due to lack of understanding. Explanations provide patients with an opportunity to re-evaluate their situation, in light of new, more valid information.

Termed informative reassurance (Morse et al., 1992), explanations and factual information restore patients' sense of control over situations, and reduce their uncertainty. Receiving factual information is a key factor in feeling reassured and gaining control (Fareed, 1996), however, because informative reassurance is cognitive, it may not address patients' emotional fears (Morse et al., 1992).

ACTIVITY 7.3

REASSURING INTERVENTIONS

Process

1. Return to activity 7.1 and randomly redistribute the recorded patient situations to each participant.

2. Each participant reviews the patient situation and records how they would provide reassurance under the circumstances.

3. The recorded situations, along with the suggested way to reassure the patient, are once more randomly distributed to all participants.

4. Each situation and suggestion for reassurance is then read aloud by the participants. The types of reassurance suggested are recorded on a tally sheet, under the broad headings provided in the text.

Discussion

1. Which methods of providing reassurance were most preferred? Discuss the possible reasons for this.

2. Which methods of providing reassurance are easy to employ? Which are more difficult? Discuss reasons for this.

SUPPORTING

To support is to provide a means of holding up something, in order to prevent its falling apart. Foundations support houses. Beams support ceilings. Their enduring presence provides the means to keep a structure intact, and prevent its collapse.

In supporting patients, nurses 'stand in the wings' awaiting a call for assistance. Being supportive is an essential quality of nurses and it is needed whenever nurses relate to patients. The foundation skills of listening and understanding are the primary means of conveying a supportive attitude. Their use demonstrates that the nurse is available, accepting and encouraging. Nurses also express their support by upholding an inherent belief in patients' capabilities and resources, and through maintaining a sense of hope. In this regard, support encompasses a variety of skills, because it is predominantly an attitude of being with and for the patient.

Types of support

There are a variety of ways in which nurses provide support to patients. Firstly, there is informational support. Sharing information with patients is supportive because information assists patients in coming to terms with their health status, making decisions about health-care and understanding what is usual and expected for a given situation. Another type of support comes in the form of direct aid and assistance. This type of support is the concrete, often observable, 'lending of a helping hand'. Helping a hospitalised patient out of bed is a clear example of this type of support. Another type of support is the provision of positive affirmation and encouragement to patients. This type of support is emotional in nature, and an example of it is the proverbial 'pat on the back'. It involves standing by and offering encouragement to the patient. The last type is the most common usage of the term 'support'.

Wortman (1984) provides a useful schema in defining support. Support is conveyed to patients through:

- expressions of positive regard and esteem
- encouragement to express and acknowledgment of feelings and points of view
- access to information
- practical and tangible assistance
- a sense of belonging

Most of what hospitalised patients describe as supportive is captured in this description of support (Edgman-Levitan, 1993). The most important aspect of support for the patients in Edgman-Levitan's study were expressions of concern, acceptance, understanding and hope. In addition, patients felt supported when they were offered useful information and realistic expectations.

From the preceding description of the types of support, it is apparent that nurses provide support to patients in a variety of ways. An effective relationship with a patient provides support. Most of the actions patients find supportive are discussed in the previous chapters of this book, for example, listening with understanding. The previous section of this chapter on comforting, or the following section on providing information are both examples of supportive nursing actions.

Nevertheless, nurses must also bear in mind that they are but one, often temporary, source of support for patients. Too much emphasis on nurses as providers of support can result in them feeling overwhelmed by patients' needs.

Mobilising patient resources

Another way for nurses to provide support for patients is through direct intervention to mobilise 'other' sources of support. This section focuses on such mobilisation. The following example is an illustration of how nurses mobilise support for patients:

> Barbara Frenzell is in hospital following the stillbirth of a baby girl at full term. The pregnancy, her first, was planned, and both she and her husband eagerly anticipated the birth. The loss and disappointment following the stillbirth was devastating for Barbara. As expected under the circumstances, she was extremely sad, upset and distraught. The nurses found her to be remote, noncommunicative and inaccessible, although her emotional pain was visible to them. They understood Barbara's sadness but were especially concerned by her lack of responsiveness when interacting. Although every effort was made to interact with Barbara, the nurses began to feel helpless because they could not 'connect' with her. They recognised that their concern was greater than usual, and assessed the need for active intervention.
>
> Of all the nurses caring for Barbara, Sue had established the most meaningful relationship with her. Although mostly unresponsive, Barbara spoke more with Sue than any of the other nurses. Through exploration Sue learnt that Barbara's husband, John, had refused to discuss the death of their daughter with her. John's attitude and approach was one of a 'stiff upper lip' style. He saw no reason to 'cry over spilt milk' and dwell on the negative; he just wanted their lives to return to normal as soon as possible. Sue noticed that, when Barbara discussed John's reaction, she became a bit more communicative and animated. More than anything, Barbara wanted to talk to John about her feelings of despair and sadness. In this situation, one of Sue's supports, John, was not available to her. What Barbara needed, more than anything, was to be able to talk to John about what had happened. Sue decided to intervene to mobilise this support for Barbara.
>
> The next time John came to visit, Sue made the effort to spend time with them both. Up to this point, the nurses had left the two of them alone during visiting time, out of respect for their needs for privacy. During the interaction with Barbara and John, Sue encouraged John to discuss his reactions to what had happened. When he stated that there was no reason to cry and feel sorry for himself, Sue suggested that, although he himself may not wish to cry, perhaps his approach was preventing Barbara from expressing how she felt. At this point, Barbara began to cry. John appeared a bit surprised, but made an effort to console her. Sue left the room, with Barbara and John in an embrace. The next day Barbara's general appearance and demeanour had changed. Although still quite sad, she was more talkative and open. Clearly, she felt better as a result of receiving support from her husband John.

This story illustrates, quite clearly, the importance of nurses perceiving support as more than something they supply directly. Through mobilising support for Barbara, rather than focusing exclusively on the patient–nurse relationship, Sue provided intervention that was helpful and effective.

ENABLING PATIENTS TO PARTICIPATE IN CARE

Patient participation has become a popular concept in nursing (Cahill, 1996) because it moves away from the notion of the patient as a passive recipient of care to the patient as an active agent in care. It shifts the role of nurse from provider of care to partner in care. Patient participation is concordant with a modern view of the patient as a collaborator in care.

Patient participation varies from involving patients in care by considering their viewpoints to having patients acting as equal partners in decisions about care. Partnership implies a working association between two people, which is usually based on a contract (Cahill, 1996). As such, both partners are knowledgeable about the work of the partnership. Involving patients in care, on the other hand, is more one-way, with the nurses being more knowledgeable, yet taking into consideration the patient's point of view. Whether at the level of partnership or involvement, there must be a relationship between patient and nurse in order for patient participation to occur (Cahill, 1996).

Having patients participate in their health-care is both an ethical ideal and a practical reality. From an ethical point of view, all patients should have a say in their care, that is, having a legitimate voice in care is a recognised patient right. From a practical standpoint, patients who participate in their health-care are more likely to commit to that care because the care takes into account their particular circumstances. In this regard, health outcomes are more likely to be successful when patients have input into that care.

But having patients participate in their own care is not simply a matter of believing in an ideal or acknowledging a reality. Although health-care practitioners acknowledge the value of patient participation, they prefer patients to be passive and are challenged to determine whether and to what extent patients want to participate (Cahill, 1998; Guadagnoli & Ward, 1998).

Do patients want to be involved in their care? Research indicates that the answer to this question is both complex and variable. In most of the research on the topic, patient participation has been viewed as patient involvement in decision-making about health-care. That is, participation is viewed as the extent to which patients are involved in health-care treatment decisions. Reviews of these studies reveal that patients want to participate to variable degrees *if* options exist and *when* they feel well informed (Cahill, 1998; Guadagnoli & Ward, 1998).

For example, hospitalised patients in Biley's (1992) study indicated that they wanted to participate in care if they felt well enough to do so, knew enough and were permitted to participate. In comparison, hospitalised patients in Waterworth and Luker's (1990) study were more interested in 'toeing the line' and fitting in with the nurses than they were with exercising their right to participate in health-care. Another study that reveals insight into patient participation involved patients who were chronically ill and not hospitalised (Thorne & Robinson, 1989). These patients involved themselves as 'team players' when they felt competent in managing their illness and when they trusted the health-care professionals. In the absence of trust and the presence of personal competence, these patients used their knowledge to manipulate the system to obtain necessary services, but did not engage with professionals.

The major theme in the literature on patient participation is the amount of information that patients have to participate. In the absence of information, patients did not feel capable of participating. Therefore, having patients participate in their care is contingent on them having knowledge about that care. Herein lies one of the major challenges to participation. Sharing information with patients is an important skill in meeting this challenge.

Sharing information

The skill of sharing information encompasses a range of actions from providing explanations, to giving instructions, to imparting knowledge, to formal teaching. When explaining to a patient the reasons for an extended delay in a scheduled procedure, the nurse is sharing information. When engaged in informing patients what they can expect to happen postoperatively, the nurse is sharing information. When teaching a patient how to care for a colostomy, the nurse is sharing information.

What nurses perceive as ordinary and everyday in the routine of health-care delivery can seem foreign to patients. Patients may have little previous knowledge and experience to draw on in trying to understand this sometimes strange, often frightening, world of health-care. Clearly, nurses are in a prime position to help patients make sense of the environment, and their experiences in it, through the sharing of information.

Nurses play a key role in keeping patients informed, not only because of their sustained, continual presence, but also because of their close proximity to the patient's specific experience. When sharing information, a nurse operates from within a patient's experience. It is the nurse who comes to know how much adjustment Mr Jones must make in order to follow a prescribed therapeutic diet. It is the nurse who appreciates the demands being placed on a new mother, who has recently arrived in the country, and is isolated from her usual support systems. Empathy and understanding of the patient's experience enable nurses to share information that is subjective to the patient, and to appreciate what the patient wants to know in relation to health status and care.

Sharing information is more than merely providing information, or imparting knowledge. In sharing, there is concern with how the information is received, understood and used. It is a two-way process. Providing information involves merely supplying information to patients and is a one-way process. In this sense, books, pamphlets and videos provide information to patients. Sharing information, on the other hand, is interactive: it connects the patients' experience with the need for information; it concerns itself with how the information is received; and it views the patient as an active participant, not as a passive recipient.

As with all the skills of intervening, sharing information is grounded in the nurse's understanding of the patient. To some patients, remaining fully informed, down to the level of minute detail of their care, is extremely important to their sense of wellbeing. Other patients prefer not to know every detail and feel best when told only the bare essentials. Nevertheless, some information, for example, orienting information about the routine of the clinical setting, is necessary, regardless of the patient's frame of reference and expressed desire to know.

Effects of sharing information

Having meaningful information about their health status and care helps patients gain a sense of control over sometimes uncontrollable, confusing or disturbing events. Frequently, information is shared when a patient is prepared for an anticipated health event. For example, knowing what can be expected following abdominal surgery assists patients in coming to terms with the usual postoperative course of events. Accurate information can do much to alleviate unnecessary anxiety stemming from false beliefs, misconceptions and even fantasies. Patients facing decisions in relation to health-care are able to determine the best course of action when they are fully informed. Explanations alleviate the anxiety of guessing what will happen next.

The skill of sharing information has been mentioned elsewhere in this chapter, in the sections on reassuring and supporting. In the case of reassuring, information is shared in order that patients remain aware of what is usual and expected in relation to their health status. In this regard, reassurance through sharing information is similar to informational support, a type of support mentioned in the section on supporting. In the next section of this chapter, sharing information is considered as a challenging skill, because of its potential to trigger patients in reappraising their situations. This section contains a general overview and discussion of how best to employ the skill of sharing information.

A nursing perspective on sharing information

Nurses sometimes show reluctance to embark on sharing information with patients, because the information to be shared is perceived as exclusively medical in nature. While it is inappropriate for nurses to assume the role of doctor in presenting initial information about a medical diagnosis, nurses frequently serve as the interpreters of such information. Patients frequently ask nurses questions that are medical in nature. Simply referring them to the appropriate doctor is often not enough. Nurses can assist patients to obtain relevant medical information by helping them to develop questions to be asked of the doctor and suggesting appropriate questions to ask. In this sense, nurses act as guides for patients.

Nevertheless, there is more to sharing information than helping patients to obtain and understand input that is medical in nature. Patients also need assistance in understanding how their health status, including their medical diagnosis (when present and known), will affect their day-to-day living. They need to learn how to adjust and adapt to the demands that are placed on them by alterations in health status. When nurses share information about these aspects of health, they are functioning within a nursing perspective. By focusing on these aspects, nurses concern themselves more with patients' responses to their health status, rather than just their health status per se.

Examples of a nursing perspective on sharing information include helping patients to:

- make sense of what is happening to them
- learn new skills in caring for self
- make adjustments and adaptations in relation to the demands placed on them by alterations in health status

In short, nurses are in a position to share information about patients' daily living in relation to health status (Carnevali, 1983).

Sharing information versus giving advice

It is easy to confuse giving advice with sharing information (this was mentioned briefly in chapter 5). In sharing information, nurses offer a range of alternatives to patients. In giving advice, nurses present solutions to patients. There are times when patients expect advice and place nurses in the role of knowledgeable expert. Before assuming this role, however, nurses need to be clear that certain risks are inherent in advising.

When functioning within the nursing perspective, nurses share information in an attempt to help patients adjust and adapt to their daily living. By advising patients about what is 'best' to do, nurses assume they are experts about each patient's life. Clearly, the patient is the most qualified expert when it comes to managing their life. The risks of playing the expert when it involves another person's life are apparent—the advice can be unsuitable, unacceptable, inappropriate or even dangerous.

It is better to present alternatives, through sharing information, and enable the patient to determine which course of action might be best. The following scenario highlights the process of presenting alternatives versus giving solutions:

June Ford has been visiting the local early childhood centre on a regular basis since her first son, Ted, was born eleven months ago. During a recent visit she related that she is becoming increasingly distressed because Ted is still waking during the night to breastfeed. Although Ted feeds quickly during the night and settles back to sleep quite easily, June is distressed by her continual broken night's sleep.

Eleanor, the registered nurse in the centre, has been working with mothers and babies for twelve years. June asks Eleanor for advice about what to do, because she is becoming desperate for an unbroken night's sleep. Eleanor begins by explaining that Ted is of sufficient weight and age to go through the night without a feed. She then proceeds to explain that June has various options. She could let Ted cry until he returns to sleep; she could use the 'controlled crying method' to get him back to sleep without a feed; June's husband could tend to Ted in the middle of the night; or she could continue to feed him, knowing that some day waking during the night will cease. Eleanor then continues, explaining how other mothers she knows have dealt with similar circumstances. Finally, she shares her own experiences learned through caring for her three children.

After presenting the options, Eleanor explains to June that only she can decide what is best for herself, Ted and the family. She finishes by stating that there are numerous theories about how to care for babies, and a variety of possible approaches, but it really comes down to what June can live with. She then explores each of the options with June, to determine what June would like to try.

Obviously, Eleanor could have advised June about what she should do, rather than share information and let June decide. In doing so, however, she would have run the risk of suggesting a solution that is unacceptable or unworkable for June. Even if the advice is acceptable, it may not work, so June would be left with no other options. Under these circumstances, June probably would not ask Eleanor again, and may even blame her for the failure of her recommendation. Most importantly, by giving advice, Eleanor becomes responsible for the outcome. June could be left with feelings of inadequacy as a result. These are the risks of presenting solutions, rather than alternatives.

Giving advice is not the same as presenting factual, clinical information to patients, or explaining the potential consequences of certain health-related behaviours. Advice offers solutions when patients are facing situations that they can potentially manage. Instructing a patient to cough and deep breathe following surgery, in order to help prevent pulmonary complications, is an example of presenting information and instructions, although this could be construed as advice. There are times when nurses effectively offer advice to patients, but this should be undertaken with full awareness of the risks involved.

Approaches to sharing information

Sharing information begins with the nurse's recognition of the patient's need for it. While it could be said that all patients need certain information in order to cope with changes in health status, the specific need within each patient may be variable. This recognition and appreciation of the patient's unique requirements for information stems from the nurse's understanding.

While the patient's unique experiences provide a useful starting point for the use of any intervening skill, there are some general situations that indicate a specific need for information. These include:

- facing new and unfamiliar situations
- coping with demands of altered health status
- developing new skills
- being misinformed

- requesting information and explanations
- expressing the need for reassurance and informational support

Readiness to learn

Timing is crucial when sharing information, and this is best expressed as capturing the patient's readiness to learn (Benner, 1984: 79). If information is shared before a patient is ready, it may fall on deaf ears or, worse, create undue anxiety in the patient. When it occurs too late, sharing information fails to achieve its desired outcome.

Capturing a patient's readiness to learn is a sophisticated process, which is described as an aspect of expert nursing practice (Benner, 1984). The degree of sensitivity to patient cues that is required for this level of practice is developed through experience and involvement with numerous patient experiences. To beginning nurses, the concept of the 'right time' to share information may seem vague and elusive. Nevertheless, an acceptance and recognition that there is a right time to 'strike while the iron is hot', enables beginning nurses to make the effort to observe and notice patient cues that indicate readiness.

A good example occurs in the teaching of patients to care for a colostomy, a complex, sometimes overwhelming, task for most patients. Because patients must first come to terms with the reality of a colostomy, they will not be ready to learn the details of caring for it and themselves until this happens. Cues indicating readiness include looking at the colostomy in more than just a fleeting manner; not reacting with disgust when looking at it; and asking questions of the nurse who is changing the colostomy bag. This is but one example of the importance of noticing when the patient seems ready to learn.

Obviously, capturing the patient's readiness means that nurses must be flexible enough to change their immediate plans, in order to accommodate this readiness.

Beginning to share information

Once the need for information is established, and the readiness to receive the information is noted, it is best to begin sharing information by establishing what the patient wants to know. Often patients will ask questions, without prompting or probing, but it may be necessary for the nurse to use exploration skills (see chapter 6) to establish what the patient wants to know first. Questions that are useful include:

- 'What questions are on your mind?'
- 'What would you like to know?'
- 'Where would you like me to begin explaining this?'

Through exploring what patients want to know, the nurse is requesting and encouraging the patient to ask the questions. It is important that these questions are answered at the depth and level at which they are asked. A simple question need not be met with a complicated, involved answer. Likewise, a complex question should not be brushed aside with a superficial answer. It is often a good idea to paraphrase (see chapter 5) the patient's question prior to attempting to answer it.

After answering a patient's question, the nurse needs to check that the response satisfied the question. This is accomplished by following the response with another question, such as 'Does that answer your question?' The nurse may be surprised when the patient answers 'No'. Under this circumstance, it is obvious that the nurse needs to develop another response, or have the patient pose the question again, using different words.

From this point, the nurse now can move into further, more focused exploration of what the patient already understands. A person who has experienced repeated hospitalisations may understand a great deal about ward routine. This exploration provides a good opportunity to correct any misinformation or misperceptions. The nurse can also use the patient's current level of understanding as a springboard for expansion and elaboration of further information. Notice how beginning in this manner encourages the patient to direct the flow of information. It also provides an opportunity for the nurse to further assess the patient's readiness to receive information.

Limiting the amount of information shared

When nurses are expanding into sharing new information, they need to appreciate that there are limits to how much information can be absorbed at one time. Too much information, presented at one time, can result in an overload of the patient's information-processing capacity. Presenting detailed, complex information all at once can create more confusion within the patient. For this reason, the general guideline of presenting no more than three new items at one time is recommended (Cormier et al., 1986).

Using appropriate language

Another important facet when sharing information is to use language that matches the patient's age, experience and cultural background. Nurses sometimes become so accustomed to the jargon of health-care that they fail to appreciate that patients do not understand some of the language used. Terms such as 'IVs', 'nil by mouth', 'obs' and even 'bedrest' can create confusion in patients. For example, some patients think 'bedrest' literally means to have a rest in bed, and liken it to an afternoon nap, thinking this is sufficient in maintaining bedrest. Not only should standard medical and nursing terms and jargon be fully explained to patients, but also their use should be kept to a minimum, if not avoided altogether.

Tailoring information to the patient

Of even greater importance, when sharing information, is the need to tailor explanations to the individual patient. Obviously, age and cultural variations (see chapters 8 and 9) need to be taken into account. But it is equally important to work from the patient's background and experience, for example, an engineer can easily relate the functioning of the heart to already acquired knowledge of closed systems that work on pressure, pumps, one-way valves and electrical conduction. Knowing a patient's background is necessary for this guideline to be enacted.

The need for reinforcement

It is often helpful to reinforce explanations and information verbally shared with prepared pamphlets, diagrams, models and spontaneously written notes. Using an alternative means of expression, such as these, provides helpful reinforcement for patients. Summarising (see chapter 5) the shared information is another helpful means of reinforcing. Often patients' anxiety levels interfere with their ability to absorb information, and reinforcing will aid in the retention of presented information.

Additionally, there may be a need to reiterate information. Repetition provides reinforcement, although the need to repeat information may prove frustrating to the nurse. The patient may need to hear it more than once in order to incorporate the information, and put it to some use.

Checking the patient's understanding

Sharing information is more than imparting knowledge, so the nurse sharing the information needs to periodically check that the patient understands the information. It is better to check frequently throughout an information-sharing interaction than to wait until it draws to a close. The skills of exploration (see chapter 6) are employed for this purpose.

Expressing understanding when sharing information

Lastly, when nurses are sharing information, they need to be sensitive to the impact of the information on the patient. For the patient, there may be surprises and challenges contained in the information received. Observing patient cues, which indicate their reactions, reflecting observed feelings and expressing empathy are all helpful skills to employ for this purpose. In the absence of patient cues, it may be necessary for nurses to explore patients' reactions to the information that is shared.

A final word on sharing information

Before embarking on sharing information, nurses must be reasonably confident with their own level of knowledge, related to the patient situation. This is not to say that nurses should 'know everything' there is to know about all patient situations, but there is little point in trying to share information when the basics of the situation are not understood. If this is the case, a cursory assessment of the patient's need for information could be undertaken; but there are limits, for example, a patient's misunderstanding might not be immediately corrected if the nurse lacks knowledge.

There are likely to be situations in which a patient's request for information is beyond what a nurse currently understands and knows. There is no real harm in nurses admitting that they do not know, as long as they are willing to find out for the patient, or refer the patient to an appropriate resource. When referral to another person, for example, the patient's doctor, is the most appropriate course of action, nurses can assist patients in framing questions to ask of this person.

➡ 320

ACTIVITY 7.4

SHARING INFORMATION

Process

1. Working in groups of five to six participants, develop a list of patient situations which indicate that the patient needs more information.

2. Each group member now writes a brief scenario, based on one of the situations from the developed list. Include patient cues indicating a need for information.

3. Distribute the scenarios to each of the group members. Members are to take the scenario away from the session and gather the information required to fully inform the patient described in the scenario.

4. At the next class gathering, participants form into groups of three. Identify one member of the group as the patient, one as the nurse who will share information and the third person as an observer.

5. For each scenario, have the 'nurse' share information with the patient. The observer uses the *Guide for sharing information* (see appendix, page 321).

Discussion

1. What was easy about sharing information? What was hard?

2. What were some of the difficulties experienced in sharing information? Refer to questions on the observer guides that were answered 'No'.

3. How did the 'nurses' assess the 'patient's' current level of knowledge?

4. How did the 'nurses' determine the 'patient's' comprehension of the information?

5. What kind of wording and language was used in sharing the information?

Enabling participation through challenging

When challenging, nurses urge patients to reconsider their current perspectives and assist them in the development of new perspectives. A challenge encourages patients to evaluate their views, feelings and interpretations of a situation. This can be achieved by directly presenting a different interpretation, or by exploring alternative perspectives with the patient. Either way, a successful challenge enables patients to reframe their experiences in a new light and therefore participate in care with this new view.

Challenging is a skill that is high in terms of influencing patients. This is because the nurse is asking patients to call into question their experiences, and to develop new perspectives on their experience. Challenging often forces patients to call on new or unused resources.

The challenging aspects of other skills

The section on reassuring skills makes reference to responses that encourage patients to reinterpret their experience. When enacted in this way, reassurance has a challenging edge to it. Sharing information can also be challenging, because the presentation of new information often results in the formation of new perspectives. Even exploration and empathy expression can be challenging. When nurses express empathy, reflect feelings and engage in exploration, the result may be that patients begin to challenge their own perspectives.

The nature of challenging

Effective challenging is beneficial because it influences patients to look at their situations in new and different ways. This reframing and reinterpretation may prove unsettling at first, and patients may experience anxiety as a result. For this reason, nurses are often uncomfortable with the notion of challenging a patient, because it seems nonsupportive to cast doubt on the patient's current perspective. Perhaps this is due to a lack of understanding of the nature and helpfulness of a challenge.

Challenging is not the same as disagreeing with or rejecting the patient's perspective, although it does rely on the nurse's judgment that another perspective may be more productive. For example, a patient may believe that having a myocardial infarction results automatically in permanent disability and dramatic alteration to previous functioning. An interpretation such as this can lead to feelings of depression and even despair. Such a patient is at risk of becoming a 'cardiac cripple'. By challenging this perspective, the nurse enables the patient to develop a more realistic view of the situation, post-infarction.

The conditions needed for effective challenging

As with all the psychosocial action skills, challenging is preceded by an understanding acknowledgment of the reality of the patient's current experience (see chapter 5). Nurses 'earn the right' (Egan, 1994) to challenge patients by first demonstrating understanding of their viewpoints and experiences. In this sense, understanding is a prerequisite to challenging.

Before embarking on challenging skills, a nurse must also consider the strength of the relationship with the patient. If little rapport, trust and understanding is developed, it is likely that a challenge will be ineffective. In fact, without trust, challenging may be counterproductive to the further development of the relationship. Patients will accept a challenge from a nurse who has demonstrated interest, accessibility, reliability and understanding. Challenging is more likely to be effective in longer term rather than shorter term relationships.

Other aspects to consider before embarking on a challenge relate to the vulnerability and fragility of the patient. Nurses must be reasonably certain that the patient being challenged has the strength, resilience and resources to develop and accept a new perspective. Minimally, the patient needs to be able to acknowledge that alternative views are possible.

The need to challenge

The need to challenge stems from the existence of patient perspectives that are unproductive, unsatisfying, poorly informed, unacceptable and/or unnecessarily painful or distressing to the patient. The importance of that final phrase, *to the patient*, cannot be stressed enough. It is important that challenges are not presented as negative judgments, which give the impression that patients 'should not' think or feel the way they do. Although nurses rely on a judgment that a new perspective may be needed, they must operate from within the patient's value system in order to be most effective. A nurse cannot decide, without consultation, that the patient's perspective needs to be altered.

Tentativeness of the challenge

Challenges are best presented in a tentative manner, but not so tentative that nurses lack assertiveness in the process. A nurse wishing to challenge a patient can begin by suggesting that there may be another way of looking at the situation. This is an effective way to determine the patient's readiness to accept alternative perspectives.

Approaches to challenging

When patients indicate, often through subtle cues, that their current view is unproductive or difficult to maintain and acknowledge the possibility of alternative perspectives, nurses can proceed by:

- exploring alternative perspectives
- presenting their own interpretation and perspective
- sharing factual information

The first approach relies on the use of exploring skills (see chapter 6). The second approach uses the skill of feedback, covered in the section on reassuring in this chapter. The third approach is also covered in this chapter, under the heading of sharing information.

Exploring consequences

Another way to begin the challenge is to explore the consequences of the patient's present perspective. While this approach relies on the effective use of exploring skills (see chapter 6), it is a focused exploration into the possible effects of the patient's current perspective, and delves into the potential risks and benefits of that perspective.

A nurse may be tempted to take the idea of consequences one step further and actually point them out to patients. This approach should be used sparingly (Ivey & Ivey, 1998), because of its potential to degenerate into a judgmental, coercive activity, which preaches warnings and punishment. Nurses need to be cautious about admonishing patients because this can translate to 'blaming the victim'. If this happens, patients may form the impressions that the nurse does not care to understand.

Assertiveness in challenging

The ability to be assertive (see chapter 3) is necessary when challenging. Some examples of assertive, challenging responses include:

- 'I see your situation in a different light than you do.'
- 'I'm concerned that if you continue along these lines, you will just wither away.'
- 'You say you are doing everything to help yourself, but I can see some more things that you could do.'

When challenging, it is important to focus on the patient's strengths and resources, not just weaknesses and failures. In this regard, challenging is employed with an attitude of respect for the patient's inherent capabilities.

Reframing through self-disclosure

Self-disclosing is a skill whereby nurses share their own thoughts, feelings, perceptions, interpretations and experiences in the interest of helping the patient. Self-disclosure is both a form of commiseration, which is a way of comforting patients (Morse et al., 1992), and a way of helping patients reframe their situations.

Reference to the use of this skill is made elsewhere in this book. In chapter 6, it is presented as a means of opening areas for exploration. Using self-disclosure to prompt patients and encourage them to express themselves is one of the most common forms of this skill. Self-disclosure is also discussed in chapter 5, as a way to clarify what patients have expressed. The skill of self-disclosure is included in this chapter because it can also be used to directly influence patients.

Sharing own experiences

One of the most frequent ways that self-disclosure is effective occurs when a nurse has experienced a situation that is similar to the patient's. For example, a nurse who has had the experience of a family member with cancer may share this experience with the family of a patient who is diagnosed with cancer. Under circumstances such as these, nurses share their experiences (commiseration) not only to demonstrate to the patient a personal understanding of the situation, but also to present an alternative perspective (reframing).

Self-disclosure also serves as a way to reassure patients that nurses are real people, with real lives. Being open enough to share their own stories with patients demonstrates that nurses trust patients as much as they want patients to trust them. The genuineness and personal involvement that is demonstrated by self-disclosure has potential to draw the nurse and patient closer together. But it also may frighten some patients, who do not desire this degree of intimacy, or who prefer nurses to remain distant.

How much of self should be shared?

This notion of sharing self with patients does challenge some notions of 'professionalism'. At times, professionalism is equated with distance, detachment and non-involvement with patients. This notion of professionalism is explored fully in chapter 2. Self-disclosure raises questions about how much information about themselves nurses should share with patients.

ACTIVITY 7.5

SELF-DISCLOSURE

 Process

1. Discuss the following:

   a. How much personal information about themselves should nurses share with patients?

   b. Is there anything of a personal nature that nurses should not share with patients? If so, what?

   c. Discuss the reasons for the answers to each of these questions.

Discussion

1. How much disagreement was there between participants in answering questions 1a–c?

2. Were there areas of agreement about what should and should not be shared with patients? What are they?

3. How do you account for the agreement and disagreement in the questions posed?

In deciding how much of self to share with patients, there will almost certainly be differences that are based on the personality factors of each nurse. Like all people, some nurses are more willing to share personal experiences than others. Irrespective of personal factors, a general rule of thumb can be applied in deciding how much of self to share. The general rule stems from the nature of the relationship between patient and nurse.

Although this relationship involves give and take, and, at times, is quite intimate, the nurse must remain oriented toward the patient. When self-disclosure is used to benefit the nurse, this orientation has shifted onto the nurse.

Pitfalls of self-disclosure

Self-disclosure does not mean that nurses should ask patients to bear some of the burden of their own personal difficulties and problems. This is one of the potential pitfalls of self-disclosure. Self-disclosing has a potential to shift the focus from the patient to the nurse and, as a result, the nurse dominates the interaction with discussions about self. In this case, the self-disclosure runs the risk of burdening the patient with the nurse's personal story. Obviously, if this happens, questions are raised about how helpful this might be for the patient. It takes awareness to recognise when this is happening, and an aware nurse will shift the focus back onto the patient, perhaps by employing an exploration skill.

When sharing their own experiences with patients, nurses need to be careful not to use the self-disclosure as a subtle way of rejecting a patient's experience, in favour of the nurse's. Nor should self-disclosure be used in a competitive manner of 'let's see who has the best/worst story to tell'. Before disclosing themselves to patients, nurses should pass the disclosure through the following proverbial gate: 'Am I sharing this in order to benefit the patient or our relationship?' If the answer is 'yes', the gate opens for self-disclosure.

Patient requests for personal information

The discussion about self-disclosure also raises the question of how nurses should respond when patients request information that is personal in nature. In this regard, the patient prompts the self-disclosure. Clearly, the decision about how much nurses share of themselves is a personal one, but there are also professional reasons to disclose or not to disclose. Firstly, the context must be considered. In an inpatient psychiatric setting, for example, there may be sound reasons for nurses to avoid too much disclosure of personal details about their lives. Other aspects of the context, which should be considered, include:

- the possible reasons the patient requests the information
- the degree of personal depth in the request
- the potential consequences of answering or not answering the question

Nurses are encouraged to reflect and explore how much or how little information about themselves they are willing to share with patients.

CHAPTER SUMMARY

The skills presented in this chapter focus on psychosocial actions of comfort, supporting and enabling. Nurses employ the skills of comforting in order to reassure patients. Effective reassurance releases patient anxiety so that energy can be used for dealing with the health event at hand. Effective support offers assistance and aid, again freeing the patient's energy to cope. Enabling patients to participate in care by sharing information and challenging helps patients to reframe their perspectives on their situation. All of these skills involve taking direct action to positively influence patients and, more importantly, free energy to cope with health events.

The power necessary for nurses to influence patients in these ways is not automatic; the nurse who has taken the time to understand fully the patient earns it. Taking action is most effective when it works from within the patient's experience, therefore the continual need to listen, explore and understand has been emphasised throughout the chapter. Nurses are most effective when they use psychosocial actions with the view that patients are capable and resourceful. With this view, the skills in this chapter are used to mobilise, utilise and reinforce patients' capabilities and resources.

REFERENCES

Benner, P. (1984). *From novice to expert: excellence and power in clinical nursing practice.* Addison-Wesley, Menlo Park CA.

Biley, F.C. (1992). Some determinants that effect patient participation in decision-making about nursing care. *Journal of advanced nursing,* 17, 414–421.

Bottorff, J.L., Gogag, M. & Engelberg-Lotzkar, M. (1995). Comforting: exploring the work of cancer nurses. *Journal of advanced nursing,* 22, 1077–1084.

Boyd, C.O. & Munhall, P.L. (1989). A qualitative investigation of reassurance. *Holistic nursing practice,* 4 (1), 61–69.

Cahill, J. (1996). Patient participation: a concept analysis. *Journal of advanced nursing,* 24, 561–571.

Cahill, J. (1998). Patient participation: a review of the literature. *Journal of clinical nursing,* 7, 119–128

Cameron, B.L. (1993). The nature of comfort to hospitalized medical surgical patients. *Journal of advanced nursing,* 18, 424–436.

Carnevali, D. (1983). *Nursing care planning: diagnosis and management,* 3rd edn. Lippincott, Philadelphia PA.

Cormier, L.S., Cormier, W.H. & Weisser, R.J. (1986). *Interviewing and helping skills for health professionals.* Jones and Bartlett, Boston MA.

Drew, N. (1986). Exclusion and confirmation: a phenomenology of patients' experiences with caregivers. *Image: journal of nursing scholarship,* 18 (2), 39–43.

Edgman-Levitan, S. (1993). Providing effective emotional support. In M. Gerteis, S. Edgman-Levitan, J. Daley & T.L. Delbanco, (eds). *Through the patients' eyes: understanding and promoting patient-centered care* (pp 154–177). Jossey-Bass, San Francisco.

Egan, G. (1994). *The skilled helper,* 5th edn. Brooks/Cole, Pacific Grove CA.

Fareed, A. (1994). A philosophical analysis of the concept of reassurance and its effect on coping. *Journal of advanced nursing,* 20, 870–873.

Fareed, A. (1996). The experience of reassurance: patients' perspectives. *Journal of advanced nursing*, 23, 272–279.

Faulkner, A. & Maguire, P. (1984). Teaching assessment skills. In A Faulkner (ed.). *Communication* (pp 130–144). Churchill Livingstone, Edinburgh.

Guadagnoli, E. & Ward, P. (1998). Patient participation in decision-making. *Social science and medicine*, 47, 329–339.

Ivey, A.E. & Ivey, M. (1998). *Intentional interviewing and counseling: facilitating client development*, 4th edn. Brooks/Cole, Pacific Grove CA.

Johnson, D. W. (2000). *Reaching out: interpersonal effectiveness and self actualization*, 7th edn. Allyn and Bacon, Boston MA.

Morse, J.M. (1992). Comfort: the refocusing of nursing care. *Clinical nursing research*, 1 (1), 91–106.

Morse, J.M., Bottoroff, J.L., Anderson, G., O'Brien, B & Solberg, S. (1992). Beyond empathy: expanding expressions of caring. *Journal of advanced nursing*, 17, 809–821.

Morse, J.M., Bottoroff, J.L. & Hutchinson, S. (1994). The phenomenology of comfort. *Journal of advanced nursing*, 20, 189–195.

Motyka, M., Motyka, H. & Wsolek, R. (1997). Elements of psychological support in nursing care. *Journal of advanced nursing*, 26, 909–912.

Proctor, A., Morse, J.M. & Khonsari, E.S. (1996). Sounds of comfort in the trauma center: how nurses talk to patients in pain. *Social science and medicine*, 42, 1669–1680.

Swanson, K.M. (1993). Nursing as informed caring for the well-being of others. *Image: journal of nursing scholarship*, 25 (4), 352–357.

Teasdale, K. (1989). The concept of reassurance in nursing. *Journal of advanced nursing*, 14, 444–450.

Thorne, S.E. & Robinson, C.A. (1989) Guarded alliance: health care relationships in chronic illness. *Journal of advanced nursing*, 21, 153–157.

Whyte, L., Motyka, M., Motyka, H., Wsolek, R. & Tune, M. (1997). Polish and British nurses' responses to patient need. *Nursing standard*, 11 (38), 34–37.

Waterworth, S. & Luker, K.S. (1990). Reluctant collaborators: do patients want to be involved in decisions concerning care? *Journal of advanced nursing*, 15, 971–976.

Wortman, C.B. (1984). Social support and the cancer patient. *Cancer*, 53 (supplement), 2339–2362.

Part III

SKILLS IN CONTEXT

Throughout chapters 3–7 various skills and concepts of interacting with patients have been presented without direct reference to situational variables that affect the use of these skills. In chapter 7 the skills of interacting are placed within the context of the relationship that develops between nurse and patient. While the various patient stories in these chapters have served as illustrations in the use of the skills, no attempt has been made to place the skills into specific nursing-care contexts.

This part places interpersonal skills in context by addressing the situational variables of patients' age, culture and personal coping style (chapters 8 and 9), as well as their responses to crisis and illness (chapter 10). The final chapter explores how developing interpersonal connections with patients has the potential to place stress on nurses and describes the ways in which nurses can cope with this stress by using interpersonal skills to enhance relationships with nursing colleagues.

CHAPTER 8

ADJUSTING INTERACTIONS TO AGE-RELATED FACTORS

Jackie Crisp
Sue Nagy

INTRODUCTION

Establishing appropriate relationships with patients is contingent upon appropriate and sensitive use of the skills discussed in the preceding chapters of this book. Deciding what 'appropriate' means, however, is not as easy as it may first appear. Nurses constantly face situations that challenge them to modify their typical approaches to interactions with patients. Modifications must be based on continuous monitoring and evaluation of the interaction, both in terms of its effectiveness and its impact on nurses and patients. It is useful, therefore, to take time to consider some of the most common factors that may affect the 'usual' course of patient–nurse interactions. One of these factors is the age of the patient.

Age-related factors challenge nurses to adjust their communication. For example, when interacting with children, nurses must consider the child's developmental age. The cognitively determined limits this brings to understanding present nurses with challenges of a different kind. The most obvious adjustments that may be made include altering the level and sophistication of the language and concepts used. Just as nurses must adjust the dosage of medication on the basis of a child's weight, so must communication be altered to adjust for the child's developmental age.

Likewise, at the other end of the human life cycle, nurses may be challenged in their interactions with older adults whose life experience has been different from their own. Adults who are a lot older than the nurse may have world views that have been developed by experiences that for the nurse are nothing more than a page in a history book.

The challenge of understanding the world from the patient's perspective is continuous. This chapter describes ways to meet the challenges that are posed by age differences between nurse and patient.

Chapter overview

A major consideration when interacting with and relating to children is the developmental age of the child. Therefore this chapter begins with a discussion of how to consider the cognitive and psychosocial developmental stage of the child, especially in relation to explaining treatment procedures. Included in this discussion is a consideration of a child's previous experience with illness, as this a factor that also affects understanding of health-related events and treatment. This is followed by a discussion of developmental aspects of interacting with the elderly. While it may come as a surprise, developmental tasks continue throughout life and old age is no different in this respect. How nurses might consider aspects specific to interacting with the elderly is reviewed in the chapter.

RELATING TO CHILDREN

Relating to children is inherently different from relating to adults for a number of reasons including the limited amount of experience most children have had in health-care situations, the negative preconceptions children commonly have of health-care and health-care workers, the power differences that exist within adult–child interactions, and the implications of age-related cognitive structures for children's capacity to assimilate and accommodate new experiences and material. It should be remembered, however, that the influence of these factors decreases as infants grow out of childhood and into adolescence. For example, the more powerful position of the adult in the interaction diminishes as children develop a stronger sense of their own identity.

Infancy to adolescence

A basic understanding of major theories of child development provides a useful framework for interacting effectively with children and enhances understanding of the major issues involved. Beginning knowledge of Piaget's theory of cognitive development and Erikson's theory of psychosocial development (Mussen et al., 1990; Santrock & Yussen, 1988; Bee, 1989) strengthens understanding of the following discussion. Readers without this background knowledge are encouraged to spend some time becoming familiar with the basic concepts of cognitive and psychosocial human development before embarking on the following section.

Cognitive development

Theories of cognitive development in children are commonly used to track the level of reasoning children demonstrate at different ages. One such theory is that of Piaget. Models or explanations based on Piagetian theory have been developed that may assist nurses in understanding how children of different ages tend to perceive and come to terms with different health-related situations.

ACTIVITY 8.1

COGNITIVE DEVELOPMENTAL LEVEL

 Process

The focus of the activity is the psychological preparation of children of different ages for the procedure of insertion of an intravenous cannula. (Participants who are not familiar with this procedure can either become so prior to the activity or select a potentially painful procedure that is familiar and understood.)

1. Form into groups of four to six participants. Each group discusses preparation of the procedure for one of the following age groups: one year, four years, nine years and fourteen years.

2. Develop the means of explaining to each child the need for the procedure.

    a. How would you describe what is involved?

    b. What would you say if the child asked how much it was going to hurt?

    c. How would you determine the best means of comforting and supporting the child throughout the procedure?

    d. What would be the best measure of the effectiveness of your preparation?

Discussion

1. The spokesperson shares the findings of the group with all the participants in a plenary session.

2. Discuss the commonalities and differences in the explanations that exist across the four age groups.

3. Relate the explanations to the theories of cognitive growth and development.

Methods of explaining health-related events have been developed on the basis of how children come to understand such events. For example, there are models describing the development of children's concepts about where babies come from (Bernstein & Cowan, 1975); medical procedures (Steward & Steward, 1981); pain (Gaffney & Dunne, 1986); the causes of illness (Burbach & Peterson, 1986); and death (Bluebond-Langer, 1978; Lansdown & Benjamin, 1985).

These models provide potential starting points when deciding how to discuss particular subjects with children, such as forthcoming procedures or how certain treatments will help to 'make them better'. At a certain stage children's thinking is not developed beyond a concrete level of understanding, which means they are unable to think in the abstract. Children at this stage of development who are diagnosed with cancer will experience difficulty in understanding both their illness and why chemotherapy and other treatments are necessary. How can their illness and treatment be explained adequately when they have a disease that often cannot be seen (they may even be feeling well), and needs to be treated with 'medicine' that makes them feel sicker than they have ever felt in their lives? On a concrete-thinking level this doesn't make sense.

The work of Bibace and Walsh (1981) provides insight into some of the major issues surrounding children's explanations for the causes of their illness. This model includes two substages within each of Piaget's pre-operational, concrete operational and formal operational stages. According to Bibace and Walsh, children within the *pre-operational*, or first, stage focus on the physical environment, with cause-effect relationships ascribed to events or factors that are spatially or temporally familiar. Magical thinking and self-centredness are characteristics of thinking within this stage. Bibace and Walsh describe the substages of *phenomenism* (for example, 'You just get it…from the bad man, by magic I think') and *contagion* (for example, 'The wind blows around and around you and you get sick') at the pre-operational level.

The second stage within the model, the *concrete operational* stage, contains the substages of *contamination* (for example, 'You get it when other kids have it and they put it on your face') and *internalisation* (for example, 'The germs go in your mouth and it feels awful'). In this stage, children are said to move from a position where they attribute the cause of illness to external objects, events or activities (contamination) to viewing the cause as the taking into the body of a harmful external agent (internalisation).

The third stage, *formal operational*, contains the substages of *physiological* (for example, 'Your lungs get filled up with mucus and stop doing their job') and *psychophysiological* (for example, 'When you're all stressed out and that makes your immune system not work properly'). Children in this stage move from a position where illness is viewed as a breakdown in the functioning of internal structures or physiology triggered by external events, to one where the potential role of thoughts and feelings in the production of some illnesses is acknowledged.

One of the major contributions made by explanations, such as the work of Bibace and Walsh (1981), is that they offer a framework to guide paediatric patient–nurse interactions. It is established that there is miscommunication between children and health-care workers (Eiser, 1984; Korsch, 1983; Lewis & Lewis, 1983). For example, children perceived that those who were caring for them did not always tell them the truth (Ross & Ross, 1984). In order for the 'truth' to be heard by children, it needs to be couched in terms that can be absorbed, and in a form that is relatively compatible with the particular child's developmental age.

Returning to the problem of children who have cancer and are not capable of abstract thinking, discussions concerning the cause of the illness need to focus on external manifestations of their disease. Internal structures and functions of their bodies are outside their understanding. In addition, because children in this group have been found to view illness as punishment for their own misbehaviour (Burbach & Peterson, 1986), nurses may need to work at dispelling this belief. The need for particular treatments should include a focus on any external or obvious symptoms of the particular cancer, and related to the child's physical environment and priorities. For example, if the child is being given a blood transfusion, a possible explanation would be: 'The new blood will make you pink and strong enough to play with the other children.' The use of 'magical' properties of the treatments ('This is a magic medicine that will make the pain go away') may be used to replace intricate explanations of complex treatments. It would be of no use, for instance, to try and explain links between intravenous therapy, the circulatory system and movement of the medicine to the affected part.

While cognitive developmental level is often closely related to age (sensorimotor 0–2 years, pre-operational 3–6 years, concrete operational 7–11 years and formal operational after 12 years), individual differences in cognitive performance exist within age groups. No recipe-like directions, therefore, are available (nor appropriate) to be used with children of particular ages. Probable cognitive developmental level, and the significance of this for the level of understanding a child *should* display, may be used as a guide only. Applying stereotypes that relate to children of certain ages, gender or temperament is as risky as any other stereotype. Taking the time to talk to children about their major concerns, understandings, expectations and fears is central to meeting the needs of individual children.

Previous illness experience

Children who have had previous hospitalisations will probably be better equipped to understand language associated with particular activities (for example, needle = injection = medication). This experience has ramifications that extend beyond simple links across common terms children will encounter. As children's experiences with aspects of health-related areas (for example, illness) increase, they may develop a relatively precocious ability to deal with difficult cognitive concepts and require relatively advanced explanations and information.

On the other hand, children of the same age, and for whom acute illness requiring hospitalisation is a novel experience, may encounter a great deal of difficulty maintaining their 'usual' level of cognitive sophistication. In fact, children faced with new and stressful situations may even regress to an earlier stage of development. For example, an eight-year-old child who usually performs at a concrete operational level of reasoning in most areas may regress to a pre-operational level when faced with such a situation.

Psychosocial development

It can be seen that children's cognitive developmental stage has a significant impact on their ability to absorb and process new material. Another factor with crucial implications for interaction is the child's stage of psychosocial development. For example, prior to attaining the ability to grasp that their caregiver exists whether they are in sight (object permanence), infants are basically content to accept anyone who is available to provide them with the things they require—food, warmth, company and so forth. Once object permanence is obtained, however, and children become attached to their primary caregiver, interactions with others become severely affected. When they encounter strangers or when their primary caregiver disappears out of sight, they become upset and often begin to cry. It is best that nurses, relative strangers, who try to relate to children do so through the child's primary caregiver, and a primary goal in caring for these children involves developing a supportive relationship that facilitates this process (see the section on intermediaries in chapter 9).

At the other end of the developmental spectrum are adolescents, primarily focused on developing a strong sense of self and their own identity. Any attempts to develop meaningful relationships with adolescents are doomed to failure if nurses ignore this very real preoccupation. Working through their parents or caregivers would be a misguided approach. Major concerns of adolescents include their peer relationships and body image, and if a pimple can disrupt the life of an average adolescent, imagine the potential impact of a major body change such as the formation of an ileostomy. No matter how necessary the procedure is seen to be by health-care professionals and the adolescent's family, convincing the adolescent of its worth will involve understanding of the situation (see chapter 4) from the perspective of the adolescent.

Failure to understand the major developmental concerns of patients may lead to a breakdown in interactions. Theories of psychosocial development, such as that developed by Erikson (1963) can provide clues to the possible concerns of patients. It should be remembered, however, that as with cognitive development, this knowledge should be used only as a base from which a picture of the patient can be developed. For example, if an adolescent has had years of intractable pain and diarrhoea due to Crohn's disease, the prospect of an ileostomy may in fact be greeted with enthusiasm.

ACTIVITY 8.2

PSYCHOSOCIAL DEVELOPMENT

 Process

This activity focuses on psychosocial stages and their relationship to interactions in health-care settings.

1. Form four groups. Each group is to choose one of following age groups: one year, four years, nine years and fourteen years. Appoint one person to act as scribe and spokesperson for the group.

2. According to Erikson's theory, what stage is the child in, and what is the major task associated with that stage? What implications does this have for the way a child may view hospitalisation? What would be the implications of chronic or long-term illness on the child's progress through this stage?

Discussion

1. The spokesperson is to share the findings of the small group with all the participants in a plenary session.

2. Discuss the commonalities and differences that emerged from the group discussion about the ways that children of different ages may adapt to chronic illness and to hospitalisation.

RELATING TO ELDERLY ADULTS

People all over the Western world are living longer. In 1900, the average life expectancy was 49 years, and only 4 per cent of the population lived to the age of 65. By 1992 the average life expectancy of non-indigenous Australian men was 73, and 79 for women (Signy & Maley, 1992). Indigenous Australians, whose health is more consistent with people in the Third World, have a life expectancy of 55 for men and 64 for women. Nurses of the future, therefore, are likely to encounter more and more elderly people among their patients. The aim of this section is to help nurses improve their interactions with elderly patients. Interacting with the elderly involves understanding the particular set of difficulties faced by them. These include the communication generation gap between the elderly and the young; the social and economic losses sustained by being elderly in an 'ageist' society; and the physical losses associated with ageing.

The generation gap

The term 'generation gap' was coined to describe the interaction difficulties that are often experienced by people of different generations (Kimmel, 1980). Problems in interacting with elderly people may arise because of generational differences in perceptions of the world. Young people, for example, tend to be oriented to the future, whereas elderly people tend to spend more time thinking about the past. This is, of course, not all that surprising since most of a young person's life is in the future and most of an old person's life is in the past. Values and attitudes to life tend to be shaped by the major economic and other world events through which people have lived.

ACTIVITY 8.3

THE GENERATION EFFECT

 Process

Consider the following brief life sketches:

Elizabeth Eden

Elizabeth was 82 years old in the year 2000. She has lived through a series of major world crises. She was born in the period following World War I, when people were enjoying life to the full, believing that peace and prosperity were their birthright. These hopes were dashed by the Great Depression, which occurred when she was a teenager, and World War II, which occurred when she was in her twenties. Like others who lived through the Depression of the 1930s, Elizabeth suffered extreme economic privations. Her father was out of work and she managed to do some casual piecework, which was very poorly paid, but she was, nevertheless, grateful for it. She learned to scrimp and make the most of limited amounts of food and clothing, and to waste nothing. She married Tom when she was in her mid twenties.

A few years later, World War II started. Tom, along with many other young husbands, went to war. Many soldiers' wives, including Elizabeth, were forced to work outside the home, taking on the work that the men had to leave. Elizabeth and Tom's first child was conceived during Tom's military leave. She had to manage the child virtually as a single working mother while at the same time coping with her anxiety about Tom who had been taken as a prisoner of war. Tom did not meet his child until he returned from a prisoner-of-war camp in 1945. After the war, their two other children were born.

After the war was over, Elizabeth gratefully retreated to the home to finish bringing up her children, and Tom returned to his former occupation. When the women's movement gained momentum in the 1970s, Elizabeth had little sympathy for the aim of equal employment opportunities for women and felt that women were better off not working outside the home.

Mark Yates

Mark was born in 1952, during the postwar baby boom. His childhood was spent during a period of economic affluence and full employment. He took economic security for granted and expected to walk straight into a job when he completed his education.

In contrast to Elizabeth, whose life spanned a number of major world crises, Mark has been beset by a number of more indefinite concerns about the future of the world. The Cold War between the Soviet Union and the United States was at its peak during his youth and, as he grew up, Mark became increasingly aware of the possibility of the world being devastated by nuclear war. He was a teenager during the period of Australia's involvement in the Vietnam War and became accustomed to news reports of the suffering and devastation suffered by the Vietnamese. During his adolescence, there was increasing public discussion of the effects of overpopulation on the world and the environment. Drugs were rife in schools, and the crime rate was increasing at a rate that was causing public alarm. The revolution in sexual attitudes and freedom was well underway.

Many of his friends, having grown up with security, shunned the exhortations of their parents to get 'a steady job'. They were vocal in their cynicism about national and international leaders.

Discussion

1. Divide into small groups and discuss how Elizabeth and Mark's views of life might differ. List these differences on large sheets of paper and post them around the room.

2. In a large group, discuss how world events may have shaped the views of people who are now in their sixties and seventies. How might they be different from people who are now in their twenties and thirties?

3. What do you fear most about growing old? What do you look forward to most?

4. How can nurses reduce interaction difficulties with their patients that are due to a generation gap?

Reminiscing

According to Erik Erikson (1963), successful ageing centres on a person's sense of satisfaction with their past life. The person develops a sense of 'ego integrity'. Remembering and talking about the past is a technique that helps ageing people to make sense of their past lives, to settle unresolved conflicts, and to develop a sense of pride in their achievements during their lifetime. Butler (1963) refers to this process as the 'life review'. The life review helps the person to develop a firmer sense of their own worth. People become more comfortable with the way they have lived their lives and correspondingly develop a more serene view of the world.

Reminiscing has been found to be very therapeutic for elderly people (Viney et al., 1988–89). Listening to reminiscences can help a nurse understand the world view of elderly patients. Looking through an old photograph album, or a local history book of the area in which people grew up or lived most of their lives, or listening to old-time music can help trigger reminiscences in the elderly. An interested listener is probably all the elderly person will need to tell their life story.

Losses associated with ageing

The process of ageing is associated with many losses (Enloe, 1986) and may contribute to the high incidence of depression in elderly people (Murphy,

1982). Some losses, such as the death of loved ones and the realisation that one's own death is closer, are social in nature. Some, such as the reduction in social roles and social status, are a direct result of negative social attitudes towards the elderly. Many older people face a decline in economic status as they retire from paid employment and become dependent on a government pension or superannuation.

Other losses, such as sensory and intellectual impairment, result from physical deterioration. Short-term memory deficits may result in comprehension difficulties and problem-solving difficulties. With ageing, reaction time increases so that older people need more time to respond to events and questions than younger people (Schuster & Ashburn, 1986). The elderly are more cautious, less impulsive and more likely to calculate the risks involved in making a decision. In late adulthood, decline in hearing and vision means that it is more difficult to process sensory input such as vision in dim lighting or conversation when there are background noises (Berger, 1988). An elderly person may find it very difficult to process rapidly presented stimuli (such as from a person speaking quickly), or to process many stimuli at once (such as a large, noisy gathering of people). They have greater difficulty in attending selectively to one stimulus and are more likely to be distracted by irrelevant stimuli (Welford, 1985). In addition, an elderly person's state of health will clearly affect functioning. A person who is not feeling well is less likely to be able to think clearly, to reason logically or to have good problem-solving abilities.

For those elderly people who experience deterioration in their ability to live independent lives, the outcome may be admission to aged-care settings. Once admitted to institutions, elderly people tend to become even more dependent, probably because people who are caring for the elderly frequently unconsciously reinforce dependent behaviour and fail to reinforce independent behaviour (Baltes et al., 1983; Baltes & Reisenzein, 1986).

ACTIVITY 8.4

EXPERIENCING SENSORY DEFICITS

 Process

1. Find an old pair of sunglasses. Cut out a piece of clear contact adhesive (the kind that is used for covering books) and attach it to the lens of the glasses. This should have the effect of allowing in some light but reducing visual acuity. Wear a pair of thin cotton gloves to simulate loss of skin sensation. Wrap elastic bandages firmly around your knees and ankles to simulate a feeling of stiffness in your joints. Place cotton wool plugs in your ears.

2. Spend at least one hour trying to carry out your normal daily activities.

Discussion

1. How difficult was it to carry out your usual activities with impaired sensory input and impaired mobility?

2. How much do you think the vagueness of old people could be attributed to difficulties in sensory perception?

Interacting with the person with a hearing impairment

There are a number of guidelines that can be applied to facilitate interactions with patients who experience hearing difficulties. Most people can lip read to some extent if they can see the speaker's mouth, so nurses should stand where the patient can see them. It is important to speak clearly, articulating the words well and refraining from shouting. If the patient does not understand, the nurse probably needs to try rephrasing sentences, using different words and shorter sentences. Soft-sounding consonants such as 'p' and 'f' are difficult to detect, therefore, using words that avoid these might be helpful. Nurses can be creative in using any means at their disposal to communicate meaning, such as using pictures, or gestures, or writing or drawing.

When nurses are interacting with patients who wear hearing aids, additional techniques are necessary to promote effective interaction. Hearing aids assist individuals with specific types of hearing impairments; they do not restore normal hearing. They are much more sensitive to background noise than natural hearing. When conversing with a patient with a hearing aid, nurses should try to find a quiet room where there are no other conversations going on in the background. Just hitting a glass on a table or clicking a pen can be a source of interference. Using hearing aids effectively requires perseverance on the part of the user and cooperation on the part of others.

CHAPTER SUMMARY

This chapter has considered how the developmental age and stage of the patient affects interactions with nurses. Children's cognitive and psychosocial development has been considered in relation to how they would view health-related events, especially illness. Some of the issues of ageing have also been discussed in relation to effects on patient–nurse interaction. Each of the topics has been reviewed in brief and readers are urged to consider age-related factors in more depth.

REFERENCES

Baltes, M.M., Honn, S., Barton, E.M., Orzech, M. & Lago, D. (1983). On the social ecology of dependence and independence in elderly nursing home residents: a replication and extension. *Journal of gerontology*, 38, 556–564.

Baltes, M.M. & Reisenzein, R. (1986). The social world in long-term care institutions: psychosocial control towards dependency? In M.M. Baltes & P.B. Baltes (eds). *The psychology of control and aging* (pp 316–343). Erlbaum, NJ.

Bee, H. (1988). *The developing child*, 5th edn. Harper & Rowe, New York.

Berger, K.S. (1988). *The developing person through the lifespan*, 2nd edn. Worth, New York.

Bernstein, A.C. & Cowan, P.A. (1975). Children's concepts of how people get babies. *Child development*, 46, 77–91.

Bibace, R. & Walsh, M.E. (1981). Children's conceptions of illness. In R. Bibace & M. E. Walsh (eds). *Children's conceptions of health, illness and bodily functions* (pp 31–48). Jossey-Bass, San Francisco CA.

Bluebond-Langer, M. (1978). *The private worlds of dying children*. Princeton University Press, Princeton NJ.

Burbach, D.J. & Peterson, L. (1986). Children's concepts of physical illness: a review and critique of the cognitive-developmental literature. *Health psychology*, 5, 307–325.

Butler, R.N. (1963). The life review: an interpretation of reminiscence in the aged. *Psychiatry*, 26, 65–76.

Eiser, C. (1984). Communicating with sick and hospitalized children. *Journal of psychology and psychiatry*, 25, 181–189.

Enloe, C. (1993). Managing living with diminishing resources and losses. In D.L. Carnevali & M. Patrick (eds). *Nursing management for the elderly*, 3rd edn (pp 250–264). Lippincott, Philadelphia PA.

Erikson, E.H. (1963). *Childhood and society*, 2nd edn. Norton, New York.

Gaffney, A. & Dunne, E.A. (1986). Developmental aspects of children's definitions of pain. *Pain*, 26, 105–117.

Kimmel, D.C. (1980). *Adulthood and aging*, 2nd edn. John Wiley, New York.

Korsch, B.M. (1983). Doctor-patient communication in acute child health care. In S. Thornton & W. Frakenburg (eds). *Child health care communications* (pp 19–31). Johnson & Johnson, New York.

Lansdown, R. & Benjamin, G. (1985). The development of the concept of death in children aged 5–9 years. *Child care, health and development*, 11, 13–20.

Lewis, M.D. & Lewis, R.N. (1983). Enhancing communication among children and adults who care for them. In S. Thornton & W. Frakenburg (eds). *Child health care communications* (pp 99–112). Johnson & Johnson, New York.

Murphy, E. (1982). Social origins of depression in old age. *British journal of psychiatry*, 141, 135–142.

Mussen, P.R., Conger, J.J., Kagan, J. & Huston, A.C. (1990). *Child development and personality*, 7th edn. Harper & Rowe, New York.

Ross, D.M. & Ross, S.A. (1984). The importance of type of question, psychological climate and subject set in interviewing children about pain. *Pain*, 19, 71–79.

Santrock, J.W. & Yussen, S.R. (1988). *Child development: an introduction*, 4th edn. W.C. Brown, Dubuque IA.

Schuster, C.S. & Ashburn, S.S. (1986). *The process of human development*, 2nd edn. Little Brown, Boston MA.

Signy, H. & Maley, K. (1992). Marriage is good for you. *The Sydney Morning Herald* 25 July, p 9.

Steward, M.S. & Steward, D.S. (1981). Children's conceptions of medical procedures. In R. Bibace & M.E. Walsh (eds). *Children's conceptions of health, illness and bodily functions: new directions for child development* (pp 61–79). Jossey-Bass, San Francisco CA.

Viney, L.L., Benjamin, Y.N. & Preston, C. (1988–89). Mourning and reminiscence: parallel psychotherapeutic processes for elderly people. *International journal of aging and human development*, 28, 237–249.

Welford, A.T. (1985). Changes of performance with age: an overview. In N. Charness (ed.). *Aging and human performance* (pp 333–369). John Wiley, New York.

FURTHER READING

Heaven, P.C.L. (1991) *Life span development*. Harcourt Brace Jovanovich, Sydney.

Marc, H.B. (1988). *Developmental psychology: an advanced textbook*. Earlbaum Associates, NJ.

Melamed, B.G., Matthews, K.A., Routh, D. K., Stabler, B. & Schneiderman, N. (1988). *Child health psychology*. Earlbaum Associates, NJ.

Newman, B.M. (1991). *Development through life: a psychosocial approach*. Brooks/Cole, Pacific Grove CA.

Rice, P. F. (1986). *Adult development and aging*. Allyn & Bacon, Boston MA.

Santrock, J. W. (1986). *Developmental psychology: a life-cycle perspective*. W C Brown, Dubuque IA.

CHAPTER 9

ADJUSTING INTERACTIONS TO CULTURAL DIFFERENCE

Sue Nagy
Jackie Crisp

INTRODUCTION

The material in the previous chapters has emphasised the importance of understanding the patient as a person with a unique perspective of the world. Nurses who come to understand an individual patient are able to work through the patient's own unique perspective of the world in order to 'see through the patient's eyes'. These perspectives of the world, be they those of nurse or patient, are based on cultural beliefs and values. Therefore, an important aspect of understanding another person is an appreciation of differences in cultural meaning.

Differences in cultural understanding commonly lie outside conscious awareness. That is, cultural understandings are often taken for granted. The purpose of this chapter is to introduce ideas that will help nurses to develop conscious awareness of culture and to begin to appreciate cultural diversity when interacting with patients.

Chapter overview

This chapter provides a basic introduction to cultural awareness, and, as such, only serves to highlight some of the major issues in communicating across cultures. The chapter begins with a brief discussion of how culture affects behaviour, especially health-related beliefs. Cultural awareness and cultural safety are discussed in this section. The problems of cultural stereotyping are discussed next, emphasising the diversity within cultural groups and the pitfalls of stereotyping. The challenges of language differences are discussed next, including guidelines for working with an interpreter. The final section deals with communicating without language and the importance of nonverbal communication.

WHAT IS CULTURE?

Culture is the total system of beliefs and values held by a society or a social group. It provides the framework for that particular society's way of life; it influences the way social life is regulated; and it guides interactions between members of a social group and influences the way they understand and make sense of the world.

How do cultural beliefs affect behaviour?

Culture has a vast influence on behaviour. A particular social group's culture is reflected in all aspects of everyday life including customs, greetings, methods of communication, attitudes to the family, beliefs about marriage, attitudes to illness and approaches to health-care. For example, Australian attitudes towards the elderly are very different from those of many European and Asian cultures (Kimmel, 1980), and Asian migrants may regard the easy familiarity that young Australian nurses display towards the elderly as indicative of a lack of respect.

Understandings of and explanations about health and illness are often culturally determined. Those explanations can be very different from the scientific explanatory model that is the basis of most clinical health-care (Allshouse, 1993). health-care is disease oriented, based on understanding of pathophysiology and psychopathology. Understanding a disease from this scientific perspective is based on notions of objectivity. Illness, on the other hand, is what a patient experiences, that is, from a subjective perspective.

Patients' personal, subjective experiences of illness are imbued with cultural meaning, which may or may not fit biomedical explanations of ill health. For example, a family might share the belief that wearing warm undergarments in winter wards off colds and flu; a 'scientific' explanation of colds and flu is that viruses cause them. Indigenous peoples of Australia believe that disharmony and discontinuity cause ill health and healing seeks to reintegrate people with one another and with the environment (Short et al., 1998: 156); knowledge developed in the field of biomedical science does not accommodate such understandings.

Nurses from social and cultural backgrounds that are different from the patient may not understand cultural meanings of health and illness, especially if they operate from an exclusively biomedical orientation. Likewise, patients whose health beliefs are different from those supported by the biomedical model may be reluctant to share their beliefs (Allshouse, 1993).

Differences in illness-related behaviour occur only because of disparity between biomedical thinking and cultural beliefs. An individual nurse's background can create barriers to understanding cultural practices that are unfamiliar. For example, some social groups hold strong beliefs that members who are well have an obligation to pay respects to the sick and to attend to their needs. Family and friends are expected to visit the sick, provide them with home-cooked food, help them to rest and regain their health. The sick, in turn, have an obligation to accept these attentions. Making brave attempts to care for oneself, and indicating that such attentions are not needed, may be regarded as ill-mannered and churlish as it prevents others from fulfilling their obligations to the patient. Social support of this kind is characteristic of Southern European, Aboriginal, Middle Eastern and Asian ethnic groups.

The approaches of these groups contrast with those who place a high value on independence and avoidance of relying on others more than is absolutely necessary, for example, the English. Attempts to get well quickly and to resume normal roles are admired and praised by other members of some groups. Patients have an obligation to make every effort to minimise the time that they are dependent on others. Nurses who, due to their own cultural backgrounds, value independence may have trouble understanding the patients who do very little for themselves while in hospital.

Culture also influences the way people understand and express pain and, therefore, the way that nurses interpret pain-related behaviour in patients. Martin and Belcher (1986), for instance, found that North Americans tend to believe that screaming is a common response when people experience intense pain, while South Africans believe that people in severe pain are more likely to be quiet and withdrawn.

In some countries, hospitalisation is beyond the means of most people, and patients are admitted only when they are severely ill. A logical consequence of this situation is a view of hospitals as places where patients are very likely to die. It is, therefore, quite understandable that patients from such countries may be terrified by the prospect of admission to hospital. Health professionals without an understanding of the basis of that fear may regard these patients as irrationally anxious.

Health-care systems are based largely on the values of the country to which they belong. Legge (1984) outlines an incident involving a non-English speaking Italian woman who was frequently given chrysanthemums by a sympathetic nurse who wanted her to feel more at home. In spite of making satisfactory progress in regaining her health, the woman seemed to be very depressed until the hospital interpreter pointed out to the nurse that, in Italy, chrysanthemums are associated with funerals.

Differences related to patients' relationships with health-care workers also vary across cultures. While in some cultures attitudes towards health professionals are largely deferential and it is rare for patients to question diagnosis or treatment, in other cultures people take a more critical view of health-care. Southern European people often actively 'shop around' for the doctor who suits them best, while many Australians may not only hesitate to do so, but believe that such behaviour demonstrates an overly critical attitude towards the doctor.

Becoming culturally aware

To interact effectively with members of different cultural groups, it is necessary to become more culturally aware and less ethnocentric. Ethnocentrism is a tendency to see the world as having one standard, that of one's own cultural group, and to judge other cultural groups in relation to it. An ethnocentric individual is unlikely to perceive or acknowledge differences in the ways that people view the world, and to fail to appreciate the advantages of living in a multicultural society.

Culturally aware nurses realise that much of their world is socially constructed and that the way it is constructed largely depends on cultural beliefs. In becoming culturally aware, nurses develop an understanding and acceptance of the differences that exist between different groups of people and are more willing to investigate the practices and rituals that are associated with different cultural groups. Some of the more fundamental of these practices include the care of the body after death, religious rituals, beliefs associated with food and childbirth customs.

One way nurses may become more culturally aware involves a process of increasing their conscious awareness of the diversity that exists across cultures, while becoming familiar with their own culturally influenced values. In order to gain this understanding, nurses need to gain experience (for example, through reading material on different cultures, travelling and social or professional interaction). In this way, nurses may develop 'a sensitivity to the similarities and differences between two different cultures' (Hodge, 1987).

Cultural safety

Not only must nurses be self-aware, but they are morally and professionally bound to provide care that is safe. The notion of safety extends beyond physical and psychological parameters to include care that is culturally safe (Polaschek, 1998; Ramsden, 1993). Cultural safety is more than simply learning about cultural practices and beliefs; it is an ethical standard that recognises the position of cultural groups and how they are perceived. Likewise, unsafe practice is any action that demeans or diminishes cultural identity and wellbeing (Polaschek, 1998). Imposing a biomedical perspective on illness while dismissing beliefs that do not fit a biomedical model is an example of culturally unsafe practice.

Cultural safety is more than a recognition of the uniqueness of cultural identity and the need for equity in health-care. Cultural safety includes recognition of social structures that disempower cultural groups. Culturally safe nurses recognise social structures that account, in part, for lack of access to adequate health-care for some cultural groups, for example, Indigenous peoples of Australia. Culturally safe nurses accommodate and respect a diverse range of views on health and healing. They are not set in one particular pattern of thinking about illness, be it a biomedical orientation or one that derives from their own cultural background.

STEREOTYPING

Stereotyping is categorising individuals into groups based on an oversimplified set of characteristics. Stereotypes are potentially useful because they can provide a sort of mental shorthand that allows processing and organisation of the enormous amounts of diverse information encountered in everyday life. The ultimate danger, however, involves generalisation of these stereotypes in their extreme forms, and an associated reluctance to recognise the extent to which individual differences do exist within all groups.

Problems arise when nurses are tempted to apply stereotypes to patients.

A nine-year-old Lebanese boy, Amal, was admitted to a surgical children's ward post-surgery for a ruptured appendix. Amal was very sick for the first three days, receiving a continuous morphine infusion for pain. As the days passed, Amal 'should' have been improving; he remained highly anxious and refused to talk to anyone other than his mother whom he would not allow to leave his side. His mother was continually at the nurses' station asking for something for his pain, and the nursing staff developed strategies to avoid administering what they considered inappropriate amounts of analgesia. At the change-of-shift handover, nurses began to talk about this 'over-anxious child and his over-anxious mother'. 'Typical of people from that part of the world.' On day seven, however, a large quantity of pus was drained from behind his suture line. Within 24 hours Amal was up playing with the other children, and the next night his mother was able to sleep at home.

The temptation for nurses to rely on stereotypes, thereby forgoing knowledge of the 'real' person, may be explained to some extent as part of the emotional cost of getting too close to individuals experiencing distress and suffering. Nevertheless, the cost of not getting close enough to patients to gain insight into their respective individualities may result in a failure to identify and meet their specific needs.

The menace inherent in stereotypes is that they are intransigent, pervasive, self-fulfilling and self-perpetuating. Stereotypes also provide convenient shortcuts when there is a perceived lack of the time and energy necessary to gain an accurate view of the needs and problems of individual patients. If a patient is viewed by nurses as 'a typical hysterical Mediterranean patient', all interactions will be coloured by that perception. When nurses apply the stereotype of a 'druggie' (that is, irresponsible, immature, needy and worthless) they avoid taking the risk of coming to know and value the patient. Nurses need to challenge continually their own use of stereotypes in order to minimise the influence they exert on patient–nurse interactions and nursing practice.

ACTIVITY 9.1

STEREOTYPING

Requirements

Prepare one card for each participant. Each card has one of the following written on it: an elderly woman; an adolescent girl; a deaf woman; a young adult man with paraplegia; a heroin addict; an adolescent with Down's syndrome; an eight-year-old boy.

Process

1. Shuffle the cards and distribute one to each participant.

2. Quickly, and without thinking about it too deeply, list all of the adjectives you can think of that relate to the individual listed on your card.

3. Form groups of four to eight participants. Share your list within the group. What stereotypes can you identify? What are some of the prevailing stereotypes of males? Females? Handicapped people? Children? The elderly?

Discussion

1. What implications would these stereotypes have for the nursing care that such an individual may receive?

2. What implications would these stereotypes have for patient–nurse interactions?

Stereotyping across different cultures

As previously noted, stereotypes are based on the view that all members of a group are identical. That is, individuals can be easily classified into meaningful and homogenous groups. Cultural groups are among the most common stereotypes.

ACTIVITY 9.2

WHAT IS THE AUSTRALIAN CULTURE?

(Adapted from the cultural game, *Who are we*? Multicultural Centre, Sydney Teachers College, now University of Sydney, Faculty of Education, Sydney, 1981)

 Process

1. Imagine that you have a friend from another country who is interested in migrating to Australia and wants to know more about the culture and way of life. What would you tell your friend about Australian attitudes to:

    a. alcohol use?

    b. celebrations?

    c. sport and leisure?

    d. family life?

    e. work?

f.   parties (what people wear and do at parties)?

g.   relationships between males and females?

h.   friendship?

i.   dating?

2.   Form groups of four to eight participants and compare answers. For each of the items considered, discuss with the group the following:

a.   'Do all Australians everywhere have similar attitudes?'

b.   'Do my parents have similar attitudes to me?'

c.   'Would a poor Australian depict a similar picture to a wealthy Australian'?

Discussion

1.   What is a typical Australian? Is there a typical Australian?

2.   Do you think that typicalities apply to other cultures? How difficult would it be to describe a 'typical English person' or a 'typical Vietnamese person?'

3.   Ask participants from non-Australian cultures how they believe their cultures have been stereotyped.

This activity should illustrate the difficulty in describing the 'typical Australian' and the futility of attempts to deny the diversity that exists within a particular group. There is always diversity within a cultural group and this is one of the problems with stereotying; it denies individual variation.

ACTIVITY 9.3

CULTURAL STEREOTYPES

 Process

1.   Refer to the following nine lists of personality traits and the names of nine cultural groups. On a separate sheet of paper, write the name of one of the cultural groups, the stereotype of which is best represented by that list. It is not necessary that you agree that each trait on the list presents an accurate picture of the group or that you personally believe in the stereotype.

2.   Compare results with other participants.

Discussion

1. Is there consistency in the participants' responses to the task?

2. To what extent do the results suggest that people adopt cultural stereotypes as a basis for their attitudes towards individuals?

3. The lists of character traits were generated by 100 North American college students in 1933 (Katz & Braly, 1933). The results of this study are summarised at the end of this chapter. How do your results compare with those of the 1933 study? How enduring are stereotypes?

4. How might your own stereotypes affect the way you care for your patients? How can you begin to alter your more prejudiced attitudes?

List 1	*List 2*	*List 3*
Scientifically minded	Artistic	Sporting
Industrious	Impulsive	Intelligent
Stolid	Passionate	Conventional
Intelligent	Quick-tempered	Tradition loving
Methodical	Imaginative	Conservative
Extremely nationalistic	Very religious	Reserved
Efficient	Talkative	Courteous
Jovial	Revengeful	Honest
Musical	Physically dirty	Industrious
Persistent	Lazy	Extremely nationalistic
Practical	Unreliable	Humourless
Progressive	Musical	Sophisticated

List 4	*List 5*	*List 6*
Superstitious	Pugnacious	Superstitious
Happy-go-lucky	Quick-tempered	Sly
Ignorant	Witty	Conservative
Musical	Honest	Tradition loving
Ostentatious	Very religious	Industrious
Very religious	Industrious	Meditative
Stupid	Superstitious	Reserved
Physically dirty	Quarrelsome	Very religious
Naive	Imaginative	Ignorant
Slovenly	Aggressive	Deceitful
Unreliable	Stubborn	Quiet
Lazy	Extremely nationalistic	Loyal to family ties

List 7	*List 8*	*List 9*
Industrious	Intelligent	Shrewd
Intelligent	Industrious	Mercenary
Materialistic	Progressive	Industrious
Ambitious	Shrewd	Grasping
Progressive	Sly	Intelligent
Pleasure loving	Quiet	Sly
Alert	Imitative	Loyal to family ties
Efficient	Alert	Persistent
Aggressive	Suave	Talkative
Straightforward	Neat	Aggressive
Practical	Treacherous	Very religious
Sporting	Aggressive	

Cultural groups

White American

Black American

Chinese

English

German

Irish

Italian

Japanese

Jewish

The tendency to stereotype can be lessened by recognising the influence that values have on behaviour (see chapter 3) and by appreciating the range of values that lie behind the behaviour of specific groups. To be truly culturally aware it is important to recognise that while there are differences *between* different cultural groups, there are also as many or even greater differences *within* them. Nevertheless, cultural stereotypes do exist and they tend to be remarkably resistant to change.

MODIFYING INTERACTIONS IN LIGHT OF LANGUAGE DIFFERENCES

In certain situations it is likely that patients will have difficulty understanding the language used by nurses. At such times it is common for nurses to use a third person to act as an intermediary.

Using intermediaries in interactions

Where the difficulty is related to a non-English speaking background of the patient, a member of a medical interpreter service may be brought in to translate. If this is not possible, a member of the patient's family who does speak English may act as an interpreter, but this has potential problems.

Where the interaction difficulty is related to the age of the patient (for example, a young child) or to specific communication problems (for example, an intellectual handicap), members of the family or individuals who are familiar with the patient are commonly used. It should always be remembered that interacting through a third person increases the likelihood of misinterpretation or reinterpretation of the content. This may be due to the filtering process associated with a third person, and the interpretations and meanings attached to the content by that person. In addition, the intermediary may make a conscious decision to alter the meaning by omitting, adding or distorting the content of the message, or patients may withhold information because of the personal relationship that exists between themselves and the intermediary.

All of the alterations to the content mentioned in the previous paragraph are more likely to occur in situations where the topic under discussion creates a high level of discomfort for those involved in the interaction. For example, if a male adolescent is asked to interpret while his mother's personal and obstetric history is taken, or an unfamiliar, middle-aged male is interpreting for a female adolescent patient who is being questioned about her sexual activity.

Using trained health interpreters

The following situation illustrates problems that may occur when an untrained interpreter is used:

> A Lebanese cleaner was asked to interpret for a couple who had given birth to an infant with Down's syndrome or 'mongolism'. The cleaner told the parents that they had given birth to a Chinese baby. This caused a great deal of conflict between the husband and wife and was not cleared up for many months. This situation would have been avoided if a trained health-care interpreter had been used.

Many areas have now established health-interpreter programs to meet the need for interpreters with the expertise required to work within health-related areas. If it is necessary to use an untrained interpreter in an emergency situation, a professional interpreter should be employed as soon as possible to check on the understanding of the patient and the family. Working effectively with an interpreter is a skilled activity, and there are enormous advantages in making the effort to acquire the skill.

Interpreters who are trained to work in the health-care system are able to translate medical terminology accurately and have proven useful in bridging gaps between the culture of the health professional and that of the patient. Misunderstandings arising both from language barriers and from differences in cultural beliefs and practices may, therefore, be prevented or minimised with the help of a trained interpreter. Whenever important or sensitive discussion is needed, or when complex information is sought or given, it is important that an interpreter, bound by the ethic of confidentiality that applies to all health-care professionals, is involved.

ACTIVITY 9.4 320

WORKING WITH AN INTERPRETER

Process

1. Form as many groups of three as possible where two members of the group are fluent in the same language, which should not be English. The remaining participants are observers.

2. Using the given situations, one foreign language speaker plays the role of a nurse and the other an interpreter. The third person plays the role of the patient. If there is more than one group, different groups can play each situation. Alternatively, the same group can play the two situations consecutively.

3. The role play is set in the Accident and Emergency Unit where a patient has been admitted with severe asthma. Emergency treatment has been instituted and the patient is now breathing more comfortably. The nurse has arranged for an interpreter to help collect information for a nursing history. For the purpose of this role play, any nursing history format may be used.

Situation A

The nurse and interpreter face each other and the nurse directs questions to the interpreter using the third person. For example, 'Has he/she ever been in hospital before?'; 'When did he/she have his/her last meal?'; 'Is he/she allergic to any medications?' The role play ends when the history is completed.

Situation B

The nurse introduces the interpreter to the patient. The interpreter sits next to the patient. The nurse addresses questions directly to the patient. After the history is completed, the nurse asks the patient if they have any questions about any aspect of treatment or care. Answers are directed to the patient, not to the interpreter. After the interview, the nurse is the first to leave while the interpreter stays and chats briefly with the patient before leaving.

Discussion

1. How did it feel to be the 'patient' in situation A? In situation B?

2. What difficulties did the 'nurses' in situation A experience? What difficulties in situation B?

3. What principles should be observed when working with an interpreter? Compare your answers with the following text about using interpreters.

Guidelines when using an interpreter

Prior to the interview, it is important that the interpreter is briefed about the purpose of the interview. The interpreter should have the opportunity to meet the patient, explain the purpose of the interview and establish a level of rapport. This is especially important if there is to be a discussion of sensitive and private matters. In instances when sexual or personal details must be discussed, it may be important that the interpreter be of the same gender as the patient. There is a general tendency for people of all cultural backgrounds to feel more comfortable discussing personal matters with a person of the same sex.

During the interview, the interpreter should be seated next to the patient. This allows the interpreter to take on the role of the patient's ally so the patient is less likely to feel outnumbered and disadvantaged. The nurse should maintain eye contact with and speak directly to the patient, not to the interpreter. This helps the nurse to develop a relationship with the patient as well as facilitate observation of the patient's nonverbal communication.

The interaction usually works best if the interpreter is able to interpret the words simultaneously, *as they are spoken*. This is the 'trailing' method of interpreting and is most likely to promote a good rapport between the patient and the nurse. In the other type of interpreting, *consecutive interpreting*, the patient completes a whole sentence or phrase before it is translated. On completion of the interview, the nurse should leave the room first, allowing opportunity for the interpreter to chat with the patient. It is important to avoid engaging the interpreter in lengthy discussions in which the patient is not involved. Further discussion between the nurse and the interpreter should be left for another time as the interpreter should be seen to be aligned with the patient, not the nurse.

COMMUNICATING WITHOUT LANGUAGE

While an interpreter should be used whenever there is important information to convey, it is often necessary to manage without an interpreter when interacting with a patient who has limited English.

ACTIVITY 9.5 ➡ 320

COMMUNICATING WITHOUT LANGUAGE

 Process

1. Form a pair with two members in the group, one of whom speaks a language other than English and who plays the role of a nurse who

is trying to take a nursing history. The other person plays the patient. Make as many pairs as there are foreign-language speakers. The remainder of the group act as observers.

2. Half the pairs use instruction A and the other half use instruction B.

Instruction A

You are feeling annoyed that you have to obtain a nursing history from a person who does not understand your language and there is no available interpreter. Your annoyance is obvious to the patient, and you behave rather impatiently, speaking in a voice louder than usual, hoping that this will help the patient better understand. No English is to be used.

Instruction B

You have to obtain a nursing history from a person who does not understand your language and there is no available interpreter. You are very patient with the person and use every means at your disposal to help the person understand what you are saying. You speak slowly, in a soft tone, and use gestures, facial expressions, drawings, diagrams or whatever is necessary to convey your meaning. No English is to be used.

Discussion

1. Compare the amount of information that was obtained for each set of instructions.

2. How did it feel to be the 'patient' in instruction A? How did it feel to be the 'nurse' in instruction A?

3. How did it feel to be the 'patient' in instruction B? How did it feel to be the 'nurse' in instruction B?

4. Have you ever been in a situation (for example, in a class or in a bank) where you were not able to make yourself understood? How did you feel? How could you have been helped to convey your message?

5. What did you learn from this exercise about interacting with non-English speaking patients?

With patience and care it is possible to convey simple information to a person who has minimal English. It is important to speak slowly and clearly. Avoid using jargon and phrases that can be readily misunderstood, such as 'that wound seems to be breaking down, we had better keep an eye on it'. It is best to use plain, correct English, avoiding ambiguities, and above all, avoiding forms of 'pidgin' English, which is used to simplify language but may actually make it more confusing. For example, a nurse may ask a patient, 'When you see doctor, what he say?' Ambiguity in tense may cause patients with little English to wonder if the interaction under discussion was in the past or is to occur in the future. Many migrant patients are proud of their English, and may be offended by the patronising stance of the nurse who speaks to them loudly or in 'pidgin'. They may even misunderstand the intent and believe that the nurse has a poor command of English. It may be difficult for patients to extend respect to such nurses and to accept them as professional people. In addition to focusing on the verbal components of interactions, remember to make full use of all forms of nonverbal communication. Write down instructions. Nonverbal, supportive feedback can show that the nurse is listening and has understood. Try not to look impatient with the patient's attempts to speak English.

When nurses have given information or instructions, it is vital that they check patients' comprehension by asking them to display their understanding of what has been said. It is important that patients do not simply repeat the nurse's words but that they use their own words to demonstrate that they truly understand. Patients may be able to repeat the words but may be too embarrassed to admit that they do not understand what they mean. It is important to remember that phrases familiar to nurses may be confusing to patients who are unfamiliar with them (for example, 'light diet'). Failure to check patients' understanding can result in unnecessary confusion and possible mishaps.

THE IMPORTANCE OF NONVERBAL COMMUNICATION

Nonverbal behaviours form an integral component of the communication process, irrespective of the verbal content. Actually, when inconsistencies exist between the verbal and nonverbal content of the message, there is a general tendency for the nonverbal aspects to be viewed as the more accurate or honest of the two.

As the opportunity for, and/or adequacy of, verbal content decreases, nonverbal communication becomes increasingly important. Throughout the human lifespan, the significance of nonverbal behaviours may in fact go full circle—from the only form of communication available in infancy, into partnership with verbal communication as language develops, and back to a relatively more significant position for those who experience deterioration of hearing and/or other senses.

In terms of individuals who, for one of any number of reasons, do not have adequate language skills (for example, hearing impairments or non-English speaking backgrounds) nonverbal communication is an even more critical element in everyday life. To a neonate the message, 'the world is not such a bad place' is conveyed by a comforting voice and a warm touch; to a patient with a hearing impairment the words, 'I'm here to help you through this' may be replaced by a confident, inspiring manner and an encouraging smile.

Nurses' nonverbal behaviour

The nature of some of the work undertaken by nurses commonly makes interactions with patients distressing and/or embarrassing. It is difficult, for instance, to conceal negative feelings associated with the ongoing invasion of personal space, or the feelings of repugnance that accompany some of the more unpleasant activities shared by the patient and nurse (Lawler, 1991).

The development of appropriate nonverbal communication skills is, therefore, of fundamental importance to the nurse. While the nonverbal component is a normal part of interpersonal interactions, conscious development of particular nonverbal behaviours and their judicious use increases significantly nurses' ability to relate effectively.

The use of an appropriate tone, pitch and rhythm will help convey or stress the importance of the content of verbal messages. An unsteady or waivering voice when discussing a required procedure for example, will hinder attempts to convey a sense of confidence and may leave patients feeling vulnerable and distressed. Once patients become emotionally upset, the verbal part of the message may become meaningless. A nurse wishing to comfort distressed patients would be more successful if a soothing vocal tone were employed. Touch is an especially important means of nonverbal communication.

ACTIVITY 9.6

NONVERBAL COMMUNICATION: TOUCH

 Process

1. Form into groups of four to six members. All members of each group should think of a situation or a 'type' of patient whereby they would find it relatively easy to touch the patient. Share and explain this choice to others within the group.

    a. Are there any commonalities between the patients or situations chosen by individual members? If so, what are they?

    b. What do you think governs individual choices?

2. Group members should now think of a situation or 'type' of patient whereby they would find it difficult to physically touch the patient.

3. As individuals, rank the patients or situations (chosen by individual members) from the easiest to the most difficult to touch.

4. Share and explain your choice within the group.

Discussion

1. How much do the lists of individual group members coincide?

2. Try to come to a group consensus on the ranking exercise.

3. Why is it easy to touch certain patients and not others?

4. Should nurses attempt to overcome or camouflage their difficulties in this area? If so, how?

Nurses' actions or behaviours can convey a sense of concern, empathy, tolerance of differences, respect, admiration or competence. A self-confident demeanour may help patients feel less concerned about a painful or technically difficult procedure; a thoughtful touch may help dispel fear; and the maintenance of eye contact should encourage patients to truly believe what is being told to them.

In order to minimise both their patients' and their own discomfort, nurses need to be aware of the messages they are sending via their actions. Insight into messages associated with particular actions allows nurses to monitor and adjust behaviours for the best possible outcomes. For example, if nurses are trying to convey a sense of acceptance and a matter-of-fact attitude when undertaking particularly repulsive dressings, their behaviours and facial expressions can play a pivotal role. Taking the time to mentally rehearse the activity (for example, the dressing), and what it will look, smell and feel like, as well as practising any specific skills, may be beneficial. In addition, thought may be given to strategies for putting the patient at ease. These may include making a mental list of topics that could be of interest to patients (nursing histories may provide valuable clues) or developing a number of age-appropriate stories or riddles for use with children.

Patients' nonverbal behaviour

A poignant reminder that nonverbal messages are open to misinterpretation is provided in the following account of the hospitalisation experience of a twelve-week-old infant:

> A victim of child abuse, Gary, a twelve-week-old infant, was admitted to a large children's hospital with a fractured left femur, seven fractured ribs and extensive bruising. Over the first two days of his hospitalisation he was given very few doses of an intramuscular narcotic for pain. As a result of his unrelieved pain, Gary became withdrawn and unresponsive. Instead of alerting the staff who were caring for him to the fact that he was in pain, Gary's behaviour was interpreted as a sign that he was pain free. 'He wouldn't be so quiet if he was in pain.' When the attending doctor changed the analgesia orders to paracetamol on the third day after admission, not one member of the nursing staff challenged the assumption that Gary's pain was resolving and therefore that the change in medication orders was appropriate.

One possible explanation for the mismanagement of Gary's pain comes from studies exploring the techniques nurses have adopted in order to cope with their work. As has been noted, the nature of the work in which nurses (and other health-care professionals) are involved is potentially distressing. A number of writers have outlined strategies developed to control anxiety (Davidson & Jackson, 1985; Lees & Ellis, 1990), and work by Menzies-Lyth (1988) and Stein (1967) provide major insights into the employment of specific coping strategies by nurses and doctors. For instance, Menzies-Lyth (1988) describes the way in which nurses distanced themselves from patients and avoided participation in decision-making.

It may be argued that interpreting Gary's somewhat ambiguous behaviour as benign is in the 'best' interests of nurses who need to protect themselves from potentially overwhelming feelings. In other words, by interpreting Gary's quietness as a sign that he was pain-free, those caring for him avoided the psychological distress that would be associated with caring for a severely abused infant.

It is perceived that one of the most common problems with nonverbal behaviour is the notion that the behaviour may be interpreted in a way that matches with the needs and world view of the observer, however, this may or may not be an accurate interpretation. Nurses' world views, among other things, can also have implications for the types of cultural stereotypes that nurses are likely to apply to patients.

CHAPTER SUMMARY

As societies become increasingly culturally diverse nurses are challenged to appreciate and accommodate the multiple perspectives on health that cultural diversity brings. This chapter is a beginning step in developing such appreciation and accommodation. Material in the chapter has focused on the importance of understanding cultural diversity and developing nursing practice that is culturally safe. In addition, the chapter has enabled nurses to consider some of the impediments to such understanding, for example, cultural stereotyping. Some of the challenges of working with interpreters and communicating nonverbally have also been reviewed. Readers should bear in mind that this chapter represents a very brief introduction to the challenges of cross-cultural communication.

NOTE ON ACTIVITY

ACTIVITY 9.3: CULTURAL STEREOTYPES

Katz and Braly (1933) found that the adjectives that were most frequently assigned to the different cultural groups were as follows:

List 1   German
List 2   Italian
List 3   English
List 4   Black American
List 5   Irish
List 6   Chinese
List 7   White American
List 8   Japanese
List 9   Jewish

REFERENCES

Allshouse, K. (1993). Treating patients as individuals. In M. Gerteis, S. Edgman-Levitan, J. Daley & Delbanco, T.L. (eds). *Through the patients' eyes:*

understanding and promoting patient-centered care, (pp 19–44). Jossey-Bass, San Francisco CA.

Davidson, P. & Jackson, C. (1985). The nurse as survivor: delayed post-traumatic stress reaction and cumulative trauma in nursing. *International journal of nursing studies*, 22, 1–13.

Hodge, A. (1987). *Communicating across cultures: an ABC of cultural awareness*. Janus Resources, Sydney.

Katz, D. & Braly, K.W. (1933). Racial stereotypes of 100 college students. *Journal of abnormal and social psychology*, 28, 280–290.

Kimmel, D.C. (1980). *Adulthood and aging*, 2nd edn. John Wiley, New York.

Lawler, J. (1991). *Behind the screens: nursing, somology and the problem of the body*. Churchill Livingstone, Melbourne.

Lees, S. & Ellis, N. (1990). The design of a stress-management programme for nursing personnel. *Journal of advanced nursing*, 15, 946–961.

Legge, V. (1984). Communication and cultural differences in the health profession. In D.J. Phillips & J. Houston. *Australian multicultural society*, (pp 186–189). Dove Communications, Melbourne.

Martin, B.A. & Belcher, J.V. (1986). Influence of cultural background on nurses' attitudes and care of the oncology patient. *Cancer nursing*, 9 (5), 230–237.

Menzies-Lyth, I.E. (1988). *Containing anxiety in institutions: selected essays*. Free Association Press, New York.

Polaschek, N.R. (1998). Cultural safety: a new concept in nursing people of different ethnicities. *Journal of advanced nursing*, 27, 452–457.

Ramsden, I. (1993). Kawa Whakaruruhau: cultural safety in nursing education in Aotearoa (New Zealand). *Nursing praxis*, 8 (3), 4–10.

Short, S., Sharman, E. & Speedy, S. (1998). *Sociology for nurses: an Australian introduction*, 2nd edn. Macmillan Education Australia, Melbourne.

Stein, L. (1967). The doctor-nurse game. *Archives of general psychiatry*, 16, 699–703

FURTHER READING

Clayton, L. (1984). *When do you bow in Australia?* AFS Australia, Sydney.

Health Commission of New South Wales (1980). *Cultural diversity and health care—a guide for health professionals*. Migrant Health Unit, Sydney.

Lee, I. (1984). *Communication, cultural diversity and the health professional*, 2nd edn. Multicultural Centre, Sydney College of Advanced Education, Sydney.

Storer, D. (ed.) (1985). *Ethnic family values in Australia*. Prentice-Hall, Sydney.

CHAPTER 10

THEMES IN HEALTH AND ILLNESS

INTRODUCTION

Nurses often interact with people who are in the throes of significant life events such as transition from health to illness. These transitions, whether major or minor, often create interruptions and disruptions in the lives of the people experiencing them. Transition means change and people experiencing change often feel uncertain and vulnerable. Nurses are in a prime position to ease the path of transition by decreasing uncertainty and vulnerability. They are also in a position to assist people in coping with the changes and challenges that accompany transition. Efforts to ease and assist are best made when nurses understand the major themes that thread through transitions. This chapter centres on such themes.

The transitions that most concern nurses involve changes from health to illness and from illness to health. Therefore, how people cope successfully with such changes are important for nurses to understand. Themes such as resilience, a sense of coherence and social support bolster this understanding. Another theme in transitions of illness and health centres on the notion of crisis. Crisis theory is useful because it shows how health events need not be negative in their impact.

The story that surrounds a patient's situation influences how the patient relates to nurses, thus creating the situational context. The health status of the patient and the circumstances surrounding it are situational variables that provide more than simply a backdrop for the relationship. These factors set the stage for the nature and type of interactions and dynamically combine with other variables to create an interpersonal context.

Chapter overview

This chapter addresses major themes in health and illness. It begins with a discussion of the process of transition through health and illness, focusing on how people cope with the consequent stress of transition. The ways people become and stay healthy are then explored through the themes of resilience, a sense of coherence (Antonovsky, 1987) and social support. The experience of illness is explored in the next section and common themes of uncertainty, vulnerability, loss and grief are highlighted. The concept of crisis, reviewed next, focuses on the factors that help to prevent a stressful event from becoming a crisis (Aguilera, 1998). The final section reviews principles of helping people cope with crisis and illness.

TRANSITIONS AND COPING

The people who are cared for by nurses often are experiencing life transitions. They may be adults moving from being independent to being permanently or temporarily dependent on others. It may be a family coming to grips with a terminal diagnosis of one of its members. Others may be awaiting a medical diagnosis after experiencing symptoms of illness. All of these circumstances imply a transition, moving from one place or way of being to another. Because of its pervasiveness in health-care, the process of transition is important for nurses to understand.

In its simplest definition, transition is passage from one place to another; in this regard transition simply refers to relocation. But in health-care settings such passages are often more far reaching. Transitions through health and illness are often transformative in the sense that lives are altered. Stress, anxiety, loss and grief may also mark health transitions, as people cope with life alterations such as being unwell, getting well again, becoming disabled and approaching death. More frequently than not, health transitions are perceived as negative situations.

Nevertheless, transitions, even those related to health events, are not all negative. Transitions bring with them tremendous opportunity for positive growth. A transition, even one from health to illness, is inherently neither positive nor negative; often a transition is both. Consider the following story:

> When Ted Johnston had a myocardial infarction (heart attack) at the age of 52, he was not surprised. Many years earlier he had witnessed his father suffer numerous myocardial infarctions that eventually left him debilitated and ultimately resulted in his death. Ted knew that there was a strong possibility that he also might experience a fate similar to his father. Because of his family history, Ted had quit smoking and reduced both his cholesterol intake and his weight, ten years prior to his infarction. Ted received early warning signals in the form of angina three years prior to his infarction and the diagnosis of coronary artery disease was confirmed at that time. When Ted had the diagnosis confirmed, he began an exercise program and visited a cardiologist regularly. None of these measures prevented his ultimate heart attack, however, Ted knew that his efforts had helped to decrease both the severity and the effects of the infarction.
>
> One aspect of Ted's life had not been altered in his efforts to reduce his risk of progressive coronary artery disease. It was his job. His work as a superintendent of a large production plant was stressful, and recent events in the industry had placed more demands than ever on Ted. When he had the heart attack, Ted realised that it was time to consider altering his current work activities. Just how he would or could do so was not immediately apparent, but the recognition that something had to be done to either reduce his work-

related stress or cope with it in different ways became clear in Ted's mind as he lay in that hospital bed inside the coronary care unit.

Ted underwent coronary artery bypass surgery just four weeks after his infarction. His recovery from a medical and surgical viewpoint was uneventful, but the experience dramatically altered Ted's life. When he returned to work six months after the surgery, he did so on a part-time basis. No longer would he spend endless hours at work. Ted also altered his attitude toward work. No longer would he react with anger and frustration at what he perceived to be improper decision-making at upper management levels. He successfully changed both his attitude and reactions to work-related demands. While still functioning effectively on the job, he successfully altered his perception of his work environment and his response to it.

After two more years as superintendent, Ted was offered and accepted a newly created position in his company. This position was more relaxed and enabled him to have more flexibility and control over his work environment. After three years in this position, Ted took an early retirement package when it was offered.

Prior to his illness the idea of retirement had frightened Ted, because he could not imagine what he would do with his time if he was not at work. His illness changed all that. He took up more leisure activities in an effort to prepare for retirement, and as his final days at work approached, Ted was ready and able to leave it all behind, eagerly anticipating his new life as a retired worker. Many years later, Ted remains content in his retirement, relaxed and able to enjoy the slower pace of life that it brings. Ted sometimes reflects back to his illness and wonders what might have happened if he had not suffered the heart attack. He now realises the learning that it triggered and is grateful that it caused him to reconsider his lifestyle and take action to alter what had become unhealthy work practices.

The story illustrates how a transition to illness can serve as a catalyst for learning and change. Ted met the challenge and opportunity presented by his illness and the illness experience ultimately served him in a positive manner. In understanding the positive and negative aspects associated with transitions, it is important that nurses have a basic understanding of how people cope.

Coping with transitions

The link between coping and transitions is premised on the notion that transitions bring change and change brings anxiety and stress. There are at least two major ways that people cope with stress (Lazarus & Folkman, 1984). They can attempt to change the situation or their perception of it, so that it does not continue to be so stressful; or they can attempt to change the way the stressful situation affects them, thus altering their response to it. The first of these attempts is known as 'problem-focused' or active coping. The second is known as 'emotion-focused' or passive coping. Active coping focuses on the problem at hand, either by solving the problem or reframing its meaning. Passive coping focuses on the emotional response to the problem at hand, for example, by pushing the problem to one side, thinking about something else or going for a walk.

Active coping efforts are related to meeting the demands of the situation through direct actions. Such efforts include problem solving; reframing the meaning of an event; seeking further information in preparation for an event; talking it over with a trusted person; finding alternative ways to meet needs and goals that are thwarted by the event; learning new skills; and altering goals or expectations.

Passive coping efforts are aimed at keeping uncomfortable feelings within manageable limits and these include the use of defence mechanisms. Examples of these types of effort include avoiding the situation; minimising the significance of the event; distancing techniques; focusing on the bright side; deriving positive value from negative events; meditating; turning to religion; laughing it off; and using physical exercise to decrease tension.

People need to be able to employ both types of coping effort. Passive coping efforts assist in maintaining emotional equilibrium by diffusing emotional responses and keeping anxiety under control. Active coping efforts enable people to change and grow through stressful experiences. Although it is a somewhat paradoxical concept, people simultaneously maintain equilibrium and grow throughout life and its transitions.

Coping effectiveness

Like transitions, coping methods are not inherently good or bad, and nurses must be able to view patients' coping efforts within the overall context of the situation. An evaluation of the effectiveness of coping efforts relies on the use of a variety of criteria, expressed in the following questions:

- Does the coping effort help to keep anxiety and distress within control?
- What are the long-term effects of the coping efforts?
- Does the coping effort help to maintain a sense of self-esteem?
- Is the coping effort helping to maintain interpersonal connections?
- Is there flexibility in the thinking about and the approach to the situation?

Effective coping is a sophisticated juggling act, which simultaneously maintains self-esteem and internal equilibrium, sustains interpersonal relationships, assists in securing adequate and relevant information, and promotes autonomy and freedom and flexibility of approach. These factors are important to take into account when nurses are considering the effectiveness of coping efforts (White, 1974).

Some characteristics of people who cope effectively

Experienced nurses who are involved with people dealing with major life transitions that are disruptive and sometimes shattering can't help but be struck by the strength of the human capacity to cope. Some people seem to have limitless capacity to psychologically weather the storm of serious physical illness, while others become overwhelmed and incapacitated by minor inconveniences. The difference is not necessarily related to the seriousness and extent of physical illness, but rather characteristics within the person.

The characteristics selected for review here are resilience, a sense of coherence and social support. Not only can nurses learn to recognise these characteristics, but they can use an understanding of them when assisting people to cope with transitions through health and illness.

Resilience

People who are resilient have the ability to 'spring back' in the face of adversity and remain optimistic in the face of threats to their wellbeing (Jacelon, 1997). Resilience is a personality characteristic that moderates the negative effects of stress (Wagnild & Young, 1993). Resilient people are capable of being injured and they bend under stress, but are equally capable of subsequent recovery (Garmezy, 1993). Consider the following story:

> Sue Campdon wouldn't rest until she had an answer that made sense to her about what she felt in her breasts. Dissatisfied with what the doctors were telling her about her symptoms, she persisted in seeing more medical specialists. She did not believe that there 'was nothing wrong'. She told herself and her friends 'Just because the tests have come back negative doesn't mean I am fine. I know there is something wrong and I am not going to settle until somebody does something.' Sue knew she could not afford to take any chances. Her family, especially her three children, needed her.
>
> She was not at all surprised by the diagnosis of cancer when finally a specialist agreed to do a breast biopsy. While the diagnosis and subsequent mastectomy were extremely distressing, at least some action was being taken. She felt strong because she knew what she was fighting. And fight she did. Through every course of radiotherapy and chemotherapy Sue remained incredibly optimistic. She reassured her friends and family members when they expressed worry or fear. In fact Sue's fortitude was an inspiration to everybody. When secondary sites of the cancer were found she was a bit disheartened, but not discouraged. She courageously endured three years of cancer therapy and never lost the beaming smile on her face. Her major frustration was a low level of energy and the need to curtail her usual activities. Sleeping during the day was not her style, but she did adjust to the change of pace in her life. Her friends and family members stepped in to assist with her daily responsibilities of caring for her children.
>
> Despite ongoing treatment the cancer gradually invaded all of Sue's body. When it became clear that no more active treatment was indicated, some of her friends and family members fell apart. Nevertheless, Sue did not. She remained an inspiration to all. Her cheerfulness was unending. Even though her 'fight' with the cancer was over, she did not feel or act defeated. She enjoyed every day that she had with her family. Sue was thankful for and cherished every moment until the end of her life. When she died peacefully and in comfort in her home, her friends and family members were grief-stricken. But they also knew that their lives had been enriched by Sue and her phenomenal strength and human spirit.

Sue showed remarkable resilience throughout her illness. Her ability to remain optimistic in the face of adversity, along with her equanimity and responsiveness to others are demonstrations of the characteristics of resilience.

Resilience is both an inherent personality trait and a learned process (Jacelon, 1997). As a personality trait, resilience is characterised by a strong sense of self, an optimistic outlook, self-reliance, and caring, strong social connections and support. As a process, resilience is a response to stress in which a person directs energy to minimise the impact of stressful events through novel approaches to problem solving and reframing their perception (active coping).

As both a personality trait and a learnt process, resilience shares common attributes. Resilient people possess a strong sense of self; they are able to find meaning and purpose in life; and they belong to a social network. Resilience is the direct opposite to the concept of vulnerability (Jacelon, 1997). When people feel vulnerable they feel inadequate to meet the demands of a situation (Clark & Driever, 1983). Resilient people feel adequate and are resourceful.

Sense of coherence

Aaron Antonovsky (1987) developed a theory about how people stay healthy in order to counteract the tendency in health-care to focus on why people get sick. In doing so he emphasised the resources that people use to successfully cope with the stresses of life. These resources combine and converge to form what Antonovsky (1987) refers to as a sense of coherence, an orientation towards life's challenges that averts tension and assists in managing life stress and transitions.

A sense of coherence (Antonovsky, 1987; Antonovsky, 1996) is marked by three attributes: an ability to understand situations that happen in life (*comprehensibility*), an abiding trust that things will work out because there are resources available to meet the demands of life's various situations (*manageability*), and the motivation to invest time and effort in life's challenges (*meaningfulness*).

People who have a strong sense of coherence perceive life's challenges as having some structure and clarity as opposed to the perception that life is a series of random events. This is what is meant by comprehensibility. Manageability, the second attribute, is the extent to which a person perceives that resources to cope successfully are available. The final characteristic, meaningfulness, is the extent to which a person believes it is worth putting time and effort into coping with life stresses (Antonovsky, 1987; Wolf & Ratner, 1999). Comprehensibility is the cognitive or thinking aspect of coherence; manageability is the behavioural or action aspect; and meaningfulness is the motivational or feeling aspect of coherence. All three— thoughts, behaviours and feelings—come together to form a sense of coherence.

Antonovsky's theory has received attention in the nursing literature (for example, Sullivan, 1993). Recent nursing studies indicate that a sense of coherence is related to: remaining healthy and socially connected (Wolf & Ratner, 1999); maintaining hope in the face of a diagnosis of cancer (Post-White et al., 1996); and returning to work following liver transplant (Newton, 1999). The positive nature of the theory, with its emphasis on health, is concordant with a nursing perspective of health-care, because nurses assist patients in dealing with the whole of a health event, not simply managing a disease.

Social support

Both resilience and a sense of coherence have a common thread, that of the presence of a social network that provides support to the person. Social support involves connection with and mutual obligation to other people. People who experience social support feel cared for, loved and esteemed (Cobb, 1976). Social support is based on the assumption that people need to have supportive relationships with other people in order to manage the demands of daily living and cope with life transitions (Norbeck, 1988). These relationships serve to fulfil social needs for affection, approval, belonging, security and identity (Thoits, 1982).

Social support is positively related to health and recovery from illness (Ell, 1996). That is, family and friends offer needed assistance and emotional support in illness, thus helping in recovery. Likewise, there is a correlation between being strongly connected through a social network and remaining healthy (Ell, 1996). People who have a strong, supportive social network remain healthier than people who are socially isolated and lacking in a social network.

Apart from the provision of tangible aid, for example, physical assistance with getting around, just how does support from other people assist with coping? There are two main hypotheses (Keeling et al., 1996). The first is that having people around who care for and about a person helps that person's self esteem and sense of security. In addition, other people may encourage healthy behaviour, such as regular exercise. Another way that other people provide support is by helping with the perception and appraisal of a situation, that is, looking at the world with different eyes. Whether by providing information or offering a different perspective, other people often help with seeing a situation in a new and different light. All of these instances of social support have a positive effect on coping and being healthy.

The concept of social support is sometimes presented as all positive, expressed through catch phrases such as 'your friends are your best medicine'. Nevertheless, this is a simplistic notion of social connections because people in a social network can place demands on each other as well as offer assistance. Friends and family can create stress as well as alleviate it. Also, support that is offered must match what is needed (Hupcey, 1998). There is no use in a friend offering help that actually hinders, for example, offering advice that is neither wanted nor useful.

Therefore social support is a complex, multidimensional concept, which means there are many aspects to it. One aspect is that social support encompasses an acknowledgment of the importance of social relationships. Other aspects include descriptions of social networks and the interrelationships between the people in that network (for example, an extended family). In addition, there are functional aspects of social relationships, the perceived availability of support and actual support that is received (Keeling et al., 1996). Because of its complexity, social support has many definitions (Hupcey, 1998; Keeling et al., 1996). At their most basic level, social connections between people are part of a healthy life.

THEMES IN ILLNESS

Illness, especially when significant enough to bring patients in contact with health professionals such as nurses, is a stressful event. Whether it is temporary or long term, an illness places demands on patients to cope and requires the use of physical, personal and social resources. Through their interactions and relationships, nurses assist patients in meeting the challenges and demands often presented by an illness. Appreciating and understanding the nature of the illness experience enables nurses to provide this assistance.

When interacting with patients, nurses' efforts are aimed at understanding the patient's experience of illness. Understanding the illness requires knowledge of the patient's physical condition, medical diagnosis and treatment (this is case knowledge, described in chapter 2). Nevertheless, understanding illness is more than simply knowing about diseases; it entails knowing something about the person who experiences illness. This is knowledge of how the person is responding to the disease (patient and person knowledge, discussed in chapter 2).

In nursing practice the focus is on the relationship between illness and disease (Benner, 1984), that is, the personal, subjective experiences of patients. Disease is a medical diagnosis that explains symptons of an illness. Illness is the experience of disease, that is, how disease affects a person's life. Illness is also the whole personal experience of a disease, the 'story' of the patient. 'Illness is the human experience of loss or dysfunction whereas disease is the manifestation of aberration at a cellular, tissue, or organ level' (Benner & Wrubel, 1989: 8). Illness is the human response to disease, however, there can be illness in the absence of disease. Similarly a person can have a disease yet not experience illness.

Whenever patients become ill there is a personal assessment of the meaning of the illness. Benner and Wrubel express this by stating that, 'Every illness has a story—plans are threatened, relationships are disturbed and symptoms become laden with meaning depending on what else is happening in the person's life' (1989: 9). 'When illness strikes, the illness and possible ways to cope with it are understood in light of personal background meanings, the situation and ongoing concerns in the patient's life' (Benner & Wrubel, 1989: 88).

Perception of illness

How patients respond to illness depends to a large degree on their perception of it. While it might be easier for nurses to consider a patient's responses in light of what they know about the clinical condition of the patient, they also need to understand how the patient is perceiving and experiencing the illness.

Illness as threat

Often there is a perception of threat or danger in illness, especially when it begins or exacerbates—threat that the person's life may no longer be the same; threat that there may be an inability to proceed with life as anticipated and planned; and threat in the sense that the body once relied on to perform and work effectively is no longer able to do so. This sense of threat is often accompanied by anxiety and fear, and if these feelings become too strong or pose too much of a disruption, they are met with efforts to keep them under control.

Of primary importance in coping with illness is the ability to maintain emotional balance. Patients must be able to keep distressing feelings within manageable limits, in order to cope with other demands of illness. If feelings of anxiety and fear become overwhelming, then patients become disorganised or almost paralysed. Passive coping efforts such as minimising, denying, rationalising and ignoring are all examples of how feelings of anxiety are kept in check.

In chapters 5 and 6 there are references to the importance of recognising when patients are trying to control their emotions and appreciating the importance of not focusing on feelings during these times. The reasons for this are reinforced in this section, and nurses who understand the importance of timing their responses will be able to refrain from discussing feelings with patients who are coping by containing and controlling their emotional responses.

Denial

Denial is frequently used as a means of containing anxiety within manageable limits. Denial can take many forms, ranging from denial of feelings about an illness to denial of the existence of a disease even when it has been diagnosed and explained to a patient. It is an effective way for patients to manage the perceived consequences of an illness. Denial is often used whenever these consequences are dire for the patient, for example, when life goals are under threat.

There is often an automatic tendency to confront and challenge denial, because it is perceived by nurses as an ineffective way of handling an illness. Before challenging denial, nurses need to understand and appreciate the benefits of it.

Denial serves as a buffer for a disturbing and disruptive reality, by allowing a temporary respite from this reality. Because patients will let reality (*their* reality) seep into their awareness at a rate that is manageable for them, the degree of denial is in keeping with this rate. This rate may be different from the nurse's desired rate. Whenever nurses are tempted to challenge a patient's denial, it is essential that the patient's readiness to accept the challenge be assessed. The nurse wishing to challenge denial must ask, 'Is this for the *patient*, or for *me*?'

Illness as challenge

Illness, either temporary or permanent, also may be viewed by patients as challenge. Illness poses many challenges: to adapt, adjust, or learn new ways of achieving life goals; to alter these goals in light of present realities; and to develop new skills and resources. When viewed as challenge, the demands of illness are met with a sense of 'fighting spirit'. This approach is characteristic of patients who meet the demands of illness head on and come to grips with adjustments and adaptations by facing the situation and 'getting on with it'.

Illness as both threat and challenge

Most patients perceive both threat and challenge through the course of an illness, especially when it is chronic in nature. In doing so, they vacillate between confronting the reality of the illness and retreating from it.

Some patients may have a characteristic style of coping that is not effective for the situation at hand. For example, when symptoms are experienced yet no definitive diagnosis can be made, or is delayed through extensive testing, patients with the tendency to attack situations head on may not cope effectively because they are essentially trying to come to grips with an unknown. As long as there is effort made to determine the cause of symptoms, patients in this situation would be better off temporarily forgetting or denying the possibilities. Focusing on 'what-if' scenarios could lead to increased distress and anxiety.

Consider the following story:

Leanne was 43 years old when she was diagnosed as having a brain tumour. Her symptoms during the three years prior to diagnosis had been annoying, puzzling and, at times, alarming to her. But, despite these symptoms, she did not see herself as ill. It was her gradual loss of hearing in her left ear and the subsequent referral to a neurologist that finally resulted in tests that confirmed the presence of the tumour. Initially she was shocked and frightened but somewhat relieved when a biopsy showed that the tumour was benign.

Nevertheless, she was informed that she would need to undergo a lengthy and complicated surgical procedure for the removal of the tumour. She began to prepare herself for this. She was accustomed to leading an active and involved life, filled with a job she enjoyed, friends and family, and extensive travel. From what the surgeon explained, Leanne realised that her life would change dramatically in the immediate months following the surgery. Although the long-term prospects for full recovery were hopeful, Leanne realised that there were no guarantees. She understood the implications of her surgery and knew her future was filled with uncertainty.

Leanne's friends and family were amazed by the way she was facing the situation. Naturally, she had periods of distress, anxiety, sadness and even anger. But most of the time she thought about and discussed her impending surgery with an informed awareness of what it would entail. She understood and accepted that her recovery would take time and require effort to relearn some daily functions that she previously took for granted.

In the weeks leading up to the surgery, however, Leanne found that she focused less and less on what was about to happen. Instead she busied herself by sewing fancy nightgowns so she would at least 'look nice' while in hospital. There was really no more for her to do but wait and try not to dwell on her worries.

Leanne's story illustrates how a combination of efforts is used to cope with an illness. Initially she focused on 'attacking' the problem by having all the necessary tests and gathering information that would help her to understand the surgery. Once plans for surgery were underway, she coped with the waiting period by focusing her energies elsewhere. Worrying seemed of little value to Leanne at this time so she coped by 'not thinking too much about' the surgery.

Commonly encountered patient situations

Nurses come into contact with patients who are facing a variety of situations, for example:

- a disease is suspected yet unknown or unclear and the patient feels unwell and is ill but no identifiable cause is known
- the patient's condition is one in which full recovery is anticipated, although the patient may be ill and incapacitated for a period of time
- although recovery is likely, the patient experiences complications that delay recovery and create the possibility of a long-term illness
- an acute condition is present for which the patient will need to make dramatic adjustments and alterations to daily living and lifestyle
- the patient's condition is one that is likely to proceed on a progressive downhill course, leaving the patient increasingly incapacitated and ill
- the patient develops a chronic condition that is usually characterised by periods of illness and periods of wellness
- there is a life-threatening condition that brings uncertainty both immediately and in the future
- the patient's condition is one in which death is likely to occur in the near future

Each of these situations represents a different set of circumstances, and each patient facing the situation will experience it differently. Nevertheless, there are commonalities that specifically relate to how nurses approach patients who are experiencing these situations. These commonalities are uncertainty, vulnerability and loss.

Uncertainty

Whenever there is an alteration to patients' health status, they are dealing with uncertainty. What is wrong? Will recovery occur? What type of medical intervention will be required? Can the demands of such intervention be met? Will there be a permanent alteration to lifestyle? Will there be pain and suffering? Uncertainty is accompanied by emotional distress and anxiety, and affects both the quality of a patient's life and the adjustment to illness (Mast, 1995).

In understanding the experience of illness, nurses are often sensitive to the uncertainty that is part of the experience. In fact, for adults uncertainty is considered to be the greatest single psychological stress in acute illness (Mishel, 1997). Perhaps the widespread existence of uncertainty in the illness experience is the reason that nurses so frequently offer false reassurance by directing patients to not worry (see chapter 5).

Factors thought to contribute to uncertainty in illness include: severity of illness, specificity of diagnosis, personality of the patient, degree of social support, and trust and confidence in health-care providers (Mast, 1995). Of these possible contributors to uncertainty in illness, the lack of a specific diagnosis is correlated through research to increasing uncertainty. Research into remaining possible causes of uncertainty is inconclusive, although the provision of relevant information by health-care professionals has been shown to decrease uncertainty. Furthermore, support from family and friends eases the anxiety that accompanies uncertainty (Mishel, 1997).

Patients who are uncertain are more likely to use passive, emotion-focused coping, although the active coping activity of seeking information is often spurred by uncertainty (Mast, 1995). Like illness, uncertainty can be perceived as both threat and opportunity. Those patients who perceive uncertainty as danger are likely to use emotion-focused coping, while those who see uncertainty as opportunity will use problem-focused coping (Mishel, 1997).

Vulnerability

When patients are experiencing illness of any nature they are likely to feel vulnerable. Vulnerability is a subjective experience in which patients perceive that their capabilities are inadequate to cope with the situation (Clark & Driever, 1983). It is based on an interpretation that the demands of a situation exceed personal capabilities for meeting these demands. In this sense, vulnerability is closely linked to the concept of crisis, presented later in this chapter.

Coming into contact with nurses can compound patients' vulnerability. The very fact that they perceive their situation as one that requires the use of health-care resources (for example, nurses) indicates that they may evaluate their own capabilities for dealing with the situation as inadequate. The potential dependence resulting from the need for health-care may further increase feelings of vulnerability. On the other hand, the fact that patients have mobilised health-care resources may indicate a sense of competence and resilience. They may still perceive themselves as capable of handling the situation but recognise the need for professional assistance.

CRISIS

Almost daily in their practice, nurses encounter people who are experiencing stressful events. Illness, especially when acute, is recognisable as stressful because it poses threats to a person's daily functioning, sense of competence, capability and self-esteem. Experiences such as the birth of a child can also be stressful because an event such as this places demands on new parents that may extend beyond their perceived capabilities for meeting these demands. Stressful events such as these may or may not result in a crisis, however, any event perceived by a patient as stressful has the potential to result in a crisis.

Common events encountered in nursing practice

Nurses deal with people experiencing actual or potential crises. Some examples of events that patients experience include:

- illness (acute and chronic)
- disability
- dying
- trauma from an accident
- ageing
- planned pregnancy
- birth of a child
- a sick child
- changes in lifestyle
- social violence
- natural disasters

When a potential or actual crisis develops, nurses are often in a position to assist and guide patients through the experience by understanding the nature of crisis situations; recognising those patients who are at risk of experiencing a crisis; and integrating this understanding and recognition into their interactions with patients. Through acknowledgment and comprehension of crisis situations, nurses are able to anticipate, even help to prevent the development of, a crisis and act to mitigate undesirable outcomes of a crisis. Such interventions are predominantly interpersonal: interactions and relationships with patients are the means through which they are enacted.

What is a crisis?

Crises are generated by situations that place demands upon a person that exceed that person's available and usable coping resources and capabilities, thus depleting energy. Although the term *crisis* is used in everyday conversation to describe a variety of circumstances, the definition used here focuses specifically on stressful situations that tax people beyond the extent of their available coping methods and supports. In this regard, a crisis is a perceived inability to meet the demands of a situation, an exhaustion of personal coping resources and supports. Crisis situations create anxiety and distress as attempts are made to cope with an event that places demands on the person. A crisis is accompanied by extreme tension, high levels of anxiety and feelings of helplessness (Brownwell, 1984).

Whenever an event is experienced as stressful and distressing, the potential for a crisis exists. But a crisis is more than simply the presence of a stressful event and the experience of distress. There also must be repeated attempts to cope with the demands of the situation. When these attempts are ineffective in keeping distress within manageable limits, meeting the challenges of the

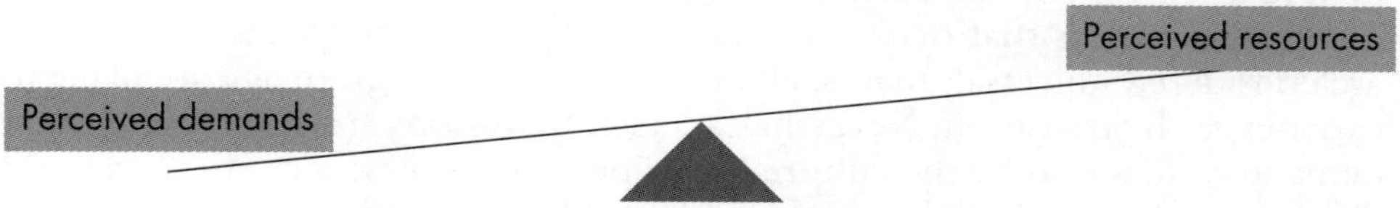

Perceived resources

Perceived demands

Figure 10.1 Crises develop when perceived demands outweigh perceived resources

situation, or altering the situation in some way to reduce its negative impact, then a crisis is likely to be experienced.

Crises are commonly thought of as negative, draining or even debilitating experiences. But challenges and opportunities for growth accompany the threatening or dangerous aspects of a crisis situation. The idea that crises have potential positive outcomes is captured in the Chinese written language. The Chinese characters for a crisis, when translated literally mean 'danger' and 'opportunity'. The wisdom expressed in this is important for nurses to recognise and appreciate.

Crises offer opportunities for growth because successful resolution enables people to extend beyond their current capabilities. Because crises occur when there is an inability to cope, successful resolution results in new or different coping methods, resources and supports being developed.

The outcome of a crisis may result in regeneration and rejuvenation because the person who has come through it successfully will have developed additional resources for coping. Focusing exclusively on stressful events and crises as negative experiences blinds nurses to the potentially positive aspects of them. While the negative side of crisis must be understood and appreciated, an awareness of the positive aspects enables nurses to maintain hope and a 'vision of possibility' when relating to patients who are experiencing actual or potential crises.

Types of crises

Stressful events that have the potential to become crises occur as a result of situations that are planned and anticipated as well as situations that occur without warning.

Maturational crises

Crises that develop from events that occur as results of usual or expected developmental demands are referred to as *developmental* or *maturational* crises. These types of events are life turning points, as people move from one phase of development to another. For example, the transition of moving from adolescence to young adulthood is one that poses many demands and may result in crisis. Ageing, with its potential loss of physical stamina, strength and energy, is another example of a developmental event that places demands on people. Without capabilities for coping with the potential demands of ageing, a crisis may develop.

With life transitions comes a break with the past (Brammer, 1988), a change in former ways of interacting with the environment and an opportunity to develop new ways of interacting. During these transitions, people often experience a sense of vulnerability and stress.

Stressful events that occur as a result of expected developmental changes are considered universal, that is, all people who reach a given age are likely to experience the transition. Nevertheless, such transitions and their consequent demands are bound by the culture of the person. Adolescence is experienced differently throughout the world, although its identification as a time of transition is universal.

Nonuniversal life transitions

There are also nonuniversal life transitions (Hoff, 1989), for example, migration to another country, marriage and the birth of a baby. Events such as these are life turning points that are not experienced by all people. Nevertheless, they are events that are usually anticipated and therefore plans can be made for their occurrence. Even though these events may be anticipated and planned, people experiencing them may be unable to meet the demands imposed by the event.

Situational crises

Another type of crisis occurs as a result of events that are not anticipated or expected, for example, the death of a child, serious illness in young adulthood and the loss of a home through a natural disaster such as a bushfire. Crises that occur as a result of events such as these are referred to as *situational* crises. These events occur unexpectedly, often suddenly, taking people by surprise and throwing them off guard.

How stressful events become crises

Not every event that is stressful and/or distressing results in crisis. Consider the following story:

> Sally Goldstein was returning home from work one rainy evening when she was involved in a low speed, head-on automobile collision close to her home. Awaiting her arrival at home were her five children, ranging in age from three to twelve years and her husband. The accident left Sally's legs severely damaged and mangled. There was a chance that one of her legs would need to be amputated. Her family, friends and neighbours were shocked and devastated by the news of Sally's condition.
>
> But Sally's outlook was positive right from the beginning of what was to become a long journey back to functioning. She was grateful to be alive, and thankful that she had not sustained injuries to her brain or other internal organs. Although her physical pain was great, especially in the early days after the accident, she remained pleasant and cheerful. Even during the time when amputation of her leg was being considered, Sally maintained that if it eventuated she could find 'other ways of getting around' despite the fact that she may do so 'with only one leg'.
>
> Friends who visited her in hospital in the early days found her attitude uplifting and remarked that they left her bedside feeling better because Sally herself was in such good spirits. Some thought that it was only a matter of time before Sally would plunge into despair, sadness and anxiety about what was happening to her. But this was not to happen, for Sally's outlook remained positive throughout the immediate and long-term recovery periods.
>
> As soon as she was able, she contacted the driver of the other vehicle involved in the collision. She expressed her concern and reassured this young man, who was not physically injured in the accident, that it was just an unfortunate incident for which no one could be blamed. Sally's family and friends rallied around and took care of her family's household needs while she was in hospital. The day she was able to get out of bed and into a wheelchair, Sally began visiting the other patients who were on the hospital ward. She

spent the remaining six weeks of her acute hospitalisation visiting other patients, bringing encouragement and showing genuine interest in each of them.

Sally's heartiness and the way she approached her situation impressed the nurses who cared for her. She remained optimistic, pleasant and understanding even when she was suffering excruciating pain. Fortunately, Sally's leg did not require amputation but she did undergo a long period of rehabilitation during which time she learnt to walk again. Throughout the entire recovery period, Sally demonstrated an ability to cope, had available resources for her assistance, and was able to maintain a realistic and positive view of the situation.

Sally's story illustrates that it is not a stressful event itself that creates a crisis situation but rather how the event is perceived and approached. In Sally's situation, her perception that she was lucky to be alive balanced the potential devastation of her injuries. Because she did not feel defeated by her circumstances, she was able to meet the many demands imposed by them. She perceived herself as capable of handling the situation and she continued to focus on 'how lucky' she felt; a crisis did not develop for Sally. Another person could have been devastated by the extent of the injuries, and could have focused attention on what was lost instead of what remained.

Sally's coping skills in the situation directly related to her ability to remain realistically focused on her remaining ability to function, rather than dwelling on her temporary loss of full functioning. Her active concern and interest in other people, her own family and friends and even the other patients on the hospital ward prevented her from becoming overly anxious about her own circumstances. She always had been an active, involved person and remained so, even though her injuries and hospitalisation limited her.

The support systems available to Sally were numerous. She had friends who provided assistance to her family during her absence from home. Not only were these people willing and able to help, but Sally and her family recognised that they needed their help and accepted it without hesitation. Sally actively encouraged people to visit her while she was in hospital because she found these visits helpful in maintaining her positive outlook.

Sally did not experience a crisis despite the fact that she did experience a stressful event which placed enormous demands on her. The factors that equipped Sally to meet the demands of the situation were her perception of the event, her coping skills and her support systems.

Aguilera (1998) describes these three factors as balancing factors, because they are critical in determining whether available resources will meet the demands of a stressful event. When there is a realistic perception of a situation, when coping skills are effective for the situation, and when support systems are available, of use and accessed in the situation, the demands of a situation and the capabilities for meeting these demands are balanced. In the absence of these factors the scales of demands and resources are tipped toward the demands, a person becomes incapable of meeting these demands, and a crisis situation develops. The effects of these balancing factors are depicted in figure 10.2.

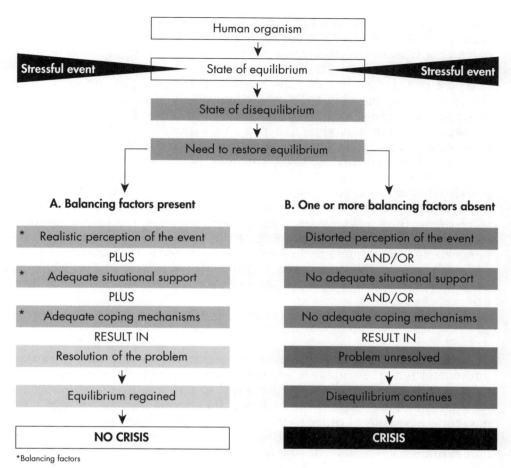

Figure 10.2 The effect of balancing factors in a stressful event (Aguilera, 1998).

Perception

How a person responds to a stressful event depends on how the event is interpreted, what meaning it has in the person's life and its perceived impact. Events have meaning in the context of the person's life. For example, had Sally been a professional dancer her view of the situation might have been quite different from what was presented in the story.

The impact and meaning of an event will influence whether or not the event will create anxiety and distress. Some patients view admission to hospital for routine surgery as a minor inconvenience. But a mother of small children who is unable to arrange adequate child care in her absence may view the same event as a major inconvenience and disruption to her daily life. For this mother, the event of hospitalisation imposes demands for which there are no available resources and therefore it may trigger a crisis.

Aguilera (1998) emphasises that the event must be perceived realistically because a distorted view of a situation creates mounting tension and anxiety.

For example, if a new mother perceives that her lack of success in easily getting her premature baby to settle is a sign of inability to be an effective parent, her tension and anxiety will mount, and she may begin to feel helpless and hopeless as a result.

There is a danger in using the notion of 'realistic' perception because nurses might be imposing their own values on the patient (see chapter 3). What may appear distorted to the nurse may be realistic for the patient. The importance of understanding the patient's experience from the patient's frame of reference (see chapter 5) is reinforced in the context of crisis.

In addition to evaluating the event itself, patients in stressful situations also evaluate their personal coping capabilities in terms of whether they perceive themselves as able to meet the demands of the situation. Even when a patient has coping resources that may be effective in the situation, a failure to recognise these resources may stifle their use. Thus, the perception of a stressful event refers to the meaning of the event as well as the perceived capabilities for responding to the event. Also included in the perception is the evaluation of available support systems. Support systems may be available but not tapped, because of a failure to perceive them, or an inability to solicit help from other people.

Coping skills

In understanding a crisis, either real or potential in nature, nurses need to understand how the patient is attempting to cope with the stressful event. Coping includes all attempts that are made in response to a stressful event. Attempts to cope range from denying the significance of an event to mastering new skills in order to meet the demands of the situation. Coping efforts may be focused on reducing the anxiety, mastering the situation, minimising its significance or simply tolerating it.

Relation of perception to coping efforts

The way an event is perceived in terms of its relevance affects how it is handled. In order to cope effectively, patients must be able to construct an interpretation of an event so that meaningful action can be taken. The perception of the event, referred to as 'cognitive appraisal' (Lazarus & Folkman, 1984), affects coping efforts that are made. Cognitive appraisal relates to how an event is evaluated in terms of its perceived outcome in relation to the patient's life goals and values. This appraisal influences a patient's coping response.

Coping efforts that are aimed at keeping anxiety under control (passive or emotion-focused coping) are effective in situations that are perceived as futile, that is, when there is considered to be a lack of control over the outcome. These types of coping efforts usually are focused on maintaining emotional control. When the outcome is perceived as overwhelming or disruptive to major life goals, and there is little that can be done to alter the outcome, then temporary denial or avoidance may be the most effective alternative.

When patients believe that they can influence the outcome of an event through some effort, they are likely to take active measures to meet the challenges and demands of the event (active or problem-focused coping). Most patients use a combination of both types of coping efforts. Patients must be able to keep emotional responses within manageable limits through the use of defence mechanisms (emotion-focused coping), while simultaneously altering, adjusting and adapting to the demands placed on them by stressful events (problem-focused coping) (Lazarus & Folkman, 1984).

Situational supports

Support from other people in the form of aid, assistance, personal affirmation and information is necessary when stressful events are experienced. During stressful events other people can provide tangible assistance as well as emotional nurturing and affiliation (see chapter 7). Without such support, a person experiencing a stressful situation may literally 'fall apart'.

While support from other people does not necessarily alter the demands of a situation, it does lessen its consequences. Support may not directly change the situation but it aids in the response to the situation, provides further capability for meeting the demands, and counteracts feelings of helplessness and hopelessness.

Support from other people helps patients to evaluate their situation realistically, to challenge and alter their existing perspectives, to maintain their self-esteem by reinforcing a belief that they are able to manage and to establish emotional balance by absorbing the impact of strong feelings. Other people's involvement can also serve as a temporary distraction from the patient's distress. Cultural and religious rituals, beliefs and practices, largely social in nature, can also provide support during stressful events.

To be effective in balancing a stressful event, support from other people must be available, usable and suitable to the context. A hospitalised patient's relative who cannot cope with the sights and sounds of a hospital will be of little value in the situation. In this sense, the effectiveness of the support needs to be evaluated in light of the current context. Supportive people must be suitable to the context and available in the situation. A supportive person who lives in another state or country may not be able to provide support regardless of how helpful this person may be.

Chapter 7 explores the concept of nurses as providers of support but emphasises the importance of nursing care, which mobilises other sources of support for patients. In the absence of support, stressful events have a greater potential to result in crises.

The following story illustrates what happens when balancing factors are absent or ineffective in preventing a stressful event from becoming a crisis. Contrast this story to that of Sally Goldstein, presented earlier.

Joanne and Harold Gray had been married 50 years when Harold suffered a heart attack. The heart attack was minor from a medical viewpoint and physical recovery was expected. Harold's hospitalisation and convalescence were following the usual pattern of recuperation, without complications. The nurses in the coronary care unit recognised that although Harold was progressing toward recovery, Joanne remained extremely anxious. Each time she visited Harold she asked the same questions over and over again. Her questions centred around the theme of Harold's recovery and she expressed fears that he was not going to be 'all right'. She kept focusing on a fear that Harold might die.

No matter how many times the nurses attempted to reassure Joanne, through offering factual, encouraging information about Harold's continued improvement, she remained visibly anxious. In fact her anxiety seemed to be escalating as Harold recovered. With each visit she appeared more distraught. One day as she was leaving the hospital, Joanne's anxiety mounted to near panic. She began to cry uncontrollably and reached a state where her behaviour became disorganised. She was making random attempts to cope with the situation and her verbalisation reflected that she was having difficulty keeping her thoughts on one track. Joanne needed immediate attention.

Victor, one of the nurses caring for Harold, took Joanne to a quiet area of the ward. He listened to Joanne in an effort to understand what was happening. It took some time to piece together the story that Joanne relayed. Victor learnt that Joanne and Harold had both been survivors of a train crash that occurred many years ago when they were young. They lived through the ordeal but lost family and friends in the accident. The event brought them close together, bonding them in a common experience that would remain significant for the rest of their lives.

Joanne's major worry now was that Harold would die. She believed the nurses were just telling her everything was all right because they did not want to worry her. She had not been sleeping or eating since Harold was in hospital because 'they always did these things together'. Harold and Joanne's only son was out of town on a business trip that had been delayed because of Harold's illness, but could not be postponed any longer. Many of Joanne and Harold's friends had either died or moved away after retirement.

Joanne's perception of the situation was that Harold would die, despite what she was hearing from the nursing and medical staff. Her major way of coping previously was to talk things over with Harold, an avenue that was not available to her under the circumstances. Joanne's son, a potential source of support, was unavailable to her at the moment. The lack of balancing factors—realistic perception of the event, adequate and usable coping skills and available situational supports—resulted in Joanne's experiencing a state of crisis.

HELPING PATIENTS THROUGH CRISIS SITUATIONS

Throughout this book there is continual emphasis on the importance of understanding a situation from the *patient's* perspective. Crisis situations are no different. Before any attempt is made to actively alter a patient's situation, nurses must be able to understand the situation from the patient's viewpoint. Even when no active intervention is possible, understanding (see chapter 5) is beneficial to a person in crisis.

Assessing a crisis

In responding to crisis situations, nurses must be able to recognise when crises are occurring in patients' lives. Awareness of situations that have a potential to create crises is the first step in recognition. But there is a danger that nurses will believe that *any* patient experiencing a stressful event will also be experiencing a crisis. Noticing a patient's distress, however significant, in itself does not mean that the patient is experiencing a crisis. A view that a stressful event is a crisis is based on the patient's perspective of the situation. Nurses need to explore the situation with the patient in order to reach this level of understanding.

The balancing factors that prevent a stressful event from becoming a crisis are useful focal points in directing such exploration. In this regard, assessing the meaning of a stressful event takes the form of focused exploration (see chapter 6). The potential for crisis can be assessed through answering the following questions, which are based on the balancing factors:

- What is the patient's perception of the event?
- What is the impact of the event on the patient's life?
- How much tension and anxiety is the patient experiencing?
- What does the patient usually do to manage stressful situations?
- Will these usual ways of coping meet the demands of this situation?
- How is the patient attempting to manage this situation?
- How effective are these attempts in meeting the demands of the situation?
- How capable does the patient feel in meeting the demands of the situation?
- How effectively is the patient keeping anxiety within manageable limits?
- What supports are usually helpful to the patient?
- How effective are these supports for *this* situation?
- Is the patient able to mobilise these supports?
- Are these supports available *at* the moment?

An understanding of each of these areas must be achieved in order for nurses to assess whether the patient is experiencing a crisis and what actions may be of assistance when they are intervening to assist the patient in managing the situation.

Intervening in a crisis

When intervening in a crisis situation, either potential or actual in nature, nurses should focus their efforts on strengthening or altering the balancing factors. Any of the intervention skills presented in chapter 7 can be employed and placed within the context of potential crisis situations. Such interventions include:

- assisting and enabling the patient to develop different and new perspectives, and altering current perspectives through the use of enabling skills
- strengthening coping skills through comforting and supporting skills
- assisting in the development of new coping skills through encouragement to try different approaches by offering information and advice
- mobilising and providing support

When intervening in a crisis it is best to remain focused on the immediate situation and limit interventions to those actions that directly relate to it

(Aguilera, 1998). The offer of suggestions and advice about how to manage the situation is often needed in crisis intervention because when patients are experiencing a crisis they are open to suggestions. In doing so, nurses must take care to provide advice that is based on an understanding of the patient's experience, culture, age, lifestyle and values.

Remain calm

Because crisis situations create tension and anxiety, it is important that nurses remain calm and confident when they interact with patients in crisis. Anxiety is often interpersonally contagious, that is, nurses who are interacting with anxious patients may themselves begin to feel anxious and unsettled. Likewise, a calm and comforting manner (see chapter 7) is also contagious, and patients will feel relaxed in the presence of a nurse who is able to remain calm.

Maintain hope

Throughout interactions with patients in crisis, it is also important that nurses maintain a sense of hope that the crisis can be resolved. Hope serves to mobilise reserve energy (Brammer, 1988) and counteracts feelings of despair. Nurses who demonstrate confidence in patients' capabilities to cope with and manage the situation promote hope. This belief in patients also demonstrates respect.

During an illness, no matter how serious or minor, a sense of hope must be promoted and maintained. Hope, that the situation will improve and that efforts to cope will meet with success, is vital to patients' perseverance. In the absence of hope, patients often give up, perceiving that their efforts to cope are in vain. This frequently occurs for brief periods during recuperation from a long-term illness or when illness is chronic. If it becomes pervasive, patients may fail to put any effort into recovering or adjusting.

While it is important that nurses maintain a sense of hope, this should not take the form of presenting false reassurance, minimising the significance of patients' distress, or promoting a false sense of wellbeing through deception. At times nurses may think that deceiving patients is in the patient's best interest. Conversely, deceit signals a lack of respect for the patient's abilities to cope and undermines any trust the patient may be feeling in the nurse. While it may be tempting to offer false hope, such actions are usually counterproductive to the establishment of an effective relationship and the resolution of a crisis.

HELPING PATIENTS COPE WITH ILLNESS

In coping with crisis or illness, patients call upon needed resources. Nurses are potential resources if they are involved, interested and concerned. But nurses can only be resources when they have taken time to understand the situation from the patient's perspective.

Nurses help patients cope with illness by assisting them in many ways, for example, nurses help patients to contain uncomfortable feelings, generate a sense of hope and redefine the situation in solvable terms. Perhaps most significant is the way in which nurses assist patients in maintaining or regaining their self-esteem.

Throughout an illness patients must be able to maintain a sense of self-esteem and their capability for meeting the demands of the situation. Illness often threatens this sense, for example, when there is loss of physical functioning or an alteration in body image. Acknowledging and understanding patients' experiences is one of the most effective ways that nurses can maintain patients' self-esteem.

Types of illness

Illnesses can be acute, critical, chronic or terminal. When interacting with patients, nurses need to consider the nature of the illness, not in an attempt to classify patients, but rather to anticipate which themes might be most relevant to the experience. Nurses still must rely on their own recognition of patients' situations and also develop understanding of how individual patients are experiencing an illness.

Acute illness

The term *acute illness* in this context refers to situations in which patients are experiencing symptoms significant enough to bring them into a health-care setting. A medical diagnosis of a specific disease may or may not be known, and regardless of this, there is a personal impact on the patient's life. Nurses need to be sensitive to this impact and how the patient is responding to the situation.

When patients come into contact with nurses because they are experiencing an acute illness *and* the cause of this illness is unknown or unclear, there is a great deal of uncertainty. Patients are usually concerned and worried about the situation and may ask numerous questions. In responding to these questions, nurses need to be sensitive to the fact that they are often asked out of uncertainty. While it might be easy to dismiss questions with, 'Let's wait and see', such a response invalidates the patient's concern. While it might not be possible for nurses to reassure patients with factual information, it is possible to reassure patients that their worries are understandable.

Not all patients in this situation will ask questions. Some will worry in silence. When this happens it is often helpful for nurses to take the lead in exploring the patient's potential uncertainty. Focused exploration or a self-disclosing statement (see chapter 6) reflecting the likelihood of uncertainty can be employed for this purpose, as long as nurses evaluate the patient's degree of comfort with discussing feelings and assess the level of trust in the relationship (see chapter 2).

If medical tests are being conducted to determine the presence or absence of a disease, nurses can inform patients about what they can expect to experience during such tests. Some patients will want to know everything about a procedure, while others will be happy to undergo a procedure with very little information.

Chapter 7 highlights the need for nurses to ascertain how much information a patient wants before actually sharing it. Sensitivity to the individual patient and understanding of the world from the patient's frame of reference are necessary if the information that is shared is to have relevance to the patient.

It is a good idea to ask patients how they would like test results communicated to them. Some patients may prefer to have family and friends present while others may prefer to hear the news, good or bad, on their own. Nurses are in the best position to understand the significance of the results in terms of their potential impact on the patient's life. This is part of understanding the experience of illness.

When the patient's condition is understood from a medical viewpoint, nurses can then focus their interpersonal efforts on understanding how the illness and consequent medical treatment may affect the patient. All of the skills presented in chapters 4–7 offer guidance on how to approach situations such as this.

Critical illness

When an illness is *critical*, it is most often life-threatening as well. During these types of experience patients are often living in 'dream world' and may even 'lose' a period in their life in the sense that, after recovery, they cannot recollect what happened. During critical illness the traditional ways of verbally communicating may be shut off, for example, because of mechanical ventilation, thus increasing the challenge for nurses to connect with patients on an interpersonal level.

In understanding the experience of critical illness it is important that nurses recognise the significance of people who know the patient on a personal level. Family and friends are often the link between the patient and the nurse, so their presence and participation during the illness can be vital. Without the information that family and friends can provide, interpersonal connections with patients become extremely difficult, if not impossible.

The sophisticated technology and equipment in the critical care environment are often unfamiliar to patients and their friends and families. The importance of providing explanations about equipment, procedures and nursing care cannot be underestimated. But again, care should be exercised by nurses to limit such explanations to a level that patients and families and friends can absorb, and to an extent that they desire.

Recovering from an acute or critical illness

During recovery from an acute or critical illness patients often want to relive their experiences and discuss them with nurses, who they perceive have an intimate understanding of the significance of illness. Feelings are often expressed because the risk of losing control over emotions is reduced. The immediate danger has passed and uncertainty is lessened. For these reasons, reflecting feelings (see chapter 5) is often effective during this time.

Frequently, patients are not prepared for the amount of time it takes to regain their strength and former ways of functioning following an acute or critical illness. An explanation from nurses that this is to be expected is reassuring, demonstrates understanding of the patient's situation and provides anticipatory guidance in the recovery experience.

Chronic illness

Chronic illnesses can be progressively deteriorating, or they can be characterised by periods of stability and instability with little or no deterioration. Chronicity places demands on patients to learn new skills, alter their lifestyles, and make adjustments and adaptations as they learn new ways of functioning. In caring for patients whose illness is chronic, nurses need to focus their efforts on helping patients to develop resources in meeting these demands. Nurses can minimise patients' sense of vulnerability through 'anticipatory guidance' that builds new worlds before old ones are destroyed (Birchfield, 1985).

Assisting patients whose illness is chronic involves helping them to learn to live with their condition. In doing so, nurses must be aware that there is often loss in the learning. They must be prepared to listen with understanding as patients whose lives have been changed as a result of their illness mourn the losses that accompany these changes. They are often in a grief process of letting go as they learn to move on.

In relating to patients, nurses need to understand the up-and-down nature of most chronic conditions. They must be able to remain with patients as they cope with losses as well as gains. It is far easier to share the triumph of success in coping with chronic illness than it is to listen with understanding to the pain that accompanies an exacerbation of the illness or a setback in recovery.

With chronic illness there is often an opportunity for nurses and patients to come to know each other over a long period of time and, therefore, the possibility that relationships will progress beyond the therapeutic level of involvement (see chapter 7), developing into a connected relationship. Through this level of relationship, patients and nurses come to understand each other as people. The pain of loss and the joy of successful adaptation that accompanies living with chronic illness is often shared on a personal level between patient and nurse.

Living with dying

The ability to form a meaningful relationship with patients whose prospects for the future are slim requires a special kind of nursing knowledge and experience. Helping patients to live with dying is a specialised area of nursing practice, but it is likely that most nurses will at some time come into contact with patients who are acutely aware of their own death.

Many people enter nursing with thoughts of helping people cope with and recover from illness, so the thought of helping people die may be somewhat alien. There is a risk that patients who are dying experience abandonment because nurses find it difficult to come to grips with the reality of death. This 'denial of death', as it is often referred to, is a reflection of societal values that revere youth, health and vitality, and look to technological advances that will 'win the battle over death'.

The reality that death is an inevitable part of life is one that nurses will find difficult to deny. While nurses may know that death is a part of life, they may not want to be reminded of this fact by coming face-to-face with a patient who is living with dying. Not all nurses are able to demonstrate the personal qualities that equip them to relate effectively to patients whose death is imminent. One of the essential personal qualities is comfort with the thought of death. The most significant aspect of interpersonally relating to patients who are living with dying is that of simply being there, unafraid and unencumbered by fears about death.

Acceptance of death and an awareness of their own thoughts, feelings and values related to dying is essential for nurses who want to connect with patients in this situation. Like self-awareness in general (see chapter 3), if these thoughts, feelings and values are left unexamined and unrecognised, they may interfere with nurses' ability to establish interpersonal contact. A discomfort with thoughts of death may result in inadvertent rejection of patients.

A popular conception of how to deal with patients who are living with dying is that they pass through various stages as they adjust to their impending death. While such stage theory provides a useful way of understanding how patients cope with dying, there is a risk that patients will be forced to conform to the theory. For example, once patients have experienced denial, nurses may relate to them with an expectation that now is the time to begin the bargaining, the next phase of dying. Rigid adherence to this type of theory forces patients to conform to nurses' expectations or may lead to consternation on the part of nurses if patients do not conform to the theory.

It is more effective for nurses to listen and understand what these patients are experiencing, and to be fully present as other human beings who are willing to be there during the period of 'waiting for death'. Listening and understanding helps to decrease the potential loneliness of this experience.

When nurses do become comfortable with the thought of death there is another risk that they will want, indeed expect, patients to discuss dying with them. Patients who are living with dying do not want to think and focus exclusively on their death, but rather be recognised as still *alive*. Patients express the need to be cared for in an atmosphere of normalcy, rather than one that is focused on the fact that they are dying (Arblaster et al., 1990). It is not that these patients want nurses to deny or ignore that they are dying, but rather they prefer that nurses do not actively direct their conversations to the subject of dying.

When patients *do* want to discuss their experience of dying, nurses need to be responsive to such discussions. This requires that nurses follow the patient's lead, that is, they should respond to the patient with comfort and ease, rather than direct their interactions to the subject of dying.

Helping patients with loss and grief

Losses are often experienced during illness. There may be loss of ability to function, loss of ability to achieve life goals, loss of hope, loss of contact and connection with significant people, or loss of flexibility and freedom to determine life goals. Coping with loss is a process of letting go, often accompanied by feelings of sadness, anxiety and sometimes guilt. Patients who are facing or experiencing loss are frequently consumed by this process and therefore are unable to focus their thoughts.

Most often there is emotional pain as patients come to grips with a loss. There is a tendency to focus on the deprivation created by the loss. Patients whose loss is acute often feel immersed in the experience. When this natural process of healing is allowed to happen, what often follows is a new sense of gain in meeting the demands of the illness.

Grief is a natural reaction to loss. It, too, is a process of letting go, mourning, reflecting, reliving memories, and eventually summoning resources to proceed with life, despite the fact that it may never be the same. Through the experience of grief, people learn to let go and adjust, and eventually adapt to changed life conditions. Grief is a process of closing a chapter of life and gathering energy to begin the next chapter. While there may be energy to begin new phases of life, unveiling the closed chapter is still possible. But this is done as a way of recollecting how it was, of choosing to remember, rather than remaining in the acute pain of loss and grief.

Nurses who understand and appreciate that grieving is a natural process of healing are able to facilitate its spontaneous progression. Through understanding, nurses are able to accept patients' expression of feelings, their reliving and reflecting, as an expected and usual progression towards healing.

A central consideration when interacting with patients who are grieving is *not* to impede the process through trying to make it all right, ignoring the suffering or dismissing the emotional pain. One of the greatest challenges to nurses is staying with the grieving patient, both emotionally and interpersonally. Remaining with patients who are in the depths of despair during a loss is often an emotionally draining experience for nurses. When the loss is real and can no longer be denied or minimised, nurses recognise that they cannot magically alter the situation and bring back what has been lost. Because of this harsh reality nurses often feel helpless and sometimes out of control. In an effort to regain control, false reassurances are sometimes uttered. 'It will be all right', 'Please don't be so upset', or 'You will learn to live again' may *sound* helpful on the surface, but do little to acknowledge the pain that is experienced in loss.

It is better for nurses to come to grips, on a personal and professional level, with the reality of the pain of loss. Accepting that loss is an aspect of nursing that cannot be denied or avoided minimises the risk of treating it as something that can be intellectually 'problem solved'. In dealing with patients who are experiencing or facing loss, nurses must be able to assist them with reviving memories of what has been lost. Nurses must be comfortable in allowing patients' feelings to emerge and be expressed. When the experience of loss is shared with and understood by nurses, patients feel consoled and nurtured.

A final word on helping patients with crisis and illness

There is another aspect that nurses need to be aware of when interacting with patients who are experiencing crisis or illness: they should *expect* patients to be self-absorbed with their situation. Crisis situations create tunnel vision that often prevents people who are experiencing them from seeing beyond the immediate circumstances. When helping patients in crisis, nurses can assist by broadening the patients' perspective and encouraging alternative perspectives. Nevertheless, what may seem obvious to the nurse may be difficult for the patient to perceive.

Likewise, because illness can be a lonely experience, people who are ill are often concerned only with themselves. The degree of self-absorption is related to the seriousness of the illness and the amount of pain and suffering that are being experienced. Nurses can help to ease the loneliness of the experience by being available, willing to listen and concerned enough to understand. But they should not expect that patients would have the same degree of concern for them.

When forming relationships with patients, nurses must consider how the health status of the patient affects the relationship and their interactions. This chapter has explored patients' health status from the viewpoint of crisis and illness. The many considerations that crisis and illness bring to the relationships between patients and nurses creates a context for these relationships. While these considerations may seem to complicate learning how to interact effectively with patients, they also add a richness to the experience. While they are interacting with patients, nurses come to appreciate and know the complexity and abundance of human experiences of crisis and illness.

CHAPTER SUMMARY

When forming relationships with patients, nurses must consider how the health status of the patient affects the relationship and their interactions. This chapter has explored patients' health status from the viewpoint of crisis and illness. The many considerations that crisis and illness bring to the relationships between patients and nurses create a context for these relationships.

While these considerations may seem to complicate the process of learning how to interact effectively with patients, they also add a richness to the experience. While nurses are interacting with patients, they come to appreciate and know the complexity and abundance of human experiences of crisis and illness.

Nevertheless, nurses must also recognise that they themselves are part of the relationship and should therefore consider how a potential drain on their personal and professional resources affects how they relate to patients.

REFERENCES

Aguilera, D.C. (1998). *Crisis intervention: theory and methodology*, 8th edn. Mosby, St Louis MS.

Antonovsky, A. (1987). *Unraveling the mystery of health: how people manage stress and stay well.* Jossey-Bass, San Francisco CA.

Antonovsky, A. (1996). The sense of coherence: an historical and future perspective. *Israel journal of medical sciences*, 32, 170–178.

Arblaster, G., Brooks, D., Hudson, R. & Petty, M. (1990). Terminally ill patients' expectations of nurses. *The Australian journal of advanced nursing*, 7 (3): 34–43.

Benner, P. (1984). *From novice to expert: excellence and power in clinical nursing practice.* Addison-Wesley, Menlo Park CA.

Benner, P. & Wrubel, J. (1989). *The primacy of caring: stress and coping in health and illness.* Addison-Wesley, Menlo Park CA.

Birchfield, M.E. (1985). *Stages of illness: guidelines for nursing care.* Brady Communications, Bowie MD.

Brammer, L.M. (1988). *The helping relationship*, 4th edn. Prentice-Hall, Englewood Cliffs NJ.

Brownwell, M.J. (1984). The concept of crisis: its utility for nursing. *Advances in nursing science*, 6 (4), 10–21.

Clark, H.F. & Driever, M.J. (1983). Vulnerability: the development of a construct for nursing. In P.L. Chinn (ed). *Advances in nursing theory development* (pp 207–220). Aspen, Rockville MD.

Cobb, S. (1976). Social support as a moderator of life stress. *Psychosomatic medicine*, 38, 300–313.

Ell, K. (1996). Social nerworks, social support and coping with serious illness: the family connection. *Social science and medicine*, 42, 173–183.

Garmezy, N. (1993). Children in poverty: resilience despite risk. *Psychiatry*, 56, 127–136.

Hoff, L. (1989). *People in crisis: understanding and helping*, 3rd edn. Addison-Wesley, Menlo Park CA.

Hupcey, J.E. (1998). Clarifying the social support theory-research linkages. *Journal of advanced nursing*, 27, 1231–1241.

Jacelon, C.S. (1997). The trait and process of resilience. *Journal of advanced nursing*, 25, 123–129.

Keeling, D.I., Price, P.E., Jones, E. & Harding, K.G. (1996). Social support: some pragmatic implications for health care professionals. *Journal of advanced nursing*, 23, 76–81.

Lazarus, R.S. & Folkman, S. (1984). *Stress, appraisal and coping.* Springer Verlag, New York.

Mast, M.E. (1995). Adult uncertainty in illness: a critical review of research. *Scholarly inquiry for nursing practice: an international journal*, 9, 3–24.

Mishel, M.H. (1997). Uncertainty in acute illness. *Annual review of nursing research*, 15, 57–80.

Newton, S.E. (1999). Relationship of hardiness and a sense of coherence to post-liver transplant return to work. *Holistic nursing practice*, 13 (3), 71–79.

Norbeck, J.S. (1988). Social support. *Annual review of nursing research*, 6, 85–109.

Post-White, J., Ceronsky, C., Kreitzer, M.J., Nickelson, K., Drew, D., Mackey, K.W., Koopmeiners, L. & Gutknecht, S. (1996). Hope, spirituality, sense of coherence, and quality of life in patients with cancer. *Oncology nursing forum*, 23, 1571–1579.

Sullivan, G.C. (1993). Towards clarification of convergent concepts: sense of coherence, will to meaning, locus of control, learned helplessness and hardiness. *Journal of advanced nursing*, 18, 1772–1778.

Thoits, P.A. (1982). Conceptual, methodological and theoretical problems in studying social support as a buffer against life stress. *Journal of health and social behavior*, 23, 145–259.

Wagnild, G. & Young, H.M. (1993). Development and psychometric evaluation of the resilience scale. *Journal of nursing measurement*, 1, 165–178.

White, R.W. (1974). Strategies of adaptation: an attempt at systematic description. In G.V. Coelho, D.A. Hamburg & J.E. Adams (eds.). *Coping and adaptation* (pp 47–68). Basic Books, New York.

Wolff, A.C. & Ratner, P.A. (1999). Stress, social support and sense of coherence. *Western journal of nursing research*, 21 (2), 182–197.

CHAPTER 11

IMPROVING COLLEAGUE INTERACTION

INTRODUCTION

The central premise of this book is that good relationships between patients and nurses are at the heart of good nursing care. Various contextual factors that need to be taken into consideration in the formation of these relationships have been described in previous chapters. These factors are embedded within the nurse (for example, self-awareness), within the patient (for example, the desire to be informed) and within the health event at hand (for example, the nature of an illness).

Nevertheless, there are considerations that extend beyond the specifics of the individual nurse, the patient and the situation. Of equal consideration is the environment of the health-care setting in which patient and nurse come together. For example, if nursing work is organised so that a patient and a nurse rarely see each other on more than one occasion, then the depth of involvement and mutual understanding is restricted by limited opportunity to get to know each other. This chapter focuses on another important consideration: promotion of supportive relationships with colleagues.

The need for supportive colleague relationships in the work environment is dealt with in this book because interpersonal involvement with patients can be professionally and personally demanding of nurses. Internal coping resources may be taxed as nurses are brought close to human vulnerability, suffering, pain, fragility, anxiety and death. These realities, potential sources of stress in nursing practice, are not easily denied or avoided when there is interpersonal connection between nurse and patient. Emotional detachment, one possible way of coping with the reality of nursing practice, is not possible under such circumstances. Alternative avenues for coping must be accessed.

Colleague support is a vehicle for travelling along these avenues of dealing with the stress of nursing. Support from others is not a coping mechanism per se, but rather a fruitful resource that reduces stress and enhances effective coping. Supportive relationships with colleagues are not automatic; they require active cultivation in order to develop and grow.

Chapter overview

This chapter firstly explores the need for social support in nursing by reviewing general aspects of nursing practice that contribute to work-related stress. Interpersonal involvement with patients is highlighted as a specific facet of this stress. The need for social support in occupational stress is briefly reviewed with specific reference to colleagues as a basis for such support. The relationship between colleague interaction and work-related stress is reviewed in the next section. Potential constraints in the formation of a supportive interpersonal work environment are explored on three levels: personal, professional and organisational. Enhancement of a supportive interpersonal work environment in nursing is a natural follow on in this discussion, and the final section of the chapter includes recommendations for the development of this environment.

STRESS AND NURSING

The provision of nursing care is both physically and emotionally demanding, and stress in nursing is acknowledged and accepted as part and parcel of the profession. The number of articles about stress that appear in the nursing literature attests to this fact.

Workload, too much to do in too little time and too few resources, and dealing with death and dying rank high on the list of factors contributing to stress in nursing (Dunn et al., 1994; Gentry & Parkes, 1982; Gray-Toft & Anderson, 1981; Hipwell et al., 1989; Kushnir et al., 1997; Ness, 1982; Snape & Cavanagh, 1993; Tyler et al., 1991). Nurses often face people who are distressed, vulnerable and in need of assistance and support. Even when not directly caring for ill people, as in the case of health promotion, nurses must still provide assistance and support in fostering others to change health patterns. Hospital care is provided on a 24-hour-a-day, 365-day-a-year basis, and nurses often provide the bulk of this care. Hours are often long and shift work can be energy depleting. Community nurses are often stretched to provide nursing care for increasing numbers of patients.

Health-care organisations impose additional demands, such as limited resources and an overdeveloped bureaucratic hierarchy. In these organisations, nurses are often accountable to multiple authorities such as supervisors, doctors' orders, professional standards and government bodies. An individual nurse also has personal standards of care and these expectations may conflict with the demands of the bureaucracy.

Thus, stress in nursing is generated from a multiplicity of sources—personal, professional and organisational. Irvine and Evans (1996) have integrated findings from a number of research studies to investigate the relationship between job satisfaction and nurses leaving their jobs (job turnover). In their meta-analysis they found that individual differences in nurses were not as pronounced as work environment variables in determining the cause of dissatisfaction with work and turnover in nursing. Rather than focusing on characteristics within individual nurses it is more fruitful to consider organisational realities such as colleague support and collaboration when considering job stress.

Interpersonal involvement

The added dimension of close interpersonal involvement with patients could be viewed as yet another demand placed on nurses. Interpersonal closeness with patients may challenge and even threaten the nurse's sense of competence and control because there are often no clear answers to patients' expressed concerns, no procedure or protocol to consult. Nurses may experience a sense of loss if patients die or fail to recover. Coming close to human suffering and pain brings into conscious awareness the nurse's own vulnerability as a human being.

Furthermore, interpersonal involvement with patients, as a professional value, may come into conflict with bureaucratic values such as tangible productivity and cost effectiveness. Spending time talking with patients is still viewed by some nurses as 'wasting time' or an activity that is done after the 'real' work is completed. A good nurse is a busy nurse and nurses who are spending time relating with patients simply do not appear busy! All of this may add to the perceived work-related stress of nurses who try to put into effect the interpersonal skills described in this book.

The experience of stress

Each of the factors mentioned, or any combination of them, can produce stress in nursing. Stress is a complex phenomenon that encompasses more than simply the factors that provide its stimulus (stressors). Stress is a transactional process involving a complex interplay between perceived demands of the environment and the perceived resources for meeting these demands (Lazarus & Folkman, 1984). It results from a perception that a demand is potentially harmful, will result in personal loss, is threatening or challenging *and* that resources for meeting the demand are inadequate, unavailable, unusable or inappropriate in the situation. A lack of balance between the perceived demands and the perceived availability of resources results in feelings of vulnerability (see chapter 10). Therefore, it is not an event itself (stressor), or the personal resources and coping capabilities alone that create stress, but rather their dynamic combination that produces a stressful experience.

Personal appraisal (perception) is critical in this process because it determines whether the demand is interpreted as harmful or threatening, and whether internal and external resources for coping are seen to be accessible and adequate (see chapter 10). These perceptions relate to questions such as: 'What is the situation?' 'What can I do to manage it?' 'Who or what can I call on to manage it?' For example, a nurse working in a critical care area may be required to wean a patient off a mechanical ventilator (demand). An experienced critical care nurse, who has weaned many patients from ventilators, may perceive this situation as relatively benign (no stress). On the other hand, a nurse who has recently completed an advanced course in critical care nursing may view the same situation as a challenge and call on available coping resources such as knowledge and problem solving. A newly graduated nurse, with little or no experience and education in critical care, may appraise the same situation as a threat for which there are no capabilities or resources. The same event results in three different responses according to how it is perceived.

The need for support

Asking nurses to become interpersonally involved with patients without addressing the need for resources to cope with this is unrealistic at best and irresponsible at worst. The perceived demands placed on nurses that occur as a result of interpersonal involvement need to be met through the cultivation of a supportive work environment that functions as a resource for coping with such demands. Other nurses are central players in this environment because support from colleagues not only helps to decrease the perceived stress, but also functions as a resource for coping.

This support comes in a variety of forms. The proverbial pat on the back, which offers personal encouragement, affirmation and validation, is the most frequent interpretation of how support for others is demonstrated. Nevertheless, there are other manifestations such as tangible aid and assistance, and informational support in the form of feedback, suggestions and advice. A final type of support, particularly relevant to the work environment, is situation-specific support (Norbeck et al., 1981). This form of support generates from another person who has experienced or is experiencing a similar situation, one who understands the complexity and nuance of the situation, one who has 'been there, done that'. This situation-specific support encompasses all the other types of support mentioned, as illustrated in the following story:

> Tom, a first-year nursing student, faints during his initial visit to the operating theatre. Mary, a veteran theatre nurse, assists Tom in recovering from the fainting episode and escorts him to the staff tearoom [tangible support]. After he recovers, she says to him, 'I bet this is embarrassing for you, and you probably wish you could crawl into a hole [emotional support]. I'll let you in on a little secret. The same thing has happened to me. I do have one question, have you eaten breakfast?'
> 'No,' Tom replies hesitantly.
> 'I knew it,' Mary responds. 'Look, let me give you a bit of advice. It's a good idea to eat breakfast before you come on duty, especially in theatre. It may help prevent this from happening again.' [informational support]

Mary's support is both emotional and informational; she reassures Tom and shares information that is useful to him. Her awareness of Tom's situation emerges from her understanding of this event, in this context, at this time. Her support is situation-specific.

THE RELATIONSHIP BETWEEN COLLEAGUE INTERACTION AND WORK-RELATED STRESS

The relationship between colleague interaction and stress in nursing is complex because co-workers function both as a resource for handling or modifying this stress *and* as a source of stress. Relationships with nursing colleagues, in that they both add to and diminish work stress, are flip sides of the same coin. Supportive interactions and relationships with colleagues have potentially positive effects; colleague interactions and relationships that lack support can add to work stress, creating negative effects.

Positive effects

What beneficial effects on work-related stress would be evident if colleague support was fully enacted in the work environment? Colleague support has the potential to alter positively the experience of stress in three identifiable ways. Firstly, support from colleagues can have the direct effect of reducing or preventing stress itself. Secondly, colleague support can buffer the negative effects of stress. And thirdly, it can function as a resource for coping.

Direct effects

Social support functions to lower the amount of perceived stress by encouraging a reappraisal of the situation. The actual perception of a situation as threatening or harmful can be altered by co-worker feedback and input. Take the example of death and dying, a commonly cited source of stress in nursing practice. While the presence of supportive nursing-staff relationships cannot change the harsh reality of death, it can mitigate some of the stressful aspects of such a loss. Death is frequently viewed as stress producing because it often threatens nurses' sense of professional competence. An appraisal of death as a natural and expected part of life lessens the likelihood that death will be viewed as a failure. The realisation that nurses are not personally responsible for a patient death from cancer, for example, is achievable through open, honest interaction with other nurses. The reappraisal of the situation is a direct effect of social support on stress because it actually lowers the level of perceived stress (MacNeil & Weisz, 1987; Mossholder et al., 1982; Norbeck, 1985; Gray-Toft & Anderson, 1983).

Buffering effects

Another result of colleague support on work-related stress is its mediating or buffering effect, that is, colleague support reduces negative effects and consequences of stress. In exploring the relationship between social support and stress-related indices in nursing, it is found that colleague support helps to reduce negative factors such as role ambiguity (Gray-Toft & Anderson, 1985); burnout (Cronin-Stubbs & Rooks, 1985; Firth et al., 1986; Lee & Henderson, 1996); accident and error rates among nurses (Gentry & Parkes,

1982); and job dissatisfaction (Decker, 1985). A New South Wales study (Battersby et al., 1990) indicates that 'friendly nurses' are a major factor in determining whether nurses stay at or leave a particular hospital. The reported strength of the buffering effect of colleague support on work-related stress is less than the reported strength of its direct effects (LaRocco et al., 1980; Norbeck, 1985). That is, colleague support helps more with emotion-focused passive coping than problem-focused active coping.

Colleague support as a coping resource

Stress in the nursing work environment cannot always be reduced or moderated, and coping efforts are activated whenever stress is present (Lazarus & Folkman, 1984). The use of colleague support as a resource or avenue for coping is another way that social support in the work environment affects the stress process. Nurses report 'talking it out' as a frequently employed coping strategy (Cross & Kelly, 1983; Oskins, 1979), and adaptive coping is correlated to being able to admit feelings of stress to self and others (Chiriboga et al., 1983). Supportive colleague interactions offer ideal opportunities for this open expression of stress.

The example of death is again a useful one because of the potential to view this event as a threat or loss. Interchange with nursing colleagues provides a forum to discuss reactions and responses to patient deaths. Sharing thoughts and feelings related to grief is an essential aspect of coping with death. Co-workers are the most logical people with whom to share these reactions because they have the greatest potential to offer situation-specific support in dealing with death.

Negative effects

The view of colleagues as supportive is encouraging, and even uplifting, but runs the risk of sounding naive and unrealistic without an acknowledgment that colleagues can also contribute to work-related stress in nursing practice.

Effective working relationships with colleagues are a necessity in nursing because of the need for collaboration and team effort in most work situations. The interdependence created by this need to pull together has potential to strain colleague relationships when nurses do not demonstrate that they operate from a similar value system. This aspect of colleague relationships is shown in a study of caring practices in nursing, in which it is highlighted that: 'Fellow staff nurses on the unit are often the greatest source of comfort and support to an emotionally burdened nurse, yet one's colleagues can also provide a real source of frustration and disappointment when their actions are seen to indicate a lack of caring for the patients' (Forrest, 1989: 818). This statement exemplifies conflicting expectations and value systems between nurses. In the absence of interdependence, this type of conflict would not be as evident. 'Supportive behaviours have a greater impact on employees who work on interdependent teams than those who work in relatively autonomous jobs' (LaRocco et al., 1980: 214).

Strained relationships and open conflict add stress to any working environment, but it is an absence of support rather than the presence of conflict that creates stress in colleague relationships in nursing. More often than not, it is that which is missing in colleague relationships that contributes to stress in nursing. Lack of support from supervisors, lack of feedback, lack of understanding in response to mistakes and lack of peer cohesion are all reported as factors that positively correlate to stress in nursing (Dunn et al., 1994; Hipwell et al., 1989; Humphrey, 1988; Linder-Pelz, 1985; Ness, 1982; Nichols et al., 1981; West & Rushton, 1986). Nurses create stress for other nurses largely by failing to provide support when it is needed.

The following story, told by a recent graduate, highlights this lack of support:

> It's as if I'm not myself when I'm at work. I don't mean with the patients. I mean with the other nurses. There were all these problems with the charge nurse when I first started. She wasn't liked by any of the other nurses on the unit and she gave the new graduates a really hard time, especially when we made mistakes.
>
> One time, I made an error in preparing a drug for a patient and, fortunately, the mistake was caught before I actually gave it to the patient. The charge nurse really reacted badly to this, and made me fill out all these incident reports. The nursing supervisor was notified and there was all this carrying on about the new college graduates. You would have thought nobody had ever made a mistake before. After all, it was bad enough that I almost hurt a patient and I dread even the thought of this ever happening.
>
> At any rate, at no time did I receive any understanding and support from the charge nurse. Some of the other nurses confided to me that they thought she (the charge nurse) had overreacted and the situation was blown out of all proportion. Mostly, they were thankful that it was me and not them.
>
> The other nurses also used the situation as a means of complaining about the charge nurse and there was constant griping and backbiting going on about this incident and other things occurring on the ward. But nobody was really being honest and open about their reactions. I suppose that's why, in the end, I just closed off. I couldn't really trust anybody.
>
> On the one hand, nobody seemed to like or respect the charge nurse and, on the other hand, none of the other nurses openly supported me either when the business with the drug error happened. It is as if we nurses are supposed to care about patients but it doesn't really matter how we treat each other.

This situation illustrates the potentially disastrous effects of an environment that is lacking support for other nurses. Lack of support compounded the stress already being experienced by this new graduate. The sad irony is that work-related stress on nurses is exacerbated when colleague support is absent, and colleague support is lacking when it is needed most—during times of increased stress. What is most disturbing is that colleague relationships add to stress, not necessarily by creating overt conflict, but by failing to provide needed support.

Most references to this lack of support in nursing-colleague relationships specify nursing supervisors and charge nurses, while less emphasis is placed on peer support. This is curious and could indicate that those with legitimate authority are expected to provide support, and there is perceived stress when it is not forthcoming. It could be that this is the case because most health-care organisations emphasise a hierarchical structure. Studies that have specifically explored supervisor support have indicated that support from those further up the hierarchy reduced stress-related factors such as role ambiguity (Gray-Toft & Anderson, 1985), emotional exhaustion, depersonalisation and thoughts of leaving (Firth et al., 1986), job dissatisfaction and propensity to leave (Decker, 1985). In addition, support from charge nurses' superiors (next up in the hierarchy) increased the support charge nurses demonstrated to the nursing staff on their wards (Firth et al., 1986). Supervisor support enhanced peer support by creating openness in work-group relationships (Gray-Toft & Anderson, 1985). This suggests a domino effect of supportive interactions between nurses that would ideally filter to patients. When nurses are supported and nourished they are better able to support and nourish others.

Added to the complexity of the relationship between stress in nursing and colleague interaction is the fact that poor colleague relationships is a sign of stress and burnout, and therefore could be an outcome of stress rather than a cause of it. The question that remains is whether poor colleague relationships is a cause of stress or its outcome (Bergagliotti & Trygstad, 1987). Either way, there is clearly a reciprocal relationship between colleague interaction and stress.

CONSTRAINTS IN DEVELOPING COLLEAGUE SUPPORT

The lack of colleague support between nurses raises questions about why and how this happens in a caring profession. Nurses risk losing their credibility as caring persons when caring for other nurses is not apparent and active in their work environment. Nurses should be able to demonstrate support for colleagues and cultivate a nourishing work environment but there are a variety of factors that inhibit these activities. Although these factors are not present in every work environment, identification of the constraints that do exist in their work environment is an initial step that nurses can take in dismantling them as barriers and decreasing their negative impact.

Lack of time

The most obvious of these constraints, and the one most likely to be cited by nurses, is a lack of time to demonstrate concern for other nurses (Kavanagh, 1989). When nurses are already overburdened with the sheer demands of the workload, how could there possibly be time to help and support other nurses? The limitation of time is often very real, but sometimes the perception of 'never any time' goes unchecked and unchallenged, for example, nurses frequently do find the time (or make the time?) to complain to each other about such things as working conditions, short staffing or supervisor insensitivity.

The time spent on complaining could be used to provide support to other nurses. Perhaps listening to a colleague's complaints is supportive—to a certain extent. Acknowledging another's perceptions through attentive listening can be helpful in and of itself. Frequently, however, complaints are used as springboards for the escalation of further complaints. The usefulness of this behaviour as a coping resource is questionable, as the outcome is often a 'churning of the guts' and an increase in stress levels. Listening to complaints for the purpose of clarifying real issues and seeking ways to address them is one helpful and supportive alternative. For example, here are two scenarios of John and Sally interacting in the medication room:

Complaining: scenario A

John: I'm sick and tired of always having to pick up after other people who can't be bothered cleaning up.

Sally: I know, some people around here would do well with a bit of manners.

John: Yes, its just common decency to clean up your own mess.

Sally: I guess we work with people who lack common decency, and, quite frankly, I'm sick of it.

The result of this interaction is that John and Sally, although feeling quite righteous in their indignation, will probably leave the medication room feeling angry and distressed.

Complaining: scenario B

John: I'm sick and tired of always having to pick up after other people who can't be bothered cleaning up.

Sally: I know, I get pretty angry as well when I come in here and spend time cleaning up before I can get my work done.

John: Yes, it's just common decency to clean up your own mess.

Sally: I agree, but wonder why it doesn't happen around here.

John: I guess it could be that we have been so busy lately that people don't have time to clean up.

Sally: I wonder if there's anything we can do about it.

This interaction has opened up the possibility of finding some solutions to a work problem, thereby decreasing the stress that John and Sally are feeling.

The other constraint related to time is the perception that supporting others takes extra time. The validity of this in the work setting is questionable. The time it takes to offer words of understanding to a colleague is less than the time it takes to understand a stranger. Other nurses already know colleagues, and the nursing work context is familiar. Empathy is easy to demonstrate under these circumstances because colleagues have shared experiences and meanings.

Repression of own needs

Even if adequate time is available, nurses may still fail to provide open support for each other, because the recognition that nurses have needs challenges the image of selfless dedication to others. Nurses often repress their own needs and feelings, while focusing their efforts on the needs of others, in what is described as the 'burden of helping'. The strength of this self-sacrificing image is waning in modern nursing but runs the risk of being replaced by a detached and distanced professionalism, whereby the nurse projects an image of one who is in control, impenetrable and dispassionate. Both of these images result in a denial of nurses' own needs, feelings and human reactions.

Difficulty in disclosing

Is there really an outright denial that nurses do have needs and feelings, or is it just that these needs and feelings are not disclosed, especially to other nurses? An open, honest acknowledgment of feelings, such as uncertainty, sadness or confusion, is often avoided out of fear that it is a sign of personal weakness and an inability to cope. This prevents nurses from seeking and offering advice and comfort with colleagues, thus closing off all other coping options except denial.

Larson (1987) uncovered difficult thoughts and feelings nurses have about their work that are kept hidden from colleagues, because of discomfort in discussing them. These secrets include concerns such as: distancing self and then feeling guilty for having done so; fears of inadequacy and incompetence; angry reactions; feeling overburdened by too many demands; wishing for a patient's death or feeling relief when a patient dies; and the desire to receive as well as give. These are understandable, even expected, reactions to the work nurses do, so there is no great surprise that these concerns exist.

It is unfortunate that such thoughts and feelings are actively concealed from colleagues because other nurses are in an ideal position to offer understanding, reassurance and guidance about these secret concerns. Presumably, they are kept secret because discussion of such feelings is considered unacceptable and unprofessional. After all, nurses cannot really admit to feeling inadequate because they are supposed to know what to do.

Overcoming fears of disclosing

More than likely, other nurses are experiencing or have experienced similar feelings and reactions, but this conspiracy of silence prevents these experiences from being shared. Keeping feelings hidden, especially fears, places nurses in the position of worrying alone and perpetuates the fallacy that, 'I am the only one who feels this way' or 'There must be something wrong with me'. There is comfort in knowing one is not alone, not the only one with fears, worries and negative reactions.

Other nurses provide a special and unique insider perspective that can challenge unrealistic fears and expectations and also allows coping options to be explored and developed. For example, if fears of incompetence and inadequacy stem from lack of knowledge, then this could be addressed through an informal sharing of knowledge or more formalised staff development programs. It is far better for nurses to acknowledge their feelings and reactions in a safe, accepting, supportive environment than to maintain a facade of immunity and control.

Organisational realities

Another constraint in the development of colleague support is the phenomenon of oppressed-group behaviour that has been observed in nursing (Roberts, 1983). The constraints outlined in the previous section assume that colleague support is available but not forthcoming because it is not actively solicited, offered and used, while oppressed-group behaviour actually stifles the development of support between nurses. As such, it is far more insidious because it creates a climate of divisiveness within nursing groups and pits nurses against each other, thus destroying camaraderie and esprit de corps. Understanding the dynamics of groups that are oppressed is essential if this negative phenomenon is to be reversed in nursing.

Nurses often perceive themselves as powerless against a system that dominates them, shouldering great responsibility within health-care organisations, without a commensurate degree of authority. The dominant culture reveres technology and devalues caring (Benner & Wrubel, 1989) and places curing as superior to caring. This oppression results in feelings of inferiority and creates the myth that the dominant group's value system and culture is 'right' and superior (Roberts, 1983). In oppression there is an internalisation of the dominant group's view of the world and a tendency within the oppressed group toward self-blame and rejection of their own values and culture as inferior. This leads to the development of a collective poor self-esteem within the group.

There are frustrations and complaints about the oppressor and the oppression, yet no direct action is taken. Instead, the anger that builds as a result of oppression is released on members of the group, rather than on the oppressor, because there is less risk of consequences in fighting each other than there is in fighting the dominant group. Oppressed groups remain submissive to those who dominate them. The lateral violence within the group keeps the group divided, prevents cohesion and maintains the status quo (Robert, 1983). The only real challenges are those that occur within the group.

Blaming and scapegoating other nurses are evidence of the behaviour of oppression in nursing work environments (DeFeo, 1987; Lartin, 1988). As long as blame can be found, and it usually is found within the oppressed group, real issues are not addressed because the culprit, another nurse, has been targeted, and there is no need to delve further into what is behind the cause of problem.

Reversing the behaviour of oppression requires recognition that the culture and value system of the oppressed group is legitimate and worthy. Currently, the discipline of nursing is rediscovering its identity as that of *caring* and this cultural reawakening is a sign that the oppression in nursing is being addressed. The concept of the value of caring and caring practices holds great promise in helping nurses to celebrate their professional culture. It would naturally follow that nurses would also begin to demonstrate caring for their colleagues as part of this cultural reawakening, not only because caring for each other would be highly regarded in a caring profession, but also because the professional self-esteem of nurses would be improved and heightened.

This caring culture places demands on the health-care system in which nurses work because 'caring as a concept is dependent on adequate time being available so that patients and nurses can interact' (Weaver, 1990: 452) and the current system does not provide ample time for nurses and patients to connect (Fry, 1988). These demands place stress on the system by upsetting the status quo and nurses need to support each other in meeting these demands and coping with the stress they create. A recognition and valuing of the culture of nursing leads to the type of collegiality that is required if nurse–nurse support is to be fully developed and used. The inspirational words of Margretta Styles sum it up: 'Collegiality is as sacred as a vow; it is a solemn promise whereby we bind ourselves to those who share our cause, our convictions, our identity, our destiny' (Styles, 1982: 143).

Other organisational issues that prevent effective colleague support need to be addressed (Kavanagh, 1989). Limited reward systems that promote competition between nurses, and overdependence on the administrative hierarchy, and even the method of patient care delivery (McMahon, 1990), all affect colleague relationships and cannot be ignored. There is a risk in asking nurses to be supportive of each other if the organisational culture does not value this. Time and resources to facilitate support between nurses need to be accessed (Kavanagh, 1989).

DEVELOPMENT OF COLLEAGUE SUPPORT

Creation of a climate of colleague support does not mean that nurses should spend most of their time focusing on the needs of other nurses and counselling their colleagues; nor does it imply that nurses should express every emotion they experience. It means paving a path by which nurses can actively share their concerns and emotions generated by the job, and be heard and understood by other nurses. All of the skills described in this book would effectively promote supportive relationships with colleagues because these skills are not exclusive to patient–nurse interactions. Being attentive, responsive, encouraging, understanding and challenging are not skills that can be switched on and off at will, and enactment of these skills on a daily basis in the work environment creates a supportive environment.

Nevertheless, there are recommendations in the use of these skills that are specific to colleague interactions. The content of supportive discussions between nursing colleagues needs to focus on specific *work-related* difficulties and the emotions they engender (Gray-Toft & Anderson, 1983; Llewelyn & Payne, 1995). These are related to the individual personalities of nurses, but are not personal problems per se. Reflective listening clarifies these difficulties and emotions, and promotes mutual understanding, but it alone is not sufficient in providing effective colleague support.

Challenging is needed in the case of colleague support (Richman, 1988) because it offers new perspectives, reframes existing perspectives, spurs nurses on to improve their work, and helps to overcome obstacles to meeting goals. Challenging can only be effective in a general climate of trust and openness, and requires an ability to be assertive. Trust is promoted between nurses when individual differences are tolerated, and feedback is given directly and honestly. Conflict is not absent within this climate; but these conditions establish a climate in which effective resolution of conflict can occur. A supportive work environment for nurses is one in which nurses are:

- acknowledged
- validated
- respected
- affirmed
- listened to
- accepted
- understood
- encouraged
- challenged
- offered feedback
- appreciated
- assisted

A supportive environment is responsive to other nurses if, and when, colleague support is requested and received. Another nurse may indicate the need for support directly or indirectly, and colleagues are in a prime position to respond to the cues indicating a need for support.

The following example, provided by a new graduate nurse, offers some insight into the benefits of responding to such cues:

I had been working for about six months, the whole time on this particular ward. I was on duty one evening with another nurse, Ruth, who was very experienced. I always liked it when I worked with Ruth because she knew what she was doing and helped me whenever I needed it.

This particular evening was busy but not really hectic. One of the patients had become really upset while on an outing and attempted to jump in front of a moving car. As a result, all of the patients on the outing returned to the unit early. I can't recall exactly what had upset her, but I was staying with her in her room, providing close one-to-one contact.

Ruth was busy feeding a patient in the room next to me. Then the patient I was with had a grand mal seizure. I had seen and even managed a few seizures prior to this, and, although a bit scared, basically knew what to do. Everything was pretty much as it usually is during a seizure, but then something strange and frightening began to happen.

The seizure hadn't stopped, wouldn't stop, and seemed to go on for an interminable time. The patient stopped breathing and began to turn blue. I began to panic inside, but kept my head while I opened her airway in the way I'd been instructed to do. I remember thinking to myself, 'CO_2 needs to build up in order to kick in the breathing response. That *is* what I learnt, isn't it?' I checked for a pulse. It was present.

After what felt like an eternity, the patient began breathing spontaneously. It was funny because it was at this point that I began to panic openly. I shouted for Ruth and she was there in a flash, asking me what was happening. I quickly explained while we positioned the patient and made her comfortable. Ruth stayed with the patient and told me to go and call the doctor. In the end it all worked out. The patient was okay but I ended up feeling terrible. Later, in the nursing station, while Ruth and I were recapping what had happened, I suddenly blurted out, 'I handled that situation so poorly. I was scared, panicked, and had to call you. I don't think I'll ever make a good nurse.'

Ruth looked at me and said, 'What do you mean?'

'Well, I couldn't manage alone. I called you', I replied.

She said, 'It seemed perfectly reasonable to me, you did everything correctly, and the whole thing was pretty frightening.' Then she turned toward me, looked me straight in the eye, and added, 'Anyway, who ever told you that you were Superwoman?'

I looked at her a bit sheepishly and said, 'Me?'

We both laughed, then had a chat, recounting the story step-by-step, with Ruth reinforcing my clinical judgment and actions. She said had it been her in that room, she would have called out for me as well, especially if I was just nextdoor. I mean, it's not like I abandoned the patient and ran down the hall.

Ruth probably never realised just how much she helped that evening. Her comment about Superwoman was right on target. It challenged me to think about my expectations of myself. Her comment still echoes in my ears whenever I get caught up in those unreal expectations. I think every nurse should have a Ruth to remind her that she can't be Superwoman.

This story illustrates a caring, concerned and helpful response from an experienced nurse to a newly graduated nurse. Ruth's reactions were based on an understanding of the situation and an awareness of this new graduate's needs. She supported this new graduate by affirming her clinical actions, but challenged her at the same time to reconsider her expectations. This demonstrates support by offering an alternative perspective, a reappraisal of the situation. Ruth could have been supportive by just saying, 'You did the right thing, you handled the situation correctly, knew what to do and did it'. While this might have sufficed, she enhanced the support by using the situation to help the new graduate learn from it. The lesson stayed with this new graduate, probably throughout her career, and helped to ease some of her stress in future situations. The power of colleague support cannot be underestimated.

CHAPTER SUMMARY

A necessary backdrop to supportive colleague interaction is an interpersonal work climate that acknowledges and validates nurses as people, and is responsive to nurses' reactions, feelings, anxieties and confusions. Interpersonal skills training is unlikely to be successful unless there is active support for nurses who employ these skills (Fielding & Llewelyn, 1987).

Nurses cannot be expected to give of themselves without such support, from other nurses and the health-care organisation that employs them, because work-related stress is addressed most effectively in the work environment.

REFERENCES

Battersby, D., Hemmings, L., Kermode, S., Sutherland, S. & Cox, J. (1990). *Factors influencing the turnover and retention of registered nurses in New South Wales hospitals.* New South Wales College of Nursing, Sydney.

Benner, P. & Wrubel, J. (1989). *The primacy of caring: stress and coping in health and illness.* Addison-Wesley, Menlo Park CA.

Bergagliotti, L.A. & Trygstad, L.N. (1987). Differences in stress and coping findings: a reflection of social realities or methodologies? *Nursing research,* 36 (3), 170–173.

Chiriboga, D.A., Jenkins, G. & Baily, J. (1983). Stress and coping among hospice nurses: test of an analytic model. *Nursing research,* 32 (5), 294–299.

Cronin-Stubbs, D., Rooks, C.A. (1985). The stress, social support, and burnout of critical care nurses: the results of research. *Heart & lung,* 14 (1), 31–39.

Cross, D.G. & Kelly, J.G. (1983). Stress and coping strategies in hospitals: a comparison of ICU and ward nurses. *The Australian nurses journal,* 13 (2), 43–46.

Decker, F.H. (1985). Socialization and interpersonal environment in nurses affective reactions to work. *Social science and medicine,* 20 (5), 449–509.

DeFeo, D. (1987). The hunt for the really bad nurse. *American journal of nursing,* 87 (2), 270.

Dunn, L.A., Rout, U., Carson, J. & Ritter, S.A. (1994). Occupational stress amongst care staff working in nursing homes: an empirical investigation. *Journal of clinical nursing,* 3, 177–183.

Fielding, R.G. & Llewelyn, S.P. (1987). Communication training in nursing may damage your health and enthusiasm: some warnings. *Journal of advanced nursing,* 12, 821–290.

Firth, H., McIntee, J., McKeown, P. & Britton, P. (1986) Interpersonal support amongst nurses. *Journal of advanced nursing,* 11, 273–282.

Forrest, D. (1989). The experience of caring. *Journal of advanced nursing,* 14, 815–823.

Fry, S. (1988) The ethics of caring: can it survive nursing? *Nursing outlook,* 36 (1), 8.

Gentry, W.D. & Parkes, K.R. (1982). Psychological stress in intensive care unit and non-intensive care unit nursing: a review of the past decade. *Heart & lung,* 11 (1), 43–47.

Gray-Toft, P.A. & Anderson, J.G. (1981). Stress among hospital nursing staff: its causes and effects. *Social science and medicine,* 15A, 639–647.

Gray-Toft, P.A. & Anderson, J.G. (1983). A hospital staff support program: design and evaluation. *International journal of nursing studies,* 20 (3), 137–147.

Gray-Toft, P.A. & Anderson, J.G. (1985). Organizational stress in the hospital: development of a model for diagnosis and prediction. *Health services research,* 19 (6), 753–774.

Hipwell, A.E., Tyler, P.A. & Wilson, C.M. (1989). Sources of stress and dissatisfaction among nurses in four hospital environments. *British journal of medical psychology*, 62, 71–79.

Humphrey, J.H. (1988). *Stress in the nursing profession*. Charles C. Thomas, Springfield IL.

Irvine, D.M. & Evans, M.G. (1996). Job satisfaction and turnover among nurses: integrating research findings across studies. *Nursing research*, 44 (4), 246–253.

Kavanagh, K.H. (1989). Nurses' networks: obstacles and challenge. *Archives of psychiatric nursing*, 3 (4), 226–233.

Kushnir, T., Rabin, S. & Azulai, S. (1997). A descriptive study of stress management in a group of pediatric oncology nurses. *Cancer nursing*, 20, 414–421.

LaRocco, J.M., House, J.S. & French, J.R.P. (1980). Social support, occupational stress, and health. *Journal of health and social behaviour*, 21, 202–218.

Larson, D.G. (1987). Helper secrets. *Journal of psychosocial nursing*, 25 (4), 20–26.

Lartin, J.M. (1988). Scapegoating: identifying and reversing the process. *Journal of nursing administration*, 18 (9), 25–31.

Lazarus, R.S. & Folkman, S. (1984). *Stress, appraisal and coping*. Springer, New York.

Lee, V. & Henderson, M.C. (1996). Occupational stress and organizational commitment in nurse administrators. *Journal of nursing administration*, 26 (5), 21–28.

Linder-Pelz, S. (1985). Occupational stressors and stress levels among Australian nurses: a review of research. *The journal of occupational health and safety— Australia and New Zealand*, 1 (1), 9–15.

Llewelyn, S. & Payne, S. (1995). Caring: the costs to nurses and relatives. In A. Broome & S. Llewelyn (eds). *Health psychology: processes and applications*, 2nd edn (pp109–122). Chapman and Hall, London.

MacNeil, J.M. & Weisz, G.M. (1987). Critical care nursing stress: another look. *Heart & lung*, 16 (3), 274–277.

McMahon, R. (1990). Power and collegial relations among nurses on wards adopting primary nursing and hierarchical ward management structures. *Journal of advanced nursing*, 15, 232–239.

Mossholder, K.W., Bedeian, A.G. & Armenakis, A.A. (1982). Group process— work outcome relationships: a note on the moderating impact of self-esteem. *Academy of management journal*, 25 (3), 575–585.

Ness, A. (1982). Stress: its effect on registered nurses and patient care. *The Australian nurses journal*, 12 (1), 47–48.

Nichols, K.A., Springford, V. & Searle, J. (1981). An investigation of distress and discontent in various types of nursing. *Journal of advanced nursing*, 6, 311–318.

Norbeck, J.S. (1985). Types and sources of social support for managing job stress in critical care nursing. *Nursing research*, 34 (4), 225–230.

Norbeck, J.S., Lindsey, A.M. & Carrieri, V.L. (1981). The development of an instrument to measure social support. *Nursing research*, 30 (5), 264–269.

Oskins, S.L. (1979). Identification of situational stressors and coping methods by intensive care nurses. *Heart & lung*, 8 (5), 953–960.

Richman, J.M. (1988). Social support groups. *Journal of nursing administration*, 18 (2) 3, 19.

Roberts, S.J. (1983). Oppressed group behaviour: implications for nursing. *Advances in nursing science*, 5, 21–31.

Snape, J. & Cavanagh, S.J. (1993). Occupational stress in neurosurgical nursing. *Intensive and critical care nursing*, 9 (3), 162–170.

Styles, M.M. (1982). *On nursing: toward a new endowment*. Mosby, St Louis MS.

Tyler, P.A., Carroll, D. & Cunningham, S.E. (1991). Stress and well-being in nurses: a comparison of the public and private sectors. *International journal of nursing studies*, 28, 125–130.

Weaver, D. (1990). Cost-effective use of professional resources: a pivotal time for nurse administrators. In N. Chaska (ed.). *The nursing profession: turning points*. Mosby, St Louis MS.

West, M. & Rushton, R. (1986). The drop-out factor. *Nursing times*, 82, December 31, 29–31.

APPENDIX

NOTES ON THE USE OF ACTIVITIES

Introduction

The information in this appendix supports the book's learning activities by presenting guidelines and suggestions about conducting the activities in a learning group. As such it is primarily for the benefit of those people who are promoting learning through the use of activities. These people are referred to as 'facilitators', rather than teachers, because this term more accurately reflects the nature of 'teaching' through the use of experiential activities.

Figure A.1 The relationship of processing (outer circle) and experiential learning (inner circle) (Stein-Parbury, J. (1992) Processing skills: enhancing experiential learning. In: Members of the 1991 Teaching Enhancement Team. *Quality of teaching matters at UTS*. Centre for Learning and Teaching. University of Technology, Sydney).

The appendix begins with a brief overview of experiential learning with specific reference to how the skills can actually be used to facilitate this method of learning. Figure A.1 illustrates the relationship between experiential learning and the skills presented in this book.

Included in this section are some suggestions for facilitators who are using experience-based learning approaches. General guidelines for employing *role play* as an experiential learning form of activity follow; and, finally, discussion and material specific to a number of the book's various activities are presented. (*Note*: each activity referred to in this final section of the appendix is highlighted in its respective chapter by the symbol ➡.)

Experiential learning

The activities in this book are designed to stimulate learning of interpersonal skills in nursing and consolidate the theory presented in the text. Some activities trigger learners to reflect on previous experiences, considering theoretical concepts in a 'there-and-then' manner. Other activities enable learners to put into practice interpersonal skills in a 'here-and-now' manner. All are designed to produce meaningful learning experiences by actively involving participants in understanding the concepts described in the text.

Learning through experience is one of the most effective ways to integrate interpersonal skills into professional behaviour. While a theoretical comprehension of the skills is essential, they are most effectively understood by participating in experiences which make them 'come to life'. By putting the skills to use in some way through experiential activities, theoretical understanding is developed in conjunction with the technical know-how of employing them.

The majority of the activities are most effective when they are conducted in a learning group situation, which is conducted by a knowledgeable and sensitive guide. This guide, the learning facilitator, is a person who not only understands the concepts illustrated in the activity but who is also able to help participants discuss the experience in a meaningful manner.

The majority of the activities include a discussion section that focuses on the processing of experiences. Processing refers to that aspect of experiential learning that enables learners to derive personalised meaning from their experiences. In processing experiences, facilitators respond rather than direct; pull ideas together rather than prescribe what they should be; and encourage reflection rather than expect automatic reactions.

When interacting with learners, facilitators who demonstrate the attitudes, skills and knowledge embedded in this book will be most effective if they use an experience-based approach to learning. In addition, facilitators of the method of learning through experience are most productive when they are knowledgeable about experiential learning.

Suggestions for facilitators of experiential learning

Sometimes experiential learning activities produce lively responses from participants. At other times, experiences designed to facilitate learning may fall flat. Here are some general suggestions for handling some of the more common difficulties, which may surface when using experience-based learning:

1. Because the meaning derived from an experience is personalised, it is difficult to become pedantic about the 'right' or correct way to respond to an experience. This may be uncomfortable for facilitators who are accustomed to presenting material in a step-wise procedural manner. Facilitators of learning through experience need to let go of procedural approaches when they are teaching interpersonal skills; allow learners to derive personally relevant meaning from their experiences; and function as a guide on a journey, rather than an expert who demonstrates how it 'should' be done.

2. When activities are conducted in a traditional classroom, it is sometimes tempting to leave the room while participants engage in an activity. As a general rule, this is not a good idea, because participants often need further guidance and assistance during the activity. It is helpful to 'float' around the room, making sure that instructions for the activity are understood. This is also a useful opportunity to discuss the associated concepts with participants.

3. Sometimes activities are ineffectual, producing a 'so what?' experience, that is, they fail to enhance participants' learning because no meaning can be constructed from it. An indication that this may be happening occurs when participants do not have much to say in response to the items in the discussion section of the activity. When an activity or its discussion seems to be 'going nowhere', it is often useful to ask a general question such as, 'What's happening here?' or 'What's going on?' When facilitators ask questions such as these, they may be surprised to learn that participants are responding to events other than the presented activity. At other times there is 'nothing happening', and at this point the activity should be abandoned. Nevertheless, when the 'so what?' experience happens once, it is not enough reason to abandon an activity altogether. Try it again with another group of participants. It may trigger significant learning in another context.

4. When participants seem hesitant to engage in an activity, make sure they understand the instructions. Most often reluctance is a result of failure to comprehend what is expected. Do not assume that hesitancy is a result of lack of interest or motivation. Always assume the participants' goodwill. It helps to establish trust.

5. It is often beneficial to begin formal classes that use an experience-based approach to learning with a 'warm-up' activity. These activities enable participants to get their minds in gear, ready to learn in an active, involved manner. Some suggestions for warm-up activities include:

    ■ Word association—have participants say the first word that comes to their mind in response to the theme of the session, for example, old age.

    ■ Brainstorm—generate as many ideas as possible about a given topic, for example, reassurance.

- Touch base—have each participant state how they are feeling at the moment.
- Tell a story—begin the session by sharing a personal anecdote about the topic of the session, for example, 'the time I became over-involved with a patient'.
- Show a picture—display a picture that depicts something of relevance to the session, for example, a patient who is crying.

These warm-up activities need to be short and snappy in order to be effective. As a general rule, they should consume no more than ten minutes of a given session.

ADDITIONAL MATERIAL FOR ACTIVITIES

Chapter 3 Knowing self: self-awareness

ACTIVITY 3.1: WHAT DO I HAVE TO OFFER TO PATIENTS?

This activity can be threatening and frightening to participants if they think they will be expected to reveal their responses. For this reason, it is essential to stress that participants will not be required to disclose the answers to the questions posed in the process section. Participants should be seated in a manner that allows their papers to remain in their view only. The discussion centres around how it felt to complete the activity, not on the answers to personal questions asked during the process.

ACTIVITY 3.5: BELIEFS ABOUT HELPING IN NURSING PRACTICE

The questionnaire used in this activity is designed to trigger thoughts about assumptions of personal responsibility for problems and how these assumptions affect approaches to helping. Participants may take issue with some of the items on the questionnaire, especially if their results are not in accordance with what they believe, want to believe, or think they 'should' believe. Much time and effort could go into discussing the items and this may detract from the purpose of the activity. Individual participant's results are therefore not the major issue and this should be stressed during the discussion of the activity.

It is equally important to emphasise that a mismatch between how patients view their responsibility and how nurses view personal responsibility can create problems in the relationship. For this reason, participants should be encouraged to develop awareness of patients' orientation to helping as well as their own orientation.

ACTIVITY 3.12: SELF-ASSESSMENT OF SPECIFIC SKILLS

This activity can only be attempted after participants have been engaged in learning specific skills.

Chapter 4 Encouraging interaction: listening

ACTIVITY 4.4: PHYSICAL ATTENDING

INSTRUCTIONS TO A

You are going to speak to person B for about five minutes on a topic of your choosing. About two minutes into the conversation inform B that you are going to share a secret with them. Make sure you say that it is a secret, then proceed to share it with B. You will need to fabricate this 'secret', so prepare yourself by thinking of something really interesting to share.

INSTRUCTIONS TO B

Seat yourself comfortably and place a seat facing you, for person A. Person A is going to talk to you for about five minutes. Act naturally during the conversation, while you listen to what A has to say.

INSTRUCTIONS TO C

Person A and person B are going to have a conversation lasting about five minutes. You are to observe and note person B's nonverbal behaviour during the conversation. You do not need to actually hear what A and B are discussing. Pay particular attention to body posture, eye contact and other behaviours, which indicate B's level of interest in the conversation. Note especially any change in B's nonverbal behaviour about two minutes into the conversation.
See *Guidelines for role play* on page 320.

ACTIVITY 4.5: ATTENDING AND NON-ATTENDING

See *Guidelines for role play* on page 320.

ACTIVITY 4.7: LISTENING FOR CONTENT

Participants often request to have stories read more than once. Stress that doing so would interfere with the purpose of the activity. While nurses may request patients to repeat what they have said (for example, when nurses cannot hear what has been said, or the patient's speech is garbled), such requests may be interpreted as a failure to listen in the first place.

Participants' responses (the who, what, when and where content) should be reviewed after each patient story is read, rather than reading all stories, then reviewing the responses. As each story is reviewed, participants become more skilled at listening for content, that is, the learning is immediate.

In answering the 'who, what, when and where' of each story, participants often become frustrated if the facilitator is pedantic about the 'correct' answers. Rather than giving the impression of right and wrong answers, it is better to focus discussion on reasons for discrepancies between participants, and between participants' answers and the ones provided at the end of the chapter. The purpose of the activity is to discover the process of listening, not to 'get' the right answers. This may need to be continually reinforced.

ACTIVITY 4.8: LISTENING FOR FEELINGS

Participants' responses should be reviewed after each patient statement is read, rather than reading all statements and then reviewing the responses. There is often great variety between participants in their interpretation of feelings. Because answers are provided at the end of the chapter, these may be perceived as 'correct' and any other answers as 'incorrect'. Take care not to give the impression that responses that are different from those presented at the end of the chapter are 'incorrect'. Rather, focus discussion on why the interpretations differ between participants. Some of the reasons for these differences include cultural variance, role expectations, personal needs, values and beliefs. Emphasise the importance of self-awareness within the context of listening for feelings.

This activity often highlights problems with the language used to describe feelings; participants sometimes find it difficult to 'find the words' to express emotions. A general discussion about the role of language in discussing feelings is useful and timely in the discussion phase of this activity. It is also beneficial to follow this activity with activity 5.5: *Building a feeling word vocabulary.*

ACTIVITY 4.9: LISTENING FOR THEMES

See *Guidelines for role play* on page 320.

ACTIVITY 4.11: RESPONSES THAT INDICATE LISTENING

Do not become overly concerned if there is a discrepancy between participants' answers and the ones provided at the end of the chapter. Sometimes such discrepancies indicate different interpretations of the words used in the responses; at other times different meanings are constructed. Sometimes participants want to argue about the answers in an effort to determine the correct one and this can become counterproductive to learning. Rather than arguing, participants should be encouraged to reflect on their interpretation of the given responses, and compare these with other participants' interpretations. As a result of this type of discussion participants are better able to understand that meanings are in people, not words.

Chapter 5 Building meaning: understanding

ACTIVITY 5.2: RECOGNITION OF THE TYPES OF RESPONSES

Participants often experience difficulty differentiating an analysing and interpreting response (A and I) from a paraphrasing and understanding response (P and U). It should be explained that an A and I response 'adds' to what the patient has expressed. When such additions are an accurate reflection of what a patient is experiencing, this is referred to as 'advanced empathy'. Advanced empathy delves into feelings and meanings that are beneath the surface. When such additions are inaccurate, they are often a reflection of the nurse's personal value judgments. A P and U response remains on the surface and does not delve more deeply into hidden and obscured meaning.

ACTIVITY 5.4: PARAPHRASING—HAVE I GOT IT RIGHT?

See *Guidelines for role play* on page 320.

ACTIVITY 5.7: CONNECTING THOUGHTS AND FEELINGS

Sometimes participants are frustrated by using the format 'You feel...when...' When this happens, encourage them to use their own style of expression, as long as the connection between thoughts and feelings is made. Emphasise that the suggested format is a useful mental aid; it is not a prescription for connecting feelings and thoughts. When adhered to rigidly, the suggested format interferes with the development of a personal style.

Chapter 6 Collecting information: exploring

ACTIVITY 6.2: WAYS OF EXPLORING: QUESTIONS VERSUS STATEMENTS

See *Guidelines for role play* on page 320.

ACTIVITY 6.3: CONVERTING PROBES INTO PROMPTS

Some participants may find it difficult to develop exploratory statements (prompts) because they are accustomed to exploring through the use of questions (probes). If this happens, it is useful to find participants who are not having difficulty converting probes to prompts and encourage these participants to assist those who are experiencing difficulty. Emphasise that the activity is not a 'test' of ability, rather a method of enhancing learning.

ACTIVITY 6.5: EFFECTS OF 'WHY?' QUESTIONS

See *Guidelines for role play* on page 320.

ACTIVITY 6.7: RECOGNISING TYPES OF QUESTIONS

Some participants may not be able to perceive the disguised 'why' question and further explanation may be necessary to complete the process. 'Why?' questions are often hidden behind statements such as 'What made you feel that way?', 'What are your reasons for thinking this way?' and 'How come?' If the word 'why' can be substituted for a word or phrase in the question without destroying its meaning, then there is a good chance that a disguised 'why?' question has been asked.

ACTIVITY 6.9: CUES AND INFERENCES

Some of the inferences presented in this activity could actually be cues. For example, item 2 would be a cue if the patient directly stated that they were uninterested in the interview. This point should be brought out during the discussion phase of the activity.

It should be stressed that inferences can be valid interpretations of cues. Sometimes participants may form the impression that inferences should be avoided at all costs. The discussion phase of this activity provides a useful opportunity to clarify this incorrect impression.

Finally, nurses must take care in supporting inferences with the cues on which they are based. In recording patient data in a chart, for example, it is essential that inferences are not stated, unless their supporting cues are also stated. On the other hand, cues can be recorded on their own, that is, they do not require an interpretation (inference).

ACTIVITY 6.11: PATIENT INTERVIEW

See *Guidelines for role play* on page 320.

Chapter 7 Comforting, supporting and enabling

ACTIVITY 7.4: SHARING INFORMATION

This activity is conducted over two sessions. In the first session, participants are given scenarios for sharing information (developed in steps 1 and 2 of the process). In doing so, they have the opportunity to familiarise themselves with the information that they will be sharing. They can come to the next session prepared to share information. Without this opportunity participants may be caught 'off guard' and feel unable to share information because they do not know enough about a given topic.
See *Guidelines for role play* on page 320.
See *Guide for sharing information* on page 321.

Chapter 9 Adjusting interactions to cultural difference

ACTIVITY 9.4: WORKING WITH AN INTERPRETER

See *Guidelines for role play* on page 320.

ACTIVITY 9.5: COMMUNICATING WITHOUT LANGUAGE

See *Guidelines for role play* on page 320.

GUIDELINES FOR ROLE PLAY

Role playing is one of the most commonly used experiential learning methods. Role playing is a process of acting 'as if' the situation is real. While it does not require formal drama skills, the patrticipants' willingness to behave in ways that may be unfamiliar is essential if the action is to proceed.

Throughout this book various activities rely on this method. Whenever it is used, it is crucial that the following guidelines be presented to participants (on a whiteboard or butchers' paper, or circulate copies) who are enacting the role play. *Remember*: the onus is on the facilitator to present this information to the learners each time a role play exercise is introduced.

Before the action

1. Assume the role. Try not to let personal thoughts and feelings about the role interfere with your ability to adopt the role; accept it for what it is—

an act designed to enhance learning. Take a few minutes prior to the action of the role play to 'put yourself' into the role.

2.   Do not be concerned if you think you cannot enact the role because you are not good at dramatising and performing. The purpose of role playing is to act naturally although you may be required to adopt a stance that feels different from your usual way of interacting with others.

3.   Once you have assumed the role, let the action flow naturally. Do not overact or exaggerate your actions in an effort to be a good role player.

4.   During the role play invent needed information, about yourself or specific details of the situation. Do not let the role play stop or flounder because you think you should know something; simply make it up in an effort to keep the action going.

5.   It is acceptable, sometimes desirable, to change your ideas and attitudes throughout the role play. Even if your role prescribes certain attitudes and feelings, these may change as a result of the progress of the action. When this happens, let it flow naturally; do not cling to your original script.

After the action

1.   Remain in the role and take a few minutes to discuss how you responded to the role and how it felt playing the role.

2.   Make sure you clarify any information or detail that was fabricated in an effort to keep the action going.

3.   Discuss any concerns you have about what others who participated in the role play may think or feel about you as a result of the role you have just assumed.

4.   When the time comes, state aloud that you are no longer in the role and are returning to who you really are.

GUIDE FOR SHARING INFORMATION

Did the nurse…

1.   Identify what the patient wants to know?
Yes No
How?

2.   Clarify what the patient already understands?
Yes No
How?

3.   Assess the accuracy of the patient's current information?
Yes No
How?

4.   Determine patient's readiness to receive the information?
Yes No
How?

5. Limit the amount of information shared (about two items at a time)?
   Yes No
   How?
6. Use understandable language?
   Yes No
   How?
7. Present information clearly?
   Yes No
   How?
8. Assess the patient's comprehension?
   Yes No
   How?
9. Request feedback from the patient?
   Yes No
   How?
10. Discuss the patient's reaction to the information?
    Yes No
    How?

INDEX

TO THE OWNER OF THIS BOOK

We are interested in your reaction to *Patient and Person,*
2nd edition by Jane Stein-Parbury.

1. What was your reason for using this book?
   _____ university course
   _____ college course
   _____ TAFE course
   _____ continuing education course
   _____ personal interest
   _____ other (please specify)

2. In which school are you enrolled? _____

3. Approximately how much of the book did you use?
   _____ ¼   _____ ½   _____ ¾   _____ all

4. What is the best aspect of the book?

5. Have you any suggestions for improvement?

6. Would more diagrams/ illustrations help?

7. Is there any topic that should be added?

Fold here

- -

(Tape shut)

Reply Paid 5
The Product Manager
Elsevier Science | Harcourt Australia
Locked Bag 16
ST PETERS 2044